Springer

Berlin
Heidelberg
New York
Barcelona
Hong Kong
London
Milan
Paris
Singapore
Tokyo

Robert F. Stärk
Joachim Schmid
Egon Börger

Java and the Java Virtual Machine

Definition, Verification, Validation

With 84 Figures, 18 Tables, and CD-ROM

 Springer

Prof. Dr. Robert F. Stärk
ETH Zentrum, Theoretische Informatik
8092 Zürich, Switzerland

Dipl.-Inf. Joachim Schmid
Siemens AG, CT SE 4, Otto-Hahn-Ring 6
81730 München, Germany

Prof. Dr. Egon Börger
Università di Pisa, Dipartimento di Informatica
Corso Italia 40, 56125 Pisa, Italy

Library of Congress Cataloging-in-Publication Data applied for

Die Deutsche Bibliothek-CIP-Einheitsaufnahme
Java and the Java virtual machine: definition, verification, validation: with 18 tables and CD-ROM/
Robert F. Stärk; Joachim Schmid; Egon Börger. - Berlin; Heidelberg; New York; Barcelona; Hong
Kong; London; Milan; Paris; Singapore; Tokyo: Springer, 2001
ISBN 3-540-42088-6

ACM Computing Classification (1998): D.3.1, D.3.4, F.3.2-3

ISBN 3-540-42088-6 Springer-Verlag Berlin Heidelberg New York

Springer-Verlag Berlin Heidelberg New York,
a member of BertelsmannSpringer Science+Business Media GmbH
http://www.springer.de

© Springer-Verlag Berlin Heidelberg 2001
Printed in Germany

Cover Design: KünkelLopka, Heidelberg
Typesetting: Computer to film by authors' data
Printed on acid-free paper   SPIN 10837750   45/3142PS 5 4 3 2 1 0

Preface

The origin of this book goes back to the Dagstuhl seminar on *Logic for System Engineering*, organized during the first week of March 1997 by S. Jähnichen, J. Loeckx, and M. Wirsing. During that seminar, after Egon Börger's talk on *How to Use Abstract State Machines in Software Engineering*, Wolfram Schulte, at the time a research assistant at the University of Ulm, Germany, questioned whether ASMs provide anything special as a scientifically well-founded and rigorous yet simple and industrially viable framework for high-level design and analysis of complex systems, and for natural refinements of models to executable code. Wolfram Schulte argued, referring to his work with K. Achatz on *A Formal Object-Oriented Method Inspired by Fusion and Object-Z* [1], that with current techniques of functional programming and of axiomatic specification, one can achieve the same result. An intensive and long debate arose from this discussion. At the end of the week, it led Egon Börger to propose a collaboration on a real-life specification project of Wolfram Schulte's choice, as a comparative field test of purely functional-declarative methods and of their enhancement within an integrated abstract state-based operational (ASM) approach.

After some hesitation, in May 1997 Wolfram Schulte accepted the offer and chose as the theme a high-level specification of Java and of the Java Virtual Machine. What followed were two years of hard but enjoyable joint work, resulting in a series of ASM models of the Java language, of the JVM, and of a provably correct compilation scheme for compiling Java programs to JVM code, which were published in [9, 8, 10, 11, 12]. When in the spring of 1999, Wolfram Schulte put this work together for his *Habilitationsschrift* at the University of Ulm, Egon Börger suggested completing and extending it to a—badly needed—full-blown ASM case study book. The book should show the ASM method at work, convincingly, for the practical design of a complex real-life system, and for its rigorous mathematical and extensive experimental analysis.

Robert Stärk and Joachim Schmid accepted to join this book project. At that time, in his Fribourg lectures [33], Robert Stärk had already elaborated part of the Java-to-JVM compilation correctness claim, namely, that the execution, on the ASM for the JVM, of every correctly compiled legal Java program is equivalent to the execution of the original Java program on the ASM for Java. In the spring of 1998, Egon Börger had proposed to Joachim Schmid a PhD thesis, hosted by Siemens Corporate Technology in Munich, on defining and implementing practically useful structuring and decomposition principles for large ASMs. It could be expected that for this work Wolfram Schulte's suggestion to make our abstract Java/JVM models executable would provide a rich test bed for validating the submachine concepts we were looking for (see [7]). The realization of these ideas led to a complete revision (completion, correction, and restructuring) of all the Java/JVM models and to their refinement by AsmGofer executable versions. The revision was triggered, not surprisingly, by three sources, namely:

- The needs of the proofs, in particular for the correctness and completeness of the verification of the bytecode resulting from the compilation, proofs which have been worked out for this book by Robert Stärk
- The needs of naturally detailing the abstractions to make them executable in AsmGofer, developed by Joachim Schmid building upon an extension of the functional programming environment Gofer by graphical user interfaces [36]
- An enhancement of the stepwise refined definition of the Java/JVM models, driven by the goal to create a compositional structure of submachines which supports incremental modularized proofs and component-wise validation (model-based testing)

All this took much more time and energy, and made us aware of more problems with bytecode verification than we had expected in the spring of 1999, and in retrospect we see that it was at the very beginning of this long journey when we lost Wolfram Schulte as the fourth author. We regret this, it was painful for the four of us to eventually recognize and accept it. We had to understand that since the moment when, just after having submitted his *Habilitationsschrift* to the University of Ulm, Wolfram joined the *Foundations of Software Engineering* group at Microsoft Research in Redmond, all his energy has been absorbed by Yuri Gurevich's challenging project to make ASMs relevant for software development at Microsoft.

Egon Börger, Joachim Schmid, Robert Stärk
Pisa, München, Zürich, March 2001

Contents

1. **Introduction** 1
    1.1   The goals of the book 2
    1.2   The contents of the book 3
    1.3   Decomposing Java and the JVM 7
    1.4   Sources and literature 11

2. **Abstract State Machines** 15
    2.1   ASMs in a nutshell 15
    2.2   Mathematical definition of ASMs 18
    2.3   Notational conventions 27

Part I. Java

---

3. **The imperative core $Java_{\mathcal{I}}$ of Java** 33
    3.1   Static semantics of $Java_{\mathcal{I}}$ 33
    3.2   Transition rules for $Java_{\mathcal{I}}$ 39

4. **The procedural extension $Java_{\mathcal{C}}$ of $Java_{\mathcal{I}}$** 47
    4.1   Static semantics of $Java_{\mathcal{C}}$ 47
    4.2   Transition rules for $Java_{\mathcal{C}}$ 63

5. **The object-oriented extension $Java_{\mathcal{O}}$ of $Java_{\mathcal{C}}$** 71
    5.1   Static semantics of $Java_{\mathcal{O}}$ 71
    5.2   Transition rules for $Java_{\mathcal{O}}$ 80

6. **The exception-handling extension $Java_{\mathcal{E}}$ of $Java_{\mathcal{O}}$** 87
    6.1   Static semantics of $Java_{\mathcal{E}}$ 87
    6.2   Transition rules for $Java_{\mathcal{E}}$ 89

7. **The concurrent extension $Java_{\mathcal{T}}$ of $Java_{\mathcal{E}}$** 95
    7.1   Static semantics of $Java_{\mathcal{T}}$ 96
    7.2   Transition rules for $Java_{\mathcal{T}}$ 98
    7.3   Thread invariants 106

8. Java is type safe 111
8.1 Structural properties of Java runs 111
8.2 Unreachable statements 117
8.3 Rules of definite assignment 121
8.4 Java is type safe 126

Part II. Compilation of Java: The Trustful JVM

9. The JVM$_\mathcal{I}$ submachine 139
9.1 Dynamic semantics of the JVM$_\mathcal{I}$ 139
9.2 Compilation of Java$_\mathcal{I}$ 142

10. The procedural extension JVM$_\mathcal{C}$ of JVM$_\mathcal{I}$ 147
10.1 Dynamic semantics of the JVM$_\mathcal{C}$ 147
10.2 Compilation of Java$_\mathcal{C}$ 153

11. The object-oriented extension JVM$_\mathcal{O}$ of JVM$_\mathcal{C}$ 155
11.1 Dynamic semantics of the JVM$_\mathcal{O}$ 155
11.2 Compilation of Java$_\mathcal{O}$ 157

12. The exception-handling extension JVM$_\mathcal{E}$ of JVM$_\mathcal{O}$ 159
12.1 Dynamic semantics of the JVM$_\mathcal{E}$ 159
12.2 Compilation of Java$_\mathcal{E}$ 163

13. Executing the JVM$_\mathcal{N}$ 165

14. Correctness of the compiler 167
14.1 The correctness statement 167
14.2 The correctness proof 178

Part III. Bytecode Verification: The Secure JVM

15. The defensive virtual machine 209
15.1 Construction of the defensive JVM 210
15.2 Checking JVM$_\mathcal{I}$ 210
15.3 Checking JVM$_\mathcal{C}$ 213
15.4 Checking JVM$_\mathcal{O}$ 214
15.5 Checking JVM$_\mathcal{E}$ 219
15.6 Checking JVM$_\mathcal{N}$ 221
15.7 Checks are monotonic 222

16. Bytecode type assignments 223
16.1 Problems of bytecode verification 224
16.2 Successors of bytecode instructions 231
16.3 Type assignments without subroutine call stacks 236
16.4 Soundness of bytecode type assignments 242
16.5 Certifying compilation 252

17. The diligent virtual machine 273
17.1 Principal bytecode type assignments 273
17.2 Verifying $JVM_\mathcal{I}$ 275
17.3 Verifying $JVM_\mathcal{C}$ 279
17.4 Verifying $JVM_\mathcal{O}$ 283
17.5 Verifying $JVM_\mathcal{E}$ 283
17.6 Verifying $JVM_\mathcal{N}$ 286

18. The dynamic virtual machine 289
18.1 Initiating and defining loaders.......................... 289
18.2 Loading classes.. 290
18.3 Dynamic semantics of the $JVM_\mathcal{D}$ 291

Appendix

A. Executable Models 305
A.1 Overview 305
A.2 Java 306
A.3 Compiler 312
A.4 Java Virtual Machine 314

B. Java 323
B.1 Rules 323
B.2 Arrays 331

C. JVM 335
C.1 Trustful execution 335
C.2 Defensive execution 343
C.3 Diligent execution 344
C.4 Check functions 347
C.5 Successor functions 348
C.6 Constraints 349
C.7 Arrays 351
C.8 Abstract versus real instructions....................... 355

D. Compiler 361
    D.1 Compilation functions 361
    D.2 maxOpd 363
    D.3 Arrays 364

References 365

List of Figures 367

List of Tables 371

Index 373

1. Introduction

This book provides a structured and high-level description, together with a mathematical and an experimental analysis, of Java and of the Java Virtual Machine (JVM), including the standard compilation of Java programs to JVM code and the security critical bytecode verifier component of the JVM. The description is structured into modules (language layers and machine components), and its abstract character implies that it is truly platform-independent. It comes with a natural refinement to executable machines on which code can be tested, exploiting in particular the potential of model-based high-level testing. The analysis brings to light in what sense, and under which conditions, legal Java programs can be guaranteed to be correctly compiled, to successfully pass the bytecode verifier, and to be executed on the JVM correctly, i.e., faithfully reflecting the Java semantics and without violating any run-time checks. The method we develop for this purpose, using Abstract State Machines which one may view as code written in an abstract programming language, can be applied to other virtual machines and to other programming languages as well.

The target readers are practitioners—programmers, implementors, standardizers, lecturers, students—who need for their work a complete, correct, and at the same time transparent definition, and an executable model of the language and of the virtual machine underlying its intended implementation. As a consequence, in our models for the language and the machine, we first of all try to directly and faithfully reflect, in a complete way, as far as possible without becoming inconsistent, and in an unambiguous yet for the human reader graspable way, the intuitions and design decisions which are expressed in the reference manuals [18, 23] and underlie the current implementations of the language and the machine. We clarify various ambiguities and inconsistencies we discovered in the manuals and in the implementations, concerning fundamental notions like legal Java program, legal bytecode, verifiable bytecode, etc. Our analysis of the JVM bytecode verifier, which we relate to the static analysis of the Java parser (rules of definite assignment and reachability analysis), goes beyond the work of Stata and Abadi [34], Qian [27, 28], Freund and Mitchell [16], and O'Callahan [26].

In this introduction, we give an overview of the general goals of the book, its contents, the structuring techniques we use for decomposing Java and the JVM, and the literature we used.

For additional information on the book and updates made after its publication, see the Home Page of Jbook at `http://www.inf.ethz.ch/~jbook`.

1.1 The goals of the book

Our main goal is not to write an introduction to programming in Java or on the JVM, but to support the practitioner's correct understanding of Java programs and of what can be expected when these programs run on the virtual machine. Therefore we provide a rigorous implementation-independent (read: a mathematical) framework for the clarification of dark corners in the manuals, for the specification and evaluation of variations or extensions of the language and the virtual machine, and for the mathematical and the experimental study and comparison of present and future Java implementations. We build stepwise refined models for the language, the virtual machine, and the compiler that are abstract, but nevertheless can in a natural way be turned into executable models, which we also provide in this book, together with the necessary run-time support. As a result, our specifications of Java and the JVM are amenable to mathematical and computer-assisted verification as well as to the experimental validation of practically important properties of Java programs when executed on the JVM.

To formulate our models for Java and the JVM as consisting of components which reflect different language and security features, we use Gurevich's *Abstract State Machines*(ASMs), a form of pseudo-code, working on abstract data structures, which comes with a simple mathematical foundation [20]. The use of ASMs allowed us:

- To express the basic Java and JVM objects and operations directly, without encoding, i.e., as abstract entities and actions, at the level of abstraction in which they are best understood and analyzed by the human reader
- To uncover the modular structure which characterizes the Java language and its implementation

At the same time, one can turn ASMs in various natural ways into executable code, so that the models can be tested experimentally and validated.

With this book we also pursue a more general goal, which uses Java and the JVM only as a practically relevant and non-trivial case study. Namely, we want to illustrate that for the design and the experimental and mathematical analysis of a complex system, the ASM method is helpful for the working software system engineer and indeed scales to real-life systems.[1] Therefore

---

[1] For a survey of numerous other applications of the method including industrial ones, we refer the reader to [3, 4].

we also include a chapter with a textbook introduction to ASMs. We provide two versions, one written for the practitioner and the other one for the more mathematically inclined reader. We hope that the framework developed in this book shows how to make implementations of real-life complex systems amenable to rigorous high-level analysis and checkable documentation—an indispensable characteristic of every scientifically grounded engineering discipline worth its name.

The three main themes of the book, namely, definition, mathematical verification, and experimental validation of Java and the JVM, fulfill three different concerns and can be dealt with separately. The *definition* has to provide a natural understanding of Java programs and of their execution on the JVM, which can be justified as representing a faithful "ground model" of the intentions of the reference manuals, although our models disambiguate and complete them and make them coherent, where necessary. The *verification* has to clarify and to prove under which assumptions, and in which sense, the relevant design properties can be guaranteed, e.g., in this case, the type safety of syntactically well-formed Java programs, the correctness of their compilation, the soundness and completeness of the bytecode verifier, etc. The *validation* of (a refinement of the ground model to) an executable model serves to provide experimental tests of the models for programs. However, as should become clear through this book, using the ASM framework, these three concerns, namely, abstract specification, its verification, and its validation, can be combined as intimately and coherently connected parts of a rigorous yet practical approach to carrying out a real-life design and implementation project, providing objectively checkable definitions, claims, and justifications. It is a crucial feature of the method that, although abstract, it is run-time oriented. This is indispensable if one wants to come up with formulating precise and reliably implementable conditions on what "auditing" secure systems [21] may mean.

It is also crucial for the practicality of the approach that by exploiting the abstraction and refinement capabilities of ASMs, one can layer complex systems, like Java and the JVM, into several natural strata, each responsible for different aspects of system execution and of its safety, so that in the models one can study their functionality, both in isolation and when they are interacting (see the explanations below).

1.2 The contents of the book

Using an ASM-based modularization technique explained in the next section, we define a structured sequence of mathematical models for the statics and the dynamics of the programming language Java (Part I) and for the Java Virtual Machine, covering the compilation of Java programs to JVM code (Part II) and the JVM bytecode verifier (Part III). The definitions clarify some dark corners in the official descriptions in [18, 23]:

- Bytecode verification is not possible the way the manuals suggest (Fig. 16.8. Fig. 16.9, Remark 8.3.1, Remark 16.5.1, bug no. 4381996 in [14])
- A valid Java program rejected by the verifier (Fig. 16.7, bug no. 4268120 in [14])
- Verifier must use sets of, instead of single, reference types (Sect. 16.1.2, Fig. 16.10)
- Inconsistent treatment of recursive subroutines (Fig. 16.6)
- Verifier has problems with array element types (Example C.7.1)
- Inconsistent method resolution (Example 5.1.4, bug no. 4279316 in [14])
- Compilation of boolean expressions due to the incompatibility of the reachability notions for Java and for JVM code (Example 16.5.4)
- Unfortunate entanglement of embedded subroutines and object initialization (Fig. 16.19, Fig. 16.20)
- Initialization problems [10]

We formulate and prove some of the basic correctness and safety properties, which are claimed for Java and the JVM as a safe and secure, platform-independent, programming environment for the internet. The safety of Java programs does not rely upon the operating system. The implementation compiles Java programs to bytecode which is loaded and verified by the JVM and then executed by the JVM interpreter, letting the JVM control the access to all resources. To the traditional correctness problems for the interpretation and the compilation of programs,[2] this strategy adds some new correctness problems, namely, for the following JVM components (see Fig. 1.4):

- The loading mechanism which dynamically loads classes; the binary representation of a class is retrieved and installed within the JVM—relying upon some appropriate name space definition to be used by the security manager—and then prepared for execution by the JVM interpreter
- The bytecode verifier, which checks certain code properties at link-time, e.g. conditions on types and on stack bounds which one wants to be satisfied at run-time
- The access right checker, i.e., a security manager which controls the access to the file system, to network addresses, to critical windowing operations, etc.

As is well known (see [21]), many Java implementation errors have been found in the complex interplay between the JVM class loader, the bytecode verifier, and the run-time system.

We show under what assumptions Java programs can be proved to be type safe (Theorem 8.4.1), and successfully verified (Theorem 16.5.2 and Theorem 17.1.2) and correctly executed when correctly compiled to JVM code (Theorem 14.1.1). The most difficult part of this endeavor is the rigorous

---

[2] See [5, 6] where ASMs have been used to prove the correctness of the compilation of PROLOG programs to WAM code and of imperative (OCCAM) programs with non-determinism and parallelism to Transputer code.

Fig. 1.1 Dependency Graph

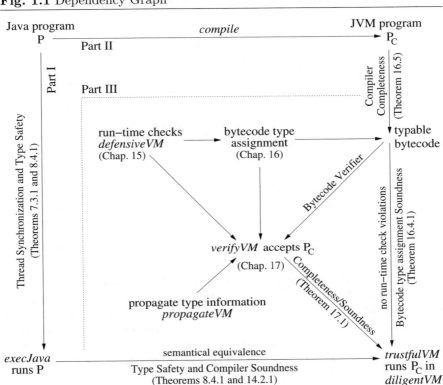

definition and verification of the bytecode verifier, which is a core part of the JVM. We define a novel bytecode verifier for which we can prove soundness (Theorem 17.1.1) and completeness (Theorem 17.1.2). We also prove that successfully verified bytecode is guaranteed to execute without violating any run-time checks (Theorem 16.4.1). We also prove the soundness of Java's thread synchronization (Theorem 7.3.1). Figure 1.1 shows how the theorems and the three parts of this book fit together. We hope that the proofs will provide useful insight into the design of the implementation of Java on the JVM. They may guide possible machine verifications of the reasoning which supports them, the way the WAM correctness proof for the compilation of Prolog programs, which has been formulated in terms of ASMs in [6], has been machine verified in [31].

Last but not least we provide experimental support for our analysis, namely, by the validation of the models in their AsmGofer executable form. Since the executable AsmGofer specifications are mechanically transformed

Fig. 1.2 Language oriented decomposition of Java/JVM

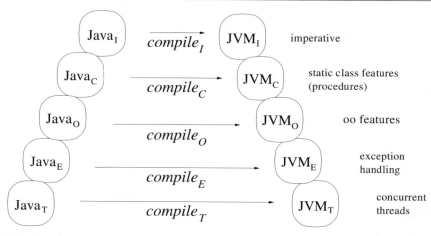

into the LATEX code for the numerous models which appear in the text, the correspondence between these specifications is no longer disrupted by any manual translation. AsmGofer (see Appendix A) is an ASM programming system developed by Joachim Schmid, on the suggestion and with the initial help of Wolfram Schulte, extending TkGofer to execute ASMs which come with Haskell definable external functions. It provides a step-by-step execution of ASMs, in particular of Java/JVM programs on our Java/JVM machines, with GUIs to support debugging. The appendix which accompanies the book contains an introduction to the three graphical AsmGofer user interfaces: for Java, for the compiler from Java to bytecode, and for the JVM. The Java GUI offers debugger features and can be used to observe the behavior of Java programs during their execution. As a result, the reader can run experiments by executing Java programs on our Java machine, compiling them to bytecode and executing that bytecode on our JVM machine. For example, it can be checked that our Bytecode Verifier rejects the program found by Saraswat [30].

The CD contains the entire text of the book, numerous examples and exercises which support using the book for teaching, the sources of the executable models, and the source code for AsmGofer together with installation instructions (and also precompiled binaries of AsmGofer for several popular operating systems like Linux and Windows). The examples and exercises in the book which are provided by the CD are marked with ⤳ CD. The executable models also contain the treatment of strings which are needed to run interesting examples.

Fig. 1.3 Multiple thread Java machine execJavaThread

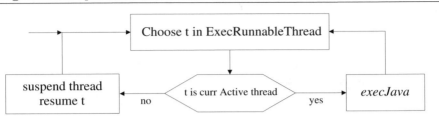

1.3 Decomposing Java and the JVM

We decompose Java and the JVM into language layers and security modules, thus splitting the overall definition and verification problem into a series of tractable subproblems. This is technically supported by the abstraction and refinement capabilities of ASMs. As a result we succeed

- To reveal the structure of the language and the virtual machine
- To control the size of the models and of the definition of the compilation scheme, which relates them
- To keep the effort of writing and understanding the proofs and the executable models, manageable

The first layering principle reflects the structure of the Java language and of the set of JVM instructions. In Part I and Part II we factor the sets of Java and of JVM instructions into five sublanguages, by isolating language features which represent milestones in the evolution of modern programming languages and of the techniques for their compilation, namely imperative (sequential control), procedural (module), object-oriented, exception handling, and concurrency features. We illustrate this in Fig. 1.2. A related structuring principle, which helps us to keep the size of the models small, consists in grouping similar instructions into one abstract instruction each, coming with appropriate parameters. This goes without leaving out any relevant language feature, given that the specializations can be regained by mere parameter expansion, a refinement step whose correctness is easily controllable instruction-wise. See Appendix C.8 for a correspondence table between our abstract JVM instructions and the real bytecode instructions.

This decomposition can be made in such a way that in the resulting sequence of machines, namely $\text{Java}_\mathcal{I}$, $\text{Java}_\mathcal{C}$, $\text{Java}_\mathcal{O}$, $\text{Java}_\mathcal{E}$, $\text{Java}_\mathcal{T}$ and $\text{JVM}_\mathcal{I}$, $\text{JVM}_\mathcal{C}$, $\text{JVM}_\mathcal{O}$, $\text{JVM}_\mathcal{E}$, $\text{JVM}_\mathcal{N}$, each ASM is a purely incremental—similar to what logicians call a conservative—extension of its predecessor, because each of them provides the semantics of the underlying language instruction by instruction. The general compilation scheme *compile* can then be defined between the corresponding submachines by a simple recursion.

Fig. 1.4 Security oriented decomposition of the JVM

Usr.java ⟶ (Compiler) ⟶ Usr.class ⟶ Internet

JVM Run–time machine

Verifier ⟵ Loader   Sys.class

Preparator ⟶ Interpreter ⟷ Input / Output

Functionally we follow a well known pattern and separate the treatment of parsing, elaboration, and execution of Java programs. We describe how our Java machines, which represent abstract interpreters for arbitrary programs in the corresponding sublanguage, are supposed to receive these input programs in the form of abstract syntax trees resulting from parsing. For each Java submachine we describe separately, in Part I, the static and the dynamic part of the program semantics. We formulate the relevant static constraints of being well-formed and well-typed, which are checked during the program elaboration phase and result in corresponding annotations in the abstract syntax tree. In the main text of the book we restrict the analysis of the static constraints to what is necessary for a correct understanding of the language and for the proofs in this book. The remaining details appear in the executable version of the Java model. We formalize the dynamical program behavior by ASM transition rules, describing how the program runtime state changes through evaluating expressions and executing statements. This model allows us to rigorously define what it means for Java to be type safe, and to prove that well-formed and well-typed Java programs are indeed type safe (Theorem 8.4.1). This includes defining rules which achieve the definite assignment of variables, and to prove the soundness of such assignments. The resulting one-thread model *execJava* can be used to build a multiple–thread executable ASM *execJavaThread* which reflects the intention of [18, 23], namely to leave the specification of the particular implementation of the scheduling strategy open, by using a choice that is a not further specified function (Fig. 1.3)[3]. For this model we can prove a correctness theorem for thread synchronization (Theorem 7.3.1).

[3] The flowchart notation we use in this introduction has the expected precise meaning, see Chapter 2, so that these diagrams provide a rigorous definition, namely of so called control state ASMs.

Fig. 1.5 Decomposing trustfulVMs into execVMs and switchVMs

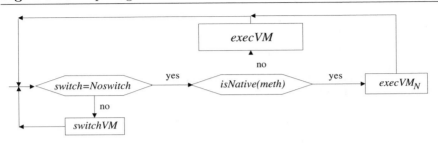

$trustfulVM = execVM_I \cup execVM_C \cup execVM_O \cup execVM_E \cup execVM_N \cup execVM_D$

$switchVM_D$ extends $switchVM_E$ extends $switchVM_C$

For JVM programs, we separate the modeling of the security relevant loading (Chapter 18) and linking (i.e., preparation and verification, see Part III) from each other and from the execution (Part II), as illustrated in Fig. 1.4.

In Part II we describe the *trustful execution* of bytecode which is assumed to be successfully loaded and linked (i.e., prepared and verified to satisfy the required link-time constraints). The resulting sequence of stepwise refined trustful VMs, namely $trustfulVM_I$, $trustfulVM_C$, $trustfulVM_O$, $trustfulVM_E$, and $trustfulVM_N$, yields a succinct definition of the functionality of JVM execution in terms of language layered submachines *execVM* and *switchVM* (Fig. 1.5). The machine *execVM* describes the effect of each single JVM instruction on the current frame, whereas *switchVM* is responsible for frame stack manipulations upon method call and return, class initialization and exception capture. The machines do nothing when no instruction remains to be executed. As stated above, this piecemeal description of single Java/JVM instructions yields a simple recursive definition of a general compilation scheme for Java programs to JVM code, which allows us to incrementally prove it to be correct (see Chapter 14). This includes a correctness proof for the handling of Java exceptions in the JVM, a feature which considerably complicates the bytecode verification, in the presence of embedded subroutines, class and object initialization and concurrently working threads.

In Chapter 17 we insert this trustfully executing machine into a *diligent* JVM which, after loading the bytecode, which is stored in class files, and before executing it using the trustfully executing component *trustfulVM*, prepares and verifies the code for all methods in that class file, using a submachine *verifyVM* which checks, one after the other, each method body to satisfy the required type and stack bound constraints (Fig. 1.6).

The machine *verifyVM* is language layered, like *trustfulVM*, since it is built from a language layered submachine *propagateVM*, a language layered

Fig. 1.6 Decomposing diligent JVMs into trustfulVMs and verifyVMs

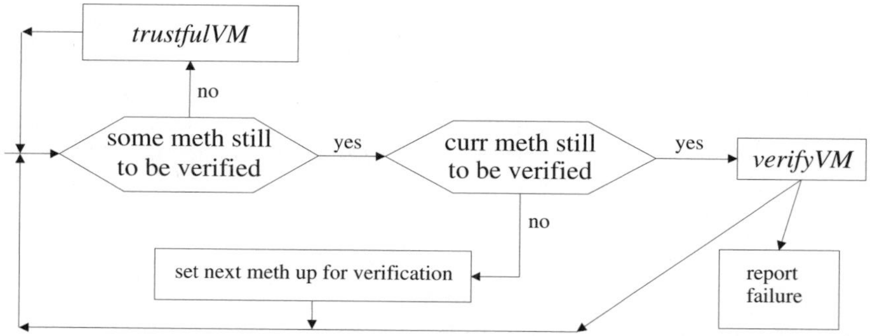

verifyVM built from submachines propagate, succ, check

predicate *check* and a language layered function *succ*. The verifier machine chooses an instruction among those which are still to be verified, checks whether it satisfies the required constraints and either reports failure or propagates the result of the checked conditions to the successor instructions (Fig. 1.7).

The submachine *propagateVM*, together with the function *succ* in the verifying submachine *verifyVM*, defines a link-time simulation (type version) of the *trustful* VM of Part II, although the checking functionality can be better defined in terms of a run-time checking machine, see Chapter 15. The *defensive* VM we describe there, which is inspired by the work of Cohen [13], defines what to check for each JVM instruction at run-time, before its trustful execution. We formulate the constraints about types, resource bounds, references to heap objects, etc., which are required to be satisfied when the given instruction is executed (Fig. 1.8).

The reason for introducing this machine is to obtain a well motivated and clear definition of the bytecode verification functionality, a task which is best accomplished locally, in terms of run-time checks of the safe executability of single instructions. However, we formulate these run-time checking conditions referring to the types of values, instead of the values themselves, so that we can easily lift them to link-time checkable bytecode type assignments (see Chapter 16). When lifting the run-time constraints, we make sure that if a given bytecode has a type assignment, this implies that the code runs on the defensive VM without violating any run-time checks, as we can indeed prove in Theorem 16.4.1. The notion of bytecode type assignment also allows us to prove the completeness of the compilation scheme defined in Part II. Completeness here means that bytecode which is compiled from a well-formed and well-typed Java program (in a way which respects our compilation scheme), can be typed successfully, in the sense that it does have type assignments

Fig. 1.7 Decomposing verifyVMs into propagateVMs, checks, succs

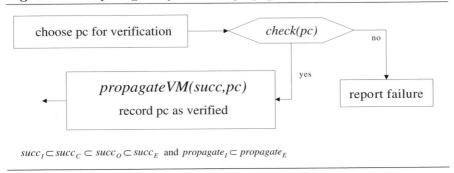

$succ_I \subset succ_C \subset succ_O \subset succ_E$ and $propagate_I \subset propagate_E$

(Theorem 16.5.2). To support the inductive proof for this theorem we refine our compiler to a certifying code generator, which issues instructions together with the type information needed for the bytecode verification.

The details of the machines outlined above are explained in this book and are summarized in appendices B and C. Putting together the properties of the language layered submachines and of the security components of Java and of the JVM, one obtains a precise yet graspable statement, and an understandable (and therefore checkable) proof of the following property of Java and the JVM.

> **Main Theorem.** Under explicitly stated conditions, any well-formed and well-typed Java program, when correctly compiled, passes the verifier and is executed on the JVM. It executes without violating any run-time checks, and is correct with respect to the expected behavior as defined by the Java machine.

For the executable versions of our machines, the formats for inputting and compiling Java programs are chosen in such a way that the ASMs for the JVM and the compiler can be combined in various ways with current implementations of Java compilers and of the JVM (see Appendix A and in particular Fig. A.1 for the details).

1.4 Sources and literature

This book is largely self-contained and presupposes only basic knowledge in object-oriented programming and about the implementation of high-level programming languages. It uses ASMs, which have a simple mathematical foundation justifying their intuitive understanding as "pseudo-code over abstract data", so that the reader can understand them correctly and successfully without having to go through any preliminary reading. We therefore

Fig. 1.8 Decomposing defensiveVMs into trustfulVMs and checks

$check_D$ extends $check_N$ extends $check_E$ extends $check_O$ extends $check_C$ extends $check_I$

invite the reader to consult the formal definition of ASMs in Chapter 2 only should the necessity be felt.

The Java/JVM models in this book are completely revised—streamlined, extended and in some points corrected—versions of the models which appeared in [9, 11]. The original models were based upon the first edition of the Java and JVM specifications [18, 23], and also the models in this book still largely reflect our interpretation of the original scheme. In particular we do not treat nested and inner classes which appear in the second edition of the Java specification, which was published when the work on this book was finished. It should be noted however that the revision of [23], which appeared in 1999 in the appendix of the second edition of the JVM specification, clarifies most of the ambiguities, errors and omissions that were reported in [10].

The proofs of the theorems were developed for this book by Robert Stärk and Egon Börger, starting from the proof idea formulated for the compiler correctness theorem in [8], from its elaboration in [33] and from the proof for the correctness of exception handling in [12]. The novel subroutine call stack free bytecode verifier was developed by Robert Stärk and Joachim Schmid. Robert Stärk constructed the proof for Theorem 16.5.2 that this verifier accepts every legal Java program which is compiled respecting our compilation scheme. The AsmGofer executable versions of the models were developed for this book by Joachim Schmid and contributed considerably towards getting the models correct.

We can point the reader to a recent survey [21] of the rich literature on modeling and analyzing safety aspects of Java and the JVM. Therefore we limit ourselves to citing in this book only a few sources which had a direct impact on our own work. As stated above, the complex scheme to implement Java security through the JVM interpreter requires a class loader, a security manager and a bytecode verifier. For a detailed analysis of the class loading mechanism, which is underspecified in [18] and therefore only sketched in this book, we refer the reader to [29, 35] where also further references on this still widely open subject can be found. We hope that somebody will use and extend our models for a complete analysis of the critical security features of Java, since the framework allows to precisely state and study the necessary system safety and security properties; the extensive literature devoted to this theme is reviewed in [21].

Draft chapters of the book have been used by Robert Stärk in his summer term 2000 course at ETH Zürich, and by Egon Börger in his *Specification Methods* course in Pisa in the fall of 2000.

2. Abstract State Machines

The notion of *Abstract State Machines* (ASMs), defined in [20], captures in mathematically rigorous yet transparent form some fundamental operational intuitions of computing, and the notation is familiar from programming practice and mathematical standards. This allows the practitioner to work with ASMs without any further explanation, viewing them as 'pseudocode over abstract data' which comes with a well defined semantics supporting the intuitive understanding. We therefore suggest to skip this chapter and to come back to it only should the need be felt upon further reading.

For the sake of a definite reference, we nevertheless provide in this chapter a survey of the notation, including some extensions of the definition in [20] which are introduced in [7] for structuring complex machines and for reusing machine components. For the reader who is interested in more details, we also provide a mathematical definition of the syntax and semantics of ASMs. This definition helps understanding how the ASMs in this book have been made executable, despite of their abstract nature; it will also help the more mathematically inclined reader to check the proofs in this book. We stick to non distributed (also called sequential) ASMs because they suffice for modeling Java and the JVM.

2.1 ASMs in a nutshell

ASMs are systems of finitely many *transition rules* of form

> **if** *Condition* **then** *Updates*

which transform abstract states. (Two more forms are introduced below.) The *Condition* (so called guard) under which a rule is applied is an arbitrary first-order formula without free variables. *Updates* is a finite set of function updates (containing only variable free terms) of form

> $f(t_1, \ldots, t_n) := t$

whose execution is to be understood as *changing* (or defining, if there was none) the value of the (location represented by the) function f at the given parameters.

Fig. 2.1 Control state ASM diagrams

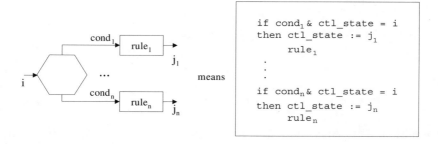

Assume disjoint $cond_i$. Usually the "control states" are notationally suppressed.

The global JVM structure is given by so called control state ASMs [3] which have finitely many control states $ctl\_state \in \{1, \ldots, m\}$, resembling the internal states of classical Finite State Machines. They are defined and pictorially depicted as shown in Fig. 2.1. Note that in a given control state i, these machines do nothing when no condition $cond_j$ is satisfied.

The notion of ASM *states* is the classical notion of mathematical *structures* where data come as abstract objects, i.e., as elements of sets (domains, *universes*, one for each category of data) which are equipped with basic operations (partial *functions*) and predicates (attributes or relations). Without loss of generality one can treat predicates as characteristic functions.

The notion of ASM *run* is the classical notion of computation of transition systems. An ASM computation step in a given state consists in executing *simultaneously* all updates of all transition rules whose guard is true in the state, if these updates are consistent. For the evaluation of terms and formulae in an ASM state, the standard interpretation of function symbols by the corresponding functions in that state is used.

Simultaneous execution provides a convenient way to abstract from irrelevant sequentiality and to make use of synchronous parallelism. This mechanism is enhanced by the following concise notation for the simultaneous execution of an ASM rule R for each x satisfying a given condition φ:

forall x **with** φ **do** R

A priori no restriction is imposed neither on the abstraction level nor on the complexity nor on the means of definition of the functions used to compute the arguments t_i and the new value t in function updates. The major distinction made in this connection for a given ASM M is between *static* functions— which never change during any run of M—and *dynamic* ones which typically do change as a consequence of updates by M or by the environment (i.e., by some other agent than M). The dynamic functions are further divided into four subclasses. *Controlled* functions (for M) are dynamic functions which are directly updatable by and only by the rules of M, i.e., functions f which appear in a rule of M as leftmost function (namely in an update $f(s) := t$ for some s, t) and are not updatable by the environment. *Monitored* functions are dynamic functions which are directly updatable by and only by the environment, i.e., which are updatable but do not appear as leftmost function in updates of M. *Interaction* functions are dynamic functions which are directly updatable by rules of M and by the environment. *Derived* functions are dynamic functions which are not directly updatable neither by M nor by the environment but are nevertheless dynamic because defined (for example by an explicit or by an inductive definition) in terms of static *and* dynamic functions.

We will use functions of all these types in this book, their use supports the principles of separation of concerns, information hiding, modularization and stepwise refinement in system design. A frequently encountered kind of static or monitored functions are choice functions, used to abstract from details of static or dynamic scheduling strategies. ASMs support the following concise notation for an abstract specification of such strategies:

choose x **with** φ **do** R

meaning to execute rule R with an arbitrary x chosen among those satisfying the selection property φ. If there exists no such x, nothing is done. For **choose** and **forall** rules we also use graphical notations of the following form:

choose x **with** φ
R

forall x **with** φ
R

We freely use as abbreviations combinations of **where, let, if then else, case** and similar standard notations which are easily reducible to the above basic definitions. We usually use the table like **case** notation with pattern matching and try out the cases in the order of writing, from top to bottom. We also use rule schemes, namely rules with variables and named parametrized rules, but only as an abbreviational device to enhance the readability or as macro allowing us to reuse machines and to display the global machine structure. For example

    if $\dots a = (X, Y) \dots$
    then $\dots X \dots Y \dots$

abbreviates

    if $\dots \mathrm{ispair}(a) \dots$
    then $\dots \mathrm{fst}(a) \dots \mathrm{snd}(a) \dots,$

sparing us the need to write explicitly the recognizers and the selectors. Similarly, an occurrence of

$$r(x_1, \ldots, x_n)$$

where a rule is expected stands for the corresponding rule R (which is supposed to be defined somewhere, say by $r(x_1, \ldots, x_n) = R$). Such a "rule call" $r(x_1, \ldots, x_n)$ is used only when the parameters are instantiated by legal values (objects, functions, rules, whatever) so that the resulting rule has a well defined semantical meaning on the basis of the explanations given above.

2.2 Mathematical definition of ASMs

In this section we provide a detailed mathematical definition for the syntax and semantics of ASMs. This definition is the basis of the AsmGofer implementation of the ASMs for Java/JVM in this book.

2.2.1 Abstract states

In an ASM state, data come as abstract elements of domains (also called universes, one for each category of data) which are equipped with basic operations represented by functions. Without loss of generality we treat relations as boolean valued functions and view domains as characteristic functions, defined on the superuniverse which represents the union of all domains. Thus the states of ASMs are *algebraic structures*, also called simply *algebras*, as introduced in standard logic or universal algebra textbooks.

Definition 2.2.1 (Vocabulary). A *vocabulary* Σ is a finite collection of function names. Each function name f has an *arity*, a non-negative integer. The arity of a function name is the number of arguments the function takes. Function names can be *static* or *dynamic*. Nullary function names are often called *constants*; but be aware that, as we will see below, the interpretation of dynamic nullary functions can change from one state to the next, so that they correspond to the variables of programming. Every ASM vocabulary is assumed to contain the static constants *undef*, *True*, *False*.

Example 2.2.1. The vocabulary Σ_{bool} of Boolean algebras contains two constants 0 and 1, a unary function name '$-$' and two binary function names '$+$' and '$*$'. The vocabulary Σ_{scm} of the programming language Scheme contains a constant *nil*, two unary function names *car* and *cdr* and a binary function name *cons*, etc.

Definition 2.2.2 (State). A *state* $\mathfrak{A}$ of the vocabulary Σ is a non-empty set X, the *superuniverse* of $\mathfrak{A}$, together with *interpretations* of the function names of Σ. If f is an n-ary function name of Σ, then its interpretation $f^{\mathfrak{A}}$ is a function from X^n into X; if c is a constant of Σ, then its interpretation $c^{\mathfrak{A}}$ is an element of X. The superuniverse X of the state $\mathfrak{A}$ is denoted by $|\mathfrak{A}|$.

Example 2.2.2. Two states $\mathfrak{A}$ and $\mathfrak{B}$ for the vocabulary Σ_{bool} of Example 2.2.1: The superuniverse of the state $\mathfrak{A}$ is the set $\{0, 1\}$. The functions are interpreted as follows, where a, b are 0 or 1:

$$
\begin{aligned}
0^{\mathfrak{A}} &:= 0 && \text{(zero)} \\
1^{\mathfrak{A}} &:= 1 && \text{(one)} \\
-^{\mathfrak{A}} a &:= 1 - a && \text{(logical complement)} \\
a +^{\mathfrak{A}} b &:= \max(a, b) && \text{(logical or)} \\
a *^{\mathfrak{A}} b &:= \min(a, b) && \text{(logical and)}
\end{aligned}
$$

The superuniverse of the state $\mathfrak{B}$ is the power set of the set of non-negative integers $\mathbb{N}$. The functions are interpreted as follows, where a, b are subsets of $\mathbb{N}$:

$$
\begin{aligned}
0^{\mathfrak{B}} &:= \emptyset && \text{(empty set)} \\
1^{\mathfrak{B}} &:= \mathbb{N} && \text{(full set)} \\
-^{\mathfrak{B}} a &:= \mathbb{N} \setminus a && \text{(set of all } n \in \mathbb{N} \text{ such that } n \notin a) \\
a +^{\mathfrak{B}} b &:= a \cup b && \text{(set of all } n \in \mathbb{N} \text{ such that } n \in a \text{ or } n \in b) \\
a *^{\mathfrak{B}} b &:= a \cap b && \text{(set of all } n \in \mathbb{N} \text{ such that } n \in a \text{ and } n \in b)
\end{aligned}
$$

Both states, $\mathfrak{A}$ and $\mathfrak{B}$, are so-called Boolean algebras.

Other examples of algebraic structures are: groups, rings, lattices, etc.

Remark 2.2.1. Formally, function names are interpreted in states as total functions. We view them, however, as being partial and define the *domain* of an n-ary function name f in $\mathfrak{A}$ to be the set of all n-tuples $(a_1, \ldots, a_n) \in |\mathfrak{A}|^n$ such that $f^{\mathfrak{A}}(a_1, \ldots, a_n) \neq undef^{\mathfrak{A}}$.

Example 2.2.3. In states for the vocabulary Σ_{scm} of Example 2.2.1, we usually have: $car^{\mathfrak{A}}(nil^{\mathfrak{A}}) = undef^{\mathfrak{A}}$, $cdr^{\mathfrak{A}}(nil^{\mathfrak{A}}) = undef^{\mathfrak{A}}$.

The constant *undef* represents an undetermined object, the default value of the superuniverse. It is also used to model heterogeneous domains. In applications, the superuniverse A of a state $\mathfrak{A}$ is usually divided into smaller *universes*, modeled by their characteristic functions. The universe represented by f is the set of all elements t for which $f(t) \neq undef$. If a unary function f represents a universe, then we simply write $t \in f$ as an abbreviation for the formula $f(t) \neq undef$.

Definition 2.2.3 (Term). The terms of Σ are syntactic expressions generated as follows:

1. Variables v_0, v_1, v_2, ... are terms.
2. Constants c of Σ are terms.
3. If f is an n-ary function name of Σ and $t_1, \ldots, t_n$ are terms, then $f(t_1, \ldots, t_n)$ is a term.

Terms are denoted by r, s, t; variables are denoted by x, y, z. A term which does not contain variables is called *closed*.

Example 2.2.4. The following are terms of the vocabulary Σ_{bool}:

$$+(v_0, v_1), \quad +(1, *(v_7, 0))$$

The are usually written as $v_0 + v_1$ and $1 + (v_7 * 0)$.

Since terms are syntactic objects, they do not have a meaning. A term can be evaluated in a state, if elements of the superuniverse are assigned to the variables of the term.

Definition 2.2.4 (Variable assignment). Let $\mathfrak{A}$ be a state. A *variable assignment* for $\mathfrak{A}$ is a function ζ which assigns to each variable v_i an element $\zeta(v_i) \in |\mathfrak{A}|$. We write $\zeta \frac{a}{x}$ for the variable assignment which coincides with ζ except that it assigns the element a to the variable x. So we have:

$$\zeta\tfrac{a}{x}(v_i) = \begin{cases} a, & \text{if } v_i = x; \\ \zeta(v_i), & \text{otherwise.} \end{cases}$$

Given a variable assignment a term can be interpreted in a state.

Definition 2.2.5 (Interpretation of terms). Let $\mathfrak{A}$ be a state of Σ, ζ be a variable assignment for $\mathfrak{A}$ and t be a term of Σ. By induction on the length of t, a value $[\![t]\!]_\zeta^{\mathfrak{A}} \in |\mathfrak{A}|$ is defined as follows:

1. $[\![v_i]\!]_\zeta^{\mathfrak{A}} := \zeta(v_i)$,
2. $[\![c]\!]_\zeta^{\mathfrak{A}} := c^{\mathfrak{A}}$,
3. $[\![f(t_1, \ldots, t_n)]\!]_\zeta^{\mathfrak{A}} := f^{\mathfrak{A}}([\![t_1]\!]_\zeta^{\mathfrak{A}}, \ldots, [\![t_n]\!]_\zeta^{\mathfrak{A}})$.

The interpretation of t depends on the values of ζ on the variables of t only: if $\zeta(x) = \xi(x)$ for all variables x of t, then $[\![t]\!]_\zeta^{\mathfrak{A}} = [\![t]\!]_\xi^{\mathfrak{A}}$ (Coincidence Lemma).

Example 2.2.5. Consider the state $\mathfrak{A}$ for Σ_{bool} of Example 2.2.2. Let ζ be a variable assignment with $\zeta(v_0) = 0$, $\zeta(v_1) = 1$ and $\zeta(v_2) = 1$. Then we have:

$$[\![(v_0 + v_1) * v_2]\!]_\zeta^{\mathfrak{A}} = 1.$$

The same term can be interpreted in the state $\mathfrak{B}$ of Example 2.2.2. Let $\xi(v_0) = \{2, 3, 5\}$, $\xi(v_1) = \{2, 7\}$ and $\xi(v_2) = \{3, 7, 11\}$. Then we have:

$$[\![(v_0 + v_1) * v_2]\!]_\xi^{\mathfrak{B}} = \{3, 7\}.$$

In the first case, the value of the term is a non-negative integer, whereas in the second case the value of the term is a set of non-negative integers.

Definition 2.2.6 (Formula). Let Σ be a vocabulary. The formulas of Σ are generated as follows:

1. If s and t are terms of Σ, then $s = t$ is a formula.
2. If φ is a formula, then $\neg \varphi$ is a formula.
3. If φ and ψ are formulas, then $(\varphi \wedge \psi)$, $(\varphi \vee \psi)$ and $(\varphi \rightarrow \psi)$ are formulas.
4. If φ is a formula and x a variable, then $(\forall x \, \varphi)$ and $(\exists x \, \varphi)$ are formulas.

The logical connectives and quantifiers have the standard meaning:

symbol	name	meaning
$\neg$	negation	not
$\wedge$	conjunction	and
$\vee$	disjunction	or (inclusive)
$\rightarrow$	implication	if-then
$\forall$	universal quantification	for all
$\exists$	existential quantification	there is

A formula $s = t$ is called an *equation*. The expression $s \neq t$ is an abbreviation for the formula $\neg\,(s = t)$.

In order to increase the readability of formulas parentheses are often omitted. For example, the following conventions are used:

$$
\begin{array}{lll}
\varphi \wedge \psi \wedge \chi & \text{stands for} & ((\varphi \wedge \psi) \wedge \chi), \\
\varphi \vee \psi \vee \chi & \text{stands for} & ((\varphi \vee \psi) \vee \chi), \\
\varphi \wedge \psi \rightarrow \chi & \text{stands for} & ((\varphi \wedge \psi) \rightarrow \chi), \text{ etc.}
\end{array}
$$

Formulas can be interpreted in a state with respect to a variable assignment. Formulas are either true or false in a state. The truth value of a formula in a state is computed recursively. The classical truth tables for the logical connectives and the classical interpretation of quantifiers are used. The equality sign is interpreted as identity.

Definition 2.2.7 (Interpretation of formulas). Let $\mathfrak{A}$ be a state of Σ, φ be a formula of Σ and ζ be a variable assignment in $\mathfrak{A}$. By induction on the length of φ, a truth value $[\![\varphi]\!]^{\mathfrak{A}}_{\zeta} \in \{\textit{True}, \textit{False}\}$ is defined as follows:

$$
[\![s = t]\!]^{\mathfrak{A}}_{\zeta} := \begin{cases} \textit{True}, & \text{if } [\![s]\!]^{\mathfrak{A}}_{\zeta} = [\![t]\!]^{\mathfrak{A}}_{\zeta}; \\ \textit{False}, & \text{otherwise.} \end{cases}
$$

$$
[\![\neg\,\varphi]\!]^{\mathfrak{A}}_{\zeta} := \begin{cases} \textit{True}, & \text{if } [\![\varphi]\!]^{\mathfrak{A}}_{\zeta} = \textit{False}; \\ \textit{False}, & \text{otherwise.} \end{cases}
$$

$$
[\![\varphi \wedge \psi]\!]^{\mathfrak{A}}_{\zeta} := \begin{cases} \textit{True}, & \text{if } [\![\varphi]\!]^{\mathfrak{A}}_{\zeta} = \textit{True} \text{ and } [\![\psi]\!]^{\mathfrak{A}}_{\zeta} = \textit{True}; \\ \textit{False}, & \text{otherwise.} \end{cases}
$$

$$
[\![\varphi \vee \psi]\!]^{\mathfrak{A}}_{\zeta} := \begin{cases} \textit{True}, & \text{if } [\![\varphi]\!]^{\mathfrak{A}}_{\zeta} = \textit{True} \text{ or } [\![\psi]\!]^{\mathfrak{A}}_{\zeta} = \textit{True}; \\ \textit{False}, & \text{otherwise.} \end{cases}
$$

$$
[\![\varphi \rightarrow \psi]\!]^{\mathfrak{A}}_{\zeta} := \begin{cases} \textit{True}, & \text{if } [\![\varphi]\!]^{\mathfrak{A}}_{\zeta} = \textit{False} \text{ or } [\![\psi]\!]^{\mathfrak{A}}_{\zeta} = \textit{True}; \\ \textit{False}, & \text{otherwise.} \end{cases}
$$

$$
[\![\forall x\,\varphi]\!]^{\mathfrak{A}}_{\zeta} := \begin{cases} \textit{True}, & \text{if } [\![\varphi]\!]^{\mathfrak{A}}_{\zeta\frac{a}{x}} = \textit{True} \text{ for all } a \in |\mathfrak{A}|; \\ \textit{False}, & \text{otherwise.} \end{cases}
$$

$$
[\![\exists x\,\varphi]\!]^{\mathfrak{A}}_{\zeta} := \begin{cases} \textit{True}, & \text{if } [\![\varphi]\!]^{\mathfrak{A}}_{\zeta\frac{a}{x}} = \textit{True} \text{ for some } a \in |\mathfrak{A}|; \\ \textit{False}, & \text{otherwise.} \end{cases}
$$

We say that a state $\mathfrak{A}$ is a *model* of φ, if $[\![\varphi]\!]_\zeta^{\mathfrak{A}} = True$ for all variable assignments ζ.

Example 2.2.6. The states $\mathfrak{A}$ and $\mathfrak{B}$ of Example 2.2.2 are models of the following equations:

$$(x + y) + z = x + (y + z), \qquad (x * y) * z = x * (y * z),$$
$$x + y = y + x, \qquad x * y = y * x,$$
$$x + (x * y) = x, \qquad x * (x + y) = x,$$
$$x + (y * z) = (x + y) * (x + z), \qquad x * (y + z) = (x * y) + (x * z),$$
$$x + (-x) = 1, \qquad x * (-x) = 0.$$

These formulas are called axioms of a Boolean algebra.

2.2.2 Transition rules and runs

In mathematics, states like Boolean algebras are static. They do not change over time. In computer science, states are dynamic. They evolve by being updated during computations. Updating abstract states means to change the interpretation of (some of) the functions in the underlying signature. The way ASMs update states is described by transitions rules of the following form which define the syntax of ASM programs.

Definition 2.2.8 (Transition rules). Let Σ be a vocabulary. The transition rules R, S of an ASM are syntactic expressions generated as follows:

1. *Skip Rule:*

   skip

   Meaning: Do nothing.

2. *Update Rule:*

   $$f(t_1, \ldots, t_n) := s$$

   Syntactic conditions:
   $-$ f is an n-ary, dynamic function name of Σ
   $-$ $t_1, \ldots, t_n$ and s are terms of Σ
   Meaning: In the next state, the value of the function f at the arguments $t_1, \ldots, t_n$ is updated to s. It is allowed that f is a 0-ary function, i.e., a constant. In this case, the update has the form $c := s$.

3. *Block Rule:*

   $R\ S$

   Meaning: R and S are executed in parallel.

4. *Conditional Rule:*

   if φ **then** R **else** S

   Meaning: If φ is true, then execute R, otherwise execute S.

5. *Let Rule:*

   let $x = t$ **in** R

   Meaning: Assign the value of t to x and execute R.

6. *Forall Rule:*

   forall x **with** φ **do** R

   Meaning: Execute R in parallel for each x satisfying φ.

7. *Call Rule:*

   $r(t_1, \ldots, t_n)$

   Meaning: Call r with parameters $t_1, \ldots, t_n$.

A *rule definition* for a rule name r of arity n is an expression

$$r(x_1, \ldots, x_n) = R,$$

where R is a transition rule. In a rule call $r(t_1, \ldots, t_n)$ the variables x_i in the body R of the rule definition are replaced by the parameters t_i.

Definition 2.2.9 (ASM). An *abstract state machine* M consists of a vocabulary Σ, an initial state $\mathfrak{A}$ for Σ, a rule definition for each rule name, and a distinguished rule name of arity zero called the *main rule name* of the machine.

The semantics of transition rules is given by sets of updates. Since due to the parallelism (in the Block and the Forall rules), a transition rule may prescribe to update the same function at the same arguments several times, we require such updates to be consistent. The concept of consistent update sets is made more precise by the following definitions.

Definition 2.2.10 (Update). An *update* for $\mathfrak{A}$ is a triple $(f, (a_1, \ldots, a_n), b)$, where f is an n-ary dynamic function name, and $a_1, \ldots, a_n$ and b are elements of $|\mathfrak{A}|$.

The meaning of the update is that the interpretation of the function f in $\mathfrak{A}$ has to be changed at the arguments $a_1, \ldots, a_n$ to the value b. The pair of the first two components of an update is called a *location*. An update specifies how the function table of a dynamic function has to be updated at the corresponding location. An *update set* is a set of updates.

In a given state, a transition rule of an ASM produces for each variable assignment an update set. Since the rule can contain recursive calls to other rules, it is also possible that it has no semantics at all. The semantics of a transition rule is therefore defined by a calculus in Fig. 2.2.

Fig. 2.2 The semantics of ASM rules

$\overline{[\![\textbf{skip}\,]\!]_\zeta^{\mathfrak{A}} \;\triangleright\; \emptyset}$

$\dfrac{}{[\![f(t) := s]\!]_\zeta^{\mathfrak{A}} \;\triangleright\; \{(f, a, b)\}}$ if $a = [\![t]\!]_\zeta^{\mathfrak{A}}$ and $b = [\![s]\!]_\zeta^{\mathfrak{A}}$

$\dfrac{[\![R]\!]_\zeta^{\mathfrak{A}} \;\triangleright\; U \qquad [\![S]\!]_\zeta^{\mathfrak{A}} \;\triangleright\; V}{[\![R\,S]\!]_\zeta^{\mathfrak{A}} \;\triangleright\; U \cup V}$

$\dfrac{[\![R]\!]_\zeta^{\mathfrak{A}} \;\triangleright\; U}{[\![\textbf{if }\varphi\textbf{ then }R\textbf{ else }S]\!]_\zeta^{\mathfrak{A}} \;\triangleright\; U}$ if $[\![\varphi]\!]_\zeta^{\mathfrak{A}} = \textit{True}$

$\dfrac{[\![S]\!]_\zeta^{\mathfrak{A}} \;\triangleright\; U}{[\![\textbf{if }\varphi\textbf{ then }R\textbf{ else }S]\!]_\zeta^{\mathfrak{A}} \;\triangleright\; U}$ if $[\![\varphi]\!]_\zeta^{\mathfrak{A}} = \textit{False}$

$\dfrac{[\![R]\!]_{\zeta\frac{a}{x}}^{\mathfrak{A}} \;\triangleright\; U}{[\![\textbf{let }x = t\textbf{ in }R]\!]_\zeta^{\mathfrak{A}} \;\triangleright\; U}$ if $a = [\![t]\!]_\zeta^{\mathfrak{A}}$

$\dfrac{[\![R]\!]_{\zeta\frac{a}{x}}^{\mathfrak{A}} \;\triangleright\; U_a \quad \text{for each } a \in I}{[\![\textbf{forall }x\textbf{ with }\varphi\textbf{ do }R]\!]_\zeta^{\mathfrak{A}} \;\triangleright\; \bigcup_{a\in I} U_a}$ if $I = \{a \in |\mathfrak{A}| : [\![\varphi]\!]_{\zeta\frac{a}{x}}^{\mathfrak{A}} = \textit{True}\}$

$\dfrac{[\![R]\!]_{\zeta\frac{a}{x}}^{\mathfrak{A}} \;\triangleright\; U}{[\![r(t)]\!]_\zeta^{\mathfrak{A}} \;\triangleright\; U}$ if $r(x) = R$ is a rule definition and $a = [\![t]\!]_\zeta^{\mathfrak{A}}$

Definition 2.2.11 (Semantics of transition rules). The semantics of a transition rule R of a given ASM in a state $\mathfrak{A}$ with respect to a variable assignment ζ is defined if and only there exists an update set U such that $[\![R]\!]_\zeta^{\mathfrak{A}} \;\triangleright\; U$ can be derived in the calculus in Fig. 2.2. In that case $[\![R]\!]_\zeta^{\mathfrak{A}}$ is identified with U.

It can happen that the update set $[\![R]\!]_\zeta^{\mathfrak{A}}$ contains several updates for the same function name f. In this case, the updates have to be consistent, otherwise the execution stops.

Definition 2.2.12 (Consistent update set). An update set U is called *consistent*, if it satisfies the following property:

If $(f, (a_1, \ldots, a_n), b) \in U$ and $(f, (a_1, \ldots, a_n), c) \in U$, then $b = c$.

This means that a consistent update set contains for each function and each argument tuple at most one value.

If an update set U is consistent, it can be fired in a given state. The result is a new state in which the interpretations of dynamic function names are changed according to U. The interpretations of static function names are the same as in the old state. The interpretation of monitored functions is given by the environment and can therefore change in an arbitrary way.

Definition 2.2.13 (Firing of updates). The result of firing a consistent update set U in a state $\mathfrak{A}$ is a new state $\mathfrak{B}$ with the same superuniverse as $\mathfrak{A}$ satisfying the following two conditions for the interpretations of function names f of Σ:

1. If $(f, (a_1, \ldots, a_n), b) \in U$, then $f^{\mathfrak{B}}(a_1, \ldots, a_n) = b$.
2. If there is no b with $(f, (a_1, \ldots, a_n), b) \in U$ and f is not a monitored function, then $f^{\mathfrak{B}}(a_1, \ldots, a_n) = f^{\mathfrak{A}}(a_1, \ldots, a_n)$.

Since U is consistent, for static and controlled functions the state $\mathfrak{B}$ is determined in a unique way. Notice that only those locations can have a new value in state $\mathfrak{B}$ with respect to state $\mathfrak{A}$ for which there is an update in U. (In this way ASMs avoid the so called frame problem.)

Definition 2.2.14 (Run of an ASM). Let M be an ASM with vocabulary Σ, initial state $\mathfrak{A}$ and main rule name r. Let ζ be a variable assignment. A *run* of M is a finite or infinite sequence $\mathfrak{B}_0, \mathfrak{B}_1, \ldots$ of states for Σ such that the following conditions are satisfied:

1. $\mathfrak{B}_0 = \mathfrak{A}$.
2. If $[\![r]\!]_{\zeta}^{\mathfrak{B}_n}$ is not defined or inconsistent, then $\mathfrak{B}_n$ is the last state in the sequence.
3. Otherwise, $\mathfrak{B}_{n+1}$ is the result of firing $[\![r]\!]_{\zeta}^{\mathfrak{B}_n}$ in $\mathfrak{B}_n$.

If we assume that for each rule definition $r(x_1, \ldots, x_n) = R$ of the machine M the free variables of R are among $x_1, \ldots, x_n$, then a run is independent of the variable assignment ζ (see Exercise 2.2.2).

2.2.3 Syntactic sugar

To extend a subuniverse of the superuniverse by new elements we use the following notation:

create x **do** R

The meaning of this construct is

let $x = f_{new}(\ldots)$ **in** R

where $f_{new}(\ldots)$ is a monitored function (possibly with parameters) which returns a new element of the superuniverse which does not belong to any of the subuniverses.

As mentioned above we sometimes use the following notation as syntactic sugar for monitored choice functions:

choose x **with** φ **do** R

We understand this notation as an abbreviation for the rule

let $x = f_{\varphi}(\ldots)$ **in** R,

where $f_\varphi(\ldots)$ is an monitored choice function updated by the environment which returns elements satisfying the selection condition φ. Of course different occurrences of **choose** have to be replaced by different choice functions (possibly with parameters) to guarantee the independence of selection.

Another approach would be to add **choose** as a basic construct to the syntax and to extend the calculus in Fig. 2.2 in the following way:

$$\frac{\llbracket R \rrbracket_{\zeta \frac{a}{x}}^{\mathfrak{A}} \; \rhd \; U}{\llbracket \textbf{choose } x \textbf{ with } \varphi \textbf{ do } R \rrbracket_{\zeta}^{\mathfrak{A}} \; \rhd \; U} \quad \text{if } \llbracket \varphi \rrbracket_{\zeta \frac{a}{x}}^{\mathfrak{A}} = \textit{True}$$

This approach has the disadvantage that the semantics of a transition rule R is no longer unique, because there can be different update sets U such that $\llbracket R \rrbracket_{\zeta}^{\mathfrak{A}} \; \rhd \; U$ is derivable in the calculus.

2.2.4 Exercises

Exercise 2.2.1. Prove the following equation:

$$\llbracket (\textbf{if } \varphi \textbf{ then } R_1 \textbf{ else } R_2) \; S \rrbracket_{\zeta}^{\mathfrak{A}} = \llbracket \textbf{if } \varphi \textbf{ then } (R_1 \; S) \textbf{ else } (R_2 \; S) \rrbracket_{\zeta}^{\mathfrak{A}}$$

Is the following equation true?

$$\llbracket S \; (\textbf{if } \varphi \textbf{ then } R_1 \textbf{ else } R_2) \rrbracket_{\zeta}^{\mathfrak{A}} = \llbracket \textbf{if } \varphi \textbf{ then } (S \; R_1) \textbf{ else } (S \; R_2) \rrbracket_{\zeta}^{\mathfrak{A}}$$

If yes, why? If not, give a counter example.

Exercise 2.2.2. The set of free variables of a term t is defined as follows:

1. $\mathrm{FV}(v_i) := \{v_i\}$
2. $\mathrm{FV}(c) := \emptyset$
3. $\mathrm{FV}(f(t_1, \ldots, t_n)) := \mathrm{FV}(t_1) \cup \ldots \cup \mathrm{FV}(t_n)$

The set of free variables of a formula φ is defined as follows:

1. $\mathrm{FV}(s = t) := \mathrm{FV}(s) \cup \mathrm{FV}(t)$
2. $\mathrm{FV}(\neg \, \varphi) := \mathrm{FV}(\varphi)$
3. $\mathrm{FV}(\varphi \wedge \psi) := \mathrm{FV}(\varphi \vee \psi) := \mathrm{FV}(\varphi \to \psi) := \mathrm{FV}(\varphi) \cup \mathrm{FV}(\psi)$
4. $\mathrm{FV}(\forall x \, \varphi) := \mathrm{FV}(\exists x \, \varphi) := \mathrm{FV}(\varphi) \setminus \{x\}$

The set of free variables of a transition rule R is defined as follows:

1. $\mathrm{FV}(\textbf{skip }) := \emptyset$
2. $\mathrm{FV}(f(t_1, \ldots, t_n) := s) := \mathrm{FV}(t_1) \cup \ldots \cup \mathrm{FV}(t_n) \cup \mathrm{FV}(s)$
3. $\mathrm{FV}(R \; S) := \mathrm{FV}(R) \cup \mathrm{FV}(S)$
4. $\mathrm{FV}(\textbf{if } \varphi \textbf{ then } R \textbf{ else } S) := \mathrm{FV}(\varphi) \cup \mathrm{FV}(R) \cup \mathrm{FV}(S)$
5. $\mathrm{FV}(\textbf{let } x = t \textbf{ in } R) := \mathrm{FV}(t) \cup (\mathrm{FV}(R) \setminus \{x\})$
6. $\mathrm{FV}(\textbf{forall } x \textbf{ with } \varphi \textbf{ do } R) := (\mathrm{FV}(\varphi) \cup \mathrm{FV}(R)) \setminus \{x\}$
7. $\mathrm{FV}(r(t_1, \ldots, t_n)) := \mathrm{FV}(t_1) \cup \ldots \cup \mathrm{FV}(t_n)$

Let $\mathfrak{A}$ be a state. Prove the following coincidence properties:

1. If $\zeta(x) = \eta(x)$ for all $x \in \mathrm{FV}(t)$, then $[\![t]\!]_\zeta^\mathfrak{A} = [\![t]\!]_\eta^\mathfrak{A}$.
2. If $\zeta(x) = \eta(x)$ for all $x \in \mathrm{FV}(\varphi)$, then $[\![\varphi]\!]_\zeta^\mathfrak{A} = [\![\varphi]\!]_\eta^\mathfrak{A}$.
3. If $\zeta(x) = \eta(x)$ for all $x \in \mathrm{FV}(R)$, then $[\![R]\!]_\zeta^\mathfrak{A} = [\![R]\!]_\eta^\mathfrak{A}$.

We assume that in a rule definition $r(x_1, \ldots, x_n) = R$ the body R contains no free variables except of $x_1, \ldots, x_n$.

Exercise 2.2.3. How can Turing machines be defined with ASMs?

2.3 Notational conventions

Throughout the book we stick to standard mathematical and programming terminology. For a quick reference we nevertheless list here some frequently used notation, in particular for list operations.

a^* denotes the set of all sequences of elements of a. We use list and sequence as synonyms.

$[a_1, \ldots, a_n]$ is the list containing the elements $a_1, \ldots, a_n$; $[\,]$ is the empty list.

$length(ls)$ returns the number of elements in list ls.

$null(ls)$ tests whether the list ls is empty (i.e., $ls = [\,]$).

$copy(i)(x)$ is the list consisting of i copies of x.

$l_1 \cdot l_2$ is the concatenation of the lists l_1 and l_2.

$push(ls, e)$ is the list $ls \cdot [e]$, the result of pushing e to (the right of) ls.

$top(ls)$ returns the right most (the last) element of the list ls.

$take(ls, n)$ generalizes $top(ls)$, returning the list consisting of the last n elements of the list ls.

$pop(ls)$ returns the list ls without the right most (the last) element.

$drop(ls, n)$ generalizes $pop(ls)$, returning the list resulting from dropping the last n elements from the list ls.

$ls(i)$ returns the ith element of the list, reading from left to right and starting counting from 0. If ls is a list $[a_0, \ldots, a_n]$, then $ls(i)$ is the element a_i.

$split(ls, n)$ splits off the last n elements of the list ls. More precisely $split(ls, n)$ is the pair (ls', ns) of two lists where $ls' \cdot ns = ls$ and $length(ns) = n$.

splits(*ls*, *ns*) is a generalization of *split*(*ls*, *n*). It splits off from the list *ls* a list of as many sublists, of appropriate length, as indicated by *ns*. More formally, the list *ns* is a list of natural numbers. The result of *splits*(*ls*, *ns*) is a pair $(ls', [ns_0, \ldots, ns_{n-1}])$ where n is the length of *ns* and $length(ns_i) = ns(i)$. The concatenation $ls' \cdot ns_1 \cdot \ldots \cdot ns_n$ is equal to the list *ls*.

tops(*ls*, *ns*) returns the list *nss* which is split off from *ls* by *splits*(*ls*, *ns*), i.e., satisfying $(\_, nss) = splits(ls, ns)$. The symbol $\_$ is the wildcard pattern and matches everything.

zip(*xs*, *ys*) is the list of pairs (x, y) where $x \in xs$ and $y \in ys$. For applying *zip*, the lists *xs* and *ys* must have the same length:

$$zip([x_1, \ldots, x_n], [y_1, \ldots, y_n]) = [(x_1, y_1), \ldots, (x_n, y_n)]$$

When parameterizing functions $f: X \to Z$ or $f: X \times Y \to Z$ we sometimes write f_x for $f(x)$ and $f_x(y)$ for $f(x, y)$.

By $Map(a, b)$ we denote the set of all (finite) mappings from domain a to range b. If f is a finite mapping, then $f(x) = y$ if $(x, y) \in f$, otherwise $f(x)$ is undefined.

$f_1 \oplus f_2$ denotes the union of the two mappings f_i where f_2 overrides values which are defined also in f_1:

$$(x, y) \in f_1 \oplus f_2 \Leftrightarrow (x, y) \in f_2 \vee (x \notin dom(f_2) \wedge (x, y) \in f_1)$$

We write $X \lhd f$ for the domain restriction of the function f to the set X; $X \ntriangleleft f$ denotes the domain restriction of f to elements in the complement of X:

$$X \lhd f := \{(x, f(x)) \mid x \in dom(f),\ x \in X\}$$
$$X \ntriangleleft f := \{(x, f(x)) \mid x \in dom(f),\ x \notin X\}$$

We write $Powerset(a)$ for the set of all subsets of a.

Part I

Java

In Part I of the book we formalize the semantics of Java. The model for the interpreter we are going to define serves three purposes, concerning the design, the verification and the validation of the language. The design goal is to provide an implementation independent definition which directly reflects the intuitions and design decisions underlying the language (see JLS [18]) and which supports the programmer's understanding of Java programs. The verification goal is to provide a sufficiently rigorous basis for proving properties of the language and of Java programs, like type safety (see Theorem 8.4.1) or the correctness of a standard scheme for the compilation of Java programs to JVM code (see Theorem 14.1.1). The validation concern is to allow for a refinement of the model into an executable version which can be used for running experiments with the model (see Appendix A).

We formally define the *semantics* of Java by providing an ASM which executes arbitrary Java programs. To make the model manageable, we factor Java into *five sublanguages*, by isolating orthogonal parts of the language, and define an ASM for each of them, namely handling the imperative, procedural, object-oriented, exception handling and concurrency features. This can be done in such a way that the ASM for each sublanguage is a purely incremental (conservative) extension of its predecessor, so that the entire machine *execJava* defined below turns out to be a parallel composition of five submachines. Intuitively speaking it expresses that given a program to be run, at each step all those submachines are called which provide rules for the interpretation of the current instruction. A similar decomposition can be made also for the JVM, see Part II.

$$
\begin{aligned}
execJava = \ &execJava_I \\
&execJava_C \\
&execJava_O \\
&execJava_E \\
&execJava_T
\end{aligned}
$$

We will denote by Java$_I$, Java$_C$, Java$_O$, Java$_E$, Java$_T$ the machines consisting of the parallel composition of the corresponding submachines $execJava_I$, $execJava_C$, $execJava_O$, $execJava_E$, $execJava_T$ up to the respective index I, C, O, E, T, in this order.

Chapter 3 defines the basic ASM $execJava_I$ for the imperative core of Java, essentially a `while` language with statements and expressions over the primitive types of Java.

In Chapter 4, we extend $execJava_I$ by $execJava_C$ which deals with Java classes. The machine $execJava_C$ supports procedural abstraction and global (module) variables through classes coming with (so called static) methods, fields and initializers.

In Chapter 5, we extend $execJava_C$ by $execJava_O$ which includes the truly object-oriented concepts of Java, namely instances, instance creation, instance field access, instance method calls with late binding, casts, and null pointers.

Chapter 6 extends *execJava$_O$* with exceptions, handled by *execJava$_E$*. We specify which exception will be thrown when semantic constraints are violated and introduce the `throw` and `try-catch-finally` statements.

In Chapter 7, we move from sequential Java to concurrent Java. The corresponding ASM model *execJava$_T$* introduces the lightweight processes of Java, called threads, their synchronization mechanism using locks, and their start, interrupt, suspension, resumption, and deletion mechanism. In terms of an abstract scheduling mechanism, we formulate and prove the correctness of the thread synchronization mechanism and related invariants which hold in Java$_T$ (Theorem 7.3.1).

In Chapter 8 we analyze some structural properties of Java statements and expressions during runs of Java, together with the values of definite assignment for local variables. We formulate and prove (Theorem 8.4.1) in which sense every legal Java program is type safe; i.e., at run-time deals only with (variable of stack) values, objects, expressions, statements, and abruptions, which satisfy the structural—in particular the compile type—constraints.

In order not to lengthen the definition of our models by tedious and routine repetitions, we skip those language constructs which can easily be reduced to the core constructs dealt with explicitly in our models; examples are alternative control structures (like `for`, `do`, `switch`), pre- and postfix operators (`++`, `--`), conditional operators (`&&`, `||`), assignments combined with operations (`+=`, `-=`, etc.), variable initialization and similar expressive sugar. The description of arrays—which is needed to run interesting examples in the executable version of our model—is given in the appendix.

We do not consider Java packages, compilation units, the visibility of names and input/output except for providing what is needed to run interesting examples in the executable version of our model. We also do not consider garbage collection. The loading and linking of classes is discussed only for the JVM in Chapter 18, although in Java dynamic loading and linking might raise exceptions, and in the presence of `finalize` methods also garbage collection is semantically visible.

3. The imperative core Java$_\mathcal{I}$ of Java

In this chapter we define the basic model *execJava$_I$*, which defines the semantics of the sequential imperative core of Java with statements (appearing in method bodies) and expressions (appearing in statements) over the primitive types of Java. Each machine is started with an arbitrary but fixed Java program it has to interpret. In Sect. 3.1 we describe the signature of Java$_\mathcal{I}$ and the static semantics of the input programs. We explain the form in which these programs are supposed to appear to the ASM, namely as annotated abstract syntax trees, resulting from parsing and elaboration. For future use in the proofs we also list the constraints which are imposed on the syntax of programs and on the types of the constructs appearing in them. In Sect. 3.2 we define the ASM rules for the dynamic semantics of Java$_\mathcal{I}$ programs.

3.1 Static semantics of Java$_\mathcal{I}$

The *primitive types* of Java$_\mathcal{I}$ are: `boolean`, `byte`, `short`, `int`, `long`, `float`, `double`, `char`. Types are denoted by capital letters A, B, C. The types `byte`, `short`, `int`, `long` and `char` are called *integral types*. The types `float` and `double` are called *floating point types*. *Numeric types* are integral types or floating point types. External representations of values of primitive type are called *literals*. Table 3.1 contains examples of literals.

A binary relation $\preceq$ is defined between primitive types. In terms of the JLS, the relation $A \preceq B$ means that there exists an *identity conversion* or a *widening primitive conversion* from A to B. In traditional terms, the relation $A \preceq B$ means that A is a *subtype* of B, i.e., each value of type A can be used as a value of type B. In some cases, however, information may be lost. For example, if a 64-bit value of type `long` is converted to a 32-bit value of type `float`, then some precision may be lost.

Definition 3.1.1. The relation $\preceq$ is the least relation on the set of primitive types which is reflexive, transitive and has the following properties:

$$\texttt{byte} \preceq \texttt{short} \preceq \texttt{int} \preceq \texttt{long} \preceq \texttt{float} \preceq \texttt{double}, \quad \texttt{char} \preceq \texttt{int}.$$

Reflexive means that $A \preceq A$ for each primitive type A. Transitive means that, if $A \preceq B$ and $B \preceq C$, then $A \preceq C$.

Table 3.1 The primitive types of Java

Type	Size	Default	Literals
boolean		false	true, false
byte	8 bit	(byte)0	
short	16 bit	(short)0	
int	32 bit	0	11, 1969, 0xff00, 017
long	64 bit	0L	11L, 0x1000L, 0777L
float	32 bit	0.0f	3.141f, 1.2e+23f
double	64 bit	0.0d	3.141, 1e-9, 0.1e10
char	16 bit	'\u0000'	'a', '?', '\n', '\uFFFF'

3.1.1 Syntax of Java$_\mathcal{I}$

The syntax of the imperative core of Java is defined in Fig. 3.1. It can also be viewed as defining corresponding domains (also called universes) of Java$_\mathcal{I}$. Although in our ASMs we will extend some of these domains by a small number of auxiliary constructs which do not appear in the syntax of Java, we use the names of Java constructs also as names for the corresponding extended ASM universes. Usually we denote domains by words beginning with a capital letter and write *dom* for elements of *Dom*, i.e., assuming without further mentioning that *dom* ∈ *Dom*.

Fig. 3.1 uses universes which represent basic syntactic constructs of Java, namely:

Exp	expressions,	*Lit*	literals,
Asgn	assignments,	*Loc*	local variables,
Stm	statements,	*Uop*	unary operators,
Block	blocks,	*Bop*	binary operators,
Bstm	block statements,	*Lab*	labels.

Local variables and labels are *identifiers*, sequences of letters and digits starting with a letter. Java programs are written in the Unicode 16-bit character set and so letters and digits may be drawn from the entire Unicode character set.

The unary operators *Uop* are listed in Table 3.2 and the binary operators *Bop* in Table 3.3. The function 'max' in the column 'Result type' of the two tables denotes the maximum of types with respect to the subtype relation $\preceq$. Although the set of primitive types is not linearly ordered by the relation $\preceq$, the maximum always exists for the special cases in Table 3.2 and Table 3.3. The type cast operator '(B)' is considered as a unary operator in Table 3.2 provided that B is a primitive type. Binary operators are associated to the left: e_1 *bop* e_2 *bop* e_3 is read as $(e_1$ *bop* $e_2)$ *bop* e_3.

Fig. 3.1 Syntax of Java$_\mathcal{I}$

$$
\begin{aligned}
Exp &:= Lit \mid Loc \mid Uop\ Exp \mid Exp\ Bop\ Exp \mid Exp\ ?\ Exp\ :\ Exp \mid Asgn \\
Asgn &:= Loc = Exp \\
Stm &:= ;\ \mid Asgn;\ \mid Lab:\ Stm\ \mid \texttt{break}\ Lab;\ \mid \texttt{continue}\ Lab; \\
&\quad\ \mid \texttt{if}\ (Exp)\ Stm\ \texttt{else}\ Stm\ \mid \texttt{while}\ (Exp)\ Stm \mid Block \\
Block &:= \{Bstm_1 \dots Bstm_n\} \\
Bstm &:= Type\ Loc;\ \mid Stm \\
Phrase &:= Exp \mid Bstm \mid Val \mid Abr \mid Norm
\end{aligned}
$$

A block statement '$A\ loc;$' is called a *local variable declaration*. The local variable *loc* is declared to be of type A. The *scope* of the declaration of *loc* consists of the statements following the variable declaration in the block. Consider the following declaration:

$$\{\dots A\ loc;\ bstm_1\ \dots\ bstm_n\}$$

Then the scope of the local variable *loc* are the statements $bstm_1, \dots, bstm_n$.

Constraint 3.1.1. A Java$_\mathcal{I}$ block must satisfy the following constraints:

1. If a variable *loc* is used in an expression, then it is in the scope of a declaration of *loc*.
2. A local variable declaration of *loc* is not in the scope of another declaration of *loc*, i.e., there are no hidden variables.
3. A labeled statement '*lab* : *stm*' does not contain proper substatements with the same label *lab*.
4. A jump statement '$\texttt{break}\ lab;$' occurs as a substatement of a labeled statement '*lab* : *stm*' with label *lab*.
5. A jump statement '$\texttt{continue}\ lab;$' occurs as a substatement of a labeled loop statement '*lab* : $\texttt{while}\ (exp)\ stm$' with label *lab*.
6. Every local variable must be initialized before it is used (*rule of definite assignment*).

In the following code fragment, for example, the compiler is able to conclude that the variable x is initialized before it is used:

```
if (0 < z)
   x = 2;
else
   x = 3;
y = x * x;
```

The rules of definite assignment are explained later in Sect. 8.3.

Table 3.2 Unary operators for operands of primitive type

Prec.	Uop	Operand type	Result type	Operation
1	+	A numeric	max(A, int)	unary plus
1	-	A numeric	max(A, int)	unary minus
1	~	A integral	max(A, int)	bitwise NOT
1	!	boolean	boolean	logical complement
1	(B)	A ≠ boolean	B ≠ boolean	type cast

Table 3.3 Binary operators for operands of primitive type

Prec.	Bop	Operand types	Result type	Operation
2	*	A and B numeric	max(A, B, int)	multiplication
2	/	A and B numeric	max(A, B, int)	division
2	%	A and B numeric	max(A, B, int)	remainder
3	+	A and B numeric	max(A, B, int)	addition
3	-	A and B numeric	max(A, B, int)	subtraction
4	<<	A and B integral	max(A, int)	left shift
4	>>	A and B integral	max(A, int)	signed right shift
4	>>>	A and B integral	max(A, int)	unsigned right shift
5	<	A and B numeric	boolean	less than
5	<=	A and B numeric	boolean	less than or equal
5	>	A and B numeric	boolean	greater than
5	>=	A and B numeric	boolean	greater than or equal
6	==	$A \preceq B$ or $B \preceq A$	boolean	equal
6	!=	$A \preceq B$ or $B \preceq A$	boolean	not equal
7	&	A and B integral	max(A, B, int)	bitwise AND
7	&	A = B = boolean	boolean	boolean AND
8	^	A and B integral	max(A, B, int)	bitwise XOR
8	^	A = B = boolean	boolean	boolean XOR
9	|	A and B integral	max(A, B, int)	bitwise OR
9	|	A = B = boolean	boolean	boolean OR

Table 3.4 Type constraints for expressions of Java$_\mathcal{I}$

$^\alpha lit$	$\mathcal{T}(\alpha)$ is the type of lit according to the JLS.
$^\alpha loc$	$\mathcal{T}(\alpha)$ is the declared type of loc.
$^\alpha(uop\ ^\beta e)$	The result of applying uop to an operand of type $\mathcal{T}(\beta)$ is of type $\mathcal{T}(\alpha)$ according to Table 3.2.
$^\alpha(^\beta e_1\ bop\ ^\gamma e_2)$	The result of applying bop to operands of type $\mathcal{T}(\beta)$ and $\mathcal{T}(\gamma)$ is of type $\mathcal{T}(\alpha)$ according to Table 3.3.
$^\alpha(loc =\ ^\beta e)$	$\mathcal{T}(\alpha)$ is the declared type of loc and $\mathcal{T}(\beta) \preceq \mathcal{T}(\alpha)$.
$^\alpha(^\beta e_0\ ?\ ^\gamma e_1 :\ ^\delta e_2)$	Let $A = \mathcal{T}(\gamma)$ and $B = \mathcal{T}(\delta)$. Then $\mathcal{T}(\beta)$ is `boolean` and one of the following conditions is true: – A, B are numeric and $\mathcal{T}(\alpha) = \max(A, B, \text{int})$ – $A \preceq B$ and $\mathcal{T}(\alpha) = B$ – $B \preceq A$ and $\mathcal{T}(\alpha) = A$

3.1.2 Type checking of Java$_\mathcal{I}$

Positions in the given program are denoted by small Greek letters α, β, γ, etc. The reader can think of positions either as positions in the source code of the program or as positions in an abstract syntax tree. Positions are displayed as superscripts, for example, as in $^\alpha exp$ or in $^\alpha stm$. The set of positions of the given program is considered as a universe of the superuniverse of the ASM for Java$_\mathcal{I}$. The universe of positions is called *Pos*.

Java programs are statically typed. The compiler has to verify that a program is well-typed. As a result of parsing and elaboration the parse tree of the program is annotated with type information. In the ASM, the annotation is modeled by a static function $\mathcal{T}$ which assigns to each position α in an expression a type. The function $\mathcal{T}$ has to satisfy the constraints in Table 3.4. Moreover, if an expression $^\alpha exp$ is the test expression in an `if` or a `while` statement, then $\mathcal{T}(\alpha)$ must be `boolean`.

During compilation and type checking explicit unary conversion operators (type casts) are inserted at places where they are necessary. For example, an explicit type cast is inserted in an assignment $loc = exp$, if the type of exp is different from the declared type of loc. The assignment is replaced by $loc = (A)exp$, where A is the declared type of loc. In this way it is ensured that during run-time a variable of declared primitive type A always holds a value of type A. Table 3.5 contains the additional type constraints which the abstract syntax tree must satisfy after parsing and elaboration.

Table 3.5 Type constraints after introduction of primitive type casts

$^\alpha(loc = {}^\beta e)$	Let A be the declared type of *loc*. If A is a primitive type, then $\mathcal{T}(\beta) = A = \mathcal{T}(\alpha)$.
$^\alpha({}^\beta e_0 \mathbin{?} {}^\gamma e_1 : {}^\delta e_2)$	If $\mathcal{T}(\gamma)$ and $\mathcal{T}(\delta)$ are primitive types, then $\mathcal{T}(\gamma) = \mathcal{T}(\delta) = \mathcal{T}(\alpha)$.

3.1.3 Vocabulary of Java$_\mathcal{I}$

The input program *body*, an annotated abstract syntax tree, is the initial value of the to be computed term *restbody*, a dynamic function which contains a) the still to be executed part of the current program (method body), b) the already computed and still needed expression values, and c) information about the current abruption or the successful termination of the computation. We view program execution as a walk through the annotated abstract syntax tree: at each position, the corresponding phrase, originally an expression or a statement, is evaluated or executed and then the control flow proceeds to the next phrase (at the same or the next position). We denote the current position by a 0-ary dynamic function

$\qquad$ *pos*: *Pos*

which represents an abstract program counter, pointing to the current expression or statement to be executed. We view *restbody* as a function which initially assigns to each position a phrase:

$\qquad$ *restbody*: *Pos* $\rightarrow$ *Phrase*

The expression *restbody/pos* denotes the currently to be computed subterm of *restbody* at *pos*. It will eventually be replaced by the computed value (element of *Val*) of the subexpression, or by a reason for abruption (element of *Abr*), or by the constant *Norm*, which we use to denote successful termination (also called normal completion) of a statement. The universe *Phrase* therefore contains semi-evaluated expressions and statements which at certain positions may contain values, reasons for abruptions or *Norm*.

The set *Abr* serves to distinguish the normal termination of the control flow from its possible abruptions, which in Java$_\mathcal{I}$ can happen due to the restricted jump statements 'break *Lab*;' and 'continue *Lab*;'. It contains elements of form *Break*(*lab*) and *Continue*(*lab*) which indicate reasons for abrupt completion of a statement in Java$_\mathcal{I}$. The notion of abruption will be extended in Java$_\mathcal{C}$ and Java$_\mathcal{E}$ to include also return and exception values.

The current value of the local variables is kept in the local environment function (association between local variables and their values)

type *Locals* = *Map*(*Loc*, *Val*)
locals: *Locals*

which is updated upon execution of assignment statements or as side effect of expression evaluation. The universe *Val*, defined by

type *Val* = `boolean` | `byte` | `short` | `int` | `long` | `float` | `double` | `char`

contains the primitive values of Java: booleans, integers in specific ranges, and floating point numbers according to IEEE 754. For simplicity, we identify the booleans of Java with the corresponding ASM values *True* and *False*, and often abbreviate *bool* = *True* to *bool*.

This concludes the definition of the core signature *restbody*, *pos*, *locals* for the states of Java$_\mathcal{I}$. Auxiliary state components and additions pertaining only to some special constructs will be presented in the corresponding sections.

3.2 Transition rules for Java$_\mathcal{I}$

Transition rules describe how the states of Java$_\mathcal{I}$, i.e., the dynamic functions *restbody*, *pos*, *locals*, change over time by evaluating expressions and executing statements of the input program. Initially *restbody* is the given method *body*, *pos* is its start position *firstPos* and *locals* is empty. The machine *execJava$_I$*, depending on its currently to be executed subterm, either evaluates an expression, or executes a statement. This work is done by two submachines *execJavaExp$_I$* and *execJavaStm$_I$* which are defined below, so that *execJava$_I$* is the following machine:

execJava$_I$ =
    execJavaExp$_I$
    execJavaStm$_I$

The machine *execJava$_I$* terminates if none of the rules of its submachines can be applied any more. Before proceeding in the next subsections to the definition of these two submachines, we explain here the basic mechanism they share, also with the other machines to be defined in this chapter, for walking through the abstract syntax tree.

When the machine encounters a *stm* to be executed or an *exp* to be evaluated, or when it comes (back) to the *firstPos* of its method body, the context of the pending subcomputation of this phrase is given by *restbody*/*pos*. After this subcomputation has been completed, either normally or abruptly, the control passes to the parent position where the decision is taken on how to continue, either by computing the next subphrase of the phrase in the parent position, or by executing on the computed subphrases the computation to be done at the parent position. In both cases the context of the completed subcomputation changes to the superphrase *restbody*/*up*(*pos*); here the auxiliary function

$$up\colon Pos \to Pos$$

yields the parent position of a position, thus allowing to retrieve for a phrase, occurring in a position, the next enclosing phrase. We capture this context switch by the following definition.

$$
\begin{aligned}
context(pos) = \ &\textbf{if } pos = firstPos \lor restbody/pos \in Bstm \cup Exp \textbf{ then}\\
&\quad restbody/pos\\
&\textbf{else}\\
&\quad restbody/up(pos)
\end{aligned}
$$

Since the context switch is often accompanied by passing to the parent position the result of the completed subcomputations, or what has to be computed from them at the parent position, we use the following rule:

$$
\begin{aligned}
yieldUp(result) = \ &\\
restbody &:= restbody[result/up(pos)]\\
pos &:= up(pos)
\end{aligned}
$$

It combines passing a result, from a substructure at pos to its direct super-structure, with an update of pos to the position of the superstructure. When a result has to be recorded without changing the value of pos, we use the following variant $yield$:

$$
\begin{aligned}
yield(result) = \ &\\
restbody &:= restbody[result/pos]
\end{aligned}
$$

To streamline the notation, we indicate that the machine is positioned on a direct subphrase t of a structure $f(\dots t \dots)$ by writing $s = f(\dots \blacktriangleright t \dots)$ for $s = f(\dots t \dots) \land pos = \blacktriangleright$. E.g. $context(pos) = uop \blacktriangleright val$ denotes that the machine is positioned on the value val, computed for the expression exp which appeared as argument to uop. Similarly we write $s = phrase(\blacktriangleright t)$ for $s = phrase(t) \land pos = \blacktriangleright \land restbody/pos = t$. When writing the rules we use the pattern matching notation which guarantees that the rules are tried to be applied, one at a time, in the order in which they appear in the text.

3.2.1 Expressions

The machine $execJavaExp_I$ in Fig. 3.2 formalizes for the imperative core of Java the condition in [18, §15.6] that all expressions are evaluated from innermost to outermost. For this purpose the current control is transfered, by updating pos, from unevaluated expressions to the appropriate subexpressions, until an atom (a literal or a variable) is reached. For binary expressions also the left-to-right evaluation strategy is taken into account, and for conditional expressions the condition is evaluated first. This reflects also that as required in [18, §15.25.1], the value of a simple assignment expression is the value of its right hand side, which becomes bound under the name of the variable of the left hand side in the local environment. When the current

Fig. 3.2 Execution of Java$_\mathcal{I}$ expressions

$execJavaExp_I = \textbf{case } context(pos) \textbf{ of}$
  $lit \rightarrow yield(JLS(lit))$

  $loc \rightarrow yield(locals(loc))$

  $uop\,^\alpha exp \rightarrow pos := \alpha$
  $uop\,^\blacktriangleright val \rightarrow yieldUp(JLS(uop, val))$

  $^\alpha exp_1 \; bop\,^\beta exp_2 \rightarrow pos := \alpha$
  $^\blacktriangleright val \; bop\,^\beta exp \quad\;\; \rightarrow pos := \beta$
  $^\alpha val_1 \; bop\,^\blacktriangleright val_2 \;\; \rightarrow \textbf{if } \neg(bop \in divMod \wedge isZero(val_2)) \textbf{ then}$
  $\qquad\qquad\qquad\qquad\quad yieldUp(JLS(bop, val_1, val_2))$

  $loc = {}^\alpha exp \rightarrow pos := \alpha$
  $loc = {}^\blacktriangleright val \rightarrow locals := locals \oplus \{(loc, val)\}$
  $\qquad\qquad\qquad yieldUp(val)$

  $^\alpha exp_0 \; ?\,^\beta exp_1 \; : \; {}^\gamma exp_2 \rightarrow pos := \alpha$
  $^\blacktriangleright val \; ?\,^\beta exp_1 \; : \; {}^\gamma exp_2 \;\; \rightarrow \textbf{if } val \textbf{ then } pos := \beta \textbf{ else } pos := \gamma$
  $^\alpha True \; ?\,^\blacktriangleright val \; : \; {}^\gamma exp \;\; \rightarrow yieldUp(val)$
  $^\alpha False \; ?\,^\beta exp \; : \; {}^\blacktriangleright val \;\; \rightarrow yieldUp(val)$

task *restbody/pos* requires to evaluate a context which is an atom or a compound expression all of whose relevant arguments are evaluated, this context is replaced by the (to be) computed value—which is determined for literals and for compound expressions by the JLS function defined in [18, §3.10] and for variables by the local environment function *locals*. For the evaluation of atoms the rule *yield(result)* is used, otherwise the rule *yieldUp(result)*.

3.2.2 Statements

The machine *execJavaStm$_I$* in Fig. 3.3 computes statements similarly to how *execJavaExp$_I$* evaluates expressions. It follows the syntactical structure of the statement to be computed by transferring, through updates of *pos*, the current control from structured statements to the appropriate substatements, until the current statement has been computed normally or abrupts the computation. This reflects the following stipulations in [18, §14.2-10]: an empty statement, a type declaration and an empty block just terminate normally; an expression statement and a labeled statement terminate normally through evaluating the expression respectively through normally terminating the execution of the direct substatement; execution of a *block* statement follows the left-to-right evaluation strategy—started by executing the first of its substatements, and followed by the execution of the remaining substatements, in their textual order—and terminates normally when all the substatements have

---

Fig. 3.3 Execution of Java$_\mathcal{I}$ statements

$execJavaStm_I = $ **case** $context(pos)$ **of**
; $\to yield(Norm)$
$^\alpha exp; \to pos := \alpha$
$^\blacktriangleright val; \to yieldUp(Norm)$

$\quad$ **break** $lab;$ $\qquad\qquad \to yield(Break(lab))$
$\quad$ **continue** $lab;$ $\qquad\quad \to yield(Continue(lab))$
$\quad lab : {}^\alpha stm$ $\qquad\qquad \to pos := \alpha$
$\quad lab : {}^\blacktriangleright Norm$ $\qquad\qquad \to yieldUp(Norm)$
$\quad lab : {}^\blacktriangleright Break(lab_b)$ $\qquad \to$ **if** $lab = lab_b$ **then** $yieldUp(Norm)$
$\qquad\qquad\qquad\qquad\qquad\qquad$ **else** $yieldUp(Break(lab_b))$
$\quad lab : {}^\blacktriangleright Continue(lab_c) \to$ **if** $lab = lab_c$ **then** $yield(body/pos)$
$\qquad\qquad\qquad\qquad\qquad\qquad$ **else** $yieldUp(Continue(lab_c))$
$\quad phrase({}^\blacktriangleright abr) \to$ **if** $pos \neq firstPos \wedge propagatesAbr(restbody/up(pos))$ **then**
$\qquad\qquad\qquad\qquad yieldUp(abr)$

$\quad \{\,\}$ $\qquad\qquad\qquad\qquad\qquad\qquad \to yield(Norm)$
$\quad \{{}^{\alpha_1} stm_1 \ldots {}^{\alpha_n} stm_n\}$ $\qquad\qquad \to pos := \alpha_1$
$\quad \{{}^{\alpha_1} Norm \ldots {}^\blacktriangleright Norm\}$ $\qquad\quad \to yieldUp(Norm)$
$\quad \{{}^{\alpha_1} Norm \ldots {}^\blacktriangleright Norm\,{}^{\alpha_{i+1}} stm_{i+1} \ldots {}^{\alpha_n} stm_n\} \to pos := \alpha_{i+1}$

$\quad$ **if** $({}^\alpha exp)\,{}^\beta stm_1$ **else** ${}^\gamma stm_2$ $\quad \to pos := \alpha$
$\quad$ **if** $({}^\blacktriangleright val)\,{}^\beta stm_1$ **else** ${}^\gamma stm_2$ $\quad \to$ **if** val **then** $pos := \beta$ **else** $pos := \gamma$
$\quad$ **if** $({}^\alpha True)\,{}^\blacktriangleright Norm$ **else** ${}^\gamma stm \to yieldUp(Norm)$
$\quad$ **if** $({}^\alpha False)\,{}^\beta stm$ **else** ${}^\blacktriangleright Norm \to yieldUp(Norm)$

$\quad$ **while** $({}^\alpha exp)\,{}^\beta stm$ $\quad \to pos := \alpha$
$\quad$ **while** $({}^\blacktriangleright val)\,{}^\beta stm$ $\quad \to$ **if** val **then** $pos := \beta$ **else** $yieldUp(Norm)$
$\quad$ **while** $({}^\alpha True)\,{}^\blacktriangleright Norm \to yieldUp(body/up(pos))$

$\quad Type\ x; \to yield(Norm)$

---

terminated normally; the execution of an **if-else** or a **while** statement is started by first evaluating the conditional expression. When the computation of the substatements terminate normally, the control switches to the statement which has to be computed next, namely by executing $yieldUp(Norm)$ or, in case a **while** statement has to be iterated, $yieldUp(body/up(pos))$.

The execution of expressions or statements can be terminated through abruptions before all steps of their execution have completed normally. In Java$_\mathcal{I}$ only the computation of a statement can be abrupted, namely due to the execution, by $execJavaStm_I$, of a jump statement (namely **break** or **continue**) which appears inside a labeled statement $lab : s$, with the effect that an element of Abr (here $Continue(lab)$ or $Break(lab)$) becomes the term at the current position pos. Then the control propagates through all the enclosing statements up to the innermost enclosing labeled statement with label *lab*—the context conditions of Java guarantee the existence of such a labeled statement, which is called the *jump target*.

More precisely the machine looks at the superstructure *restbody/up(pos)* of the current position *pos* during whose execution the abruption did occur. If this enclosing structure is not a labeled phrase (so that it has to propagate the abruption), but also if it is a labeled phrase whose label does not agree with the label of the reason of abruption, then the abruption is propagated upwards. Otherwise, in case the reason is a *Break(lab$_b$)*, the execution proceeds normally at the next phrase of the target, in case of a *Continue(lab$_c$)* the execution proceeds with the next iteration of the corresponding `while` statement, which is available in the method *body* at *pos* [18, §14.13,14.14,14.10]. This guarantees in particular that all statements complete abruptly which are passed through during the transfer of an abruption.

The concept of propagation is defined here in such a way that it can be extended easily to the abruptions in Java$_\mathcal{C}$ and Java$_\mathcal{E}$ where *abrupt completion* can also be due to return from procedure execution respectively to raising and handling of exceptions.:

$$propagatesAbr(phrase) =$$
$$phrase \neq lab : s$$

Example ($\leadsto$ CD) 3.2.1. Abrupt transfer of control is illustrated in the following example:

```
l1: while (ᵅexp) {
       ⋮
    l2: while (ᵝexp) {
           ⋮
        break l1;      // control goes to δ
           ⋮
        continue l1;   // control goes to α
           ⋮
        break l2;      // control goes to γ
           ⋮
        continue l2;   // control goes to β
           ⋮
    }
    ᵞ ...
}
ᵟ ...
```

Table 3.6 Derived language constructs

Derived	Java$_\mathcal{I}$
exp_1 && exp_2	exp_1 ? exp_2 : false
exp_1 || exp_2	exp_1 ? true : exp_2
++loc	$loc = (A)(loc + 1)$, where loc has type A
--loc	$loc = (A)(loc - 1)$, where loc has type A
if (exp) stm	if (exp) stm else;

3.2.3 Derived language constructs

Table 3.6 contains some Java constructs that can be syntactically reduced to the core language. Other Java constructs like the do, for, switch statements as well as the postincrement operator loc++ and the postdecrement operator loc-- cannot be transformed to the core language. They have to be treated separately (see Exercises 3.2.5–3.2.8).

The JLS points out that the 'if statement without else' suffers from the so-called 'dangling else problem'. Consider the following statement:

if (exp_1) if (exp_2) stm_1 else stm_2

This statement can be read in two different ways:

if (exp_1) {if (exp_2) stm_1 else stm_2}

if (exp_1) {if (exp_2) stm_1} else stm_2

Java reads it the first way. The problem disappears if one restricts the 'if statement without else' to:

if (exp) $block$

Note, that $block$ is surrounded with a pair of braces and cannot be an if statement.

For almost every binary operator bop there exists an assignment operator bop=. This operator is reduced in the following way (where A is the declared type of loc):

loc bop= exp is reduced to $loc = (A)(loc$ bop $exp)$

For example, if the variable c is declared of type char, then

c += 32   is reduced to   c = (char)(c + 32)

3.2.4 Exercises

Exercise 3.2.1. Which expressions can be typed in Java$_\mathcal{I}$ under the following variable declaration?

```
byte b; char c; int i; long l;
```

What is the type of the expressions?

1. i + (i * l)
2. b << l
3. (boolean)i
4. c & 0x1f
5. (char)(c & 0x1f)
6. (b == 0) ? 1 : 3.141
7. (~ b) + 1
8. b = (i = b + 1)
9. !(i = 2)
10. !(c < 'G')

Exercise ($\leadsto$ CD) 3.2.2. What is the value of j in the following block?

```
{ int i = 2; int j = (i = i * i) + i; }
```

Exercise ($\leadsto$ CD) 3.2.3. Consider the following Java$_\mathcal{I}$ block:

```
0{
    int i 1= 25;
    int j 3= 40;
    5while (6(7(8i % 92) != 100)) 11{
        i 12= 13(14i / 152);
        j 16= 17(18j + 191);
    }
}
```

What is the trace of *pos* when the block is executed in *execJava$_I$* starting with *pos* = 0?

Exercise 3.2.4. Use the definitions of && and || of Table 3.6 and extend the ASM rule *execJavaExp$_I$* to the two operators.

Exercise 3.2.5. Postincrement- and postdecrement expressions have the following syntax [18, §15.13]:

```
loc++,     loc--
```

What are the type constraints? Extend the ASM rule *execJavaExp$_I$* to both kind of expressions.

Exercise 3.2.6. The do statement has the following syntax [18, §14.11]:

> do *stm* while (*exp*);

Extend the ASM rule *execJavaStm$_I$* to the do statement.

Exercise 3.2.7. The for statement has the following syntax [18, §14.12]:

> for (*init*; *test*; *update*)*stm*

Extend the ASM rule *execJavaStm$_I$* to the for statement.

Exercise 3.2.8. A switch statement has the following syntax [18, §14.9]:

> $^\alpha$ switch ($^\beta exp$) $\{^{\gamma_1} grp_1 \dots {}^{\gamma_m} grp_m\}$

The groups of a switch statement have the following syntax:

> grp := lab: $stm_1 \dots stm_n$
> lab := case *lit* | default

The value *val*(γ) of a switch label $^\gamma lab$ is defined as follows:

1. *val*(γ) = *JLS*(*lit*), if $^\gamma lab$ is 'case *lit*'.
2. *val*(γ) = *default*, if $^\gamma lab$ is 'default'.

The following constraints must be satisfied:

1. $\mathcal{T}(\beta) \preceq$ int.
2. *val*(γ_i) $\neq$ *val*(γ_j) for all i, j with $1 \le i < j \le m$.
3. If *val*(γ_i) has type A, then $A \preceq \mathcal{T}(\beta)$.

As a consequence of these constraints a switch statement contains at most one *grp* with label default. Extend the ASM rule *execJavaStm$_I$* to the switch statement.

4. The procedural extension Java$_\mathcal{C}$ of Java$_\mathcal{I}$

Java$_\mathcal{C}$ extends Java$_\mathcal{I}$ by classes and interfaces, more precisely by class fields, class methods and class initializers, also called static fields, static methods and static initializers. Classes play the role of modules: class variables correspond to global variables, class methods to procedures (also called subroutines or functions) and class initializers to module initializers. In Sect. 4.1 we describe the static and in Sect. 4.2 the dynamic part of the semantics of Java$_\mathcal{C}$.

4.1 Static semantics of Java$_\mathcal{C}$

The capital Latin letters A, B, C have been used to denote primitive types. We use the same letters now to denote classes and interfaces. This is on purpose, since in the next chapter, classes and interfaces will be used as types, too. In the present chapter, classes and interfaces are treated as modules only. By convention, classes or interfaces A, B, C are identifiers starting with an upper case letter. Interfaces are often denoted by I, J.

4.1.1 Syntax of Java$_\mathcal{C}$

Fig. 4.1 contains a schematic definition of a Java class. The parts in angle brackets are optional. The keywords `public`, `abstract` and `final` are called *modifiers*. We say that the class is m, if the modifier m appears in the definition of the class.

Constraint 4.1.1. The class definition in Fig. 4.1 must satisfy the following constraints:

1. The type B must be a class and $I_1, \ldots, I_n$ must be different interfaces.
2. The class B is not `final`.
3. If A is `final`, then it is not `abstract`.
4. If $A = $ `Object`, then there is no `extends` clause.

If the `extends` clause is present, we say that A *is a direct subclass of* B or B *is a direct superclass of* A and define $A \prec_{\mathrm{d}} B$. If the `extends` clause is

---

Fig. 4.1 Syntax of a Java class

⟨public⟩ ⟨abstract⟩ ⟨final⟩
class A ⟨extends B⟩ ⟨implements $I_1, \ldots, I_n$⟩ {

   ⋮

   constructor declarations

   ⋮

   field declarations

   ⋮

   method declarations

   ⋮

   static initializers

   ⋮

}

---

missing and $A \neq$ Object, we define $A \prec_d$ Object. If the implements clause is present, we say that $I_1, \ldots, I_n$ are *direct superinterfaces of* A and define $A \prec_d I_i$ for $i = 1, \ldots, n$.

The syntax of interfaces in Fig. 4.2 differs slightly from the syntax of classes. If the extends clause is present, we say that I *is a direct subinterface of* J_i or J_i *is a direct superinterface of* I and define $I \prec_d J_i$ for $i = 1, \ldots, n$.

Constraint 4.1.2. The interface definition in Fig. 4.2 must satisfy the following constraints:

1. The types $J_1, \ldots, J_n$ are different interfaces.
2. The interface I is implicitly abstract.

Let $\prec_h$ be the transitive closure of $\prec_d$. This means that $A \prec_h B$ holds if, and only if, B can be reached by a finite number of direct $\prec_d$ steps. The relation $\prec_h$ is called the *inheritance relation*. The following terminology is used for classes A, B and interfaces I, J:

− If $A \prec_h B$: A *is a subclass of* B or B *is a superclass of* A
− If $A \prec_h I$: A *implements* I or I *is superinterface of* A
− If $I \prec_h J$: I *is a subinterface of* J or J *is a superinterface of* I

It is not allowed that $A \prec_h A$. Cycles in the inheritance relation are detected at compile-time or at run-time when classes are dynamically loaded.

Constraint 4.1.3. The inheritance relation $\prec_h$ must be acyclic.

The relation $A \preceq_h B$ is defined as $A \prec_h B$ or $A = B$. If $A \preceq_h B$, then one can say that each A 'is-a' B.

Fig. 4.2 Syntax of a Java interface

⟨public⟩ interface I ⟨extends $J_1, \ldots, J_n$⟩ {

    ⋮

    constant declarations

    ⋮

    abstract method declarations

    ⋮

}

Lemma 4.1.1. The relation $\preceq_h$ is a partial ordering:

1. $A \preceq_h A$.
2. If $A \preceq_h B$ and $B \preceq_h C$, then $A \preceq_h C$.
3. If $A \preceq_h B$ and $B \preceq_h A$, then $A = B$.

The relation $\preceq_h$ restricted to classes is a finite tree. The root of the tree is the class `Object`. In mathematical terms, this can be expressed as follows.

Lemma 4.1.2. Let A, B and C be classes. Then we have:

1. $A \preceq_h$ `Object` (every class is a subclass of `Object`).
2. If $A \prec_d B$ and $A \prec_d C$, then $B = C$.
3. If $A \preceq_h B$ and $A \preceq_h C$, then $B \preceq_h C$ or $C \preceq_h B$.

Not much can be said with respect to interfaces except that interfaces have no superclasses but only superinterfaces.

Lemma 4.1.3. If A is an interface and $A \preceq_h B$, then B is an interface, too.

Classes and interfaces are collected in so-called packages.

Definition 4.1.1. A *package* is a collection of classes and interfaces.

Definition 4.1.2. A Java$_C$ program is a set of packages.

The usual way to tell the compiler to which package a class or interface belongs is to prepend a `package` statement to the file in which the class or interface is defined. A `package` statement has the following form:

    package *PackageName*;

A package name is a sequence of identifiers separated by dots. The JLS proposes a unique way to name packages using Internet domains. For example:

    package ch.ethz.inf.staerk;

Fig. 4.3 Syntax of Java$_\mathcal{C}$

$$
\begin{array}{ll}
Exp & := \ldots \mid Field \mid Class.Field \mid Invk \\
Asgn & := \ldots \mid Field = Exp \mid Class.Field = Exp \\
Exps & := Exp_1, \ldots, Exp_n \\
Invk & := Meth(Exps) \mid Class.Meth(Exps) \\
Stm & := \ldots \mid Invk; \mid \texttt{return } Exp; \mid \texttt{return}; \\
Phrase & := \ldots \mid \texttt{static } Block
\end{array}
$$

Inside the package one can refer to a class by its simple name, e.g. `Point3D`. Outside the package one has to use the full qualified name, e.g.

   `ch.ethz.inf.staerk.Point3D`.

Since the dot is overloaded, an expression '$x.x.x$' can denote different things in different contexts [18, §6.5].

Definition 4.1.3. We say that a type B is *accessible* from A, if one of the following conditions is true:

1. B is a primitive type (Table 3.1), or
2. B is in the same package as A, or
3. B is `public`.

Constraint 4.1.4. The inheritance relation must satisfy the following constraint: If $A \prec_\mathrm{d} B$, then B is accessible from A.

Fig. 4.3 defines what is added in Java$_\mathcal{C}$ to the syntax of Java$_\mathcal{I}$, namely return statements and expressions for fields and method invocations. Method invocations can occur inside expressions or as top-level statements. Fig. 4.3 uses the following universes:

   Class .... (fully qualified) class and interface names,
   Field .... field names (identifiers),
   Meth .... method names (identifiers),
   Invk ..... method invocations.

4.1.2 Class members

Class members are constructor declarations, field declarations, method declarations and static initializers. Constructor declarations will be introduced in the next chapter.

Field declarations. A field declaration in a class C has the following syntax:

⟨public | protected | private⟩ ⟨final⟩ ⟨static⟩ *A field* ⟨= *exp*⟩;

We refer to the field as C/*field*. The type A is called the *declared type* of the field. We say that the field is m, if the modifier m appears in the declaration of the field. If the optional part '= *exp*' is present, then the assignment *field* = *exp* is called *the initializer of the field*.

Constraint 4.1.5. A field declaration must satisfy the following constraints:

1. The type A is accessible from C.
2. The field is declared at most once in C.
3. If the field is final, then a variable initializer must appear in the declaration of *field*.

Fields are classified according to whether they are static or not:

– If the field is static, then it is called a *class field*
– If the field is not static, then it is called an *instance field*

Class fields correspond to global variables in a module, whereas instance fields correspond to fields in a record.

Method declarations. A method declaration in a class C has the following syntax:

⟨public | protected | private⟩
⟨abstract⟩ ⟨final⟩ ⟨static⟩ ⟨native⟩
A *meth*(B_1 *loc*$_1$, ..., B_n *loc*$_n$) *body*

The method body can be:

body := ';' | *block*

We refer to the method as C/*msig*, where *msig* is the signature of the method, i.e., *msig* is the expression *meth*(B_1, ..., B_n). We say that C/*msig* is m, if the modifier m appears in the declaration of *msig* in C. The universe *MSig* consists of method signatures, i.e., method names together with the number of arguments and the types of the arguments.

Constraint 4.1.6. A method declaration must satisfy the following constraints:

1. The name A is a type or the keyword void. It is called the *declared return type* of the method.
2. The types A, B_1, ..., B_n are accessible from C.
3. The identifiers *loc*$_1$, ..., *loc*$_n$ are pairwise different. They are called the *formal parameters* of the method. We say that the parameter *loc*$_j$ is declared of type B_j.

4. The formal parameters $loc_1, \ldots, loc_n$ are different from identifiers in local variable declarations of *body*.
5. If a variable *loc* is used in an expression in *body*, then *loc* is a formal parameter of the method or *loc* is in the scope of a local variable declaration of *loc*.
6. If the declared return type A is different from `void`, then each execution path of *body* must be terminated with a statement 'return *exp*;' (see also Sect. 8.2).
7. If the declared return type A is `void`, then each execution path of *body* must be terminated by the statement 'return;'. (Otherwise, the compiler inserts a `return` statement at the end of the body.)
8. The method *msig* is declared at most once in C.
9. The method is `abstract` if, and only if, its body is the semicolon.
10. If $C/msig$ is `abstract`, then C is `abstract`.
11. If $C/msig$ is `private`, `final` or `static`, then it is not `abstract`.

Note, that `void` is not a real type. It is not allowed to declare a formal parameter or a local variable to be of type `void`.

Methods are classified according to whether they are `static` or not:

− If the method is `static`, then it is called a *class method*
− If the method is not `static`, then it is called an *instance method*

Class methods correspond to procedures in a module.

Static initializers. A static initializer has the following syntax:

> `static` *block*

We assume that all static initialization blocks and all static field initializers of a class are combined in textual order in one single static initialization block. This block is called *the initializer* of the class or interface. It is executed when the class is initialized.

Constraint 4.1.7. The keyword `return` is not allowed to appear in the *block* of a static initializer.

4.1.3 Interface members

The members of an interface are constant declarations and abstract method declarations.

Constant declarations. A constant declaration in an interface I has the following syntax:

> A *field* = *exp*;

The expression *exp* can be an arbitrary non-constant expression. It is evaluated when the interface is initialized. Usually the identifier *field* consists of upper case letters only.

Constraint 4.1.8. A constant declaration must satisfy the following constraints:

1. The type A is accessible from I.
2. A field is declared at most once in I.
3. The field is implicitly `public`, `static` and `final`.

Although an interface does not contain static initialization blocks, we assume that all field initializers are combined in textual order as a sequence of assignments in one block which is called *the initializer* of the interface I.

Abstract method declarations. An abstract method declaration in an interface I has the following syntax:

$$A\, meth(B_1\, loc_1, \ldots, B_n\, loc_n);$$

If a class implements an interface, then all abstract methods of the interface must be implemented in the class. What this means will be explained below.

Constraint 4.1.9. An abstract method declaration must satisfy the following constraints:

1. The types A and $B_1, \ldots, B_n$ must be accessible from I.
2. The method is implicitly `public` and `abstract` (and not `static`).

4.1.4 Accessibility, visibility, hiding and overriding

A class inherits members from its superclasses and superinterfaces. A declaration of a field or `static` method, however, may *hide* a member of a superclass with the same name. A declaration of an instance method is said to *override* a declaration of a method with the same signature. Members which are *visible* in a class can be referred to by their simple names. In the following definitions, x denotes a field or a method signature.

Definition 4.1.4. We say that x has `default` access in class C, if x is neither `private` nor `public` nor `protected` in C.

Definition 4.1.5. An element C/x is *accessible* from A means:

1. x is `private` in C and $A = C$, or
2. x is not `private` in C and C is in the same package as A, or
3. x is `public` in C, or
4. x is `protected` in C and $A \prec_h C$.

Some consequences of these definitions are:

1. If x is `private` in C, then C/x is accessible from class C only. Outside of C, the element C/x is not accessible.

2. If x has `default` access in C, then C/x is accessible from all classes in the same package. Outside of the package, the element C/x is not accessible.
3. If x is `public` in C, then C/x is accessible from everywhere.
4. If x is `protected` in C, then C/x is accessible from the same package or outside of the package from subclasses of C.
5. Elements of interfaces are accessible from everywhere, because they are `public` by definition.

The next definition is almost identical with the previous definition except that the clause for the modifier `protected` has an additional condition [18, §6.6.2].

Definition 4.1.6. An element C/x is *accessible* from A with respect to B means:

1. x is `private` in C and $A = C$, or
2. x is not `private` in C and C is in the same package as A, or
3. x is `public` in C, or
4. x is `protected` in C and $B \preceq_h A \prec_h C$.

In the next definition we define what it means that an element is *visible* in a class or interface A. In terms of the JLS this means that it is a *member* of A.

Definition 4.1.7. The visibility of members is defined inductively:

1. If x is declared in A, then A/x is visible in A.
2. If $A \prec_d B$, C/x is visible in B, x is not declared in A and C/x is accessible from A, then C/x is visible in A.

Example ($\rightsquigarrow$ CD) 4.1.1. Consider the following two classes:

```
class A {
  public  static int i = 2;
  private static int j = 3;
}
class B extends A {
    public static int i = 4;
}
```

The field `A/i` is not visible in class B, because i is defined in class B, too. The field `A/j` is not visible in class B, because it is `private` in A and therefore not accessible from B.

It is possible that two fields with the same identifier are visible in a class, since a class can implement several interfaces.

Example ($\rightsquigarrow$ CD) 4.1.2. Both, the field `I/MAX` and the field `J/MAX` are visible in class A.

```
interface I {
  int MAX = 100;
}
interface J {
  int MAX = 99;
}
class A implements I, J {}
```

As long as the constant `MAX` is not accessed in `A` by its simple name, no syntax error occurs.

Example (⤳ CD) 4.1.3. A field can be visible in a class through different paths:

```
interface I {
  int MAX = 100;
}
class A implements I {}
class B extends A implements I {}
```

The field `I/MAX` is visible in class `B` through its superclass `A` as well as directly, since B implements I.

The JLS uses the term 'override' for instance methods only. We use it here for class methods, too.

Definition 4.1.8. A method $A/msig$ is said to *directly override* a method $C/msig$, if there is a class or interface B such that

1. $A \prec_d B$,
2. $C/msig$ is visible in B and
3. $C/msig$ is accessible from A.

When a new method possibly overrides or hides a method with the same signature in a superclass or superinterface several conditions have to be satisfied, for example, the return type has to be the same.

Constraint 4.1.10. If $A/msig$ directly overrides $C/msig$, then the following constraints must be satisfied:

1. The return type of $msig$ in A is the same as in C.
2. Method $msig$ is not `final` in C.
3. Method $msig$ is `static` in A if, and only if, it is `static` in C.
4. Method $msig$ is not `private` in A.
5. If $msig$ is `public` in C, then $msig$ is `public` in A.
6. If $msig$ is `protected` in C, then $msig$ is `public` or `protected` in A.

The last three constraints say that access may not decrease according to the following ordering:

$$\texttt{private} < \texttt{default} < \texttt{protected} < \texttt{public}$$

The relation 'overriding' is the reflexive, transitive closure of 'direct overriding'.

Definition 4.1.9. The relation $A/msig$ *overrides* $B/msig$ is inductively defined as follows:

1. If $msig$ is declared in A, then $A/msig$ overrides $A/msig$.
2. If $A/msig$ directly overrides $B/msig$ and $B/msig$ overrides $C/msig$, then $A/msig$ overrides $C/msig$.

It is possible that a method $msig$ is declared in several superinterfaces of a class A. It is also possible that $msig$ is declared in a superinterface and in a superclass of A. In order to avoid inconsistencies one has to require that the return type of $msig$ is always the same.

Constraint 4.1.11. If two methods $B/msig$ and $C/msig$ with the same signature are both visible in A, then the following constraints must be satisfied:

1. $msig$ has the same return type in B and C,
2. If $msig$ is `public` in B, then $msig$ is `public` in C.
3. If $msig$ is not `static` in B, then $msig$ is not `static` in C.

The following constraint for `abstract` methods is not contained in the JLS. The constraint is natural, since `abstract` methods in interfaces are `public` by definition. The constraint is later used in the Lookup Lemma 8.4.1.

Constraint 4.1.12. If $C/msig$ is `abstract`, then it is `public` or `protected`.

The JLS allows `abstract` methods with `default` access. Such methods, however, are strange, because they cannot be implemented in a different package.

Definition 4.1.10. A class A *implements* a method $msig$, if there exists a class B such that

1. $A \preceq_{\mathrm{h}} B$ and $msig$ is declared in B,
2. $B/msig$ is visible in A,
3. $msig$ is not `abstract` in B.

Unless a class A implements all methods of its superinterfaces the class has to be declared `abstract`. Also if an `abstract` method of a superclass is visible in A, then A has to be declared `abstract`.

Constraint 4.1.13. If the `abstract` method $C/msig$ is visible in class A and A does not implement $msig$, then A is `abstract`.

In other words, if a non abstract class A implements an interface I, then A implements each method declared in the interface I.

Example ($\rightsquigarrow$ CD) 4.1.4. Class A inherits from its direct superclass B a non-abstract method m(int). Therefore, class A implements method m(int).

```
interface I { int m(int i); }
class B {
  public int m(int i) {
    return i * i;
  }
}
class A extends B implements I { }
```

The abstract method I/m(int) is visible in class A. Since A implements m(int), class A is not abstract.

Example ($\rightsquigarrow$ CD) 4.1.5. If the method m(int) is declared private in class B, then it is no longer visible in class A.

```
interface I { int m(int i); }
class B {
  private int m(int i) {
    return i * i;
  }
}
abstract class A extends B implements I { }
```

Since class A does not implement method m(int), class A has to be declared abstract.

Example ($\rightsquigarrow$ CD) 4.1.6. If the method m(int) is declared with default access in class B, then Constraint 4.1.11 is violated, because m(int) is public in interface I:

```
interface I { int m(int i); }
class B {
  int m(int i) {
    return i * i;
  }
}
abstract class A extends B implements I { }
```

The compiler reports an error because the access modifier of m(int) is made more restrictive.

4.1.5 Static type checking

For the rest of this chapter we assume that all fields and methods of classes are static. Static field access expressions are replaced at compile-time by abstract expressions $C.field$, where *field* is a class field declared in class or interface I. There are two possibilities to access a static field:

1. $B.field$, where B is a class or interface.
2. *field*

These expressions are replaced at compile-time as follows:

1. In an expression $B.field$ the identifier *field* can denote a field of the class or interface B or a field of one of B's superclasses or superinterfaces which is visible in B. At compile-time, the expression $B.field$ in class A is replaced by $C.field$, if the class or interface C is unique with the property that $C/field$ is visible in B and accessible from A. If there is no such class C or if *field* is not static in C, then a syntax error occurs.
2. If a simple expression *field* in class A is not in the scope of a local variable declaration or formal parameter with the same name, then it denotes a field of A or field of one of A's superclasses or superinterfaces which is visible in A. The simple expression *field* is replaced by the expression $C.field$, if the class or interface C is unique with the property that $C/field$ is visible in A, and if *field* is static in C.

The type of a static field access expressions $C.field$ is the declared type of *field* in C (see Table 4.1).

4.1.6 Overloaded methods

A method invocation expression can refer to a method in the current class or to a visible method of one of its superclasses. Since methods can be overloaded, during compile-time the most specific method is chosen which is applicable to the types of the arguments of the invocation. The type of the method invocation is then the return type of the chosen method. A method is more specific, if it is defined in a subclass or in the same class and if the argument types are subtypes. The return type of the method is ignored in the comparison. The relation 'more specific' is a partial ordering. If a set of methods has a least element, then this element is unique.

Definition 4.1.11. A method $C/meth(A_1, \ldots, A_n)$ is *more specific* than a method $D/meth(B_1, \ldots, B_n)$, if $C \preceq_h D$ and $A_i \preceq B_i$ for $i = 1, \ldots, n$.

There are two kinds of method invocations:

1. $^\alpha meth^\beta(exps)$
2. $^\alpha C.meth^\beta(exps)$, where C is a class.

Table 4.1 Type constraints for Java$_C$

$^\alpha C.field$	$\mathcal{T}(\alpha)$ is the declared type of *field* in C.
$^\alpha(C.field = {}^\beta exp)$	$\mathcal{T}(\alpha)$ is the declared type of *field* in C, *field* is not `final` in C, $\mathcal{T}(\beta) \preceq \mathcal{T}(\alpha)$.
$^\alpha C.msig(exps)$	$\mathcal{T}(\alpha)$ is the declared return type of *msig* in class C.
`return` $^\alpha exp;$	If the position α is in the body of a method with return type A, then $\mathcal{T}(\alpha) \preceq A$.

As a result of parsing and elaboration each kind of expression is replaced by $^\alpha D.m^\beta(exps)$, where D and the method signature m are determined as follows: Assume that the position α is in class A and that $^\beta(exps)$ is $^\beta(^{\gamma_1} exp_1, \ldots, {}^{\gamma_n} exp_n)$. Let *msig* be the signature $meth(\mathcal{T}(\gamma_1), \ldots, \mathcal{T}(\gamma_n))$. A set of applicable methods $app(\alpha)$ is determined as follows:

1. Let $app(\alpha)$ be the set of all methods D/m such that
   a) $A/msig$ is more specific than D/m and
   b) D/m is visible in A.
2. Let $app(\alpha)$ be the set of all methods D/m such that
   a) $C/msig$ is more specific than D/m and
   b) D/m is visible in C and accessible from A with respect to C.

Assume that $app(\alpha)$ contains a most specific element D/m, i.e.,

– $D/m \in app(\alpha)$
– If $E/k \in app(\alpha)$, then D/m is more specific than E/k

Assume that m is `static` in D. Then D/m is the method chosen by the compiler. Moreover, the type at position α is the declared return type of m in D (see Table 4.1).

Example ($\leadsto$ CD) 4.1.7. In the following program the method `m` is overloaded. It can take arguments of type `double` as well as arguments of type `long`. The most specific method is chosen during compile-time:

```
class A {
  static void m(double d) {}
  static void m(long l) {}
  static void test(int i) {
    m(i); // Method m(long) is chosen during compile-time.
  }
}
```

Since i is declared to be of type int, the most specific method for the method invocation m(i) is m(long). In order to ensure type safety, the compiler inserts automatically a type cast: the method invocation m(i) is replaced by m((long)i). Hence, before the method m(long) is invoked, the argument is converted from type int to long.

Example (⤳ CD) 4.1.8. It can happen that there exists no most specific method which is applicable to a method invocation.

```
class A {
  static void m(int x,long y) {}
  static void m(long x,int y) {
    m(0,0); // Reference to m is ambiguous.
  }
}
```

In this case, the compiler reports that the reference to the method is ambiguous. Note, that the literal 0 is of type int.

Example (⤳ CD) 4.1.9. In the following example A/m(int) and B/m(long) are both applicable to the method invocation expression m(0):

```
class A {
  static void m(int x) {}
}

class B extends A {
  static void m(long x) {
    m(0); // Reference to m is ambiguous.
  }
}
```

Since B $\preceq_h$ A and int $\preceq$ long the two methods are not comparable and therefore there is no most specific method for m(0).

Example (⤳ CD) 4.1.10. The type of the expression in the return statement can be a subtype of the declared return type of the method:

```
class Test {
  static long m(int i) {
    return i;
  }
}
```

In this example, the value of i is automatically converted to type long: the compiler replaces 'return i' by 'return (long)i' (see Table 4.2).

Table 4.2 Type constraints after introduction of primitive type casts

$^\alpha(C.field = {}^\beta exp)$	Let D be the declared type of *field* in C. If D is primitive, then $\mathcal{T}(\beta) = D = \mathcal{T}(\alpha)$.
$^\alpha C.msig({}^{\beta_1} exp_1, \ldots, {}^{\beta_n} exp_n)$	If $msig = meth(B_1, \ldots, B_n)$ and B_i is a primitive type, then $\mathcal{T}(\beta_i) = B_i$.
`return` $^\alpha exp;$	If the position α is in the body of a method with a primitive return type A, then $\mathcal{T}(\alpha) = A$.

4.1.7 Vocabulary of Java$_C$

The extension of the vocabulary we describe in this section for Java$_C$ reflects that this machine comes with a class environment, including a class initialization mechanism, that it deals with different methods which can be invoked and be returned from, and that with method return it introduces a new reason of abruption of normal program execution.

For the sake of simplicity, but without loss of generality, we assume that any class C has a class initializer C/`<clinit>`()—its body (whose function is to initialize the class fields at the first active use of the class, see below) is a phrase `static` *block*, where *block* may be empty. Non constant class field initializations are syntactically reduced to assignments and are placed at the beginning of the class initializer. Java$_C$ abstracts from initializations of constant fields; the latter are `final` class fields, whose values are compile-time constants [18, §15.27]. The value of constant fields is precomputed (as part of the elaboration phase) and stored in the class and interface environment of the given program.

We assume also that there are only field access expressions of the kind $C.field$, where *field* is a `static` field declared in C. Other field access expressions are replaced during parsing and type checking. Moreover, method invocations are of the kind $C.msig(exps)$, where *msig* is a method signature of a `static` method of class C. The method signature as well as the class C have been determined during type-checking (see Sect. 4.1.5).

Java$_C$ programs are executed w.r.t. a static *class environment* which is set up during parsing and elaboration. The following static functions look up information in this environment, possibly traversing the inheritance hierarchy from bottom to top (from subtype to supertype).

The function *super* returns the direct superclass of a given class, provided there is a superclass, i.e., $C \prec_d super(C)$. We use the function *classNm* to access the class name of a compound identifier (e.g. $classNm(c/m) = c$). The function *methNm* accesses the method name (e.g. $methNm(c/m) = methNm(m)$). The function *body* yields the body of the given method in the given class.

$super$: $Class \to Class$
$body$: $Class/MSig \to Block$

In Java$_C$ we distinguish four initialization states for a class: either the initialization of the class has not yet started (but the class is *Linked*), it is *InProgress*, it is already *Initialized* or during the initialization an error occured. Therefore we introduce a universe

data $ClassState = Linked \mid InProgress \mid Initialized \mid Unusable$

together with a dynamic function

$classState$: $Class \to ClassState$

which records the current initialization status of a class. A class is *initialized*, if the initialization state for the class is *InProgress* or *Initialized*.

$initialized(c) =$
      $classState(c) = Initialized \lor classState(c) = InProgress$

To model the dynamic state of class fields, we have to reserve storage for these variables. The dynamic function *globals* yields the value stored under a field specification.

$globals$: $Class/Field \to Val$

In Java$_C$ we have to deal with different methods which can be invoked and be returned from. We use the dynamic function *meth* to denote the currently executed method.

$meth$: $Class/MSig$

A method may call other methods. We use the usual stack technique to implement method calls. When a new method is invoked, the *frame* of the invoking method *meth*, consisting of *meth*, *restbody*; *pos*, and *locals*, is pushed onto the stack to be resumed after the invoked method has finished. We denote by a dynamic function *frames* the sequence of currently still to be executed frames on the stack.

type $Frame = (Class/MSig, Phrase, Pos, Locals)$
$frames$: $Frame^*$

In Java$_C$ there are two new reasons for abruption, namely *Return* and *Return(Val)*, occurring through the execution of **return** statements which by definition complete the body of a method abruptly and possibly return a result value to the invoker of the method. They will be used in the extension of the abruption handling rules of *execJavaStm$_I$* in *execJavaStm$_C$*.

data $Abr = Break(Lab) \mid Continue(Lab) \mid Return \mid Return(Val)$

4.2 Transition rules for Java$_C$

The machine *execJava$_C$* of *execJava* extends the machine *execJava$_I$* by the rules which define the semantics of the new Java$_C$-expressions and Java$_C$-statements. Therefore like *execJava$_I$* it consists of two submachines, for expression evaluation and statement execution, which are defined below.

> *execJava$_C$* =
>   *execJavaExp$_C$*
>   *execJavaStm$_C$*

For the initial state of Java$_C$ we assume that the environment of the respective lookup functions and predicates is defined by the given program which consists of a list of classes and interfaces. All class fields of all classes are set to their default or constant values. The run of Java$_C$ starts with *meth* being the class method

```
public static void main()
```

which is supposed to be part of the environment; *pos* denotes the first position of the *body* of main which defines *restbody*, *locals* is undefined (because main is invoked without parameters). The run terminates, if no rule of Java$_C$ can be applied any more.

The machine *execJavaExp$_C$* is defined in Fig. 4.4. We first look at its effect for expressions belonging to initialized classes. In this case the evaluation of class fields is defined similarly to the evaluation of local variables in *execJavaExp$_I$*, but using the memory function *globals* instead of *locals*. The value of a class field access is the value bound under the name of the class and of the field in the global environment [18, §15.10]. To execute a class field assignment is to compute the value of its right-hand side [18, §15.25], followed by binding it as new value to the class and field name in the global environment. When a class method is called [18, §15.11], *execJavaExp$_C$* triggers the evaluation of the actual arguments of the invocation, respecting the left-to-right strategy; their values are then bound by *invokeMethod* (see below) to the parameters of the method, to start the execution of the called method and at the same time preparing the return to *up(pos)* in the calling method.

Now we explain the class initialization mechanism in *execJavaExp$_C$*. The program execution starts in a state in which no class or interface is initialized (except for Object). The initialization is required to be done at the *first active use* of any class or interface C, namely by executing its static initializer. The first active use of C can occur in the following situations:

– A class method declared in C is invoked
– A static field declared in C is used or assigned which is not a primitive constant
– A new instance of class C is created (see Chapter 5)

Fig. 4.4 Execution of Java$_C$ expressions

$$
\begin{aligned}
&execJavaExp_C = \textbf{case } context(pos) \textbf{ of}\\
&\quad c.f \qquad\qquad \to \textbf{if } initialized(c) \textbf{ then } yield(globals(c/f)) \textbf{ else } initialize(c)\\
&\quad c.f = {}^{\alpha}exp \to pos := \alpha\\
&\quad c.f = {}^{\blacktriangleright}val \to \textbf{if } initialized(c) \textbf{ then}\\
&\qquad\qquad\qquad\qquad globals(c/f) := val\\
&\qquad\qquad\qquad\qquad yieldUp(val)\\
&\qquad\qquad\qquad \textbf{else } initialize(c)\\
\\
&\quad c.m^{\alpha}(exps) \to pos := \alpha\\
&\quad c.m^{\blacktriangleright}(vals) \to \textbf{if } initialized(c) \textbf{ then } invokeMethod(up(pos), c/m, vals)\\
&\qquad\qquad\qquad \textbf{else } initialize(c)
\end{aligned}
$$

$$
\begin{aligned}
&()   &&\to yield([\,])\\
&({}^{\alpha_1}exp_1, \ldots, {}^{\alpha_n}exp_n)   &&\to pos := \alpha_1\\
&({}^{\alpha_1}val_1, \ldots, {}^{\blacktriangleright}val_n) &&\to yieldUp([val_1, \ldots, val_n])\\
&({}^{\alpha_1}val_1, \ldots, {}^{\blacktriangleright}val_i, {}^{\alpha_{i+1}}exp_{i+1} \ldots {}^{\alpha_n}exp_n) &&\to pos := \alpha_{i+1}
\end{aligned}
$$

A *primitive constant* is a field that is both `static` and `final`, and that is initialized with a compile-time constant expression. A constant expression is built up from literals and other primitive constants using unary and binary operators. Primitive constants are replaced in the source code, at compile-time, by the corresponding literals with the same value (so called inlining of primitive constants).

Before a class is initialized, its superclasses must be initialized. As a consequence, when *execJavaExp$_C$* accesses fields, or assigns to fields, or calls methods, as first active use of a not yet initialized class C, it invokes the class initializer of C which is described by the following rule *initialize(C)*.

$$
\begin{aligned}
&initialize(c) =\\
&\quad \textbf{if } classState(c) = Linked \textbf{ then}\\
&\qquad classState(c) := InProgress\\
&\qquad \textbf{forall } f \in staticFields(c)\\
&\qquad\quad globals(f) := defaultVal(type(f))\\
&\qquad invokeMethod(pos, c/\texttt{<clinit>}, [\,])
\end{aligned}
$$

This rule records that starting from now, the initialization of class C is *InProgress*. All static fields (*staticFields*) of the class are initialized with their default value. Through the macro *invokeMethod* defined below, the rule pushes the current computation state on the frame stack, with unchanged *pos* (since after the initialization the computation has to proceed where the initialization was started) and without parameters (since class initialization methods have no arguments), and it transfers the control to the first position of the body of the static initialization code (where *firstPos* can be considered as a system constant).

The statement execution submachine *execJavaStm$_C$* of *execJava$_C$*, defined in Fig. 4.5, starts the execution of `static` initialization blocks—unless the current class has a superclass which is not yet initialized, in which case *execJavaStm$_C$* invokes the initialization of that superclass. When a `static` block of class C is executed, accesses to the fields of C and invocations of methods of C should not trigger a new first use of C. This is the reason why *InProgress* is included in the definition of the predicate *initialized*.

When returning from a method, in case an expression is returned, the submachine *execJavaStm$_C$* first transfers the control to the expression evaluation submachine *execJavaExp$_C$*; in case no expression is returned, or after the value *val* of the returned expression has been computed, the computation abrupts, with the possible return value encoded into the reason *Return(val)* for abruption, and the current method has to be exited. In the extension *execJava$_E$* of *execJava$_C$*, this method exit will be subject to prior execution of so called finally code, which may be present in the current method. Therefore, instead of transferring the control from a return statement directly to the invoker, we let *execJavaStm$_C$* propagate the return abruption up to the starting point *firstPos* of the current method body, from where the method will be exited. However, the return from a class initialization method has to be excluded from this propagation. Therefore we refine the predicate *propagatesAbr* from *execJava$_I$* in *execJava$_C$* as follows:

propagatesAbr(phrase) =
  phrase ≠ *lab* : *s* ∧
  phrase ≠ `static` *s*

In *execJava$_E$ propagatesAbr* will be further refined to take also finally code into account.

The rule *invokeMethod*, which is used in Fig. 4.5, pushes the current frame, with the position given as parameter, on the frame stack and creates a new current frame to start executing the body of the invoked method. The argument values are bound to the formal parameters of the method in the new local environment. We use the submachine *invokeNative* which describes the invocation of native methods and is defined in Sect. 7.2.2. The function *modifiers* returns the method modifiers (*Native, Public, . . .*), as specified in the class definition.

invokeMethod(nextPos, c/m, values)
  | *Native* ∈ *modifiers(c/m)* =
    invokeNative(c/m, values)
  | **otherwise** =
    frames   := *push(frames, (meth, restbody, nextPos, locals))*
    meth   := *c/m*
    restbody := *body(c/m)*
    pos   := *firstPos*
    locals   := *zip(argNames(c/m), values)*

Upon return from the execution of a method, the rule *exitMethod(result)* passes control back to the current position of the invoker, reestablishes the

---

Fig. 4.5 Execution of Java$_C$ statements

$execJavaStm_C = $ **case** $context(pos)$ **of**
   static $^\alpha stm \to$ **let** $c = classNm(meth)$
    if $c = $ Object $\vee\ initialized(super(c))$ **then** $pos := \alpha$
    else $initialize(super(c))$
   static $^\alpha Return \to yieldUp(Return)$

   return $^\alpha exp;$ $\to pos := \alpha$
   return $^\blacktriangleright val;$ $\to yieldUp(Return(val))$
   return; $\to yield(Return)$
   $lab : {}^\blacktriangleright Return$ $\to yieldUp(Return)$
   $lab : {}^\blacktriangleright Return(val) \to yieldUp(Return(val))$
   $Return$ $\to$ **if** $pos = firstPos \wedge \neg null(frames)$ **then**
                             $exitMethod(Norm)$
   $Return(val)$ $\to$ **if** $pos = firstPos \wedge \neg null(frames)$ **then**
                             $exitMethod(val)$

   $^\blacktriangleright Norm; \to yieldUp(Norm)$

---

method and local variables of the invoker and replaces in its *restbody* the method invocation statement by the result of the invoked method (i.e., the value to be returned if there is one or the information on normal completion of the method body)—except for the normal return from a class initialization whereupon the execution proceeds with the previous *restbody* and the class state is updated to *Initialized*.

$exitMethod(result) = $
   let $(oldMeth, oldPgm, oldPos, oldLocals) = top(frames)$
   $meth$ $:= oldMeth$
   pos $:= oldPos$
   $locals$ $:= oldLocals$
   $frames := pop(frames)$
   if $methNm(meth) = $ "<clinit>" $\wedge\ result = Norm$ **then**
     $restbody$ $:= oldPgm$
     $classState(classNm(meth)) := Initialized$
   else
     $restbody := oldPgm[result/oldPos]$

4.2.1 Exercises

Exercise ($\rightsquigarrow$ CD) 4.2.1. Which field is selected at position α?

```
interface I {
  int i = 11;
}
class A implements I {
  private static int i = 7;
```

```
   void m() {
     i = ᵅB.i;
   }
}
class B extends A {}
```

Exercise ($\rightsquigarrow$ CD) 4.2.2. Which field is selected at position α?

```
interface I {
  int i = 11;
}
class A {
  private static int i = 7;
}
class B extends A implements I {
  static int j = ᵅi + 1;
}
```

Exercise ($\rightsquigarrow$ CD) 4.2.3. What are the applicable methods at positions α, β, γ? Which method is selected by the compiler?

```
class A {
  static void m(int x) {}
  static void m(char x) {}
}
class B extends A {
  static void m(long x) {
    ᵅm(0);
    ᵝm('A');
    ᵞm(0L);
  }
}
```

Exercise ($\rightsquigarrow$ CD) 4.2.4. What is the order of initialization?

```
class A {
  static int x = 7;
  static { System.out.println("Initialization of A"); }
}
class B extends A {
  static { System.out.println("Initialization of B"); }
}
class Test {
  public static void main(String[] argv) {
    System.out.println(B.x);
  }
}
```

Exercise ($\rightsquigarrow$ CD) 4.2.5. What is the order of initialization?

```
class A {
  static int x = 7;
  static { System.out.println("Initialization of A"); }
}
class B extends A {
  static int x = 3;
  static { System.out.println("Initialization of B"); }
}
class Test {
  public static void main(String[] argv) {
    System.out.println(B.x);
  }
}
```

Exercise ($\rightsquigarrow$ CD) 4.2.6. What is the order of initialization?

```
class A {
  static int x = 7;
  static { System.out.println("Initialization of A"); }
}
class B extends A {
  static final int x = 3;
  static { System.out.println("Initialization of B"); }
}
class Test {
  public static void main(String[] argv) {
    System.out.println(B.x);
  }
}
```

Exercise ($\rightsquigarrow$ CD) 4.2.7. What is the output of the following program?

```
interface I {
  int c = 1 + A.x;
  int d = 1 + A.y;
}
class A implements I {
  static int x = 2;
  static int y = I.d;
}
class Test {
  public static void main(String[] args) {
    System.out.println("I.c = " + I.c);
    System.out.println("I.d = " + I.d);
    System.out.println("A.x = " + A.x);
```

```
    System.out.println("A.y = " + A.y);
  }
}
```

Exercise ($\leadsto$ CD) 4.2.8. What is the output of the following program?

```
interface I {
  int c = 1 + A.x;
  int d = 1 + A.y;
}
class A implements I {
  static int x = 2;
  static int y = I.d;
}
class Test {
  public static void main(String[] args) {
    System.out.println("A.x = " + A.x);
    System.out.println("A.y = " + A.y);
    System.out.println("I.c = " + I.c);
    System.out.println("I.d = " + I.d);
  }
}
```

5. The object-oriented extension Java$_\mathcal{O}$ of Java$_\mathcal{C}$

Java$_\mathcal{O}$ extends Java$_\mathcal{C}$ to an object-oriented language, supporting the following new features to form expressions: instance fields, instance methods, creation of new instances, method overriding, type casts, type checks and null pointers. Correspondingly *execJava$_\mathcal{O}$* introduces new rules for expression evaluation and handling of values. In Sect. 5.1 we describe the static and in Sect. 5.2 the dynamic part of the semantics of Java$_\mathcal{O}$.

5.1 Static semantics of Java$_\mathcal{O}$

In the previous chapter, classes and interfaces played the role of modules. In the present chapter, classes and interfaces will be types, too. This means that the type of a variable can be a class or interface and not only a primitive type. The return type of a method can be a class or interface, too.

Definition 5.1.1. Types A, B, C are generated as follows:

1. Primitive types are types (see Table 3.1).
2. Classes and interfaces are types.
3. Null and void are types.
4. If A is a type different from Null and void, then $A[\,]$ is a type.

The type Null is not allowed to appear explicitly in a program. The type void can only be used as a return type of a method. The type $A[\,]$ is called *array of A. Reference types* are class types, interface types, array types and the type Null. The default value for all reference types is the constant null.

The subtype relation $\preceq$ of Def. 3.1.1 is extended to reference types.

Definition 5.1.2. For reference types, the relation $\preceq$ is the least reflexive and transitive relation satisfying the following conditions:

1. If $A \prec_d B$, then $A \preceq B$.
2. If A is a reference type, then Null $\preceq A$ and $A \preceq$ Object.
3. $A[\,] \preceq$ Cloneable and $A[\,] \preceq$ Serializable.
4. If $A \preceq B$ and A, B are reference types, then $A[\,] \preceq B[\,]$.

Table 5.1 Binary operators for references

Bop	Operand types	Result type	Operation
+	A or B is `String`	`String`	String concatenation
==	$A \preceq B$ or $B \preceq A$	`boolean`	equal (references)
!=	$A \preceq B$ or $B \preceq A$	`boolean`	not equal (references)

`Null` is the least reference type and `Object` is the top element. For classes and interfaces A, B the following is true (see Exercise 5.2.5):

$$A \preceq B \iff A \preceq_h B \text{ or } B = \texttt{Object}.$$

In terms of the JLS, the relation $A \preceq B$ for reference types means that there is an *identity conversion* or a *widening reference conversion* from A to B (see [18, §5.1.4]).

Example 5.1.1. Although every reference type is a subtype of `Object`, this is not true for primitive types. For example, `int` is not considered as a subtype of `Object`, i.e., `int` $\npreceq$ `Object`. There exists, however, a standard class `Integer` which is a subtype of `Object`,

$$\texttt{java.lang.Integer} \preceq \texttt{Object}.$$

Note, that although `int` is a subtype of `long` the type array of `int` is not a subtype of array of `long`, i.e., we have `int` $\preceq$ `long`, but `int[]` $\npreceq$ `long[]`.

5.1.1 Operators for reference types

The binary operators `+`, `==` and `!=` can be applied to arguments of reference type. The type of the result is indicated in Table 5.1. Note, that to test whether two strings s_1 and s_2 are equal one has to use s_1`.equals(`s_2`)` and not s_1 `==` s_2.

5.1.2 Syntax of Java$_\mathcal{O}$

The syntax of the object-oriented sublanguage Java$_\mathcal{O}$ of Java is given in Fig. 5.1. Expressions with `this` or `super` are allowed in the following contexts only:

1. in the body of an instance method,
2. in the initializer of an instance field,
3. in the body of a constructor.

Expressions with `super` are not allowed to appear in the class `Object`.

Fig. 5.1 Syntax of Java$_\mathcal{O}$

$$Exp \; := \ldots \mid \texttt{null} \mid \texttt{this} \mid Exp.Field \mid \texttt{super}.Field$$
$$\mid Exp \; \texttt{instanceof} \; Class \mid (Class)Exp$$
$$Asgn := \ldots \mid Exp.Field = Exp \mid \texttt{super}.Field = Exp$$
$$Invk \; := \ldots \mid \texttt{new} \; Class(Exps) \mid Exp.Meth(Exps) \mid \texttt{super}.Meth(Exps)$$

5.1.3 Constructor declarations

A constructor declaration in a class A has the following syntax:

$$\langle\texttt{public} \mid \texttt{protected} \mid \texttt{private}\rangle \; A(B_1 \; loc_1, \ldots, B_n \; loc_n) \; cbody$$

The name of the constructor is the simple name of the class, in our case A. A constructor declaration has no return type. Constructors are not inherited and, therefore, cannot be overridden. Several constructors with different signatures may be defined in the same class. The body of a constructor has the following grammar:

$$cbody := block \mid \{\texttt{this}(exps); \; bstm \ldots\} \mid \{\texttt{super}(exps); \; bstm \ldots\}$$

The first statement of the constructor body can be an *explicit constructor invocation* of a constructor of the same class or of a constructor of the direct superclass:

1. `this`($exps$);   [constructor of the same class]
2. `super`($exps$);   [constructor of the direct superclass]

An explicit constructor invocation statement may not refer to any instance variables or instance methods declared in the class or any superclass, or use `this` or `super` in any expression. It is not allowed that there is a cycle through explicit constructor invocations.

The compiler does the following:

1. If *cbody* does not begin with an explicit constructor invocation, then the constructor invocation 'super();' is inserted.
2. The instance variable initializers of class A are inserted in textual order as assignments immediately after the explicit invocation of a superclass constructor.
3. If the class A does not have a constructor, then the following default constructor is inserted:

   $$A() \; \{\texttt{super}();\}$$

   The default constructor is `public`, if the class A is `public`.

The default constructor of the class `Object` is:

$$\texttt{Object}() \; \{\}$$

Example ($\leadsto$ CD) 5.1.2. Consider the following class A:

```
class A {
  private int x;
  private int y = 17;
  static int z = 3;

  A(int x) {
    this.x = x;
  }
}
```

The compiler replaces the constructor A(int) by the following code:

```
A(int x) {
  super();
  y = 17;
  this.x = x;
}
```

The static field A/z is initialized when the class A is initialized, not when a constructor is invoked.

5.1.4 Field access expressions

Instance field access expressions are transformed at compile-time into the abstract form *exp.C/field*, where *field* is an instance field declared in class *C*. Instance fields can be accessed in three different ways:

1. *exp.field*
2. super.*field*
3. *field*

Assume that the expressions are in class *A*. Then they are transformed in the following way:

1. Let *B* be the type of *exp* in the expression *exp.field*. Then *field* denotes an instance field of *B* or of one of *B*'s superclasses. The expression *exp.field* is replaced by *exp.C/field*, if the class *C* is unique with the property that *C/field* is visible in *B* and accessible from *A* with respect to *B* (Def. 4.1.6), and if *field* is not static in *C*. If there exists no such class *C*, a syntax error occurs.
2. An expression super.*field* in class *A* denotes an instance field of the direct superclass *B* of *A* or of one of *B*'s superclasses. The expression super.*field* is replaced by this.*C/field*, if the class *C* is unique with the property that *C/field* is visible in *B* and accessible from *A* (Def. 4.1.5), and if *field* is not static in *C*.

3. If a simple expression *field* in class A is not in the scope of a local variable declaration or formal parameter with the same name, then it denotes a field of A or of one of A's superclasses. The simple expression *field* is replaced by the expression $\texttt{this}.C/\textit{field}$, if the class C is unique with the property that $C/\textit{field}$ is visible in A, and if *field* is not $\texttt{static}$ in C. The simple field access expression *field* must be in a context where $\texttt{this}$ is allowed.

The type of an abstract field access expression $exp.C/\textit{field}$ is the declared type of *field* in class C (see Table 5.2).

5.1.5 Overloaded methods

As a result of the parsing and elaboration phase instance method invocations are attributed as specified in [18, §15.11.1–3]. They are transformed at compile-time into the abstract form $exp.D/msig(exps)$, where *msig* is a method signature of an instance method declared in class or interface D. Instance method invocations have an additional *callKind* which is used for method lookup.

data $Kind = Virtual \mid Special \mid Super$

The invocation kind *Static* is not needed here, since it is already handled by class methods. Instance methods can be invoked in three different ways:

1. $^{\alpha}(^{\beta}exp.meth^{\gamma}(exps))$
2. $^{\alpha}\texttt{super}.meth^{\gamma}(exps)$
3. $^{\alpha}meth^{\gamma}(exps)$

Assume that α is in class A and that $^{\gamma}(exps)$ is $^{\gamma}(^{\delta_1}exp_1, \ldots, {}^{\delta_n}exp_n)$. Let *msig* be the method signature $meth(\mathcal{T}(\delta_1), \ldots, \mathcal{T}(\delta_n))$. In a first step the compiler computes a set $app(\alpha)$ of applicable and accessible methods as follows:

1. Let $C = \mathcal{T}(\beta)$. Then $app(\alpha)$ is the set of all D/m such that
   a) $C/msig$ is more specific than D/m,
   b) D/m is visible in C and accessible from A with respect to C,
   c) if D is an interface, then C does not implement m.[1]
2. Let C be the direct superclass of A, i.e., $A \prec_{\mathrm{d}} C$. Then $app(\alpha)$ is the set of all methods D/m such that
   a) $C/msig$ is more specific than D/m,
   b) D/m is visible in C and accessible from A,
   c) if D is an interface, then C does not implement m.
3. Let $app(\alpha)$ be the set of all methods D/m such that
   a) $A/msig$ is more specific than D/m,
   b) D/m is visible in A,

---

[1] The last condition is not contained in the JLS [18, §15.11]. In [19, §15.12.2.2] the problem is solved in a slightly more general way.

   c) if D is an interface, then A does not implement m.

In a next step a most specific method is selected, if there exists one, and an invocation mode is determined. Assume that $app(\alpha)$ contains a most specific element D/m. Assume that m is not static in D. Then D/m is the method chosen by the compiler and the invocation mode is determined as follows:

1. The method invocation expression is replaced by

   $$\alpha(^\beta exp.D/m^\gamma(exps)).$$

   If the method m is private in D, then $callKind(\alpha) = Special$, otherwise $callKind(\alpha) = Virtual$.
2. The method invocation expression is replaced by

   $$\alpha(^\beta\texttt{this}.D/m^\gamma(exps)).$$

   The invocation mode is $callKind(\alpha) = Super$. In this case it is not allowed that m is abstract in D.
3. The method invocation expression is replaced by

   $$\alpha(^\beta\texttt{this}.D/m^\gamma(exps)).$$

   If the method m is private in D, then $callKind(\alpha) = Special$, otherwise $callKind(\alpha) = Virtual$.

The method chosen during compile-time determines the type of a method invocation expression: $\mathcal{T}(\alpha)$ is the return type of method m in D (see Table 5.2). The compile-time information associated with the method invocation is later used at run-time. If the invocation mode is

– *Special*, overriding is not allowed and the instance method m in class D is called directly
– *Virtual*, then the instance method m is looked up dynamically starting at the class of the target reference
– *Super*, the instance method m in class D is called directly

Example ($\rightsquigarrow$ *CD*) *5.1.3.* In the following example the method A/m(int) is applicable at the method invocation m(i) in the method test in class B.

```
interface I { void m(int i); }
class A {
  public void m(int i) { }
}
class B extends A implements I {
  void test(int i) {
    m(i);
  }
}
```

The method I/m(int) is not applicable, because it is implemented by B.

Example ($\leadsto$ CD) 5.1.4. In the body of method `test` in the following class `A`, the JDK 1.2 compiler accepts the first two invocations of `m(x)` and rejects the third one as ambiguous. In all three cases, however, both methods `I/m(J)` and `J/m(I)` are applicable, hence all three method invocations are ambiguous.

```
interface I {
  void m(J x);
}
interface J extends I {
  void m(I x);
}
abstract class A implements J {
  void test(J x) {
   this.m(x);
   ((A)x).m(x);
   x.m(x);
  }
}
```

If we use abstract classes instead of interfaces, then the JDK 1.2 compiler correctly reports all three method invocations as ambiguous.

```
abstract class I {
  abstract void m(J x);
}
abstract class J extends I {
  abstract void m(I x);
}
abstract class A extends J {
  void test(J x) {
    this.m(x);    // Reference to m is ambiguous.
    ((A)x).m(x);  // Reference to m is ambiguous.
    x.m(x);       // Reference to m is ambiguous.
  }
}
```

5.1.6 Instance creation expressions

Instance creation expressions are treated like ordinary method invocations. An instance creation expression `new` $C(exps)$ is transformed at compile-time into the abstract form

$$(\text{new } C).C/msig(exps),$$

where *msig* is a signature of a constructor of class C with name `<init>`. The abstract expression `new` C creates a new reference to an instance of class C which is the target reference of the invoked constructor. Since constructors

Table 5.2 Type constraints for Java$_\mathcal{O}$

$^\alpha$`null`	$\mathcal{T}(\alpha) = $ `Null`
$^\alpha$`this`	$\mathcal{T}(\alpha) = A$, if the position α is in class A.
$^\alpha(^\beta exp$ `instanceof` $A)$	$\mathcal{T}(\alpha) = $ `boolean`. A is a reference type. It must be possible that there is a class or array type C with $C \preceq A$ and $C \preceq \mathcal{T}(\beta)$ (see Exercise 5.2.6).
$^\alpha((A)\,^\beta exp)$	$\mathcal{T}(\alpha) = A$. A is a reference type. It must be possible that there is a class or array type C with $C \preceq A$ and $C \preceq \mathcal{T}(\beta)$ (see Exercise 5.2.6).
$^\alpha(exp.C/field)$	$\mathcal{T}(\alpha)$ is the declared type of *field* in class C.
$^\alpha(exp_1.C/field = {}^\gamma exp_2)$	$\mathcal{T}(\alpha)$ is the declared type of *field* in C, *field* is not `final` in C, $\mathcal{T}(\gamma) \preceq \mathcal{T}(\alpha)$.
$^\alpha$`new` $C.C/msig(exps)$	$\mathcal{T}(\alpha) = C$. C is a class and C is not `abstract`.
$^\alpha(exp.C/msig(exps))$	$\mathcal{T}(\alpha)$ is the declared return type of method *msig* in class or interface C.

Table 5.3 Type constraints after introduction of primitive type casts

$exp_1.C/field = {}^\gamma exp_2$	Let A be the declared type of *field* in C. If A is primitive, then $\mathcal{T}(\gamma) = A$.
$exp_0.C/msig(^{\beta_1} exp_1, \ldots, {}^{\beta_n} exp_n)$	If $msig = meth(B_1, \ldots, B_n)$ and B_i is a primitive type, then $\mathcal{T}(\beta_i) = B_i$.

are not inherited, applicable constructors are always in the same class. The *callKind* of a constructor invocation is *Special*.

5.1.7 Type checking of Java$_\mathcal{O}$

The type constraints for Java$_\mathcal{O}$ are listed in Table 5.2. Some casts can be proven incorrect at compile-time; such casts result in a compile-time error. Consider a cast expression '$(A)\,exp$'. Assume that *exp* has type B. At run-time the value of *exp* will belong to a class or array type $C \preceq B$. The cast will be allowed at run-time only if $C \preceq A$. Hence, if the compiler is able to prove that there exists no class or array type C such that $C \preceq A$ and $C \preceq B$, the cast is not allowed. Details can be found in Exercise 5.2.6.

5.1.8 Vocabulary of Java$_\mathcal{O}$

The following static functions look up compile-time information in the environment:

$$
\begin{aligned}
\textit{instanceFields}&: \textit{Class} \rightarrow \textit{Powerset}(\textit{Class}/\textit{Field}) \\
\textit{defaultVal}\quad &: \textit{Type} \rightarrow \textit{Val} \\
\textit{type}\quad\quad\;\; &: \textit{Class}/\textit{Field} \rightarrow \textit{Type} \\
\textit{lookup}\quad\quad\; &: (\textit{Class}, \textit{Class}/\textit{MSig}) \rightarrow \textit{Class}
\end{aligned}
$$

The function *instanceFields* calculates the set of instance fields declared by the specified class and all of its superclasses (if any). Hence $D/\textit{field}$ belongs to *instanceFields*(C) iff $C \preceq_h D$ and *field* is an instance field of D.

Example ($\rightsquigarrow$ CD) 5.1.5. Consider the following two classes:

```
class A {
  private int x;
  public int y;
  public static int z;
}
class B extends A {
  private int x;
}
```

Then *instanceFields*(B) $= [\text{A}/\text{x}, \text{A}/\text{y}, \text{B}/\text{x}]$. An object of type B has fields A/x, A/y, B/x. The field A/z is `static` and therefore not an instance field.

The function *defaultVal* maps types to their default values as specified in [18, §4.5.4]. The function *type* returns the declared type of the field in the class. The function *lookup* yields the class where the given method specification is defined with respect to the class hierarchy. The function *lookup*$(A, B/\textit{msig})$ is computed as follows:

1. If class A contains a non **abstract** declaration of *msig* and
   a) B is an interface, or
   b) $A/\textit{msig}$ overrides $B/\textit{msig}$ (cf. Def. 4.1.9),
   then *lookup*$(A, B/\textit{msig}) = A$.
2. Otherwise, if C is the direct superclass of A, then
   lookup$(A, B/\textit{msig}) = \textit{lookup}(C, B/\textit{msig})$.
3. Otherwise, $A = \texttt{Object}$ and *lookup*$(A, B/\textit{msig}) = \textit{undef}$.

Example 5.1.6. This example illustrates some details of the dynamic method lookup. Consider the following two packages:

```
package p;

public class A  {
  String m() { return "p"; }

  public String n() { return this.m(); }
}
```

```
package q;

public class B extends p.A {
  public String m() { return "q"; }

  public static void main(String[] _) {
    B x = new B();
    System.out.println(x.n());
  }
}
```

The method p.A/m() is not visible in package q. Therefore the method q.B/m() does not override p.A/m(). Although the variable x contains at run-time a reference of type q.B, the output of the program is p. If the method p.A/m() is declared public, then the output of the program will be q.

An object is an instance of a non abstract class. Objects are represented by references (pointers). References belong to the dynamic universe *Ref*. We extend the universe *Val* in Java$_\mathcal{O}$ to include references and the value *null*.

> **type** *Val* $= \ldots \mid Ref \mid null$

To model the dynamic state of objects, we have to reserve storage for all instance variables and have to store to which class an object belongs. The dynamic function *heap* records the class together with the field values of an object. The function *classOf* returns the class of the object that is referred to by the reference.

> **data** *Heap* $=$ *Object*(*Class*, *Map*(*Class*/*Field*, *Val*))
>
> *heap*   : *Ref* $\rightarrow$ *Heap*
> *classOf* : *Ref* $\rightarrow$ *Class*
> *classOf*(*ref*) $=$ **case** *heap*(*ref*) **of**
>   *Object*(*c*, *fields*) $\rightarrow$ *c*

More precisely, if *heap*(*ref*) $=$ *Object*(*C*, *fields*), then *fields* is a finite map which assigns a value to each field in the list *instanceFields*(*C*).

5.2 Transition rules for Java$_\mathcal{O}$

The initial state and the termination conditions of Java$_\mathcal{O}$ are the same as for Java$_\mathcal{C}$. Since Java$_\mathcal{O}$ has only new expressions and no new statements, the rules for Java$_\mathcal{O}$ extend only the expression evaluation rules of Java$_\mathcal{I}$ and Java$_\mathcal{C}$.

> *execJava$_O$* $=$
>   *execJavaExp$_O$*

Fig. 5.2 Execution of Java$_O$ expressions

$$execJavaExp_O = \textbf{case } context(pos) \textbf{ of}$$
$$\texttt{this} \rightarrow yield(locals(\texttt{"this"}))$$

$$\texttt{new } c \rightarrow \textbf{if } initialized(c) \textbf{ then create } ref$$
$$heap(ref) := Object(c, \{(f, defaultVal(type(f)))$$
$$\mid f \in instanceFields(c)\})$$
$$yield(ref)$$
$$\textbf{else } initialize(c)$$

$${}^{\alpha}exp.c/f \rightarrow pos := \alpha$$
$${}^{\blacktriangleright}ref.c/f \rightarrow \textbf{if } ref \neq null \textbf{ then } yieldUp(getField(ref, c/f))$$

$${}^{\alpha}exp_1.c/f = {}^{\beta}exp_2 \rightarrow pos := \alpha$$
$${}^{\blacktriangleright}ref.c/f = {}^{\beta}exp \rightarrow pos := \beta$$
$${}^{\alpha}ref.c/f = {}^{\blacktriangleright}val \rightarrow \textbf{if } ref \neq null \textbf{ then}$$
$$setField(ref, c/f, val)$$
$$yieldUp(val)$$

$${}^{\alpha}exp \textbf{ instanceof } c \rightarrow pos := \alpha$$
$${}^{\blacktriangleright}ref \textbf{ instanceof } c \rightarrow yieldUp(ref \neq null \wedge classOf(ref) \preceq c)$$

$$(c)^{\alpha}exp \rightarrow pos := \alpha$$
$$(c)^{\blacktriangleright}ref \rightarrow \textbf{if } ref = null \vee classOf(ref) \preceq c \textbf{ then } yieldUp(ref)$$

$${}^{\alpha}exp.c/m^{\beta}(exps) \rightarrow pos := \alpha$$
$${}^{\blacktriangleright}ref.c/m^{\beta}(exps) \rightarrow pos := \beta$$
$${}^{\alpha}ref.c/m^{\blacktriangleright}(vals) \rightarrow \textbf{if } ref \neq null \textbf{ then}$$
$$\textbf{let } c' = \textbf{case } callKind(up(pos)) \textbf{ of}$$
$$Virtual \rightarrow lookup(classOf(ref), c/m)$$
$$Super \rightarrow lookup(super(classNm(meth)), c/m)$$
$$Special \rightarrow c$$
$$invokeMethod(up(pos), c'/m, [ref] \cdot vals)$$

An additional rule extends *exitMethod*, describing the special case of a return from a constructor initialization method.

The expression evaluation machine *execJavaExp$_O$* defined in Fig. 5.2 passes the control from object related expressions to the evaluation of the corresponding object expression, namely for field access, field assignment, type check, type cast, instance method invocation and creation of a parametrized new class instance (if the class is initialized). The machine *execJavaExp$_O$* treats this the way *execJavaExp$_I$* handles local variables, upon invoking an instance method it binds the value of this keyword to the reference for the object for which the instance method is invoked [18, §15.7.2]. The expression null is a literal with value *null*.

execJavaExp$_O$ treats the access and the assignment to instance fields similarly to how *execJavaExp$_I$* deals with local variables, checking in addition that the previously computed object, pointed to by the target reference, is not *null*. The value of the computed expression, in the case of a field access, is the value *fields*(f) which is stored in the heap for the object pointed to by the target reference *ref* [18, §15.10]; it is described by the function *getField* below. In the case of a field assignment, the value of the computed expression is the value of the right-hand side of this assignment [18, §15.25] which, using *setField*, is stored in the heap to the field for the object pointed to by the target reference.

$$getField(ref, f) = \textbf{case } heap(ref) \textbf{ of}$$
$$Object(c, fields) \rightarrow fields(f)$$

$$setField(ref, f, val) =$$
$$heap(ref) := Object(c, fields \oplus \{(f, val)\})$$
$$\textbf{where } Object(c, fields) = heap(ref)$$

For type check and cast expressions *execJavaExp$_O$* passes the dynamic type condition of the computed subexpression up to the expression. The semantics of instance method calls as defined by *execJavaExp$_O$* [18, §15.11] is similar to that defined by *execJavaExp$_C$* for static method calls in that the evaluation of the arguments of the call (which includes the binding of the reference target to **this**) is guaranteed to happen before the values of these arguments are bound through *invokeMethod* to the method parameters. In addition, before applying *invokeMethod*, the machine checks that the target reference is defined; it determines dynamically the method body to be executed [18, §15.11.4].

For the creation of a parametrized new class instance, *execJavaExp$_O$* guarantees that the class get initialized before the parameter values are evaluated in the left-to-right order. Only then a reference to the newly created object of the specified class type is stored on the heap, together with new instances (instantiated with their default values) of all the fields declared in the specified class and its superclasses [18, §15.8], and the constructor method is invoked.

The *exitMethod* rule has to be extended for constructors. The result of a constructor invocation with **new** is the newly created object which is stored in the local environment as value for **this**.

$$exitMethod(result) =$$
$$\dots$$
$$\textbf{elseif } methNm(meth) = \texttt{"<init>"} \wedge result = Norm \textbf{ then}$$
$$restbody := oldPgm[locals(\texttt{"this"})/oldPos]$$
$$\dots$$

The effect of the *execJavaExp$_O$*-extension of the *exitMethod* rule is the same as if during the parsing and elaboration phase a 'return this' is inserted at the end of each constructor. Exercise 5.2.7 shows why we have to adapt the *exitMethod* rule.

5.2.1 Exercises

Exercise 5.2.1. Which of the following subtype relations are true in Java$_\mathcal{O}$?

1. int[] $\preceq$ Object[]
2. java.lang.Integer[] $\preceq$ Object[]
3. int[][] $\preceq$ Object[]
4. int[][][] $\preceq$ Cloneable[]
5. byte[][] $\preceq$ long[][]

Exercise ($\leadsto$ CD) 5.2.2. What is the output of the following program? How many fields has an object of type B?

```
class A { int i = 0; }
class B extends A { int i = 1; }
class Test {
  public static void main(String[] args) {
    B b = new B();
    System.out.println(b.i);
    System.out.println(((A)b).i);
  }
}
```

What are the abstract forms of the field access expressions b.i and ((A)b).i after parsing and elaboration?

Exercise ($\leadsto$ CD) 5.2.3. What is the output of the following program?

```
class A {
  private String m() { return "A/m()"; }
  public String n() { return "A/n()"; }
  void test() {
    System.out.println(this.m());
    System.out.println(this.n());
  }
}

class B extends A {
  public String m() { return "B/m()"; }
  public String n() { return "B/n()"; }
}

class Test {
  public static void main(String[] argv) {
    B b = new B();
    b.test();
  }
}
```

Which methods are selected by the compiler? What is their invocation mode? Which methods are invoked at run-time?

Exercise ($\rightsquigarrow$ CD) 5.2.4. What is the output of the following program?

```
class Cell {
  private int content;
  public int get(){ return content; }
  public void set(int i){ content = i; }
  public void inc(int i){ set(get() + i); }
}

class BackupCell extends Cell {
  private int backup;
  public void set(int i){ backup = get(); super.set(i); }
  public void restore(){ super.set(backup); }
}

class Test {
  public static void main(String[] args){
    BackupCell c = new BackupCell();
    c.set(1);
    c.inc(2);
    System.out.println(c.get());
    c.restore();
    System.out.println(c.get());
  }
}
```

Explain how backup cells work.

Exercise 5.2.5. The subtype relation $\preceq$ for reference types is inductively defined in Def. 5.1.2. It can be characterized directly as follows. Let $A \rho B$ iff one of the following conditions is true:

1. $A \preceq_\mathrm{h} B$, or
2. $B = \texttt{Object}$, or
3. $A = \texttt{Null}$, or
4. A is an array type and $B \in \{\texttt{Cloneable}, \texttt{Serializable}\}$, or
5. there is an $n \in \mathbb{N}$ and C, D such that $n > 0$, $A = C[]^n$, $B = D[]^n$ and
   a) D is a primitive type and $C = D$, or
   b) D is a class or interface and $C \preceq_\mathrm{h} D$, or
   c) $D = \texttt{Object}$ and C is a reference type , or
   d) $D \in \{\texttt{Cloneable}, \texttt{Serializable}\}$ and C is an array type.

Show that the relation ρ has the following properties:

1. $A \rho A$.

2. If $A \, \rho \, B$ and $B \, \rho \, C$, then $A \, \rho \, C$.
3. If $A \, \rho \, B$, then $A[\,] \, \rho \, B[\,]$.
4. If $A \, \rho \, B$, then $A \preceq B$.
5. If $A \, \rho \, B$ and $B \, \rho \, A$, then $A = B$.

It follows that $A \, \rho \, B \Leftrightarrow A \preceq B$. Hence the relation ρ is a direct characterization of the subtype relation $\preceq$.

Exercise 5.2.6. Let A, B, C reference types with $C \neq \texttt{Null}$, $C \preceq A$ and $C \preceq B$. Show that at least one of the following conditions is satisfied:

1. $A \preceq B$, or
2. $B \preceq A$, or
3. A and B are interfaces which do not contain methods with the same signature but different return type, or
4. A is an interface and B is a non-**final** class, or
5. B is a Interface and A is a non-**final** class, or
6. there is an $n \in \mathbb{N}$ and types E, F such that $n > 0$, $A = E[\,]^n$, $B = F[\,]^n$ and
   a) E and F are interfaces which do not contain methods with the same signature but different return type, or
   b) E is a interface and F is a non-**final** class, or
   c) F is a Interface and E is a non-**final** class.

The conditions above are listed in the JLS [18, §5.5].

Exercise 5.2.7. Consider the following Java statement:

```
Test t = new Test();
```

Assume we have not extended the *exitMethod* rule for constructor invocation. Explain why our Java ASM would stop after evaluating the expression **new Test()** instead of assigning the result to variable t.

6. The exception-handling extension Java$_{\mathcal{E}}$ of Java$_{\mathcal{O}}$

Java$_{\mathcal{E}}$ extends Java$_{\mathcal{O}}$ with exceptions, designed to provide support for recovering from abnormal situations. In this extension of the previous machines it becomes transparent how **break** and **continue** statements (in Java$_{\mathcal{I}}$), **return** statements (in Java$_{\mathcal{C}}$) and the initialization of classes and interfaces (in Java$_{\mathcal{O}}$) interact with catching and handling exceptions. When a Java program violates certain semantic constraints at run-time, the JVM signals this error to the program as an *exception*. The control is transferred, from the point where the exception occurred, to a point that can be specified by the programmer. An exception is said to be *thrown* from the point where it occurred, and it is said to be *caught* at the point to which control is transferred. Exceptions are represented in Java by instances of subclasses of the class **Throwable**. Java distinguishes between *run-time exceptions* (which correspond to invalid operations violating the semantic constraints of Java, like an attempt to divide by zero or to index an array outside its bounds), *errors* (which are failures detected by the executing machine), and *user-defined exceptions*. We consider here only run-time and user-defined exceptions, since errors belong to the JVM and are therefore ignored in the dynamic semantics of Java.

In Sect. 6.1 we describe the static and in Sect. 6.2 the dynamic part of the semantics of Java$_{\mathcal{E}}$.

6.1 Static semantics of Java$_{\mathcal{E}}$

The direct subclasses of **Throwable** are **Error** and **Exception**. One of the direct subclasses of **Exception** is the class **RuntimeException**. A class E is called a *checked exception class*, if

1. $E \preceq_{\mathrm{h}}$ **Throwable**,
2. $E \npreceq_{\mathrm{h}}$ **Error**,
3. $E \npreceq_{\mathrm{h}}$ **RuntimeException**.

The checked exceptions which a method may throw have to be declared in the **throws** clause of the method. A **throws** clause has the following syntax:

$$meth(D_1\, x_1, \ldots, D_n\, x_n)\, \textbf{throws}\, E_1, \ldots, E_n\; body$$

Fig. 6.1 Syntax of Java$_{\mathcal{E}}$

Stm ::= ... | **throw** *Exp*;
| **try** *Block* **catch** (*Class$_1$ Loc$_1$*) *Block$_1$* ... **catch** (*Class$_n$ Loc$_n$*) *Block$_n$*
| *Stm* **finally** *Block*

The classes E_i must be subclasses of **Throwable**, i.e., $E_i \preceq_h$ **Throwable**.

Definition 6.1.1. Let A and B be classes or interfaces. We say that a method *msig* throws *more specific exceptions* in A than in B, if for each class E occurring in the **throws** clause of *msig* in A there exists a class F in the **throws** clause of *msig* in B such that $E \preceq_h F$.

It is allowed to restrict the exceptions that might be thrown when a method is overridden or implemented. It is not allowed to introduce new exceptions in the **throws** clause when a method is overridden or implemented.

Constraint 6.1.1 (Overriding). If a method $A/msig$ directly overrides $B/msig$, then *msig* throws more specific exceptions in A than in B.

Constraint 6.1.2 (Implementing). Assume that I is an interface and

1. $I/msig$ is visible in A,
2. $C/msig$ is visible in A.

Then *msig* throws more specific exceptions in C than in I.

The syntax of Java$_{\mathcal{E}}$ in Fig. 6.1 defines the extension of Java$_{\mathcal{O}}$ by the two statements of Java which are related to exceptions. A **try-catch** statement can have an arbitrary number of **catch** clauses. A **catch** clause is also called an *exception handler*. The scope of the parameter *loc* of a **catch** clause is the block of the clause. The statement *stm* in a **finally** statement '*stm* **finally** *block*' must be a **try-catch** statement.

Definition 6.1.2. We say that an exception E is *allowed* at a position α, if one of the following conditions is true:

1. $E \preceq_h$ **Error**, or
2. $E \preceq_h$ **RuntimeException**, or
3. the position α is in a **try** block and at least one **catch** clause of the **try** statement has a parameter of type F such that $E \preceq_h F$, or
4. the position α is in the body of a method or constructor declaration and there exists a class F in the **throws** clause of the declaration such that $E \preceq_h F$.

The following lemma is used in the proof of the type soundness theorem (Theorem 8.4.1).

Table 6.1 Type constraints for Java$_\mathcal{E}$

`catch` $(E\ loc)\ block$	$E \preceq_\text{h}$ `Throwable`.
`throw` $^\alpha exp;$	$\mathcal{T}(\alpha) \preceq_\text{h}$ `Throwable` and $\mathcal{T}(\alpha)$ is allowed at position α according to Def. 6.1.2.
$^\alpha(exp_0.\,C/msig(exps))$	Each class E occurring in the `throws` clause of $msig$ in C is allowed at position α according to Def. 6.1.2.
$^\alpha C.msig(exps)$	Each class E occurring in the `throws` clause of $msig$ in C is allowed at position α according to Def. 6.1.2.

Lemma 6.1.1. If E is allowed at position α and $F \preceq_\text{h} E$, then F is allowed at position α.

The static type constraints for exceptions are listed in Table 6.1. The subclasses of class `RuntimeException` are unchecked exception classes and are therefore exempted from compile-time checking. Many of the operations and constructs of Java can result in runtime exceptions.

6.1.1 Vocabulary of Java$_\mathcal{E}$

Since throwing an exception completes the computation of an expression or a statement abruptly, we introduce a new type of reasons of abruptions, namely references $Exc(Ref)$ to an exception object.

> **data** $Abr = Break(Lab)\mid Continue(Lab)\mid Return\mid Return(Val)\mid Exc(Ref)$

Exceptions propagate through the grammatical block structure of a method and up the method call stack to the nearest dynamically enclosing `catch` clause of a `try-catch` statement that handles the exception. A `catch` clause handles an exception, if the exception object is compatible with the declared type. The `try-finally` statements provided by Java are generally used to clean-up after the `try` clause. A `try-finally` statement is executed when its `try` block—regardless of how it completes—has been executed.

6.2 Transition rules for Java$_\mathcal{E}$

Java$_\mathcal{E}$ is initialized like Java$_\mathcal{O}$ the execution is assumed to start normally. Java$_\mathcal{E}$ provides new statements and handling of run-time exceptions, which may occur during expression evaluation. Therefore the machine $execJava_E$ consists of two submachines, to be defined below, consisting of additional rules for the new statements and for the handling of some characteristic expression evaluation exceptions.

$$exec Java_E =$$
$$exec JavaExp_E$$
$$exec JavaStm_E$$

The execution of **throw**, **try**, **finally** statements is started by the submachine $exec JavaStm_E$, defined in Fig. 6.2, by passing the control to the evaluation of the related exception expression or to the execution of the first direct substatement. When the exception value *ref* of a **throw** statement has been computed, and if it turns out to be *null*, a **NullPointerException** is reported to the enclosing phrase using *failUp*, which allocates a new object for the exception and throws the exception (whereby the execution of the corresponding **finally** code starts, if there is some, together with the search for the appropriate exception handler). When appropriate we use *fail* instead of *failUp* to substitute the current phrase by the corresponding exception.

$$failUp(exc) = yieldUp(\textbf{throw new } exc();\,)$$
$$fail(exc) \quad = yield(\textbf{throw new } exc();\,)$$

If the exception value *ref* of a **throw** statement is not *null*, the abruption $Exc(ref)$ is passed up to the (position of the) **throw** statement, thereby abrupting the control flow with the computed exception as reason [18, §14.16].

Upon normal completion of a **try** statement, the machine passes the control to the parent statement, whereas upon abrupted completion the machine attempts to catch the exception by one of the **catch** clauses. The catching condition is the compatibility of the class of the exception with one of the catcher classes. If the catching fails, the exception is passed to the parent statement, as is every other abruption which was propagated up from within the **try** statement; otherwise the control is passed to the execution of the relevant **catch** statement. Upon normal completion of this statement, the machine passes the normal control up, whereas upon abrupted completion the new exception is passed up to the parent statement.

For a **finally** statement, upon normal or abrupted completion of the first direct substatement, the control is passed to the execution of the second direct substatement, the **finally** statement proper. Upon normal completion of this statement, the control is passed up, together with the possible reason of abruption, the one which was present when the execution of **finally** statement proper was started, and which in this case has to be resumed after execution of the **finally** statement proper. However, should the execution of this **finally** statement proper abrupt, then this new abruption is passed to the parent statement.

Exceptions are passed up when they have been propagated to the position directly following a label.

There is a special case which has to be added, namely uncaught exceptions in class initializers. For them Java specifies the following strategy. If,

---

Fig. 6.2 Execution of Java$_\mathcal{E}$ statements

$execJavaStm_E = $ **case** $context(pos)$ **of**
    throw $^\alpha exp; \rightarrow pos := \alpha$
    throw $^\blacktriangleright ref; \rightarrow$ **if** $ref = null$ **then** $failUp(\texttt{NullPointerException})$
                  else $yieldUp(Exc(ref))$

    try $^\alpha stm$ **catch** $\ldots$ $\rightarrow pos := \alpha$
    try $^\blacktriangleright Norm$ **catch** $\ldots \rightarrow yieldUp(Norm)$
    try $^\blacktriangleright Exc(ref)$ **catch** $(c_1\,x_1)\,^{\beta_1} stm_1 \ldots$ **catch** $(c_n\,x_n)\,^{\beta_n} stm_n \rightarrow$
        if $\exists 1 \leq j \leq n : classOf(ref) \preceq_{\mathrm{h}} c_j$ **then**
            let $j = \min\{i \mid classOf(ref) \preceq_{\mathrm{h}} c_i\}$
            pos $:= \beta_j$
            $locals := locals \oplus \{(x_j, ref)\}$
        else $yieldUp(Exc(ref))$
    try $^\blacktriangleright abr$ **catch** $(c_1\,x_1)\,^{\beta_1} stm_1 \ldots$ **catch** $(c_n\,x_n)\,^{\beta_n} stm_n \rightarrow yieldUp(abr)$
    try $^\alpha Exc(ref) \ldots$ **catch** $(c_i\,x_i)\,^\blacktriangleright Norm \ldots \rightarrow yieldUp(Norm)$
    try $^\alpha Exc(ref) \ldots$ **catch** $(c_i\,x_i)\,^\blacktriangleright abr \ldots$ $\rightarrow yieldUp(abr)$

    $^\alpha stm_1$ **finally** $^\beta stm_2 \rightarrow pos := \alpha$
    $^\blacktriangleright Norm$ **finally** $^\beta stm \rightarrow pos := \beta$
    $^\blacktriangleright abr$ **finally** $^\beta stm$ $\rightarrow pos := \beta$
    $^\alpha s$ **finally** $^\blacktriangleright Norm \rightarrow yieldUp(s)$
    $^\alpha s$ **finally** $^\blacktriangleright abr \rightarrow yieldUp(abr)$

    $lab :$ $^\blacktriangleright Exc(ref)$ $\rightarrow yieldUp(Exc(ref))$
    static $^\alpha Exc(ref) \rightarrow$
        if $classOf(ref) \preceq_{\mathrm{h}}$ **Error** **then**
            $yieldUp(Exc(ref))$
        else
            $failUp(\texttt{ExceptionInInitializerError})$
    $Exc(ref) \rightarrow$ **if** $pos = firstPos \wedge \neg null(frames)$ **then**
                        $exitMethod(Exc(ref))$
                        if $methNm(meth) = $ `"<clinit>"` **then**
                            $classState(classNm(meth)) := Unusable$

---

during execution of the body of a `static` initializer, an exception is thrown, and if this is not an `Error` or one of its subclasses, throw `ExceptionIn-InitializerError`. If the exception is compatible with `Error`, then the exception is rethrown in the directly preceding method on the frames stack.

    If the attempt to catch a thrown exception in the current method fails, i.e., when *pos* reaches *firstPos*, the exception is passed to the invoker of this method (if there is some), to continue the search for an exception handler there. If the current method is a class initializer, then the corresponding class becomes unusable.

    A `throw` statement can be user-defined, whereby an exception is thrown explicitly. A `throw` statement can also be due to the occurrence of run-time exceptions which are thrown, if certain semantic constraints for binary op-

---

Fig. 6.3 Execution of Java$_{\mathcal{E}}$ expressions

$execJavaExp_E = $ **case** $context(pos)$ **of**
$\quad ^{\alpha}val_1\ bop\ ^{\blacktriangleright}val_2\quad \rightarrow$ **if** $bop \in divMod \wedge isZero(val_2)$ **then**
$\qquad\qquad\qquad\qquad\qquad failUp(\texttt{ArithmeticException})$
$\quad ^{\blacktriangleright}ref.c/f\qquad\qquad \rightarrow$ **if** $ref = null$ **then** $failUp(\texttt{NullPointerException})$
$\quad ^{\alpha}ref.c/f = {}^{\blacktriangleright}val \rightarrow$ **if** $ref = null$ **then** $failUp(\texttt{NullPointerException})$
$\quad ^{\alpha}ref.c/m^{\blacktriangleright}(vals) \rightarrow$ **if** $ref = null$ **then** $failUp(\texttt{NullPointerException})$
$\quad (c)^{\blacktriangleright}ref\qquad\qquad \rightarrow$ **if** $ref \neq null \wedge classOf(ref) \not\preceq c$ **then**
$\qquad\qquad\qquad\qquad\qquad failUp(\texttt{ClassCastException})$

---

erations, target expressions and reference type cast expressions do not hold. The submachine $execJavaExp_E$ in Fig. 6.3 defines the semantics of three characteristic run-time exceptions which can occur. A binary expression throws an **ArithmeticException**, if the operator is an integer division or remainder operator and the right operand is 0 [18, §15.13, 15.14]. An instance target expression throws a **NullPointerException**, if the operand is *null*. A reference type *cast expression* throws a **ClassCastException**, if the value of the direct subexpression is neither *null* nor *compatible* with the required type [18, §15.15].

If the current class is in an erroneous state, then initialization is not possible and a **NoClassDefFoundError** is thrown. This is expressed by the following extension in Java$_{\mathcal{E}}$ of the rule *initialize* from Java$_{\mathcal{C}}$:

$initialize(c) =$
$\quad \ldots$
$\quad$ **if** $classState(c) = Unusable$ **then**
$\qquad fail(\texttt{NoClassDefFoundErr})$

In Java$_{\mathcal{E}}$ the definition of propagation of abruptions is refined for jump and return instructions, to the effect that **try** statements suspend these abruptions for execution of relevant **finally** code. As explained above, after the execution of this **finally** code, that abruption will be resumed (unless during the **finally** code a new abruption did occur which cancels the original one).

$propagatesAbr(phrase) =$
$\quad phrase \neq lab : s \wedge$
$\quad phrase \neq \texttt{static}\ s \wedge$
$\quad phrase \neq \texttt{try} \ldots \wedge$
$\quad phrase \neq s_1\ \texttt{finally}\ s_2$

Example ($\rightsquigarrow$ CD) 6.2.1. The following program shows that, if a **return** expression is included in a **try** block, then the **finally** block is executed before the expression is returned.

```
int m(int i) {
  try {
    return i + i;
  } finally {
    return i * i;
  }
}
```

Since the `finally` block contains another `return` expression, the value of
`i * i` is returned and the value `i + i` is discarded.

6.2.1 Exercises

Exercise (⤳ CD) 6.2.1. What is the output of the following program?

```
class Test {
  public static void main(String[] argv) {
    int i = 0;
    l1: while (i < 5) {
      try {
        if (i == 2) break l1;
      }
      finally { i = i + 1; }
    }
    System.out.println(i);
  }
}
```

Exercise (⤳ CD) 6.2.2. What is the output of the following program?

```
class E extends Exception {
  public int contents;
  public E(int i) { contents = i; }
  public String toString() {
    return "E(" + contents + ")";
  }
}

class Test {
  public static void main(String[] argv) {
    for (int i = 0; i < 4; i++) {
      try { test(i); }
      catch (Exception e) {
        System.out.println("test(" + i + ") threw " + e);
      }
    }
```

```
    }
    public static int test(int i) throws E {
      try {
        if (i < 3)
          throw new E(10 / i);
        else
          return 0;
      }
      finally {
        System.out.println("test(" + i + ") done");
      }
    }
  }
```

Exercise ($\leadsto$ CD) 6.2.3. What is the output of the following program?

```
public class Test {
  public static void main(String[] argv) {
    for (int i = 0; i < 4; ++i) {
      try { m(i); }
      catch (Exception e) {
        System.out.println(e + " handled in main");
      }
    }
  }
  public static void m(int i) throws Exception {
    try {
      System.out.println("m(" + i + ") called");
      if (i % 2 == 0) throw new Exception("m(" + i + ")");
    }
    catch (Exception e) {
      System.out.println(e + " handled in m(" + i + ")");
      throw e;
    }
    finally {
      System.out.println("m(" + i + ") done");
    }
  }
}
```

7. The concurrent extension Java$_\mathcal{T}$ of Java$_\mathcal{E}$

The abstract state machine *execJava* defines the behavior of Java executing a single phrase at a time and by a single thread. In this chapter we extend Java$_\mathcal{E}$ to Java$_\mathcal{T}$ so that *execJava* can be embedded into a machine *execJavaThread*, for multithreaded Java, which provides support for execution of multiple tasks with shared main and local working memory. We consider the mechanisms Java provides for thread creation and destruction, for synchronizing the concurrent activity of threads using locks, and for waiting and notification introduced for an efficient transfer of control between threads. We describe the methods for starting (*start*), interrupting (*interrupt*), suspending (*wait*), and resuming (*notify*) threads as normal methods, which for the purpose of executability are included here into native methods.

The reference manual [18] specifies a memory model for shared memory multiprocessors that support high performance implementations. It allows objects to reside in main and local working memory, and presents rules specifying when a thread is permitted or required to transfer the contents of its working copy of an instance variable into the master copy in main memory, or vice versa. To separate this memory model—which "details the low-level actions that may be used to explain the interaction of Java Virtual Machine threads with a shared memory" [23, page 371]—from the semantics of the mechanisms defined by the language for thread creation, destruction, synchronization and for waiting and notification, we define here a model which uses only the main memory for storing objects, and which agrees for best practice programs with the memory model in [18].

In Sect. 7.1 we describe the static semantics of Java$_\mathcal{T}$ and in Sect. 7.2 the rules which define its dynamic semantics. In Sect. 7.3 we formulate and prove some thread invariants, expressing in particular the correctness of the thread synchronization mechanism without commitment to any particular scheduling scheme.

Fig. 7.1 Syntax of Java$_\mathcal{T}$

$Stm := \ldots \mid$ **synchronized** $(Exp)\ Stm$

7.1 Static semantics of Java$_\mathcal{T}$

7.1.1 Vocabulary of Java$_\mathcal{T}$

Threads are concurrent, independent processes, running within a single program. We describe them as elements of a universe *Thread*, i.e., the domain of objects belonging to the class **Thread** through which threads are represented and controlled in Java. Since threads are objects, the universe *Thread* is a subset of *Ref*. A pointer q is in *Thread* iff $q \in dom(heap)$ and $classOf(q) \preceq_\mathrm{h}$ **Thread**. Every thread q executes the machine *execJava*, but it does it on its own continuation $cont(q)$, consisting of its frame stack *frames* and its current frame $(meth, restbody, pos, locals)$. The continuation is local to the thread and cannot be accessed by other threads. It is used to restore the values of *meth*, *restbody*, *pos*, *locals* and *frames*, when q becomes the current thread.

$cont\colon Thread \to (Frame^*, Frame)$

Threads exchange information among each other by operating on objects residing in shared *main memory*, which is modeled by the functions *globals* and *heap*.

The extension of the syntax of Java$_\mathcal{E}$ in Java$_\mathcal{T}$ by synchronization statements is given in Fig. 7.1. The type of the expression *Exp* in a **synchronized** statement must be a reference type.

To synchronize threads, Java uses *monitors*, a mechanism for allowing only one thread at a time to execute a region of code protected by the monitor. The behavior of monitors is formulated in terms of locks, which are uniquely associated with objects. When a **synchronized** statement is processed, the executing thread must grab the lock which is associated with the target reference, to become the owner of the lock, before the thread can continue. Upon completion of the block, the mechanism releases that very same lock. We use a dynamic function *sync* to keep track of the dynamic nestings of synchronized statements; $sync(q)$ denotes the stack of all references grabbed by thread q. Since a single thread can hold a lock more than once, we have to define also dynamic lock counters.

$sync\ :\ Thread \to Ref^*$
$locks\ :\ Ref \to Nat$

To assist communication between threads, each object also has an associated *wait set* of threads, which are waiting for access to this object. Wait sets are used by the **wait** and **notify** methods of class **Object**. The **wait** method allows a thread to wait for a notification condition. Executing **wait** adds the current thread to the wait set for this object and releases the lock—which is reacquired, to continue processing, after the thread has been notified by another thread. Wait sets are modeled by a dynamic function

$$waitSet\colon Ref \rightarrow Powerset(Thread)$$

Every thread can be in one of five *execution modes*. This is modeled using the following dynamic function:

$$exec\colon Thread \rightarrow ThreadState$$

where the universe *ThreadState* of thread execution modes is defined by

data *ThreadState* = *NotStarted* | *Active* | *Synchronizing*
    | *Waiting* | *Notified* | *Dead*

As will be defined below, a thread T is in the state $exec(T) = NotStarted$, from the moment it is created, until the **start** method of the **Thread** object is called, whereby it becomes *Active*. A thread gets into the *Synchronizing* state by execution of a synchronization statement on an object of which it does not have a lock. The object it is competing for is stored using the dynamic function *syncObj*.

$$syncObj\colon Thread \rightarrow Ref$$

A thread in the *Waiting* state cannot be run, because a **wait** method has been called. The thread is waiting for the notification of an object. The object it is waiting for is given by the dynamic function *waitObj*.

$$waitObj\colon Thread \rightarrow Ref$$

A thread who is waiting for regaining the abandoned locks on an object gets *Notified* (and thereby leaves its waiting mode and can compete for being selected again for execution) through the action of another thread, who executes the *notify* method. A thread in the *Notified* state is re-enabled for thread scheduling. A thread becomes *Dead* when it has terminated the execution of its code.

The **interrupt** method is an asynchronous method which may be invoked by one thread to affect the execution of another thread. We use a dynamic function to signal if a thread has been interrupted:

$$interruptedFlag\colon Thread \rightarrow Bool$$

The Java reference manual [18] leaves the *scheduling* strategy open. Although the language designers had a pre-emptive priority-based scheduler in mind, they explicitly say that there is no guarantee for threads with highest priority to be always running. Therefore we abstract from priority based scheduling and formalize the scheduling strategy by a not furthermore specified selection function "choose", which is used in the machine *execJavaThread* below. That machine will call the submachine *execJava*, to be executed by the thread which has been chosen to be the currently running active thread and is kept in the dynamic constant *thread*. To achieve this goal we define in the next section the submachine *execJava$_T$* of *execJava*, which provides the semantics for the new statement appearing in Java$_\mathcal{T}$.

7.2 Transition rules for Java$_\mathcal{T}$

The initial state of Java$_\mathcal{T}$ is defined as for Java$_\mathcal{E}$, but started with a single thread, namely the runnable, active, current *thread*. Execution of the machine *execJavaThread*, into which *execJava* is embedded, continues until there are no more runnable threads. We first define Java$_\mathcal{T}$ then *execJavaThread* and finally the rules for starting, interrupting, notifying, and putting threads to waiting.

The additional rules for Java$_\mathcal{T}$ define the semantics for the new synchronization statement and for the extension of the rules for exiting an initialization method or for exiting the code of a thread.

$$execJava_T =$$
$$execJavaStm_T$$

The rules for *execJavaStm$_T$* in Fig. 7.2 start the execution of a **synchronized** statement by passing the control to the evaluation of the synchronization expression.

Once the synchronization expression has been evaluated, *execJavaStm$_T$* attempts to grab the lock of the object denoted by the target reference, provided it is not *null*. If it is *null*, a **NullPointerException** is thrown. Otherwise *execJavaStm$_T$* checks whether the current thread already holds the lock of that object. In case it does, the current thread grabs the lock once more, namely by pushing it onto the *sync* stack, it increments the lock counter and passes the control to the execution of the protected statement. Otherwise the current thread is put into synchronization mode (and its continuation and its synchronization object are stored), so that it now participates in the competition on getting activated by *execJavaThread*.

Upon normal completion of the protected statement, using the rule *releaseLock*, the lock which was grapped last by the thread is released, by popping it from the *sync* stack, the lock counter is decremented, and the control is passed up.

$$releaseLock(phrase) =$$
$$\textbf{let } [p] \cdot rest = sync(thread)$$
$$sync(thread) := rest$$
$$locks(p) \qquad := locks(p) - 1$$
$$yieldUp(phrase)$$

Fig. 7.2 Execution of Java$_{\mathcal{T}}$ statements

$execJavaStm_T = \mathbf{case}\ context(pos)\ \mathbf{of}$
  $\mathbf{synchronized}\ (^{\alpha}exp)^{\beta}stm \to pos := \alpha$
  $\mathbf{synchronized}\ (^{\blacktriangleright}ref)^{\beta}stm \to$
    $\mathbf{if}\ ref = null\ \mathbf{then}\ failUp(\texttt{NullPointerException})$
    $\mathbf{else}$
      $\mathbf{if}\ ref \in sync(thread)\ \mathbf{then}$
        $sync(thread) := [ref] \cdot sync(thread)$
        $locks(ref)\ \ \ := locks(ref) + 1$
        $pos\ \ \ \ \ \ \ \ \ \ := \beta$
      $\mathbf{else}$
        $exec(thread)\ \ \ \ \ := Synchronizing$
        $syncObj(thread) := ref$
        $cont(thread)\ \ \ \ := (frames, (meth, restbody, \beta, locals))$
  $\mathbf{synchronized}\ (^{\alpha}ref)^{\blacktriangleright}Norm \to releaseLock(Norm)$
  $\mathbf{synchronized}\ (^{\alpha}ref)^{\blacktriangleright}abr \to releaseLock(abr)$

  $\mathbf{static}^{\blacktriangleright}abr \to notifyThreadsWaitingForInitialization$
  $abr \to \mathbf{if}\ pos = firstPos \wedge null(frames)\ \mathbf{then}\ killThread$

Similarly, when an abruption is detected during the execution of a **synchronized** statement, *releaseLock* passes the abruption up. For this purpose, in Java$_{\mathcal{T}}$ the definition of *propagatesAbr* is refined to its final version, including also **synchronized** statements into those which do not propagate abruptions.

$propagatesAbr(phrase) =$
  $phrase \neq lab : s\ \wedge$
  $phrase \neq \mathbf{static}\ s\ \wedge$
  $phrase \neq \mathbf{try} \ldots \wedge$
  $phrase \neq s_1\ \mathbf{finally}\ s_2\ \wedge$
  $phrase \neq \mathbf{synchronized}\ s$

Should the attempt to handle the abruption reaches the starting position of the code of the current thread, with an empty frame stack, the thread notifies all the threads who are waiting for him and dies.

$killThread =$
  $waitSet(thread) := \emptyset$
  $exec(thread)\ \ \ := Dead$
  $\mathbf{forall}\ q \in waitSet(thread)$
    $exec(q) := Notified$

Except for the remaining case of a thread which abrupts an initialization method, which will be explained below, this concludes the extension of *execJava* by the submachine *execJava$_{\mathcal{T}}$*, which defines the behavior of any current single thread. What remains to do is to refine some of the rules in the previous machines.

When creating a new thread, i.e., a member of class **Thread** its mode has to be initialized (to *NotStarted*) and its locks stack and is wait set have to be initialized to empty. Formally this comes up to extend the definition of **new** which was given in the submachine *execJavaExp$_O$* of Java$_\mathcal{O}$ on Page 81 by the following new definition:

$$waitSet(ref) := \emptyset$$
$$locks(ref) \quad := 0$$
if $c \preceq_\text{h}$ **Thread then**
$$\quad exec(ref) := NotStarted$$
$$\quad sync(ref) := [\,]$$
$$\quad interruptedFlag(ref) := False$$

Similarly we have to extend the definition of initialization. Initialization of a class or interface in Java$_\mathcal{T}$ requires synchronization, since several threads may be trying simultaneously to do this initialization. If initialization by one thread is *InProgress*, other threads have to wait, until the initialization is done or an *Error* occurs. To distinguish the thread that actually initializes a class from those that wait for it, we use two dynamic functions; *initThread(c)* is the thread that initializes class c; *initWait(c)* is the set of threads waiting for the initialization of class c.

$$initThread : Class \rightarrow Thread$$
$$initWait \quad : Class \rightarrow Powerset(Thread)$$

The definition of the predicate *initialized* has to be sharpened by adding the description of the initializing thread in case an initialization is *InProgress*.

$$initialized(c) =$$
$$\quad classState(c) = Initialized \vee$$
$$\quad classState(c) = InProgress \wedge initThread(c) = thread$$

Hence, a class c is not *initialized*, if one of the following is true:

- $classState(c) = Linked$
- $classState(c) = Unusable$
- $classState(c) = InProgress$ and $initThread(c) \neq thread$

To initialize a class or interface, one has first to synchronize on the **Class** object. When a class is linked, the current *thread* is recorded as the initializing thread, and no other threads are waiting for initializing this class. If initialization is *InProgress*, then upon attempting to initialize the class, the currently executing *thread* is set to mode *Waiting*, it is put into the list of threads which are waiting to initialize the class, and its current state is stored. This is formalized by the following two new rules to be added to the definition of *initialize(c)* which was defined in Page 64:

    if $classState(c) = Linked$ **then**
      $initWait(c)$ $:= \emptyset$
      $initThread(c) := thread$
    if $classState(c) = InProgress \land initThread(c) \neq thread$ **then**
      $exec(thread) := Waiting$
      $cont(thread) := (frames, (meth, restbody, pos, locals))$
      $initWait(c)$ $:= initWait(c) \cup \{thread\}$

Upon abrupting an initialization method of a class c, the current thread has to notify the threads in $initWait(c)$. This is captured by the following rule which is used in that case in Fig. 7.2:

    $notifyThreadsWaitingForInitialization =$
    let $c = classNm(meth)$
    $initWait(c)$ $:= \emptyset$
    $initThread(c) := undef$
    forall $q \in initWait(c)$
      $exec(q) := Active$

7.2.1 Scheduling of multiple threads

There are various ways to incorporate *execJava* into a machine which handles the scheduling of multiple threads. The machine defined in [9] uses for this purpose distributed ASMs, but it does not lead to an executable model. We therefore choose here a different approach and define a machine *execJavaThread*, which can and has been made executable by AsmGofer (see Chapter A), and which provides an abstract scheduling mechanism through which, at each moment, one thread is selected to execute *execJava*. In order not to commit, at the level of specification, to any particular selection mechanism, we use instead a not furthermore specified choice function.

    At each moment one of the runnable threads is chosen. If it happens to be the currently executed and still active *thread*, then it is confirmed as agent to execute the machine *execJava* defined above. Otherwise the current *thread* gets its state stored for future continuation of its computation, and it is replaced by the newly chosen thread, which is started to run *execJava* (see the definition below).

    $execJavaThread =$
    choose $q \in dom(exec), runnable(q)$
      if $q = thread \land exec(q) = Active$ **then**
        $execJava$
      else
        if $exec(thread) = Active$ **then**
          $cont(thread) := (frames, (meth, restbody, pos, locals))$
        $thread := q$
        $run(q)$

The *runnable* threads among which the next one is chosen for executing *execJava* are those who are either active, or trying to synchronize on an object, or whose waiting period has ended (through a notification from some other thread, so that they can again compete for execution).

$runnable(q) =$
  case $exec(q)$ **of**
    $Active$ $\to True$
    $Synchronizing \to locks(syncObj(q)) = 0$
    $Notified$ $\to locks(waitObj(q)) = 0$

The rule used by *execJavaThread* for putting a thread back to run *execJava* switches the context back and synchronizes or wakes up the thread, depending on its current mode.

$run(q) =$
  $switchCont(q)$
  if $exec(q) = Synchronizing$ **then**
    $synchronize(q)$
  if $exec(q) = Notified$ **then**
    $wakeup(q)$

The rules to switch context, to synchronize, and to wakeup a thread which has been selected for being run, reestablish the state of the thread as current state and make the thread active; *synchronize* also puts the synchronizing expression value on top of the *sync* stack and updates the *lock* counter, whereas *wakeup* lets the woken up thread reacquire all its synchronization claims on the synchronizing object.

$switchCont(q) =$
  let $(frames', (meth', restbody', pos', locals')) = cont(q)$
  $exec(q)$ $:= Active$
  $meth$ $:= meth'$
  $restbody := restbody'$
  pos $:= pos'$
  $locals$ $:= locals'$
  $frames$ $:= frames'$

The rules *synchronize* and *wakeup* do not need to include the update $exec(q) := Active$ because this update is executed as part of *switchCont*, which is executed each time *synchronize* or *wakeup* is called in $run(q)$.

$synchronize(q) =$
  $sync(q)$ $:= [syncObj(q)] \cdot sync(q)$
  $locks(syncObj(q)) := 1$

$wakeup(q) =$
  $locks(waitObj(q)) := occurrences(waitObj(q), sync(q))$

The function $occurrences(x, l)$ returns the number of occurrences of the element x in the list l.

Our abstract scheduling mechanism does not exclude the possibility that the machine *execJavaThread* stops executing threads and switches contexts only. It could happen that it continuously switches the contexts of two threads without executing any computation steps of the single threads.

7.2.2 Thread methods

In this section we specify the thread methods for starting, interrupting, suspending and resuming threads. They all belong to the Java class **Thread** and are incorporated here as native methods, to make them usable in the executable version of our model *execJavaThread*. A native method is called with a list *values* of arguments; the first argument *values*(0) is the value of the object on which the method is called except **Thread/interrupted** which is a static method.

$\textit{invokeNative}(\textit{meth}, \textit{values})$
| $\textit{meth} = \textbf{Thread/start}()$ | $= \textit{start}(\textit{values}(0))$
| $\textit{meth} = \textbf{Thread/interrupt}()$ | $= \textit{interrupt}(\textit{values}(0))$
| $\textit{meth} = \textbf{Thread/interrupted}()$ | $= \textit{interrupted}$
| $\textit{meth} = \textbf{Thread/isInterrupted}()$ | $= \textit{isInterrupted}(\textit{values}(0))$
| $\textit{meth} = \textbf{Object/wait}()$ | $= \textit{wait}(\textit{values}(0))$
| $\textit{meth} = \textbf{Object/notify}()$ | $= \textit{notify}(\textit{values}(0))$
| $\textit{meth} = \textbf{Object/notifyAll}()$ | $= \textit{notifyAll}(\textit{values}(0))$

There are two possibilities to create a new thread. The first one is to define a subclass of class **Thread** and to create a new instance of the subclass. The second possibility is to use the constructor **Thread(Runnable)** of class **Thread**. For this purpose one has to define a class that implements the interface **Runnable**. In each case, the **start** method of class **Thread** is used to cause a thread to compete, by becoming active, for execution of the **run** method of its **Thread** object [18, §20.20.14]. If the thread to be started has already been started, an **IllegalThreadStateException** is thrown. The result of the invocation of **start** is that two threads are running concurrently, namely the current thread, which returns from the call to the **start** method, and the thread represented by the **target** field, which executes its **run** method.

$\textit{start}(\textit{ref}) =$
  if $\textit{exec}(\textit{ref}) \neq \textit{NotStarted}$ **then**
    $\textit{fail}(\textbf{IllegalThreadStateException})$
  else
    let q $= \textit{getField}(\textit{ref}, \textbf{Thread}/\,\texttt{"target"})$
      $\textit{meth} = \textit{lookup}(\textit{classOf}(q), \textbf{Thread/run}())/\textbf{run}()$
    $\textit{exec}(\textit{ref}) := \textit{Active}$
    $\textit{cont}(\textit{ref}) := ([\,], (\textit{meth}, \textit{body}(\textit{meth}), \textit{firstPos}, \{(\,\texttt{"this"}, q)\}))$
    $\textit{yieldUp}(\textit{Norm})$

The **interrupt** method of class **Thread** may be invoked by one thread to interrupt another thread. An **InterruptedException** is thrown, if the thread is waiting and not trying to initialize a class. If the thread is not waiting, then the interrupt is asynchronous. The *interruptFlag* of the thread is set. It is the programmer's responsibility to check the flag from time to time, to respond to the interrupt request. A thread therefore does not immediately react to an interrupt signal.

$interrupt(q) =$
  $yieldUp(Norm)$
  if $exec(q) = Waiting \land \neg classInitialization(q)$ **then**
    let $(frames', (meth', restbody', pos', locals')) = cont(q)$
    let $fail = restbody'[\textbf{throw new InterruptedException}(); /pos']$
    let $ref = waitObj(q)$
    $waitSet(ref) := waitSet(ref) \setminus \{q\}$
    $exec(q)$ $:= Notified$
    $cont(q)$ $:= (frames', (meth', fail, pos', locals'))$
    $interruptedFlag(q) := False$
  else
    $interruptedFlag(q) := True$

$classInitialization(q) = q \in ran(initThread) \lor q \in \bigcup ran(initWait)$

The method `interrupted` of class `Thread` is `static` and can be used to check whether the current thread has been interrupted. The *interruptedFlag* is cleared thereby.

$interrupted =$
  if $interruptedFlag(thread)$ **then**
    $interruptedFlag(thread) := False$
    $yield(True)$
  else
    $yield(False)$

The method `isInterrupted` of class `Thread` is an instance method, used to check whether a given thread has been interrupted.

$isInterrupted(q) =$
  if $interruptedFlag(q)$ **then**
    $yieldUp(True)$
  else
    $yieldUp(False)$

The `wait` method of class `Object` causes the current *thread* to enter mode *Waiting*, until some other thread invokes the `notify` method for the underlying object. The method can be called only when the current thread is already synchronized on this object (in which case the method completes normally), otherwise an `IllegalMonitorStateException` is thrown. Executing `wait` adds the current thread to the wait set for the considered object, releases the *locks* and stores the state of the current *thread*. The rule *wait* is executed when the method `wait` is called.

$wait(ref) =$
  if $ref \notin sync(thread)$ **then**
    $fail(\texttt{IllegalMonitorStateException})$
  else
    let $ret = restbody[Norm/up(pos)]$
    $waitSet(ref) \quad := waitSet(ref) \cup \{thread\}$
    $locks(ref) \qquad := 0$
    $exec(thread) \quad := Waiting$
    $waitObj(thread) := ref$
    $cont(thread) \quad := (frames, (meth, ret, up(pos), locals))$
    $yieldUp(Norm)$

The `notify` method of class `Object` chooses one thread among those waiting on the current object. The choice is left unspecified by the Java language reference manual; we reflect this by using yet another not furthermore specified choice function. The chosen thread is removed from the wait set, and its mode is changed from *Waiting* to *Notified*. The `notify` method may be called only when the current thread is already synchronized on this object (in which case the `notify` method completes normally), otherwise an `IllegalMonitorStateException` is thrown.

$notify(ref) =$
  if $ref \notin sync(thread)$ **then**
    $fail(\texttt{IllegalMonitorStateException})$
  else
    $yieldUp(Norm)$
    choose $q \in waitSet(ref)$
      $waitSet(ref) := waitSet(ref) \setminus \{q\}$
      $exec(q) \qquad := Notified$

There is a variant of the `notify` method which notifies *all* the threads which are waiting on the current object, and empties its waiting set.

$notifyAll(ref) =$
  if $ref \notin sync(thread)$ **then**
    $fail(\texttt{IllegalMonitorStateException})$
  else
    $waitSet(ref) := \emptyset$
    $yieldUp(Norm)$
    forall $q \in waitSet(ref)$
      $exec(q) := Notified$

7.2.3 Exercises

Exercise 7.2.1. Extend the rule *execJavaThread* such that each thread performs at least one execution step when it is selected by the abstract scheduler.

Exercise 7.2.2. What happens if a thread is interrupted when it is waiting for the initialization of a class, i.e., when it is in the set *initWait*(c) of some class c?

Exercise 7.2.3. Can a thread be interrupted when it is initializing a class?

Exercise 7.2.4. Assume that the interrupt flag of thread q has been set by an invocation of the `interrupt` method. Assume that thread q continues its execution ignoring the state of its interrupt flag. Assume that thread q puts itself into the *Waiting* state by invoking the `wait` method on some object and the interrupt flag is still *True*. What happens now if the `interrupt` method is invoked on q?

7.3 Thread invariants

The list $sync(q)$ of objects the thread q is synchronized on can be reconstructed from the context of q. We start in the bottom frame of the stack of q with an empty list. The bottom frame contains a position α and a rest-body. Starting at the root position of the restbody we go downwards to α. Each time we encounter a

> `synchronized` (ref) *phrase*,

where the path to α leads into *phrase*, we prepend the object ref to the list. When we reach the position α, we continue with the second frame, and so on, including the current frame. The list we obtain, on the way up in the frame stack and down in the restbodies, is called $syncFromCont(q)$ and will always be the same as $sync(q)$.

For the formulation of the invariants we use several predicates. The predicate $synchronizing(q, ref)$ means that thread q is synchronizing on the object ref. Thread q does not yet hold the lock of ref and is competing for it with other threads. The predicate $waiting(q, ref)$ means that thread q has called the wait method of the object ref and is waiting to be notified. The predicate $notified(q, ref)$ means that another thread has called the notify method of the object ref and thread q has been chosen to be notified.

> $synchronizing(q, ref) =$
> $exec(q) = Synchronizing \wedge syncObj(q) = ref$
> $waiting(q, ref) =$
> $exec(q) = Waiting \wedge waitObj(q) = ref$
> $notified(q, ref) =$
> $exec(q) = Notified \wedge waitObj(q) = ref$

What does it mean that a thread holds the lock of an object? If q is synchronized on ref, then q holds the lock of ref. However, if q is waiting for ref or has been notified by ref, then q temporarily releases the lock of the object ref. This is expressed by the predicate $locked(q, ref)$.

> $locked(q, ref) =$
> $ref \in sync(q) \wedge \neg waiting(q, ref) \wedge \neg notified(q, ref)$

We say that an object *ref* is locked, if there exists a thread q holding the lock of *ref*.

$locked(ref) =$
$\quad \exists q \in dom(exec)(locked(q, ref))$

In Java$_\mathcal{T}$, the following invariants are satisfied (they are formalized in the theorem below):

1. The current thread is a valid thread.
2. The elements of the domain of *exec* are threads.
3. If the execution state of a thread is *NotStarted*, then the thread is not synchronized on any object and is not in the wait set of any object.
4. If a thread is synchronized on an object, then the object is a valid reference in the *heap*.
5. If the state of a thread is synchronizing, then the thread is not already synchronized on the object it is competing for. It can hold the lock of other objects, and therefore block other threads from execution.
6. The list of synchronized objects, obtained from the context of a thread, is the same as the *sync* list of the thread.
7. If a thread is waiting for an object, then it is synchronized on the object and is in the wait set of the object. By definition, it does not hold the lock of the object it is waiting for. However, it can hold the lock of other objects, and therefore block other threads from execution.
8. A thread cannot be in the wait set of two different objects.
9. If a thread has been notified on an object, then it is no longer in the wait set of the object. It is still synchronized on the object, but it does not hold the lock of the object. It can hold the lock of other objects, and therefore block other threads from execution.
10. If a thread has terminated normally or abruptly, then it does not hold the lock of any object.
11. If a thread holds the lock of an object, then the lock counter of the object is exactly the number of occurrences of the object in the list of synchronized objects of the thread. It follows that, if the lock counter of an object is zero, then no thread holds the lock of the object.
12. It is not possible that two different threads hold the lock of the same object.
13. If the lock counter of an object is greater than zero, then there exists a thread which holds the lock of the object.

Theorem 7.3.1 (Synchronization). The following invariants are satisfied for each thread q:

(thread) $classOf(thread) \preceq_h$ Thread.

(exec1) $dom(exec)$ is exactly the set of all threads.

(exec2) If $exec(q) = NotStarted$, then $sync(q) = [\,]$.

(sync1) If $ref \in sync(q)$, then $ref \in dom(heap)$.

(sync2) If $synchronizing(q, ref)$, then $ref \in dom(heap)$, $ref \notin sync(q)$ and $[ref] \cdot sync(q) = syncFromCont(q)$.

(sync3) If $exec(q) \notin \{Synchronizing, NotStarted\}$, then $sync(q) = syncFromCont(q)$.

(wait1) If $waiting(q, ref)$, then $q \in waitSet(ref)$ and $ref \in sync(q)$.

(wait2) If $q \in waitSet(ref)$, then q is a thread and $waiting(q, ref)$.

(notified) If $notified(q, ref)$, then $q \notin waitSet(ref)$ and $ref \in sync(q)$.

(dead) If $exec(q) = Dead$, then the frame stack of q is empty, $waitSet(q) = \emptyset$ and $sync(q) = [\,]$.

(lock1) If $locked(q, ref)$, then $locks(ref) = occurrences(ref, sync(q))$.

(lock2) If $locked(q_1, ref)$ and $locked(q_2, ref)$, then $q_1 = q_2$.

(lock3) If $locks(ref) > 0$, then $locked(ref)$.

Proof. By induction on the number of steps in the run of the ASM. The predicates *synchronizing*, *waiting*, *notified*, and *locked* depend on the dynamic functions *sync*, *exec*, *syncObj*, and *waitObj* only. These functions as well as the dynamic functions *cont*, *thread*, *locks* and *waitSet* are not updated in *execJava*, except in *execJava$_\mathcal{T}$* or when new instances of objects are created. Hence the critical cases are in *execJavaThread* and *execJava$_\mathcal{T}$*. □

Exercise 7.3.1. Derive the following statements from the thread invariants:

1. If $exec(q) = NotStarted$, then q is in no *waitSet*.
2. No thread is in the *waitSet* of two objects.

Exercise 7.3.2. Prove that a thread which has terminated abruptly or normally has no lock on any object.

Example ($\leadsto$ CD) 7.3.1. The following example models a common situation. Several authors are writing together a book. If an author holds the lock of the book and the book is not yet finished, he does the following:

1. he appends a piece of text to the book;
2. he notifies another author (or the publisher);
3. he releases the lock of the book;
4. he waits until he gets notified himself.

If the book is finished, he notifies another author (or the publisher) and terminates his work.

```
class Author extends Thread {
  private char letter;
  private StringBuffer book;

  Author(StringBuffer b,char c) { book = b; letter = c; }

  public void run() {
    synchronized (book) {
      while (book.length() < 40) {
        book.append(letter);
        book.notify();
        try { book.wait(); }
        catch (InterruptedException e) { }
      }
      book.notify();
    }
  }
}
```

The publisher waits until the book is finished. He then prints the book and notifies all waiting authors.

```
class Publisher extends Thread {
  private StringBuffer book;

  Publisher(StringBuffer b) { book = b; }

  public void run() {
    synchronized (book) {
      while (book.length() < 40) {
        book.notify();
        try { book.wait(); }
        catch (InterruptedException e) { }
      }
      System.out.println(book);
      book.notifyAll();
    }
  }
}
```

The following program creates a book, 10 authors 'A', 'B', 'C', ..., 'J' and a publisher.

```
class Test {
  public static void main(String[] _) {
    StringBuffer book = new StringBuffer(40);
    for (int i = 0; i < 10; ++i) {
```

```
      new Author(book,(char)('A' + i)).start();
   }
   new Publisher(book).start();
 }
}
```

A possible output of the program is:

```
ABACDEFGHIJBACDEFGHIJBACDEFGHIJBACDEFGHI
```

The JLS does not specify the order of the letters. There are no constraints. For example, the output of the program could start with a 'J'. Or in an extreme case, the publisher and the author 'J' could alternately lock the book such that at the end the book consists of forty letters 'J'. [In fact, this happens sometimes with certain versions of Sun's JDK.]

8. Java is type safe

In this chapter we analyze and prove some structural properties of Java runs which are needed for the proof that Java is type safe (Theorem 8.4.1), and for the correctness proof of the compilation of Java to JVM bytecode (Chapter 14). This includes the reachability analysis for expressions and statements (Sect. 8.2) and the rules of definite assignment for local variables (Sect. 8.3, where we correct two inconsistencies in the rules defined in the JLS [19]).

8.1 Structural properties of Java runs

Most structural properties of Java runs are intuitively clear. Therefore a reader not interested in the technical details of mathematical proofs should skip this section and move directly to Sect. 8.3. Some structural properties proved in this section are used for the proof that Java is type safe in Sect. 8.4. Most structural properties are used later in the correctness proof of the compilation of Java to bytecode of the JVM in Chapter 14.

The evaluation of expressions or statements may not terminate at all. An expression can contain an invocation of a recursive function which does not return. A statement can contain a loop which does not terminate. Our main goal is to prove a theorem relating the states of a possibly infinite run of the ASM of Java with the recursive structure of expressions and statements.

In order to prove properties about runs of ASMs it is convenient to add the time as a subscript to the dynamic functions. Therefore by f_n we denote the dynamic function f in the nth state of the run of the ASM. For example, pos_n is the value of the dynamic function pos in the nth state of a run of $execJavaThread$.

To some dynamic functions we add threads as superscripts. For example, pos_n^q is the value of pos for thread q in the nth state of the run. The thread superscripts allow us to make statements about the local states of threads without distinguishing between the current thread and other threads.

Definition 8.1.1 (Context functions). For each thread q the functions $frames_n^q$, $meth_n^q$, $restbody_n^q$, pos_n^q, $locals_n^q$ are defined in such a way that, if the current thread in state n is q, then

$$frames_n = frames_n^q, \quad meth_n = meth_n^q, \quad restbody_n = restbody_n^q,$$
$$pos_n \quad = pos_n^q, \qquad locals_n = locals_n^q.$$

If the current thread in state n is different from q, then

$$cont_n(q) = (frames_n^q, (meth_n^q, restbody_n^q, pos_n^q, locals_n^q)).$$

The functions are defined only if q is a valid pointer of type **Thread** in the nth state of the run, i.e., if $q \in \mathrm{dom}(heap_n)$ and $classOf_n(q) \preceq_h$ **Thread**.

When a thread executes Java code, control walks through the abstract syntax trees of method bodies. It enters expressions and statements, evaluates them and yields the results upwards for further processing. When methods are invoked or classes are initialized, new frames are pushed on the stack of the thread. When the methods return, the frames are popped again.

What does it mean that a thread is inside a phrase (expression or statement) in a certain interval of the run of the ASM? It means that during the interval the current position of the thread is always inside the phrase. Since methods may be invoked inside the phrase, new frames are created and the current position walks through the bodies of the invoked methods. Hence the current position leaves the phrase, although in the view of the parent frame the position is still inside the phrase.

We write $l_1 \sqsubseteq_{\mathrm{pre}} l_2$, if the list l_1 is a prefix of l_2. For positions α and β, $\alpha \sqsubseteq_{\mathrm{pre}} \beta$ means that β is below α in the abstract syntax tree. For stacks, $frames_1 \sqsubseteq_{\mathrm{pre}} frames_2$ means that $frames_2$ is an extension of $frames_1$.

Definition 8.1.2 (Inside). Thread q is *inside* α on the interval $[m, n]$, if for all i with $m \leq i \leq n$

1. $frames_m^q \sqsubseteq_{\mathrm{pre}} frames_i^q$,
2. if $frames_m^q = frames_i^q$, then $\alpha \sqsubseteq_{\mathrm{pre}} pos_i^q$.

What does it mean that a thread enters a phrase in a certain state of the run of the ASM? It means that in that state in the run, the thread is the active thread and the phrase is the phrase at the current position in the body of the current method, and it is unevaluated. At some positions, however, static initializers are called for the initialization of classes. When control returns from the class initialization, the phrase at the current position is still the same as before the initialization and so the thread 'enters' the expression a second time. This second 'entering' is excluded in the following definition.

Definition 8.1.3 (Enter). Thread q *enters* α at m, if

1. $thread_m = q$,
2. $pos_m = \alpha$,
3. there is no $k < m$ such that q is inside α on the interval $[k, m]$.

What does it mean that a thread evaluates a phrase in a certain interval of the run of the ASM? It means that the thread enters the phrase at the beginning of the interval and stays inside the phrase during the interval. The only changes made to *restbody* are inside the phrase. The local environment can be changed and extended during the evaluation because expressions and statements have side effects. The stacks of frames at the beginning and at the end of the interval are the same.

Definition 8.1.4 (Evaluation). Thread q *evaluates* α on $[m, n]$, if

1. q enters α at m,
2. q is inside α on the interval $[m, n]$,
3. $restbody_n^q = restbody_m^q[\varphi/\alpha]$, where $\varphi = restbody_n^q/\alpha$,
4. $frames_n^q = frames_m^q$,
5. $\mathrm{dom}(locals_m^q) \subseteq \mathrm{dom}(locals_n^q)$.

Given the endpoint of the evaluation of an expression or statement, the beginning of the evaluation is uniquely determined, since it is not allowed that the thread just returned from a class initialization.

Lemma 8.1.1. If q evaluates α on the interval $[m, n]$ and q evaluates α on the interval $[m', n]$, then $m = m'$.

The ASM formalism allows us to speak about steps in a run of a machine. Since the steps in the run of Java$_\mathcal{T}$ are different from the steps of the single threads, we need some terminology to speak about the steps of an individual thread. The *previous step* of a thread is (the number of) its step which was done in the last state in the run of the ASM where the thread has been the current thread.

Definition 8.1.5 (Previous step). The *previous step* of thread q before n is m, if

1. $m < n$,
2. $thread_m = q$,
3. for each i, if $m < i < n$, then $thread_i \neq q$.

The walk of the current position through the body of a method can branch at certain positions. For most positions in the abstract syntax tree, however, when they are entered the preceding position is uniquely determined. It is called the *predecessor* of the position.

Definition 8.1.6 (Predecessor). Position α is a *predecessor* of position β in method μ (written $\alpha \prec_\mu \beta$), if for each thread q of state n which is in μ at n and enters β at n there is a previous step m of q before n such that

1. $pos_m^q = \alpha$,
2. $frames_m^q = frames_n^q$,

Table 8.1 The direct subexpressions of an expression

Expression at position α	Direct subexpressions of α
$^\alpha(uop\ ^\beta exp)$	$^\beta exp$
$^\alpha(^\beta exp_1\ bop\ ^\gamma exp_2)$	$^\beta exp_1,\ ^\gamma exp_2$
$^\alpha(c.f = {}^\beta exp)$	$^\beta exp$
$^\alpha(^{\beta_1} exp_1, \ldots, {}^{\beta_n} exp_n)$	$^{\beta_1} exp_1, \ldots, {}^{\beta_n} exp_n$
$^\alpha(c.m^\beta(exps))$	$^\beta(exps)$
$^\alpha(^\beta exp\ \text{instanceof}\ c)$	$^\beta exp$
$^\alpha((c)\ ^\beta exp)$	$^\beta exp$
$^\alpha(^\beta exp.c/f)$	$^\beta exp$
$^\alpha(^\beta exp_1.c/f = {}^\gamma exp_2)$	$^\beta exp_1,\ ^\gamma exp_2$
$^\alpha(^\beta exp.c/m^\gamma(exps))$	$^\beta exp,\ ^\gamma(exps)$
$^\alpha\text{new}\ c.c/m^\beta(exps)$	$^\beta(exps)$
$^\alpha(^\beta exp_1[^\gamma exp_2])$	$^\beta exp_1,\ ^\gamma exp_2$
$^\alpha(^\beta exp_1[^\gamma exp_2] = {}^\delta exp_3)$	$^\beta exp_1,\ ^\gamma exp_2,\ ^\delta exp_3$
$^\alpha(\text{new}\ A[^{\beta_1} exp_1]\ldots[^{\beta_n} exp_n][]\ldots[])$	$^{\beta_1} exp_1, \ldots, {}^{\beta_n} exp_n$

3. $restbody_m^q = restbody_n^q$,
4. $locals_m^q = locals_n^q$.

Lemma 8.1.2 (Predecessor). If the direct subexpressions (Table 8.1) of $^\alpha exp$ in the body of μ are $^{\beta_1} exp_1, \ldots, {}^{\beta_n} exp_n$, then $a \prec_\mu \beta_1$ and $\beta_i \prec_\mu \beta_{i+1}$ for each i with $1 \leq i < n$. For other kinds of phrases the predecessors are listed in Table 8.2.

Proof. By induction on the run of *execJavaThread*. If the rule executed in the step of the ASM moves the current position upwards or does not move the position at all, nothing has to be shown, because in that case by definition, the thread in the current position does not enter an expression or statement. Hence the rules which move the current positions inwards or forwards have to be considered only.   □

The stack of a thread may grow and shrink. New frames are pushed on the stack when class or instance methods are invoked, when class initializers are executed, or when new instances are created and a constructor is called. The positions which cause the growth of the stack are categorized as follows:

Definition 8.1.7 (Position categories). We say that

1. position β is a *method invocation position* for α in:

$$^\alpha c.m^\beta(exps)$$
$$^\alpha(exp.c/m^\beta(exps))$$

Table 8.2 The predecessors of expressions and statements

Phrase at α in μ	Predecessors
$^\alpha(loc = {}^\beta exp)$	$\alpha \prec_\mu \beta$
$^\alpha({}^\beta exp_0 \,?\, {}^\gamma exp_1 : {}^\delta exp_2)$	$\alpha \prec_\mu \beta,\ \beta \prec_\mu \gamma,\ \beta \prec_\mu \delta$
$^\alpha({}^\beta exp;)$	$\alpha \prec_\mu \beta$
$^\alpha\{{}^{\beta_1} stm_1\ \ldots\ {}^{\beta_n} stm_n\}$	$a \prec_\mu \beta_1,\ \beta_i \prec_\mu \beta_{i+1}$ for $1 \le i < n$
$^\alpha\texttt{if}\ ({}^\beta exp)\ {}^\gamma stm_1\ \texttt{else}\ {}^\delta stm_2$	$\alpha \prec_\mu \beta,\ \beta \prec_\mu \gamma,\ \beta \prec_\mu \delta$
$^\alpha\texttt{while}\ ({}^\beta exp)\ {}^\gamma stm$	$\alpha \prec_\mu \beta,\ \beta \prec_\mu \gamma$
$^\alpha lab\!:{}^\beta stm$	$\alpha \prec_\mu \beta$
$^\alpha\texttt{return}\ {}^\beta exp$	$\alpha \prec_\mu \beta$
$^\alpha\texttt{throw}\ {}^\beta exp$	$\alpha \prec_\mu \beta$
$^\alpha\ \texttt{try}\ {}^\beta block_t$ $\quad\texttt{catch}\ (E_1\ x_1)\ {}^{\gamma_1} block_1$ $\quad\quad\vdots$ $\quad\texttt{catch}\ (E_n\ x_n)\ {}^{\gamma_n} block_n$	$\alpha \prec_\mu \beta,\ \beta \prec_\mu \gamma_i$ for $1 \le i \le n$
$^\alpha({}^\beta stm\ \texttt{finally}\ {}^\gamma block)$	$\alpha \prec_\mu \beta,\ \beta \prec_\mu \gamma$
$^\alpha\texttt{synchronized}\ ({}^\beta exp)\ {}^\gamma stm$	$\alpha \prec_\mu \beta,\ \beta \prec_\mu \gamma$
$^\alpha\ \texttt{static}\ {}^\beta block$	$\alpha \prec_\mu \beta$

2. position β is a *constructor invocation position* for α in:

$$^\alpha\texttt{new}\ c.c/m^\beta(exps)$$

3. position β is a *class initialization position* in:

$^\beta\texttt{static}\ block$	[static initializer]
$^\beta c.f$	[access to class field]
$c.f = {}^\beta exp$	[assignment to class field]
$c.m^\beta(exps)$	[invocation of class method]
$^\beta\texttt{new}\ c.c/m(exps)$	[new instance creation]

For each thread the current method is either a class method, an instance method, a constructor, or a class initialization method. If the stack of the thread is empty, then the current method is the run method of the thread.

Definition 8.1.8 (Run method). We say that C/m is the *run method* of thread q, if

1. $m = \texttt{run}()$,
2. $getField(q, \texttt{Thread/target}) = r$,
3. $classOf(r) = A$,
4. $lookup(A, \texttt{Thread/run}()) = C$.

The ASM rules which change the stack of a thread are *invokeMethod* and *exitMethod*. A new frame is pushed with *invokeMethod* when a class is initialized, when a class or instance method is invoked, or when a new instance is created and a constructor is invoked. A frame is popped with *exitMethod* when a value is returned to the invoking frame or when an exception is passed to the invoking frame. The next lemma simply states, that the current method has been called at some point in the past. The lemma must be proved simultaneously with Lemma 8.1.4.

Lemma 8.1.3 (Invocation). For each thread q of state n in the run of *execJavaThread*, either $meth_n^q$ is the run method of q and $frames_n^q$ is the empty stack, or there exists k and m such that $k \leq m < n$ and

1. $frames_n^q = frames_m^q \cdot (\_, \_, \alpha, \_)$,
2. one of the following is true:
   a) $meth_n^q$ is a class or instance method and pos_m^q is a method invocation position for α in the body of $meth_m^q$, or
   b) $meth_n^q$ is a constructor and pos_m^q is a constructor invocation position for α in the body of $meth_m^q$, or
   c) $meth_n^q$ is a `<clinit>` method, $pos_m^q = \alpha$ and α is a class initialization position in the body of $meth_m^q$,
3. for each i, if $m < i \leq n$, then $frames_n^q \sqsubseteq_{\mathrm{pre}} frames_i^q$,
4. q evaluates α on the interval $[k, m]$.

Proof. By induction on the run of *execJavaThread*. In most steps of the run the frame stack of a thread remains unchanged and nothing has to be shown. A class or instance method is invoked at a method invocation position. A constructor is invoked at a constructor invocation position. A `<clinit>` method is invoked at a class initialization position. □

The following lemma says that *execJavaThread* respects the recursive structure of expressions and statements. At each point in the computation there is a unique point in the past where control entered the expression or statement at the current position. In the interval between the entry point and the current point the expression is evaluated according to Def. 8.1.4. This means that all changes made to *restbody* occur in the subtree rooted at the current position. Outside of this area, *restbody* is not touched.

Lemma 8.1.4 (Evaluation). For each thread q of state n in the run of *execJavaThread*, if $pos_n^q = \alpha$, then there exists an $m \leq n$ such that thread q evaluates α on the interval $[m, n]$.

Proof. By induction on the run of *execJavaThread*. Lemma 8.1.3 is used when values or exceptions are returned to the parent frame. □

It is not possible that control enters an expression or statement and returns to the root position of the expression or statement before it is completely evaluated. At the current position in *restbody* there is always an unevaluated expression, an unevaluated statement, a value, the constant *Norm*, or an abruption.

Lemma 8.1.5. For each thread q of state n in the run of *execJavaThread*, if $restbody_n^q/pos_n^q$ is neither a value nor the constant *Norm* nor an abruption, then $restbody_n^q/pos_n^q$ is an unevaluated expression or an unevaluated statement.

Proof. By induction on the run of *execJavaThread*. Lemma 8.1.4 is used when the current position moves to the next subexpression.   □

8.2 Unreachable statements

It is not allowed to drop off the end of a method body. A compile-time error occurs if the body of a method can complete normally. It is also a compile-time error if a statement cannot be executed because it is unreachable. Every Java compiler must carry out a conservative flow analysis to make sure that all statements are reachable. For this purpose two static predicates *reachable* and *normal* are computed at compile-time. The predicates have the following intended meanings:

reachable(α)
    The phrase at position α is reachable.
normal(α)
    The phrase at position α can complete normally.

The predicates are defined such that *normal*(α) implies *reachable*(α). Moreover, if a substatement is reachable, then the statement is reachable.

The reachability analysis is also used in Sect. 16.5 in the proof that bytecode generated by the Java compiler of Part II is accepted by the bytecode verifier. There, one has to show that execution cannot jump out of the code of a method.

At the root position of a method body the predicate *reachable* is determined by the following initial conditions: Let $^\alpha block$ be the body of an instance method, constructor or class method or a static initializer. Then *reachable*(α) is *True*.

For the other positions in the block the predicates *reachable* and *normal* can then be computed in a top-down manner. Instead of explaining exactly how the functions are computed, in Table 8.3 we just state the equivalences the predicates have to satisfy. Constant boolean expressions are not treated the same way in all control structures. For example, in the while statement

Table 8.3 Reachability constraints

$^\alpha;$	$normal(\alpha) \Leftrightarrow reachable(\alpha)$
$^\alpha(^\beta exp;)$	$normal(\alpha) \Leftrightarrow reachable(\alpha)$
$^\alpha\{^{\beta_1} stm_1 \ldots {}^{\beta_n} stm_n\}$	$reachable(\beta_1) \Leftrightarrow reachable(\alpha)$, $reachable(\beta_{i+1}) \Leftrightarrow normal(\beta_i)$, $normal(\alpha) \Leftrightarrow normal(\beta_n)$
$^\alpha\texttt{if}\,(^\beta exp)\,{}^\gamma stm_1\,\texttt{else}\,{}^\delta stm_2$	$reachable(\gamma) \Leftrightarrow reachable(\alpha)$, $reachable(\delta) \Leftrightarrow reachable(\alpha)$, $normal(\alpha) \Leftrightarrow normal(\gamma) \vee normal(\delta)$
$^\alpha\texttt{while}\,(^\beta exp)\,{}^\gamma stm$	$reachable(\gamma) \Leftrightarrow reachable(\alpha)$ and $^\beta exp$ is not a constant expression with value *False*, $normal(\alpha) \Leftrightarrow reachable(\alpha)$ and $^\beta exp$ is not a constant expression with value *True*
$^\alpha lab{:}\,{}^\beta stm$	$reachable(\beta) \Leftrightarrow reachable(\alpha)$, $normal(\alpha) \Leftrightarrow normal(\beta)$ or there exists a reachable statement **break** lab inside $^\beta stm$ that can exit $^\beta stm$ (Def. 8.2.2)
$^\alpha\texttt{break}\,lab;$	$\neg\,normal(\alpha)$
$^\alpha\texttt{continue}\,lab;$	$\neg\,normal(\alpha)$
$^\alpha\texttt{return};$	$\neg\,normal(\alpha)$
$^\alpha\texttt{return}\,{}^\beta exp;$	$\neg\,normal(\alpha)$
$^\alpha\texttt{throw}\,{}^\beta exp;$	$\neg\,normal(\alpha)$
$^\alpha\texttt{try}\,{}^\beta block_t$ $\quad\texttt{catch}\,(E_1\,x_1)\,{}^{\gamma_1} block_1$ $\quad\vdots$ $\quad\texttt{catch}\,(E_n\,x_n)\,{}^{\gamma_n} block_n$	$reachable(\beta) \Leftrightarrow reachable(\alpha)$, $reachable(\gamma_i) \Leftrightarrow reachable(\alpha)$ and $E_i \not\preceq_{\mathrm h} E_j$ for $1 \leq j < i$ and $block_t$ can throw an exception F (Def. 8.2.3) with $F \preceq_{\mathrm h} E_i$ or $E_i \preceq_{\mathrm h} F$, $normal(\alpha) \Leftrightarrow normal(\beta) \vee \bigvee_{1\leq i\leq n} normal(\gamma_i)$
$^\alpha(^\beta stm\,\texttt{finally}\,{}^\gamma block)$	$reachable(\beta) \Leftrightarrow reachable(\alpha)$, $reachable(\gamma) \Leftrightarrow reachable(\alpha)$, $normal(\alpha) \Leftrightarrow normal(\beta) \wedge normal(\gamma)$
$^\alpha\texttt{synchronized}\,(^\beta exp)\,{}^\gamma stm$	$reachable(\gamma) \Leftrightarrow reachable(\alpha)$, $normal(\alpha) \Leftrightarrow normal(\gamma)$

```
while (false) stm
```

the statement *stm* is not considered as reachable. In the if-then-else statement

```
if (false) stm
```

the statement *stm*, however, is considered as reachable. The reason for this difference is to allow programmers to use the if-then-else statement for "conditional compilation".

For positions in expressions the predicate *reachable* is determined by the following definition.

Definition 8.2.1 (Reachable expression). An expression is *reachable* iff the innermost statement containing it is reachable.

If an abruption occurs in a `try` block, the corresponding `finally` block is executed before the abruption moves upwards. If the `finally` block does not complete normally, the old abruption is discarded and cannot exit the `try-finally` statement.

Definition 8.2.2 (Abruption can exit statement). An abruption at position α can exit *stm*, if for every substatement ${}^{\beta}({}^{\gamma}s$ `finally` ${}^{\delta}b)$ of *stm* such that α is in s the predicate *normal*(δ) is true.

We say that a `break` statement at position α can exit *stm*, if an abruption at position α can exit *stm*.

Definition 8.2.3 (Statement can throw exception). A statement *stm* can throw an exception E, if one of the following conditions is true:

1. $E = $ `RuntimeException` or $E = $ `Error`, or
2. *stm* contains a reachable statement ${}^{\alpha}$`throws` ${}^{\beta}exp$ such that $\mathcal{T}(\beta) = E$, the exception E is not caught in *stm* and an abruption at position α can exit *stm*, or
3. *stm* contains a reachable method invocation ${}^{\alpha}c/m(exps)$ such that E occurs in the `throws` clause of m in c, the exception E is not caught in *stm* and an abruption at position α can exit *stm*.

At run-time the current position is always *reachable*. If a statement completes normally, then the statement is *normal* (see Theorem 8.4.1). The converse is not true. There are *normal* statements which can complete abruptly. For example, in an if-then-else-statement one branch may be normal whereas the other branch completes abruptly.

8.2.1 Exercises

Exercise (⤳ CD) 8.2.1. Is the `catch` clause reachable in the following program?

```
class E extends Exception { }

class Test {
  public static void main(String[] argv) {
    try {
      try { throw new E(); } finally { return; }
    } catch (E x) { return; }
  }
}
```

Exercise ($\leadsto$ CD) 8.2.2. Which catch clauses are reachable in the following code?

```
class E extends Exception { }

class F extends E { }

class G extends Exception { }

class Test {
  static void test(E e) {
    try { throw e; }
    catch (F x) { }
    catch (E x) { }
    catch (G x) { }
    catch (Error x) { }
    catch (RuntimeException x) { }
    catch (Exception x) { }
  }
}
```

Exercise ($\leadsto$ CD) 8.2.3. Can the body of the method m complete normally?

```
class Test {
  int m() {
    l: try {
      break l;
    } finally { return 0; }
  }
}
```

Exercise ($\leadsto$ CD) 8.2.4. Can the body of the method m complete normally?

```
class Test {
  int m(int i) {
    if (i < 0) return 0;
    else
      while (i != 0) {
        if (i == 0) return 1;
        i = i - 1;
      }
  }
}
```

8.3 Rules of definite assignment

Each local variable must have a definitely assigned value when any access of its value occurs. An access to its value consists of using the identifier of the variable occurring anywhere in an expression except as the left-hand operand of the simple assignment operator =. A Java compiler must carry out a specific conservative flow analysis to make sure that, for every access of a local variable, the local variable is definitely assigned before the access; otherwise a compile-time error must occur.

Since local variables are not initialized with default values like class variables or instance fields, a Java program that does not obey the rules of definite assignment could violate the invariants of Theorem 8.4.1 below and would not be type safe. For example, a local pointer variable which is not initialized could point to an undefined location on the heap. Moreover, the rules of definite assignment ensure that the bytecode generated by a correct Java compiler is not rejected by the bytecode verifier (Theorem 16.5.2 and 17.1.2).

The rules of definite assignment have been changed in the second edition of the JLS [19, §16]. Boolean operators &, |, ^, == as well as assignments of boolean expressions to boolean variables are no longer treated in a special way. We take the rules of the second edition, because it simplifies the task of writing a compiler that generates code that is accepted by the verifier.

In order to precisely specify all the cases of definite assignment, static functions *before*, *after*, *true*, *false* and *vars* are computed at compile-time. These functions assign sets of variables (identifiers) to each position in the body of a method. The static functions have the following intended meanings (the functions $true(\alpha)$ and $false(\alpha)$ are defined for expressions of type **boolean** only):

$x \in before(\alpha)$
> The variable x is definitely assigned before the evaluation of the statement or expression at position α.

$x \in after(\alpha)$
> The variable x is definitely assigned after the statement or expression at position α when this statement or expression completes normally.

$x \in true(\alpha)$
> The variable x is definitely assigned after the evaluation of the expression at position α when this expression evaluates to true.

$x \in false(\alpha)$
> The variable x is definitely assigned after the evaluation of the expression at position α when this expression evaluates to false.

$x \in vars(\alpha)$
> The position α is in the scope of the local variable, formal parameter or **catch** parameter x.

The functions satisfy the following inclusions:

Table 8.4 Definite assignment for boolean expressions

$^{\alpha}$`true`	$true(\alpha) = before(\alpha),\ false(\alpha) = vars(\alpha)$
$^{\alpha}$`false`	$true(\alpha) = vars(\alpha),\ false(\alpha) = before(\alpha)$
$^{\alpha}(!\ ^{\beta}e)$	$before(\beta) = before(\alpha),$ $true(\alpha) = false(\beta),\ false(\alpha) = true(\beta)$
$^{\alpha}(^{\beta}e_0\ ?\ ^{\gamma}e_1\ :\ ^{\delta}e_2)$	$before(\beta) = before(\alpha),$ $before(\gamma) = true(\beta),\ before(\delta) = false(\beta),$ $true(\alpha) = true(\gamma) \cap true(\delta),\ false(\alpha) = false(\gamma) \cap false(\delta)$
$^{\alpha}(^{\beta}e_1\ \&\&\ ^{\gamma}e_2)$	$before(\beta) = before(\alpha),\ before(\gamma) = true(\beta),$ $true(\alpha) = true(\gamma),\ false(\alpha) = false(\beta) \cap false(\gamma)$
$^{\alpha}(^{\beta}e_1\ ||\ ^{\gamma}e_2)$	$before(\beta) = before(\alpha),\ before(\gamma) = false(\beta),$ $true(\alpha) = true(\beta) \cap true(\gamma),\ false(\alpha) = false(\gamma)$

1. $before(\alpha) \subseteq after(\alpha) \subseteq vars(\alpha)$.
2. If $type(\alpha) =$ `boolean`, then $before(\alpha) \subseteq true(\alpha) \cap false(\alpha)$.
3. If $type(\alpha) =$ `boolean`, then $true(\alpha) \cup false(\alpha) \subseteq vars(\alpha)$.

At the root position of a method body the function *before* is determined by the following initial conditions: Let $^{\alpha}block$ be the body of an instance method, constructor or class method with declaration $m(c_1\ loc_1, \ldots, c_n\ loc_n)$. Then $before(\alpha) = \{loc_1, \ldots, loc_n\}$, because when the body is invoked there are always values assigned to the formal parameters $loc_1, \ldots, loc_n$. If $^{\alpha}block$ is a static initializer, then $before(\alpha)$ is the empty set.

For the other positions in the block the functions *before*, *after*, *true* and *false* can then be computed in a top-down manner. Instead of explaining exactly how the functions are computed, we just state the equations the functions have to satisfy.

Table 8.4 contains the equations for boolean expressions (see Table 3.6 for the boolean operators). It is assumed that $type(\alpha) =$ `boolean` in each row. There are no conditions for *after* in Table 8.4, since by definition in all cases $after(\alpha) = true(\alpha) \cap false(\alpha)$. Constant boolean expressions with value true (resp. false) are treated like the literal `true` (resp. `false`). If $type(\alpha)$ is `boolean` and $^{\alpha}exp$ is not an instance of one of the expressions in Table 8.4, then $true(\alpha) = after(\alpha)$ and $false(\alpha) = after(\alpha)$.

Table 8.5 contains the equations for non-boolean expressions. The most important condition is the first one for local variables. It requires for a local variable loc at a position α that $loc \in before(\alpha)$. Hence loc must be definitely assigned before it is used.

In addition to the constraints in Table 8.5 there are the following conditions for an expression $^{\alpha}exp$ with direct subexpressions $^{\beta_1}exp_1, \ldots, ^{\beta_n}exp_n$ (Table 8.1):

Table 8.5 Definite assignment for arbitrary expressions

$^\alpha loc$	$after(\alpha) = before(\alpha),\ loc \in before(\alpha)$
$^\alpha lit$	$after(\alpha) = before(\alpha)$
$^\alpha(loc = {}^\beta e)$	$before(\beta) = before(\alpha),\ loc \in vars(\alpha),$ $after(\alpha) = after(\beta) \cup \{loc\}$
$^\alpha({}^\beta e_0 \mathbin{?} {}^\gamma e_1 : {}^\delta e_2)$	$before(\beta) = before(\alpha),\ before(\gamma) = true(\beta),$ $before(\delta) = false(\beta),\ after(\alpha) = after(\gamma) \cap after(\delta)$
$^\alpha c.f$	$after(\alpha) = before(\alpha)$

1. $before(\beta_1) = before(\alpha)$,
2. $before(\beta_{i+1}) = after(\beta_i)$ for $i = 1, \ldots, n-1$,
3. $after(\alpha) = after(\beta_n)$.

Table 8.6 contains the constraints for statements. For a statement with label *lab* at position α a set $break(\alpha, lab)$ is needed.

Definition 8.3.1. A variable x belongs to $break(\alpha, lab)$ if the following two conditions are true:

1. x is in $before(\beta)$ for each statement $^\beta$**break** *lab* inside the statement at position α that can exit α (Def. 8.2.2) and
2. x is in $after(\beta)$ for each statement $^\beta(s$ **finally** $b)$ inside α such that s contains a **break** *lab* that can exit α.

If there are no substatements **break** *lab* inside $^\beta stm$, then $break(\beta, lab) = vars(\beta)$.

In a block statement the variables which are definitely assigned after the normal execution of the statement are the variables which are definitely assigned after the last substatement of the block. However, the variables must still be in the scope of a declaration. Consider the following example:

```
{ α{ int i; i = 3; } { int i; i = 2 * βi; } }
```

The set $after(\alpha)$ is empty and does not contain the variable i because at the end of block α, i is not in the scope of a declaration. Thus $before(\beta)$ is empty, too, and the block is rejected by the compiler. Note that in Java it is not allowed to declare the same variable again in the scope of another declaration (Constraint 3.1.1).

What does it mean that the rules for definite assignment are sound? It means that at run-time all variables of the compile-time computed set $before(pos)$ are defined in the local environment. If there is a normal value at the current position *pos* in *restbody*, then all variables of the set $after(pos)$ are defined in the local environment. If the value is the boolean value *True*, then the variables of the set $true(pos)$ are defined in the local environment;

Table 8.6 Definite assignment for statements

$\alpha;$	$after(\alpha) = before(\alpha)$
$\alpha(^{\beta} exp;)$	$before(\beta) = before(\alpha),\ after(\alpha) = after(\beta)$
$\alpha\{^{\beta_1} stm_1\ \ldots\ ^{\beta_n} stm_n\}$	$before(\beta_1) = before(\alpha),$ $before(\beta_{i+1}) = after(\beta_i)$ for $i = 1, \ldots, n-1,$ $after(\alpha) = after(\beta_n) \cap vars(\alpha)$
$\alpha\mathtt{if}\ (^{\beta} exp)\ ^{\gamma} stm_1\ \mathtt{else}\ ^{\delta} stm_2$	$before(\beta) = before(\alpha),$ $before(\gamma) = true(\beta),\ before(\delta) = false(\beta),$ $after(\alpha) = after(\gamma) \cap after(\delta)$
$\alpha\mathtt{while}\ (^{\beta} exp)\ ^{\gamma} stm$	$before(\beta) = before(\alpha),\ before(\gamma) = true(\beta),$ $after(\alpha) = false(\beta)$
$\alpha lab:\ ^{\beta} stm$	$before(\beta) = before(\alpha),$ $after(\alpha) = after(\beta) \cap break(\beta, lab)$
$\alpha\mathtt{break}\ lab;$	$after(\alpha) = vars(\alpha)$
$\alpha\mathtt{continue}\ lab;$	$after(\alpha) = vars(\alpha)$
$\alpha\mathtt{return};$	$after(\alpha) = vars(\alpha)$
$\alpha\mathtt{return}\ ^{\beta} exp;$	$before(\beta) = before(\alpha),\ after(\alpha) = vars(\alpha)$
$\alpha\mathtt{throw}\ ^{\beta} exp;$	$before(\beta) = before(\alpha),\ after(\alpha) = vars(\alpha)$
$\alpha\mathtt{try}\ ^{\beta} block_t$ $\quad\mathtt{catch}\ (E_1\ x_1)\ ^{\gamma_1} block_1$ $\quad\vdots$ $\quad\mathtt{catch}\ (E_n\ x_n)\ ^{\gamma_n} block_n$	$before(\beta) = before(\alpha),$ $before(\gamma_i) = before(\alpha) \cup \{x_i\},$ $after(\alpha) = after(\beta) \cap \bigcap_{1 \le i \le n} after(\gamma_i)$
$\alpha(^{\beta} stm\ \mathtt{finally}\ ^{\gamma} block)$	$before(\beta) = before(\alpha),\ before(\gamma) = before(\alpha),$ $after(\alpha) = after(\gamma)\ \cup$ $\{x \in after(\beta) \mid$ there is no $x = exp$ in $^{\gamma} block\}$
$\alpha\mathtt{synchronized}\ (^{\beta} exp)\ ^{\gamma} stm$	$before(\beta) = before(\alpha),\ before(\gamma) = after(\beta),$ $after(\alpha) = after(\gamma)$

if the value is *False*, then the variables of the set $after(pos)$ are defined in the local environment. The soundness of the rules of definite assignment is included in Theorem 8.4.1 below.

Remark 8.3.1. The constraints in Table 8.6 differ from the rules of definite assignment in [19, §16] in two points. First, the official JLS defines for a `try-finally` statement $^{\alpha}(^{\beta} stm\ \mathtt{finally}\ ^{\gamma} block)$:

$$after(\alpha) = after(\beta) \cup after(\gamma).$$

Our definition in Table 8.6 is more restrictive. A variable x in $after(\beta)$ belongs to $after(\alpha)$ only if there is no subphrase $x = exp$ in $^{\gamma} block$. Why do we restrict the set in this way? The reason is the program in Fig. 16.8 which is legal according to the JLS. If we compile the program following [23, §7.13], then the resulting bytecode is rejected by any bytecode verifier we tried. If we take our constraints in Table 8.6, then the program in Fig. 16.8 is no longer legal, since there is an assignment i = 3 in the finally block and the variable i is not regarded as definitely assigned after the try-finally statement. Hence, it cannot be used in the return statement. The effect of our restriction of the rules of definite assignment for the try-finally statement is that a variable which is definitely assigned after the try-finally statement but not after the finally block is—in the eyes of the bytecode verifier—not modified by the subroutine that implements the finally block.

The second difference between Table 8.6 and the rules of definite assignment in the official JLS affects the labeled statement. The second clause of Def. 8.3.1 is not contained in the official JLS. Hence, according to the JLS a variable is definitely assigned after a labeled statement, if it is definitely assigned after the statement and before every break that can exit the labeled statement. We restrict the set further. The reason for our restriction is that the program in Fig. 16.9 which is legal according to the JLS is rejected by all known bytecode verifiers. Therefore we exclude the (rather exotic) program in Fig. 16.9 from the Java programming language. Both of our restrictions of the rules of definite assignments are chosen so that we can prove in Sect. 16.5 that our compiler in Part II generates verifiable code.

8.3.1 Exercises

Exercise (⤳ CD) 8.3.1. An attacker wants to fool the Java type system. His idea is simple. A pure Object is type casted into an array of integers. The ClassCastException which is thrown at run-time is caught so that in the handler of the catch clause the Object can be used as an array.

```
class Test {
  public static void main(String[] _) {
    int[] a;
    try {
      a = (int[])(new Object());
    }
    catch (ClassCastException e) {
      System.out.println(a[0]);
    }
  }
}
```

Explain why the idea does not work.

Exercise 8.3.2. What are the conditions for the functions *before* and *after* for the do, for and switch statement (see [18, §16])?

Exercise 8.3.3. Show that the equations for the operators !, && and || in Table 8.4 can be derived from the equations for conditional expressions using the following equivalences:

$$
\begin{aligned}
! \, e &\equiv e \, ? \, \texttt{false}\!:\!\texttt{true} \\
e_1 \,\&\&\, e_2 &\equiv e_1 \, ? \, e_2 \, :\! \texttt{false} \\
e_1 \,||\, e_2 &\equiv e_1 \, ? \, \texttt{true}\!: e_2
\end{aligned}
$$

Exercise ($\rightsquigarrow$ CD) 8.3.4. Is the following method correct with respect to the rules of definite assignment? What happens if we define $false(\alpha) = \emptyset$ in $^{\alpha}\texttt{true}$?

```
int m() {
  int i;
  if (true)
    return 0;
  else
    return i;
}
```

8.4 Java is type safe

What does it mean that Java is type safe? It means that if an expression is evaluated, then the resulting value is of the type of the expression. This statement alone, however, is not sufficient. Consider the case of a local variable. If the variable is not defined in the local environment, it is evaluated to the constant *undef*. The constant *undef* is then propagated in the evaluation tree until the abstract Java machine stops and the execution fails.

In a real implementation of Java the constant *undef* does not exist. There is also no notion of definedness of variables in the local environment. In a situation like above, execution proceeds with the (arbitrary) value which was at the memory position of the undefined local variable. This value could be of any type and the type safety of Java would be violated. Hence, type safety means more. It also means that the constant *undef* never occurs at run-time in the state of the ASM. This implies, for example, that pointers must always be defined in the heap, since an undefined pointer is evaluated to *undef*, too.

Type safety means that when a legal, well-typed Java program is executed on the ASM described in the previous chapters, then its state is always in good shape; local variables, class variables, instance fields and array elements always contain values of the declared types; references to objects are always defined in the heap (there are no dangling pointers); expressions are evaluated to values of the compile-time type; even when exceptions are thrown and later caught, the invariants remain valid. Type safety means that the invariants of Theorem 8.4.1 below are always satisfied during the run of the Java program.

Why is the soundness of the rules of definite assignment important for the type safety of Java? Consider again the case of a local variable *loc* at the current position α of the execution of a Java program. If we know that the set $before(\alpha)$ is contained in the domain of the local environment, we can conclude that *loc* is defined in the local environment and therefore is not evaluated to *undef*, because the equations for local variables in Table 8.5 require that *loc* belongs to the set $before(\alpha)$. Hence the soundness of the rules of definite assignment are an essential ingredient for the proof of the Java type safety theorem below.

What does it mean that a value v is of type A? For primitive values like integers and floats it means that A is equal to the type of the value v. For references it means that $classOf(v)$ is a subtype of A. Since this notion of run-time compatibility does not agree with the subtype relation $\preceq$ for primitive types (Def. 3.1.1), we introduce a new relation $\sqsubseteq$ between the types of Java.

Definition 8.4.1 (Run-time compatible). The relation $A \sqsubseteq B$ holds iff one of the following conditions is true:

1. A and B are primitive types and $A = B$, or
2. A and B are reference types and $A \preceq B$ (see Def. 5.1.2).

The relation $\sqsubseteq$ is a partial ordering. We have:

1. $A \sqsubseteq A$.
2. If $A \sqsubseteq B$ and $B \sqsubseteq C$, then $A \sqsubseteq C$.
3. If $A \sqsubseteq B$ and $B \sqsubseteq A$, then $A = B$.
4. $A[\,] \sqsubseteq B[\,] \Leftrightarrow A \sqsubseteq B$.

The invariants of the type safety theorem have to be proved simultaneously for the current frame and for the frames on the stack, for each thread. Therefore we define what we mean by a frame and a parent frame in the state of the computation.

Definition 8.4.2 (Frame in a state). We say that f is a *frame in state n* of thread q, if one of the following conditions is true:

1. $f = (meth_n^q, restbody_n^q, pos_n^q, locals_n^q)$, or
2. f is an element of $frames_n^q$.

Definition 8.4.3 (Parent frame). We say that g is the *parent frame* of f in thread q, if one of the following conditions is true:

1. $frames_n^q = [\ldots, g, f, \ldots]$, or
2. $f = (meth_n^q, restbody_n^q, pos_n^q, locals_n^q)$ and $g = top(frames_n^q)$.

As we have seen above, for the type safety of Java it is important that there are no dangling references. Therefore we have to define what it means that a reference is *used* in the state. A reference is used if there exists something which refers to it. The term 'is used' does not mean the same as 'is reachable'. A reachable reference is a reference that can be accessed in the continuation of the computation.

Definition 8.4.4 (Used reference). We say that a reference *ref* is *used* in state n, if one of the following conditions is true:

1. there exists a field c/f such that $globals_n(c/f) = ref$, or
2. there exists an r and a field c/f such that $getField_n(r, c/f) = ref$, or
3. there exists an r and an $i \in \mathbb{N}$ such that $getElement_n(r, i) = ref$, or
4. there exists a frame $(\_, restbody^*, \_, locals^*)$ in state n of a thread q and one of the following conditions is true:
   a) there exists a variable *loc* such that $locals^*(loc) = ref$, or
   b) there exists a position α such that $restbody^*/\alpha = ref$, or
   c) there exists a position α such that $restbody^*/\alpha = Return(ref)$, or
   d) there exists a position α such that $restbody^*/\alpha = Exc(ref)$.

Now we have all the notions to formulate the invariants of the type safety theorem. We split the invariant into invariants for the frames of a thread, invariants of the dynamic method chain of a thread, and global invariants.

The *global invariants* state that run-time values of (static or instance) fields and of array elements are compatible with their types (**global, object2, array**), that there are no dangling references (**ref**), and that references to class instances are for non-abstract classes and have the correct class instance fields (**object1**).

The dynamic method *chain invariants* express that at any method invocation position on the frame stack, the invoked method's return type is compatible with the type at the method invocation position (**chain1**), and that the exceptions in the invoked method's `throws` clause are allowed at that position (**chain2**). If a constructor is invoked, then the value of `this` in the local environment is the newly created reference which is stored at the position of the `new`-expression in the invoking frame (**chain3**).

The *frame invariants* guarantee that each run-time position is compile-time reachable (**reach**) and contains in its restbody, if not an unevaluated phrase, either a value or an abruption or a normally completed statement (**undef**) which satisfies the compile-time constraints. In fact, the variables computed as definitely assigned at the current position of the frame are well-defined local variables at run-time (**def1**)–(**def6**) with values compatible with the declared types (**loc1**)–(**loc5**). Expressions evaluate to values which are compatible with the compile-time type associated to their position (**val**), and the positions of statements which complete normally are compile-time normal (**norm**).

Run-time abruptions occur in accordance with the corresponding compile-time constraints for jumps, returns or exceptions. Every run-time position where $Break(l)$ occurs is within a statement with label l that contains a `break` l that can exit (Def. 8.2.2) the statement (**abr1**). Every run-time position where $Continue(l)$ occurs is within a `while` statement which label l (**abr2**). Every run-time position where $Return$ or $Return(v)$ occurs is within a method body, with a return value of a type which is compatible with the return type of the method (**abr3, abr4**). The class of any exception thrown at run-time is a subclass of `Throwable`, and if it is neither an error nor a run-time exception, then the position where the exception occurs is protected by a `catch` or `throws` clause with compatible type and the thrown exception is more specific than some exception that a statement at the position can throw at compile-time (**abr5**) (Def. 8.2.3).

Theorem 8.4.1 (Java is type safe). Assume that

$$(meth^*, restbody^*, pos^*, locals^*)$$

is a frame in state n of thread q. Then the following invariants are satisfied:

(**def1**) $before(pos^*) \subseteq dom(locals^*)$.

(**def2**) If $restbody^*/pos^*$ is normal, then $after(pos^*) \subseteq dom(locals^*)$.

(**def3**) If $restbody^*/pos^* = True$, then $true(pos^*) \subseteq dom(locals^*)$.

(**def4**) If $restbody^*/pos^* = False$, then $false(pos^*) \subseteq dom(locals^*)$.

(**def5**) If $restbody^*/pos^* = Break(l)$, then $break(pos^*, l) \subseteq dom(locals^*)$.

(**def6**) If the frame is not the current frame of q and $body(meth^*)/pos^*$ is a method invocation then $after(pos^*) \subseteq dom(locals^*)$.

(**reach**) $reachable(pos^*)$.

(**norm**) If $restbody^*/\alpha = Norm$, then $normal(\alpha)$.

(**val**) If $restbody^*/\alpha$ is a value of type B, then $B \sqsubseteq \mathcal{T}(\alpha)$, where $\mathcal{T}(\alpha)$ is the compile-time type of position α in $body(meth^*)$.

(**undef**) The constant $undef$ does not occur in $restbody^*$.

(**loc1**) If $x \in dom(locals^*)$, then $locals^*(x) \in Val$.

(**loc2**) If pos^* is in the scope of a local variable declaration of a variable x of type A and $x \in dom(locals^*)$, then $locals^*(x)$ is a value of type $B \sqsubseteq A$.

(**loc3**) If pos^* is in the scope of a formal parameter x of type A, then $locals^*(x)$ is a value of type $B \sqsubseteq A$.

(**loc4**) If pos^* is in the scope of a `catch` parameter x of type E, then $locals^*(x)$ is a value of type $F \preceq_h E$.

(**loc5**) If pos^* is in class A and pos^* is in the body of an instance method or in the body of a constructor, then $locals^*(\mathtt{this})$ is a value of type $B \preceq_h A$.

(**abr1**) If $restbody^*/\alpha = Break(l)$, then α is in a statement with label l and $body(meth^*)/\alpha$ contains a reachable `break` lab which can exit $body(meth^*)/\alpha$ (Def. 8.2.2).

(**abr2**) If $restbody^*/\alpha = Continue(l)$, then α is in a `while` statement with label l.

(abr3) If $restbody^*/\alpha = Return$, then α is in the body of a method with return type `void`.

(abr4) If $restbody^*/\alpha = Return(v)$, then α is in the body of a method with return type A and v is a value of type $B \sqsubseteq A$.

(abr5) If $restbody^*/\alpha = Exc(ref)$, then $classOf(ref) = E$, $E \preceq_h$ `Throwable`, E is allowed at position α (Def. 6.1.2) and $body(meth^*)/\alpha$ can throw an exception F (Def. 8.2.3) such that $E \preceq_h F$.

Assume that $(\_, restbody^*, \beta, \_)$ is the parent frame of $(c/m, \_, \_, locals^*)$ in state n of thread q. Then the dynamic method invocation chain has the following properties:

(chain1) If the return type of c/m is A and $A \neq$ `void`, then $type(\beta) = A$.

(chain2) If E occurs in the `throws` clause of c/m, then E is allowed at position β (see Def. 6.1.2).

(chain3) If c/m is a constructor and $restbody^*/\beta = ref.c/m(\_)$, then $locals^*(\texttt{this}) = ref$.

The following global invariants are true in state n:

(global) If c/f is a `static` field of declared type A, then $globals_n(c/f)$ is a value of type $B \sqsubseteq A$.

(ref) If a reference ref is used in state n, then $ref \in dom(heap_n)$.

(object1) If $heap_n(ref) = Object(c, fields)$, then c is a non `abstract` class and $dom(fields) = instanceFields(c)$.

(object2) If $heap_n(ref) = Object(\_, fields)$, $fields(f) = v$ and f is of declared type A, then v is a value of type $B \sqsubseteq A$.

(array) If $heap_n(ref) = Array(A, elems)$ and $elems(i) = v$, then v is a value of type $B \sqsubseteq A$.

Proof. By induction on the number of steps in the run of the ASM. We first consider invariants (def1)–(def6) which express the soundness of the rules of definite assignment. Why is Lemma 8.1.5 used in the proof? Consider the case where

$$restbody_n^q/pos_n^q = {}^\alpha(uop \; {}^\beta exp) \text{ and } pos_{n+1}^q = \beta.$$

By the induction hypothesis (def1) we know that $before(\alpha) \subseteq dom(locals_n^q)$. Since $before(\beta) = before(\alpha)$, we obtain that $before(pos_{n+1}^q) \subseteq dom(locals_{n+1}^q)$ and invariant (def1) remains valid. What about invariant (def2)? By assumption, we have $restbody_{n+1}^q/pos_{n+1}^q = {}^\beta exp$. What happens if ${}^\beta exp$ is a value? Fortunately this is not possible, because by Lemma 8.1.5 we know that ${}^\alpha(uop \; {}^\beta exp)$ is an unevaluated expression and therefore ${}^\beta exp$ cannot be a value. Hence, invariant (def2) is trivially satisfied and also the remaining invariants (def3)–(def6).

Invariant (def5) about $Break(l)$ requires special care. A $Break(l)$ can occur inside statements only. When it is propagated upwards in $restbody$, the set $break(pos^*, l)$ gets smaller. When a $Break(l)$ is propagated upwards from a `try` statement, then the corresponding `finally` block has terminated normally and thus, by invariant (norm) it is *normal*. Hence the $Break(l)$ can exit the `try-finally` statement in the sense of Def. 8.2.2. Therefore invariant (def5) remains true. Similarly, the set $before(pos^*)$ gets smaller when other abruptions are propagated upwards.

Unfortunately the positions of $restbody_n^q$ are not contained in $body(meth_n^q)$. For example, the rule $fail(exc)$ of Sect. 6.2 inserts a new piece of code into restbody and possibly generates positions which are not present in the body of $meth_n^q$. In this case, we assume that $before$ and $after$ are computed on the fly for the new positions in the inserted code.

Now we consider the remaining invariants. Consider the case where the current position pos_n^q is at a local variable $^\alpha loc$ which is replaced by $locals_n^q(loc)$ in the computation step of the ASM. Because the program satisfies the equations for definite assignment in Table 8.5, it follows that loc is in the set $before(\alpha)$. By invariant (def1), the set $before(\alpha)$ is contained in $\mathrm{dom}(locals_n^q)$. Therefore the variable loc is in $\mathrm{dom}(locals_n^q)$. By invariant (loc1), $locals_n^q(loc)$ is a value v. Hence, $locals_n^q(loc)$ is not the constant $undef$ and invariant (undef) remains valid. Moreover, the local variable loc at the current position pos_n^q is either in the scope of a local variable declaration, a formal method parameter or a catch parameter. In each case we can apply the appropriate induction hypothesis (loc2)–(loc4) and obtain that the value v is of type $\mathcal{T}(\alpha)$, hence invariant (val) is satisfied.

The transitivity of the run-time compatibility relation $\sqsubseteq$ is used several times. Consider, for example, the case where pos_n^q is at position γ in a conditional expression $^\alpha(^\beta True\,?\,^\gamma v\ :\ ^\delta exp)$ and the value v is moved upwards to position α in the computation step of the ASM. Let B be the type of v. By the induction hypothesis (val) we know that $B \sqsubseteq \mathcal{T}(\gamma)$. Since the program is well-typed (see Tables 3.4 and 3.5), we have $\mathcal{T}(\gamma) \sqsubseteq \mathcal{T}(\alpha)$. Since the relation $\sqsubseteq$ is transitive, it follows that $B \sqsubseteq \mathcal{T}(\alpha)$ and hence invariant (val) remains valid.

If an abruption $Break(l)$ or $Continue(l)$ is generated by executing the corresponding statement, then the invariants (abr1) and (abr2) are initially satisfied because of Constraint 3.1.1. An abruption $Return$ can only be generated in a method with return type `void` because of Constraint 4.1.6 hence invariant (abr3) is satisfied. If an abruption $Return(v)$ is generated, then invariant (abr4) is initially satisfied because of the type constraints in Tables 4.1 and 4.2.

Since the type of a method invocation expression is the return type of the invoked method (see Tables 4.1, 4.2, 5.2, 5.3), the invariant (chain1) is satisfied when a method is invoked. The Lookup Lemma 8.4.1 below ensures that the return type of a dynamically invoked method is the same as the return type of the compile-time method.

Consider the case where pos_n^q is at position γ in a method invocation expression ${}^\alpha({}^\beta ref.B/m^\gamma(vals))$. By the induction hypothesis (ref) we know that ref is defined in $heap_n$, because ref is used in state n according to Def. 8.4.4. Let $A = classOf(ref)$. Then, by the induction hypothesis (object1), it follows that A is a non abstract class. By the induction hypothesis (val) we know that $A \sqsubseteq \mathcal{T}(\beta)$. The compiler did choose the most specific applicable method B/m in such a way that $\mathcal{T}(\beta) \preceq_h B$ and m is declared in B. If follows that $A \preceq_h B$ and the assumptions of the lookup lemma below are satisfied. Hence the function $lookup(A, B/m)$ does not return $undef$ and invariant (undef) remains valid.

The lookup lemma ensures also invariant (chain2). The method found by the $lookup$ function throws more specific exceptions than the method B/m determined at compile-time. The classes in the throws clause of B/m are all allowed at position α because of the type constraints in Table 6.1. Hence (chain2) is satisfied.

If an exception is not caught in the body of a method, it is propagated upwards to the first position. Consider the case where pos_n^q is with an exception $Exc(ref)$ at the first position of a method body. By the induction hypothesis (abr5), it follows that $classOf(ref) = E$, where E is allowed at the first position. According to Def. 6.1.2, if E is not an error or a run-time exception, then there must exists a class F in the throws clause of the current method with $E \preceq_h F$. By the induction hypothesis (chain2) it follows that F is allowed at the position of the parent frame waiting for the return of the method. Lemma 6.1.1 yields that E is allowed at that position, too. Hence invariant (abr5) remains valid after the exception is propagated to the parent frame.   □

Remark 8.4.1. For the formulation of the invariants (loc1)–(loc3) it is essential that in Java it is not allowed to hide a local variable, a formal parameter or a catch parameter with a new declaration of the same identifier (see Constraint 3.1.1).

For the dynamic method lookup procedure, the following lemma is needed. It states that when the $lookup$ function is used to search in the class hierarchy for the current definition of a method declared in a class B, it yields a method with the correct return type and with a compile-time compatible throws clause.

Lemma 8.4.1 (Lookup lemma). Assume that A is a non abstract class, m is a method signature and B is a class or interface such that

1. $A \preceq_h B$,
2. m is declared in B.

Then there exists a class C such that

1. $lookup(A, B/m) = C$,
2. m has the same return type in B and C,
3. m throws more specific exceptions in C than in B (see Def. 6.1.1).

Proof. There are two cases. Either B is a class or an interface.

Case 1. B is a class:

Let C be the least class (w.r.t. $\preceq_h$) such that

1. $A \preceq_h C \preceq_h B$,
2. m is declared in C,
3. C/m overrides B/m (see Def. 4.1.9).

Suppose that m is **abstract** in C. By Constraint 4.1.12, it follows that m is **public** or **protected** in C. Hence by Def. 4.1.7 and Def. 4.1.5, C/m is visible in A and, by Constraint 4.1.13, A is an **abstract** class. Contradiction.

Thus, m is not **abstract** in C and therefore (by clause 1 of the algorithm for computing $lookup$ in Sect. 5.1.8) $lookup(A, B/m) = C$.

Using Constraints 4.1.10 and 6.1.1 and Def. 4.1.9 it follows that m has the same return type in C and B and that m throws more specific exceptions in C than in B.

Case 2. B is an interface:

Since B is an interface, m is **public** in B by Constraint 4.1.9.

Let D be a minimal (w.r.t. $\preceq_h$) class *or interface* such that

1. $A \preceq_h D \preceq_h B$,
2. m is declared in D.

By Constraints 4.1.10 and 6.1.1, it follows that

1. m is **public** in D,
2. m has the same return type in D and B,
3. m throws more specific exceptions in D than in B.

If D is a class, we can proceed as in Case 1. Otherwise, D is an interface and, by Constraint 4.1.9, D/m is **abstract**.

Since D/m is visible in A and A is not **abstract**, by Constraint 4.1.13, it follows that A implements m.

Hence by Def. 4.1.10, there exists a class C such that $A \preceq_h C$, m has a non **abstract** declaration in C and C/m is visible in A.

Since C/m is visible in A and B is an interface, $lookup(A, B/m) = C$.

By Constraint 4.1.11, it follows that m has the same return type in C and in D and by property 2 above also in C and in B.

By Constraint 6.1.2, it follows that m throws more specific exceptions in C than in D and by property 3 above m throws more specific exceptions in C than in B.

In both cases we have shown that the dynamic lookup procedure finds a non-**abstract** method declaration and this declaration is consistent with the given declaration B/m.   □

The type safety theorem is also useful for proving the completeness of the ASM rules for Java. For example, there is no rule that can be applied in case that the current position *pos* is *firstPos* and *restbody* is *Norm*. There is no need for such a rule, because this case is not possible in a run of the ASM for a legal Java program due to invariant (norm) of Theorem 8.4.1. Invariant (norm) says that, if *restbody* is *Norm*, then the body of the current method would be *normal*. This is not allowed in Java.

There is also no rule for the case that *pos* is *firstPos* and *restbody* is *Break(l)* or *Continue(l)*. That this case is not possible follows from invariants (abr1) and (abr2) of Theorem 8.4.1, because the body of a method cannot be enclosed by a statement with label l.

Part II

Compilation of Java: The Trustful JVM

Every justification showing that a proposed compiler behaves well is relative to a definition of the semantics of source and target language. In Part I we have developed a mathematical (read: rigorous and platform independent) definition for an interpreter of Java programs, which captures the intuitive understanding Java programmers have of the semantics of their code. In this part we provide a mathematical model of an interpreter for the Java Virtual Machine, which formalizes the concepts presented in the JVM specification [23], as far as they are needed for the compilation of Java programs. We also extract from the JVM specification the definition of a scheme for the compilation of Java to JVM code and prove its correctness (see Theorem 14.1.1).

Since the JVM as used in this chapter is a machine to run compiled Java programs, we abstract here from checking the constraints on the JVM code (bytecode verification) and from dynamic loading. These aspects are discussed in Part III. The resulting *trustful* JVM runs well for statically loaded, well formed and well-typed JVM programs. If the translation is done following the scheme we define here, then we are able to prove that the generated target JVM program is also well formed and well typed. This proof however is deferred to Part III, where we introduce the checking component and dynamic loading.

The JVM specification and the definition of the compilation scheme in this chapter can be read independently from Part I—only the correctness proof relies upon an exact definition of the semantics of Java programs. We suppose the reader to have basic knowledge in modern programming language compilation.

We split the JVM and the compilation function into an incremental sequence of machines whose structure corresponds to the submachines we have introduced for Java. In Chapters 9 to 12 we define the sequence of successively extended JVM machines $JVM_\mathcal{I}$, $JVM_\mathcal{C}$, $JVM_\mathcal{O}$ and $JVM_\mathcal{E}$ for the compilation of programs from the imperative core $Java_\mathcal{I}$ of Java and its extensions $Java_\mathcal{C}$ (by classes and procedures), $Java_\mathcal{O}$ (by object-oriented features) and $Java_\mathcal{E}$ (by exceptions). As part of $JVM_\mathcal{C}$ we introduce the submachine *switchVM_C*— extended in $JVM_\mathcal{E}$ to *switchVM_E* and in $JVM_\mathcal{D}$ to *switchVM_D*—which takes care of frame stack manipulations, as opposed to the execution submachine which deals with operations on the current frame. We discuss here only the single threaded JVM, although our approach could easily include also multiple threads (see the Java model with threads in Chapter 7). In Chapter 13 we add native methods to $JVM_\mathcal{E}$.

9. The JVM$_\mathcal{I}$ submachine

In this chapter we define the JVM submachine JVM$_\mathcal{I}$ which can execute compiled Java$_\mathcal{I}$ programs. We also define a standard compilation scheme for translating Java$_\mathcal{I}$ programs to JVM$_\mathcal{I}$ code.

9.1 Dynamic semantics of the JVM$_\mathcal{I}$

The basic machine JVM$_\mathcal{I}$ is an untyped word-oriented stack-machine supporting all instructions for implementing a *while*-language. JVM$_\mathcal{I}$ provides instructions to load constants, to apply various unary and binary operators, to load and store a variable, to duplicate and to remove values, and to jump unconditionally or conditionally to a label. A JVM$_\mathcal{I}$ program is a sequence of instructions.

$$
\begin{aligned}
\textbf{data } \textit{Instr} = \ & \textit{Prim}(\textit{PrimOp}) \\
| \ & \textit{Load}(\textit{MoveType}, \textit{RegNo}) \\
| \ & \textit{Store}(\textit{MoveType}, \textit{RegNo}) \\
| \ & \textit{Dupx}(\textit{Size}, \textit{Size}) \\
| \ & \textit{Pop}(\textit{Size}) \\
| \ & \textit{Goto}(\textit{Offset}) \\
| \ & \textit{Cond}(\textit{PrimOp}, \textit{Offset}) \\
| \ & \textit{Halt}
\end{aligned}
$$

The universe *PrimOp* contains literals, unary and binary functions and relations. *Offset* and *Size* denote code offsets and the amount of words to move. These universes are synonyms for the universe of natural numbers *Nat*. And so is the universe *RegNo*, which stands in for variable locations in the JVM.

$$
\begin{aligned}
\textbf{type } \textit{Offset} &= \textit{Nat} \\
\textbf{type } \textit{Size} \ \ &= \textit{Nat} \\
\textbf{type } \textit{RegNo} &= \textit{Nat}
\end{aligned}
$$

Load and *Store* instructions are also parametrized by the types they move. Possible types of values in JVM$_\mathcal{I}$ are:

$$
\textbf{data } \textit{MoveType} = \texttt{int} \mid \texttt{long} \mid \texttt{float} \mid \texttt{double}
$$

Real JVM instructions can be obtained by expanding the (parameter) universes *PrimOp*, *Size*, and *MoveType*. Appendix C.8 defines this correspondence in detail. In fact the abstract instructions above already comprise about 150 of the 200 bytecode instructions of the JVM.

Environment. JVM$_\mathcal{I}$'s static environment consists only of the bytecode for the currently executed method.

> *code*: *Code*
> **type** *Code* = *Instr**

We assume for simplicity of exposition and without loss of generality that the last instruction of *code* is *Halt*. [1] In Chapter 10 we will write this function more precisely as parametrized (namely by the current *meth*od).

Values. JVM$_\mathcal{I}$ supports integers, floats, longs and doubles. Integers are 32-bit, longs are 64-bit signed two complement values. Floats are 32-bit, doubles are 64-bit IEEE 754 floating point numbers. The universe of *Word*s is supposed to hold 32-bit values.[2] 64-bit values are mapped to sequences of length two of words in an implementation dependent way. Thus JVM values are sequences of length one or two of words. The *Size* of a value is its length in words. The function *size* can also be applied on *MoveTypes*, in which case it returns the number of words to move.

JVM$_\mathcal{I}$ implements values and operations on the introduced data types in the usual way, the only exception being boolean. Booleans are represented as integers: 0 is used for *False*, and 1 for *True*. We denote by *JVMS*(*s*) the semantic value corresponding to syntactic arguments *s*.

State. JVM$_\mathcal{I}$'s dynamic state consists of a single frame, containing a program counter *pc*, registers *reg* (i.e., a local variable environment), and an operand stack *opd*. In the declaration below, the first column defines the state, and the second column defines the condition on the initial state.

pc : *Pc*	*pc* = 0
reg : *Map*(*RegNo*, *Word*)	*reg* = $\emptyset$
opd : *Word**	*opd* = [ ]
type *Pc* = *Nat*	

---

[1] *Halt* is not an instruction of the real JVM, but its introduction simplifies the exposition.

[2] The real JVM also supports bytes and shorts, which are 8-bit and 16-bit signed two complement values, and 16-bit uni-code characters. However, there are (almost) no instructions for these values—instead when such a value is read from or written to the store, it is automatically cast into an integer or truncated to the relevant size, respectively.

Fig. 9.1 Trustful execution of JVM$_\mathcal{I}$ instructions

---

$execVM_I(instr) =$
   case $instr$ **of**
       $Prim(p)$ $\rightarrow$ **let** $(opd', ws) = split(opd, argSize(p))$
                      if $p \in divMod \Rightarrow sndArgIsNotZero(ws)$ **then**
                          $opd := opd' \cdot JVMS(p, ws)$
                          $pc\;\; := pc + 1$
       $Dupx(s_1, s_2)$ $\rightarrow$ **let** $(opd', [ws_1, ws_2]) = splits(opd, [s_1, s_2])$
                      $opd := opd' \cdot ws_2 \cdot ws_1 \cdot ws_2$
                      $pc\;\; := pc + 1$
       $Pop(s)$ $\rightarrow$ **let** $(opd', ws) = split(opd, s)$
                      $opd := opd'$
                      $pc\;\; := pc + 1$
       $Load(t, x)$ $\rightarrow$ **if** $size(t) = 1$ **then** $opd := opd \cdot [reg(x)]$
                      else $opd := opd \cdot [reg(x), reg(x + 1)]$
                  $pc := pc + 1$
       $Store(t, x)$ $\rightarrow$ **let** $(opd', ws) = split(opd, size(t))$
                      if $size(t) = 1$ **then** $reg := reg \oplus \{(x, ws(0))\}$
                        else $reg := reg \oplus \{(x, ws(0)), (x + 1, ws(1))\}$
                      $opd := opd'$
                      $pc\;\; := pc + 1$
       $Goto(o)$ $\rightarrow$ $pc := o$
       $Cond(p, o)$ $\rightarrow$ **let** $(opd', ws) = split(opd, argSize(p))$
                      $opd := opd'$
                      if $JVMS(p, ws)$ **then** $pc := o$ **else** $pc := pc + 1$
       $Halt$ $\rightarrow$ $halt :=$ `"Halt"`

Rules. Fig. 9.1 specifies the dynamic semantics of JVM$_\mathcal{I}$ instructions by ASM rules. The *trustfulVM$_I$* halts, if the pc points to *Halt* where we update the dynamic function *halt* (see Remark 9.1.1 below). In the defensive VM and the diligent VM there are other reasons for halting. As long as the *trustfulVM$_I$* does not halt, it fires *execVM$_I$* rules.

$$trustfulVM_I = execVM_I(code(pc))$$

Remark 9.1.1. For the sake of brevity, we suppress notationally the main guard of all our machines, namely *halt* $=$ *undef*. As soon as *halt* gets a defined value (e.g. `"Halt"`, `"Verification failed"`, etc.) the machines stop executing, as do their executable versions.

The *execVM$_I$* rules define the effect of executing a single instruction. The *Prim(p)* instruction takes n values from the top of the operand stack, where n is determined using *argSize(p)* that returns the sum of the sizes of the parameters of p, e.g. $argSize(\texttt{iadd}) = 2$ and $argSize(\texttt{dadd}) = 4$. If p is an element of the *divMod* operator set (that denotes integer and long division and modulo operators) and the right operand is 0, then the execution of the instruction is undefined. Otherwise, the result of the semantic function

$JVMS(p, ws)$ applied on the popped values ws is pushed onto the operand stack. For instance the value of $JVMS(\mathtt{iadd}, [1, 2])$ is 3. The function $JVMS$ takes care of the semantic effect of all arithmetic and type conversion instructions of the real JVM [23]. The instruction Pop removes the top stack value. A $Dupx$ instruction duplicates the top value ws_2 and inserts the duplicate below the second value ws_1 on the stack. For example, the instruction $Dupx(0, 1)$ is the $\mathtt{dup}$ instruction of the real JVM. A $Load$ instruction loads the value stored under the location x on top of the stack. If x denotes a double word, the next two locations are pushed on top of the stack. A $Store$ instruction stores the top (double) word of the operand stack in the registers x (and $x + 1$). A $Goto$ instruction causes execution to jump to the next instruction determined by the provided parameter. The $Cond$ instruction is a conditional goto. If the relation for the values on top of the operand stack holds, execution continues at the specified instruction, otherwise execution proceeds with the next instruction.

9.2 Compilation of Java$_{\mathcal{I}}$

This section describes a standard scheme to translate a Java$_{\mathcal{I}}$ source language program, expressed by an abstract syntax tree, into a sequence of low-level instructions for the target machine JVM$_{\mathcal{I}}$. More efficient compilation schemes can be introduced by further refinement steps. By a simultaneous recursion we define four functions $\mathcal{B}_1$, $\mathcal{B}_0$, $\mathcal{E}$, $\mathcal{S}$ for the compilation of expressions and statements, where the expressions are treated differently depending on whether they are formed by non strict ("Boolean") or by strict operators. The definition uses a case distinction; the cases appearing in Fig. 9.2, 9.3, 9.4 are thought of as disjoint and ordered from top to bottom. To improve readability, we suppress the details of a consistent assignment of JVM variable numbers $\overline{x}$ to (occurrences of) Java variables x and of the generation of labels. We use functions $\mathcal{T}$ to return the type of (occurrences of) variables and expressions.

The compilation $\mathcal{E} \colon Exp \to Code$ of (occurrences of) Java$_{\mathcal{I}}$ expressions to JVM$_{\mathcal{I}}$ instructions yields a sequence of instructions which, as we will prove below, has the effect of storing the value of the expression on top of the operand stack. (For the proof we assume that JVM$_{\mathcal{I}}$ supports the same constants as Java$_{\mathcal{I}}$.) Executing $Prim(lit)$ pushes its argument on top of the stack, similarly for translating variables. In the compilation of variable assignments, the expression value is first duplicated before it is stored, because a $Store$ instruction consumes the topmost element of the operand stack.

Expressions which are used to describe the control flow of a program—namely $\mathtt{true}$, $\mathtt{false}$, expressions formed by negation or by the non strict logical primitives ($\mathtt{\&\&}$, $\mathtt{||}$), and if-then-else expressions—are translated using the functions $\mathcal{B}_1$, $\mathcal{B}_0 \colon (Exp, Label) \to Code$. These functions translate expressions in the context of a given target label l in such a way that if the evaluation of the given expression yields **true**, then the execution of the code compiled by $\mathcal{B}_1$ jumps to the provided label l, otherwise the execution continues at the next instruction that follows the compiled expression. Symmetrically for $\mathcal{B}_0$ and expressions evaluating to **false**. In particular for conditional expressions, in case the expression exp_0 evaluates to **true**, $\mathcal{B}_1$ sends the execution to continue at the label if$_1$ where the compilation of the then part e_1 starts; otherwise it sends the execution to continue where the compilation of the else part exp_2 starts. After the execution of either the then or the else part, if this part evaluates to **true**, the execution will continue at the given label lab, otherwise it will jump to the next instruction following the compilation of the if-then-else expression (instruction $Goto(\text{if}_2)$). For non-control flow expressions exp, the intended control flow effect of $\mathcal{B}_1$, $\mathcal{B}_0$ is achieved by adding after the compilation of exp a zero test conditioned jump to the given target label.

We illustrate the use of $\mathcal{B}_1$ for the compilation of negations. If the evaluation of an expression exp yields **true**, executing the $\mathcal{E}$-compilation of the negation of exp makes JVM$_\mathcal{I}$ jump to the label una$_1$ which is followed by an instruction pushing 0 (the JVM-value of the negation of exp) on the stack. Otherwise 1 is pushed on the stack and the execution is sent by a jump to the next instruction that follows the $\mathcal{E}$-compilation of the negation. The compilation of the other control flow expressions is similar. When compiling expressions which are formed by a strict operator, all the arguments are translated from left to right, followed by the application of the operator. Constant boolean expressions with value *True* (resp. *False*) are treated like the literal **true** (resp. **false**) in Fig. 9.3.

The compilation $\mathcal{S} \colon Stm \to Code$ of Java$_\mathcal{I}$ statements to JVM$_\mathcal{I}$ instructions takes a Java$_\mathcal{I}$ statement stm as input and produces an equivalent JVM$_\mathcal{I}$ instruction sequence as output. The instructions for any stm are generated in such a way that after their execution, the operand stack is reestablished to what it was when their execution had been started. The compilation of an empty statement produces no instructions. The compilation of an expression statement consists of the compilation of the expression followed by an additional *Pop* instruction, which erases the computed value from the top of the operand stack. The compilation of a block of statements results in the sequence of the compilation of these statements. The compilation of an if-then-else statement is similar to the one for conditional expressions. The compilation of a while statement starts with a jump to the label while$_1$, which is followed by the compilation of the condition. If this condition evaluates to **true**, the execution continues with the compiled body and is followed by testing the condition again. This compilation of a while statement needs only one conditional jump. The compilation of a labeled instruction generates continue and break labels which are used as target labels for compiling the corresponding **break** lab and **continue** lab statements.

Fig. 9.2 Compilation of Java$_\mathcal{I}$ expressions

$$
\begin{aligned}
\mathcal{E}(lit) &= Prim(lit) \\
\mathcal{E}(loc) &= Load(\mathcal{T}(loc), \overline{loc}) \\
\mathcal{E}(loc = exp) &= \mathcal{E}(exp) \cdot Dupx(0, size(\mathcal{T}(exp))) \cdot Store(\mathcal{T}(exp), \overline{loc}) \\
\mathcal{E}(!\ exp) &= \mathcal{B}_1(exp, \text{una}_1) \cdot Prim(1) \cdot Goto(\text{una}_2) \cdot \\
&\quad\ \text{una}_1 \cdot Prim(0) \cdot \text{una}_2 \\
\mathcal{E}(uop\ exp) &= \mathcal{E}(exp) \cdot Prim(uop) \\
\mathcal{E}(exp_1\ bop\ exp_2) &= \mathcal{E}(exp_1) \cdot \mathcal{E}(exp_2) \cdot Prim(bop) \\
\mathcal{E}(exp_0\ ?\ exp_1\ :\ exp_2) &= \mathcal{B}_1(exp_0, \text{if}_1) \cdot \mathcal{E}(exp_2) \cdot Goto(\text{if}_2) \cdot \text{if}_1 \cdot \mathcal{E}(exp_1) \cdot \text{if}_2
\end{aligned}
$$

Fig. 9.3 Compilation of Java$_\mathcal{I}$ expressions for control flow

$$
\begin{aligned}
\mathcal{B}_1(\mathbf{true}, lab) &= Goto(lab) \\
\mathcal{B}_1(\mathbf{false}, lab) &= \epsilon \\
\mathcal{B}_1(!\ exp, lab) &= \mathcal{B}_0(exp, lab) \\
\mathcal{B}_1(exp_0\ ?\ exp_1\ :\ exp_2, lab) &= \mathcal{B}_1(exp_0, \text{if}_1) \cdot \mathcal{B}_1(exp_2, lab) \cdot Goto(\text{if}_2) \cdot \\
&\quad\ \text{if}_1 \cdot \mathcal{B}_1(exp_1, lab) \cdot \text{if}_2 \\
\mathcal{B}_1(exp, lab) &= \mathcal{E}(exp) \cdot Cond(\mathbf{ifne}, lab) \\[1em]
\mathcal{B}_0(\mathbf{true}, lab) &= \epsilon \\
\mathcal{B}_0(\mathbf{false}, lab) &= Goto(lab) \\
\mathcal{B}_0(!\ exp, lab) &= \mathcal{B}_1(exp, lab) \\
\mathcal{B}_0(exp_0\ ?\ exp_1\ :\ exp_2, lab) &= \mathcal{B}_1(exp_0, \text{if}_1) \cdot \mathcal{B}_0(exp_2, lab) \cdot Goto(\text{if}_2) \cdot \\
&\quad\ \text{if}_1 \cdot \mathcal{B}_0(exp_1, lab) \cdot \text{if}_2 \\
\mathcal{B}_0(exp, lab) &= \mathcal{E}(exp) \cdot Cond(\mathbf{ifeq}, lab)
\end{aligned}
$$

Fig. 9.4 Compilation of Java$_\mathcal{I}$ statements

$$
\begin{aligned}
\mathcal{S}(;) &= \epsilon \\
\mathcal{S}(exp;) &= \mathcal{E}(exp) \cdot Pop(size(\mathcal{T}(exp))) \\
\mathcal{S}(\{stm_1 \ldots stm_n\}) &= \mathcal{S}(stm_1) \cdot \ldots \cdot \mathcal{S}(stm_n) \\
\mathcal{S}(\mathbf{if}\ (exp)\ stm_1\ \mathbf{else}\ stm_2) &= \mathcal{B}_1(exp, \text{if}_1) \cdot \mathcal{S}(stm_2) \cdot Goto(\text{if}_2) \cdot \\
&\quad\ \text{if}_1 \cdot \mathcal{S}(stm_1) \cdot \text{if}_2 \\
\mathcal{S}(\mathbf{while}\ (exp)\ stm) &= Goto(\text{while}_1) \cdot \text{while}_2 \cdot \mathcal{S}(stm) \cdot \\
&\quad\ \text{while}_1 \cdot \mathcal{B}_1(exp, \text{while}_2) \\
\mathcal{S}(lab:\ stm) &= lab_c \cdot \mathcal{S}(stm) \cdot lab_b \\
\mathcal{S}(\mathbf{continue}\ lab;) &= Goto(lab_c) \\
\mathcal{S}(\mathbf{break}\ lab;) &= Goto(lab_b)
\end{aligned}
$$

Why do we use the functions $\mathcal{B}_1$ and $\mathcal{B}_0$ for compiling boolean test expressions and not the function $\mathcal{E}$? A simple compiler could compile an if-statement in the following way:

$$\mathcal{S}(\texttt{if } (exp)\, stm_1 \texttt{ else } stm_2) =$$
$$\mathcal{E}(exp) \cdot Cond(\texttt{ifne}, \text{if}_1) \cdot \mathcal{S}(stm_2) \cdot Goto(\text{if}_2) \cdot \text{if}_1 \cdot \mathcal{S}(stm_1) \cdot \text{if}_2$$

It generates the code for the expression exp using the function $\mathcal{E}$. If the result of the test is *True* (different from integer 0), then control jumps to the code of stm_2. Otherwise, stm_1 is executed.

Semantically the simple compilation scheme is correct. The problem is that code generated by the simple scheme is not always accepted by the bytecode verifier (Chapter 17), as shown in the following example (see also Example 16.5.4):

Example ($\leadsto$ CD) 9.2.1. Consider the following method:

```
boolean m(boolean x, boolean y) {
  boolean z;
  if (x && (z = y))
    return z;
  else
    return x;
}
```

According to the rules of definite assignment in Sect. 8.3, the variable z is definitely assigned when it is used in the return statement, hence the program is a legal Java program. When we compile the method using the equivalence

x && (z = y) $\equiv$ x ? z = y : false,

we obtain the following two variants:

Simple compilation	Compilation with $\mathcal{B}_i$
$Load(\texttt{int}, x)$	$Load(\texttt{int}, x)$
$Cond(\texttt{ifne}, A)$	$Cond(\texttt{ifne}, A)$
$Prim(0)$	$Goto(B)$
$Goto(B)$	$A: Load(\texttt{int}, y)$
$A: Load(\texttt{int}, y)$	$Dupx(0,1)$
$Dupx(0,1)$	$Store(\texttt{int}, z)$
$Store(\texttt{int}, z)$	$Cond(\texttt{ifne}, L)$
$B: Cond(\texttt{ifne}, L)$	$B: Load(\texttt{int}, x)$
$Load(\texttt{int}, x)$	$Return(\texttt{int})$
$Return(\texttt{int})$	$L: Load(\texttt{int}, z)$
$L: Load(\texttt{int}, z)$	$Return(\texttt{int})$
$Return(\texttt{int})$	

The bytecode in the right column, generated using the functions $\mathcal{B}_i$, is accepted by the verifier, whereas the bytecode in the left column, generated using the simple scheme, is rejected. The reason for the rejection is that the bytecode verifier does not treat the truth value *False* (generated by $Prim(0)$) in a special way, as the rules for definite assignment do in Table 8.4. The bytecode verifier cannot deduce that, on the left-hand side, the variable z has an assigned value at label L, because there exists a path from the first instruction to label L which does not store any value in z.

10. The procedural extension JVM$_{\mathcal{C}}$ of JVM$_{\mathcal{I}}$

In this chapter we extend the machine JVM$_{\mathcal{I}}$ to a JVM submachine JVM$_{\mathcal{C}}$ which can execute compiled Java$_{\mathcal{C}}$ programs. The extension consists in adding rules for handling class variables, and for method invocation and return. We introduce a submachine *switch VM$_C$* which takes care of frame stack manipulations—upon method invocation or return and upon implicit class initialization—and which will be extended in *switch VM$_E$* for frame manipulations due to capturing exceptions. We also extend the Java$_{\mathcal{I}}$-to–JVM$_{\mathcal{I}}$ compilation scheme by translating the new Java$_{\mathcal{C}}$ expressions and statements to JVM$_{\mathcal{C}}$ code.

10.1 Dynamic semantics of the JVM$_{\mathcal{C}}$

JVM$_{\mathcal{C}}$ extends JVM$_{\mathcal{I}}$ by instructions to read and write class fields, to invoke and to return from class methods and to initialize classes. Methods can either return nothing (i.e., they return void) or they return real values like integers.

> **data** *Instr* = ...
> | *GetStatic*(*Type*, *Class* / *Field*)
> | *PutStatic*(*Type*, *Class* / *Field*)
> | *InvokeStatic*(*Type*, *Class* / *MSig*)
> | *Return*(*MoveType*)
>
> **data** *MoveType* = ...
> | void

We define in *exec VM$_C$* a rule for each of the new instructions. We also introduce a submachine *switch VM$_C$* which takes care of the context switch upon calling or returning from a method. This separation of method call and return from the execution of instructions in the method body is extended in Part III to separate the instruction execution proper from checking concerns in the refinement of the trustful to a defensive machine and to the diligent machine coming with a bytecode verifier.

As long as we only consider statically linked programs, classes are denoted by their class name. Field and method references are pairs of class and field or method names.

type $MSig = (Meth, Type^*)$

The abstract universes *Field* and *Meth* stand for field and method identifiers. *Type* denotes the types supported by the JVM. The JVM supports overloading. Fields can have the same identifier, as long as the classes they are declared in are different. Methods within the same class can also be overloaded, as long as the argument types differ.[1]

We use selector functions *classNm*, *fieldNm*, *methSig*, *methNm* and *argTypes* and overload selectors, as long as their meaning is not ambiguous. For instance *classNm* is used to select the class name of a field reference as well as of a method reference. Similarly we use *methNm* to get the method identifier of a method reference. We write tuples of field and method references in the form c/f and c/m, where c, f and m are elements of the universes *Class*, *Field* and *MSig*, respectively. Likewise we write method signatures as $m(ts)$, where m and ts denote a method identifier and a type sequence, respectively.

Environment. JVM$_\mathcal{C}$ programs are executed with respect to a static environment *cEnv*, which is a mapping of classes and interfaces to class files. (The following description does not distinguish interfaces and classes, unless explicitly stated.) Each class file provides for every class its name, its kind (whether it is a class or an interface), its superclass (if there is any, otherwise *super* is undefined), the set of the interfaces the class implements, a table for fields, and a table for methods. In JVM$_\mathcal{C}$ every member of a class file is static; this is extended in JVM$_\mathcal{O}$, which also supports instances.

Class files do not include definitions for fields or methods provided by any superclass, unless the definitions are overwritten.

$cEnv$: $Class \to ClassFile$

$$
\begin{aligned}
\textbf{data } ClassFile = CFile(\ &classNm &&: Class, \\
&isInterface &&: Bool, \\
&modifiers &&: Powerset(Modifier), \\
&super &&: Class, \\
&implements &&: Powerset(Class), \\
&fields &&: FieldTab, \\
&methods &&: MethTab)
\end{aligned}
$$

Field declarations have a type and a set of modifiers. The type of a method is its result type, which can be void. If a method is implemented in the class, the function *code* defines a nonempty sequence of instructions, otherwise the sequence is empty. An implemented method can include an exception table. Exception handling is introduced in Chapter 12. Methods can have constraints on the maximum depth of their operand stacks and the number of

---

[1] The types of fields and return types of methods are not used. However, types will play an important role when considering the security aspects of the JVM. This is the subject of Part III.

registers they use ($maxOpd$ and $maxReg$). This information is only exploited in the secure JVM, which is the subject of Part III.

> **type** $FieldTab = Map(Field, FDec)$
> **type** $MethTab = Map(MSig, MDec)$
>
> **data** $FDec = FDec(modifiers : Powerset(Modifier),$
> $\qquad\qquad\qquad type \qquad : Type)$
>
> **data** $MDec = MDec(modifiers \qquad\qquad : Powerset(Modifier),$
> $\qquad\qquad\qquad\quad returnType \qquad : Type,$
> $\qquad\qquad\qquad\quad code \qquad\qquad\quad : Code,$
> $\qquad\qquad\qquad\quad excs \qquad\qquad\quad : Exc^*,$
> $\qquad\qquad\qquad\quad (maxOpd, maxReg) : (Nat, Nat))$

We assume that for any class file selector there is a derived function having the same name, that suppresses the class environment $cEnv$ and abbreviates the data path to select the corresponding component. For instance, the overloaded function $super : Class \rightarrow Class$ returns the direct superclass of the specified class, that is $super(c) = super(cEnv(c))$. Another example is the derived function $code(c/m)$ that returns the code of the given method, that is $code(c/m) = code(methods(cEnv(c))(m))$.

State. JVM$_C$ adds procedural abstraction in the form of class methods. Due to their presence we have not only a single JVM$_\mathcal{I}$ frame (pc, reg, opd) but many of them of type

> **type** $Frame = (Pc, Map(RegNo, Word), Word^*, Class/MSig)$

which are stored in a stack. Note that the frame information is enriched by a fourth component, that always describes the method to which the frame belongs. The dynamic function $stack$ holds the stack of active method incarnations. The dynamic function $meth$ holds the currently active method.

> $meth : Class/MSig$
> $stack : Frame^*$
> $meth = (\texttt{Object/<entrypoint>}())$
> $stack = [\,]$

The first method to execute is $\texttt{Object/<entrypoint>}()$. Its code is:

> $Prim(\texttt{null})$
> $InvokeStatic(\texttt{void}, Main/\texttt{main}(\texttt{String}))$
> $Halt$

where $Main$ is a not furthermore specified class (in ASM terminology: a static 0-ary function) given by the invoker of the application.[2]

---

[2] Conceptually, the internal method is not needed. It can be substituted by corresponding conditions on the initialization.

Method invocation and return as well as implicit class initialization (see below) change the current frame (the context). In order to obtain a uniform treatment of checking and verifying of methods (see Part III), we explicitly separate here method transfer from the execution of instructions within method bodies. For this purpose we introduce a new universe

> **data** *Switch* = *Noswitch*
> | *Call*(*Class*/*MSig*, *Args*)
> | *Result*(*Val*)
> | *InitClass*(*Class*)

> **type** *Args* = *Word**
> **type** *Val* = *Word**

that comes together with a dynamic function *switch* characterizing the context switch the machine is currently performing. The machine either performs no switch (*Noswitch*–the initial value) or it calls (*Call*) or returns (*Result*) from a method, or it initializes (*InitClass*) a class.

> *switch*: *Switch*
> *switch* = *Noswitch*

The JVM uses symbolic field and method references to support binary compatibility, see also [18]. As a consequence, the calculation of field offsets and of method offsets is implementation dependent. Therefore, we keep the class field access as abstract as in Java (see Chapter 4) and define the storage function for class fields by the same abstract function *globals* which initially holds the default value for each static field. The environment based function *staticFields*(*c*) returns the static fields of a class *c*, the function *defaultVal*(*f*) returns *null* for fields holding references, and 0 otherwise. (Depending on the type of the field different representations of 0 are chosen.)

> *globals*: *Class*/*Field* → *Val*
> ∀ *c* ∈ *dom*(*cEnv*) : ∀ *f* ∈ *staticFields*(*c*) : *globals*(*f*) = *defaultVal*(*f*)

Before a class can be used it must be loaded, linked, and its class initializers must be executed. Loading and linking is introduced in Chapter 18. At the JVM level class initializers appear as class methods with the special name `<clinit>`. In JVM$_C$ a class can either be linked or initialized, similarly to the Java model in Chapter 4 which also keeps track of the initialization state of a class so that we can repeat the definition here:

> **data** *ClassState* = *Linked* | *Initialized*

The JVM also comes with a dynamic function *classState*, which records the current class state. Initially all classes, except the root class `Object`, are *Linked*. The class `Object` is initially initialized.

Fig. 10.1 Trustful execution of JVM$_C$ instructions

$trustfulScheme_C(exec\,VM, switch\,VM) =$
  if $switch = Noswitch$ **then**
    $exec\,VM(code(pc))$
  else
    $switch\,VM$

$exec\,VM_C(instr) =$
  $exec\,VM_I(instr)$
  case $instr$ **of**
    $GetStatic(\_, c/f) \rightarrow$ **if** $initialized(c)$ **then**
                    $opd := opd \cdot globals(c/f)$
                    $pc\ \ := pc + 1$
                else $switch := InitClass(c)$
    $PutStatic(\_, c/f) \rightarrow$ **if** $initialized(c)$ **then**
                    let $(opd', ws) = split(opd, size(c/f))$
                    $globals(c/f) := ws$
                    $opd := opd'$
                    $pc\ \ := pc + 1$
                else $switch := InitClass(c)$
    $InvokeStatic(\_, c/m) \rightarrow$ **if** $initialized(c)$ **then**
                        let $(opd', ws) = split(opd, argSize(c/m))$
                        $opd\ \ \ := opd'$
                        $switch := Call(c/m, ws)$
                    else $switch := InitClass(c)$
    $Return(t) \rightarrow$ **let** $(opd', ws) = split(opd, size(t))$
                $switch := Result(ws)$

$classState: Class \rightarrow ClassState$
$\forall\, c \in dom(cEnv) \setminus \{\texttt{Object}\} : classState(c) = Linked$
$classState(\texttt{Object}) = Initialized$

A class is initialized, if its class state is *Initialized*. Formally:

$initialized(c) = (classState(c) = Initialized)$

Rules. Fig. 10.1 defines $trustfulScheme_C$. The scheme can be read as a macro with two parameters $exec\,VM$ and $switch\,VM$. For JVM$_C$ we instantiate the parameters with $exec\,VM_C$ and $switch\,VM_C$.

$trustful\,VM_C = trustfulScheme_C(exec\,VM_C, switch\,VM_C)$

As long as a context switch is requested, $switch\,VM_C$ rules fire. Otherwise $exec\,VM_C$ rules are executed.

We first explain the new $exec\,VM_C$ rules for the case that the referenced class of the field or method is already initialized. A *GetStatic* instruction loads, on top of the operand stack, the value (one or two words) which is

Fig. 10.2 Trustful switch machine

$$
\begin{aligned}
&switch\,VM_C = \\
&\quad \textbf{case } switch \textbf{ of} \\
&\qquad Call(meth, args) \rightarrow \textbf{if } \neg isAbstract(meth) \textbf{ then} \\
&\qquad\qquad\qquad\qquad\qquad\quad pushFrame(meth, args) \\
&\qquad\qquad\qquad\qquad\qquad\quad switch := Noswitch \\
&\qquad Result(res) \;\;\rightarrow \textbf{if } implicitCall(meth) \textbf{ then } popFrame(0, [\,]) \\
&\qquad\qquad\qquad\qquad\quad \textbf{else } popFrame(1, res) \\
&\qquad\qquad\qquad\qquad switch := Noswitch \\
&\qquad InitClass(c) \rightarrow \textbf{if } classState(c) = Linked \textbf{ then} \\
&\qquad\qquad\qquad\qquad\quad classState(c) := Initialized \\
&\qquad\qquad\qquad\qquad\quad \textbf{forall } f \in staticFields(c) \\
&\qquad\qquad\qquad\qquad\qquad globals(c/f) := default(type(c/f)) \\
&\qquad\qquad\qquad\qquad\quad pushFrame(c/\texttt{<clinit>}()) \\
&\qquad\qquad\qquad\qquad\quad \textbf{if } c = \texttt{Object} \vee initialized(super(c)) \textbf{ then} \\
&\qquad\qquad\qquad\qquad\qquad switch := Noswitch \\
&\qquad\qquad\qquad\qquad\quad \textbf{else} \\
&\qquad\qquad\qquad\qquad\qquad switch := InitClass(super(c))
\end{aligned}
$$

stored under the field in the global environment. A *PutStatic* instruction stores the top (two) word(s) of the operand stack in the global environment at the given field. An *InvokeStatic* instruction pops the arguments from the operand stack and triggers a context switch. The *switch VM$_C$* machine in Fig. 10.2 then stores the current frame in the frame stack and places the arguments of the invoked method in the registers of the new frame, and execution continues at the first instruction of the new method[3]. When *exec VM$_C$* interprets *Return*, it takes the required number of words (0, 1 or 2) from the top of the operand stack and triggers a context switch. Upon returning from a class initializer (*implicitCall*), no return value is passed and *switch VM$_C$* makes the execution continue with the frame and the instruction which triggered the class initialization; otherwise *switch VM$_C$* discards the topmost frame, pushes the returned words onto the invoker's operand stack and increments the invoker's pc. We therefore define (see the refinement for class loading method `<cload>` in Sect. 18.3.2):

$$implicitCall(m) = methNm(m) = \texttt{"<clinit>"}$$

Pushing and popping frames, as required by the *switch VM$_C$*, are defined by the following rules:

$$
\begin{aligned}
&pushFrame(newMeth, args) = \\
&\quad stack := stack \cdot [(pc, reg, opd, meth)] \\
&\quad meth := newMeth \\
&\quad pc \quad := 0 \\
&\quad opd \quad := [\,] \\
&\quad reg \quad := makeRegs(args)
\end{aligned}
$$

---

[3] In Fig. 12.1 an error is raised should the invoked method happen to be abstract.

Fig. 10.3 Compilation of Java$_C$ expressions/statements

$$\mathcal{E}(c.f) \qquad = GetStatic(\mathcal{T}(c/f), c/f)$$
$$\mathcal{E}(c.f = exp) = \mathcal{E}(exp) \cdot Dupx(0, size(\mathcal{T}(exp))) \cdot PutStatic(\mathcal{T}(c/f), c/f)$$
$$\mathcal{E}(c.m(exps)) = \mathcal{E}(exps) \cdot InvokeStatic(\mathcal{T}(c/m), c/m)$$

$$\mathcal{E}((exp_1, \ldots, exp_n)) = \mathcal{E}(exp_1) \cdot \ldots \cdot \mathcal{E}(exp_n)$$

$$\mathcal{S}(\texttt{static } stm) = \mathcal{S}(stm)$$
$$\mathcal{S}(\texttt{return};) \qquad = Return(\texttt{void})$$
$$\mathcal{S}(\texttt{return } exp;) = \mathcal{E}(exp) \cdot Return(\mathcal{T}(exp))$$

$$popFrame(offset, result) =$$
$$\quad \textbf{let } (stack', [(pc', reg', opd', meth')]) = split(stack, 1)$$
$$\quad pc \quad := pc' + offset$$
$$\quad reg \quad := reg'$$
$$\quad opd \quad := opd' \cdot result$$
$$\quad meth := meth'$$
$$\quad stack := stack'$$

The function *makeRegs* converts an argument sequence to a finite mapping:

$$makeRegs(args) = \{(l, v) \mid (l, v) \in zip([0..length(args) - 1], args)\}$$

Initialization starts, that is a class initialization method `<clinit>` is implicitly called by triggering a context switch to *InitClass*(c), when the class referred to in a *Get-*, *Put-* or *InvokeStatic* instruction is not initialized. Before a class is initialized, its superclass has to be initialized, if there is any. Interfaces can be initialized at this time, although this is not specified in the Java language reference manual [18]. This strategy is reflected by the *InitClass*(c) rule in *switchVM$_C$*. It pushes `<clinit>` frames on the stack and at the same time records that the class is initialized. The machine *switchVM$_C$* executes this rule until in the inheritance hierarchy either the class `Object` or an initialized superclass is reached. Since the class state is set to initialized as soon as a frame is pushed, the finiteness of the inheritance hierarchy implies that this recursive initialization always terminates.[4]

10.2 Compilation of Java$_C$

The compilation of Java$_I$ expressions is extended by defining the compilation of class field access, class field assignment, and by the compilation of calls of class methods. This extension refers to the compiling function $\mathcal{E}$, see Fig. 10.3. The compilation of class field access and assignment follows the

---

[4] In a concurrent setting, an additional class state variant is needed, see Chapter 7.

pattern for local variable access and assignment. For calls of class methods, first all arguments are pushed on the stack from left to right followed by an *InvokeStatic* instruction.

Likewise we extend the compiling function $\mathcal{S}$ to translate static initializations and **return** statements.

11. The object-oriented extension JVM$_\mathcal{O}$ of JVM$_\mathcal{C}$

In this chapter we extend the machine JVM$_\mathcal{C}$ to a JVM submachine JVM$_\mathcal{O}$ which can execute compiled Java$_\mathcal{O}$ programs. We also extend the Java$_\mathcal{C}$-to–JVM$_\mathcal{C}$ compilation scheme by translating the new Java$_\mathcal{O}$ expressions and statements to JVM$_\mathcal{O}$ code.

11.1 Dynamic semantics of the JVM$_\mathcal{O}$

In this section we extend the machine JVM$_\mathcal{C}$ to JVM$_\mathcal{O}$. This machine handles the result of the compilation of object-oriented features of Java programs, namely instances, instance creation and initialization, instance field access, instance method calls, type casts and null pointers. Therefore the extension consists in adding to the *execVM$_C$* rules for the new instructions of JVM$_\mathcal{O}$ and extending the *Store*, *Load* and *Return* instructions to handle addresses.

> **data** *Instr* = ...
> | *New(Class)*
> | *GetField(Type, Class/Field)*
> | *PutField(Type, Class/Field)*
> | *InstanceOf(Type)*
> | *Checkcast(Type)*
> | *InvokeSpecial(Type, Class/MSig)*
> | *InvokeVirtual(Type, Class/MSig)*
>
> **data** *MoveType* = ...
> | addr

JVM$_\mathcal{O}$ distinguishes two kinds of instance method calls. If the method is early bound (*InvokeSpecial*), the class which implements the method is embedded in the method reference. In the case of late binding (*InvokeVirtual*), the method must be looked up dynamically.

Environment. JVM$_\mathcal{O}$ uses the same environment and abstract class file as JVM$_\mathcal{C}$. However, instance fields and instance methods—in opposite to class fields and class methods—are not static but dynamic. Java constructors appear in the JVM as instance initialization methods with the special name `<init>`.

Fig. 11.1 Trustful execution of JVM$_\mathcal{O}$ instructions

$execVM_O(instr) =$
  $execVM_C(instr)$
  case $instr$ **of**
    $New(c) \rightarrow$
      if $initialized(c)$ **then create** r
        $heap(r) := Object(c, \{(f, defaultVal(f)) \mid f \in instanceFields(c)\})$
        $opd := opd \cdot [r]$
        $pc := pc + 1$
      else $switch := InitClass(c)$
    $GetField(\_, c/f) \rightarrow$ **let** $(opd', [r]) = split(opd, 1)$
                            if $r \neq null$ **then**
                                $opd := opd' \cdot getField(r, c/f)$
                                $pc := pc + 1$
    $PutField(\_, c/f) \rightarrow$ **let** $(opd', [r] \cdot ws) = split(opd, 1 + size(c/f))$
                            if $r \neq null$ **then**
                                $setField(r, c/f, ws)$
                                $pc := pc + 1$
                                $opd := opd'$
    $InvokeSpecial(\_, c/m) \rightarrow$
      let $(opd', [r] \cdot ws) = split(opd, 1 + argSize(c/m))$
      if $r \neq null$ **then**
        $opd := opd'$
        $switch := Call(c/m, [r] \cdot ws)$
    $InvokeVirtual(\_, c/m) \rightarrow$
      let $(opd', [r] \cdot ws) = split(opd, 1 + argSize(c/m))$
      if $r \neq null$ **then**
        $opd := opd'$
        $switch := Call(lookup(classOf(r), c/m), [r] \cdot ws)$

    $InstanceOf(c) \rightarrow$ **let** $(opd', [r]) = split(opd, 1)$
                        $opd := opd' \cdot (r \neq null \wedge classOf(r) \sqsubseteq c)$
                        $pc := pc + 1$
    $Checkcast(c) \rightarrow$ **let** $r = top(opd)$
                        if $r = null \vee classOf(r) \sqsubseteq c$ **then**
                            $pc := pc + 1$

Values. References uniquely denote instances and belong to the abstract universe *Ref*, which is assumed to be a subset of *Word*. We assume that also *null* is an element of *Word*.

State. JVM$_\mathcal{O}$ memorizes the class of an instance and the values of instance fields in the heap. The heap is structured as in Java$_\mathcal{O}$.

data $Heap = Object(Class, Map(Class/Field, Val))$

$heap: Ref \rightarrow Heap$

Two derived functions *classOf* and *getField* access the heap to select the class of the instance and the values of its fields. The rule *setField* is used to assign to an instance field, see Chapter 5 for the definition.

Rules. The *trustfulVM* for JVM$_\mathcal{O}$ is the one for JVM$_\mathcal{C}$ extended with the new *execVM$_O$* rules appearing in Fig. 11.1.

$$trustfulVM_O = trustfulScheme_C(execVM_O, switchVM_C)$$

If upon executing a *New* instruction the referenced class is initialized, a fresh reference $r \notin dom(heap)$ is allocated. The class of the reference is set to the given class with its instance fields set to the *default* values. The new reference is pushed on the operand stack.[1] A *GetField* instruction pops the target reference from the stack and pushes the value of the field, determined using the function *getField*, from the dynamic store on the operand stack. A *PutField* instruction pops a value and the target reference from the stack; using the rule $setField(r, c/f, ws)$ it sets the dynamic store at the point of the target reference and the given field to the popped value. The instructions *InvokeSpecial* and *InvokeVirtual* pop from the stack the arguments and the target reference (which denotes the instance whose method is called). The class which implements the method is determined as follows: If the method is early bound (*InvokeSpecial*), the class specified by the instruction parameter is selected, otherwise the method is late bound (*InvokeVirtual*) and the implementing class is looked up dynamically, starting at the class of the given reference. (The function *lookup* returns, starting at the given class, the first (super) class for the given method reference that implements this method, see Sect. 5.1.8.) The arguments for the invoked method are stored in the registers of the new stack frame, starting at the target reference which is placed in $reg(0)$. Execution continues at the first instruction of the new method. An *InstanceOf* instruction pops a reference from the operand stack. If the reference is not *null* and compatible with the required class, the integer 1 is pushed on the operand stack, otherwise 0 is pushed. A *Checkcast* instruction validates that the top value on the stack is an instance of the given class.

11.2 Compilation of Java$_\mathcal{O}$

We extend here the compilation of Java$_\mathcal{C}$ expressions to the new Java$_\mathcal{O}$ expressions, see Fig. 11.2. The reference **this** is implemented as the distinguished local variable with register number 0. Expressions which create new instances are compiled in such a way that first an uninitialized object is created. This object is then duplicated so that after calling the constructor for the initialization of the object—this call consumes the topmost stack element—one

---

[1] For the checking mechanism in the defensive JVM$_\mathcal{O}$ (Fig. 15.4) we will refine the *New*(c)-rule by providing the to be checked information on the initialization status for the newly created reference to an object of class c.

Fig. 11.2 Compilation of Java$_\mathcal{O}$ expressions

$$
\begin{aligned}
\mathcal{E}(\texttt{this}) &= Load(\texttt{addr}, 0) \\
\mathcal{E}(\texttt{new } c) &= New(c) \cdot Dupx(0, 1) \\
\mathcal{E}(exp.c/f) &= \mathcal{E}(exp) \cdot GetField(\mathcal{T}(c/f), c/f) \\
\mathcal{E}(exp_1.c/f = exp_2) &= \mathcal{E}(exp_1) \cdot \mathcal{E}(exp_2) \cdot Dupx(1, size(\mathcal{T}(c/f))) \cdot \\
&\quad PutField(\mathcal{T}(c/f), c/f) \\
\mathcal{E}(exp.c/m(exps)) &= \mathcal{E}(exp) \cdot \mathcal{E}(exps) \cdot \\
&\quad \textbf{case } callKind(exp.c/m) \textbf{ of} \\
&\qquad Virtual \rightarrow InvokeVirtual(\mathcal{T}(c/m), c/m) \\
&\qquad Super \;\;\rightarrow InvokeSpecial(\mathcal{T}(c/m), c/m) \\
&\qquad Special \rightarrow InvokeSpecial(\mathcal{T}(c/m), c/m) \\
\\
\mathcal{E}(exp \texttt{ instanceof } c) &= \mathcal{E}(exp) \cdot InstanceOf(c) \\
\mathcal{E}((c)exp) &= \mathcal{E}(exp) \cdot Checkcast(c)
\end{aligned}
$$

reference to the new object is left on the stack. The compilation of instance field access and assignment is similar to the compilation of static fields (see Chap. 9), except that first the target reference must be pushed on the stack. For instance method calls, the target reference can be accessed in the caller using register number 0. Reference type cast and **instanceof** expressions are translated like unary operators (see Chap. 9) using the corresponding specific JVM instructions. The literal **null** is compiled into the instruction $Prim(\texttt{null})$.

12. The exception-handling extension JVM$_\mathcal{E}$ of JVM$_\mathcal{O}$

In this chapter we extend the machine JVM$_\mathcal{O}$ to a JVM submachine JVM$_\mathcal{E}$ which can execute compiled Java$_\mathcal{E}$ programs. This includes extending the submachine $switchVM_C$ to $switchVM_E$ which copes with frame stack manipulations due to exception handling. We also extend the Java$_\mathcal{O}$-to-JVM$_\mathcal{O}$ compilation scheme by translating the new Java$_\mathcal{E}$ statements to JVM$_\mathcal{E}$ code.

12.1 Dynamic semantics of the JVM$_\mathcal{E}$

In the JVM exceptions are objects that can be thrown and caught. JVM$_\mathcal{E}$ extends JVM$_\mathcal{O}$ by instructions dealing with exceptions, namely to raise an exception, to jump to and to return from subroutines.

> **data** $Instr = \ldots$
> $\qquad | \;\; Athrow$
> $\qquad | \;\; Jsr(\mathit{Offset})$
> $\qquad | \;\; Ret(\mathit{RegNo})$

The extension JVM$_\mathcal{E}$ of JVM$_\mathcal{O}$ consists in adding to the $execVM_O$ a rule for each of the error handling instructions and in adding to $switchVM_C$ a new rule which describes the context switch when an exception is thrown.

> $trustfulVM_E = trustfulScheme_C(execVM_E, switchVM_E)$

Environment. To implement the try/catch construct of Java, JVM$_\mathcal{E}$ provides exception tables. They list the exceptions of a method. When an exception is raised, these tables are searched for the handler.

> **data** $Exc = Exc(\mathit{from} \quad : Pc,$
> $\qquad\qquad\quad\; upto \quad\; : Pc,$
> $\qquad\qquad\quad\; handle : Pc,$
> $\qquad\qquad\quad\; type \quad\;\; : Class)$

Any quadruple (f, u, h, t) describes the range of instructions $\{f..u-1\}$ where an exception is handled that is compatible with t.[1]

---

[1] In the real JVM if the exception entry describes a finally block, the *type* component is undefined. We assume that the corresponding class name is *Throwable*. Since any exception is a subclass of *Throwable*, this definition has the desired effect.

When an exception is raised, the run-time system searches the exception table of the current method. If no handler is found, the frame of the current method is discarded and the invoker frame is re-instantiated to continue the search for an exception handler. If a handler is found, the operand stack is cleared and the reference of the exception is pushed onto the stack. The execution continues from the address of the handler (within the current method and with the current register values). This propagation of exceptions terminates since we assume that *Main* has a "default" exception handler. It catches any exception and points to *Halt*. Its exception table is $[(0, 2, 2, \texttt{Throwable})]$.

State. Exception handling modifies the frame stack. The universe *Switch* is extended to signal the handling of a thrown exception:

data $Switch = \ldots \mid Throw(Ref) \mid ThrowInit(Ref)$

When an exception occurs in a `<clinit>` method the *switch* will be set to *ThrowInit* and the method's class must be marked as *Unusable*. We extend the universe *ClassState* as follows:

data $ClassState = \ldots \mid Unusable$

$unusable(c) = (classState(c) = Unusable)$

Values. To implement Java try/finally constructs, JVM$_\mathcal{E}$ supports embedded subroutines. The corresponding instructions push 32-bit program counters onto the stack or load them from local variables. This requires that *Pc* is injected in *Word*.

Rules. Fig. 12.1 defines the rules of *switchVM$_E$*. The *switchVM$_E$* rules search for the handler of the thrown exception. If the current *pc* and exception match an exception entry of the current method, *switchVM$_E$* sets the program counter to the first matching handler and replaces the operand stack with the thrown exception. The function *handler* selects the appropriate error handler (if any) where the function *excs* returns the exception table of the given method (see definition of methods in Chapter 10.1).

$$handler(m, pc, c) = e$$
$$\textbf{where } [e] \cdot \_ = [e \mid e \in excs(m), match(pc, c, e)]$$
$$escapes(m, pc, c) = \not\exists e \in excs(m) : match(pc, c, e)$$
$$match(pc, c, Exc(f, u, h, t)) = f \leq pc \wedge pc < u \wedge c \preceq_{\text{h}} t$$

If the exception *escapes* from the current method, the top method frame is discarded and it is checked whether the invoker frame has defined a handler. If an exceptpin thrown in a `<clinit>` method is not compatible with **Error**, an **ExceptionInInitializerError** replaces the thrown one.[2] If a `<clinit>` method frame is popped, the declared class becomes *Unusable*. The exception

---

[2] In the real JVM the **ExceptionInInitializerError** embeds the thrown exception.

Fig. 12.1 Switch machine for JVM$_\mathcal{E}$

$switchVM_E =$
$\quad switchVM_C$
$\quad$**case** $switch$ **of**
$\qquad Call(meth, args) \rightarrow$ **if** $isAbstract(meth)$ **then**
$\qquad\qquad\qquad\qquad\qquad raise(\text{"AbstractMethodError"})$
$\qquad InitClass(c) \rightarrow$ **if** $unusable(c)$ **then**
$\qquad\qquad\qquad\qquad\qquad raise(\text{"NoClassDefFoundError"})$
$\qquad Throw(r) \rightarrow$ **if** $\neg escapes(meth, pc, classOf(r))$ **then**
$\qquad\qquad\qquad\qquad$ **let** $exc = handler(meth, pc, classOf(r))$
$\qquad\qquad\qquad\qquad pc \quad\;\; := handle(exc)$
$\qquad\qquad\qquad\qquad opd \quad := [r]$
$\qquad\qquad\qquad\qquad switch := Noswitch$
$\qquad\qquad\qquad$ **else**
$\qquad\qquad\qquad\qquad$ **if** $methNm(meth) = \text{"<clinit>"}$ **then**
$\qquad\qquad\qquad\qquad\qquad$ **if** $\neg(classOf(r) \preceq_h \text{Error})$ **then**
$\qquad\qquad\qquad\qquad\qquad\qquad raise(\text{"ExceptionInInitializerError"})$
$\qquad\qquad\qquad\qquad\qquad\qquad pc := undef$
$\qquad\qquad\qquad\qquad\qquad$ **else** $switch := ThrowInit(r)$
$\qquad\qquad\qquad\qquad$ **else** $popFrame(0, [])$
$\qquad ThrowInit(r) \rightarrow$ **let** $c = classNm(meth)$
$\qquad\qquad\qquad\qquad classState(c) := Unusable$
$\qquad\qquad\qquad\qquad popFrame(0, [])$
$\qquad\qquad\qquad\qquad$ **if** $\neg superInit(top(stack), c)$ **then**
$\qquad\qquad\qquad\qquad\qquad switch := Throw(r)$

$superInit((\_, \_, \_, m), c) =$
$\quad methNm(m) = \text{"<clinit>"} \wedge super(classNm(m)) = c$

NoClassDefFoundError is thrown, if an unusable class should be initialized. The macro $raise(c)$ is a short hand for the following code template:

$\quad New(c)$
$\quad Dupx(0, 1)$
$\quad InvokeSpecial(\textbf{void}, c/\texttt{<init>}())$
$\quad Athrow$

This code can be implemented as a static method defined for instance in class Object.

$\quad fail(c) \;\;\, = (\texttt{Object}/(\text{"<fail"} \cdot c \cdot \text{">"}, []))$
$\quad raise(c) = (switch := Call(fail(c), []))$

The $execVM_E$ rules in Fig. 12.2 specify the effect of the JVM$_\mathcal{E}$ instructions on the current frame. The *Athrow* instruction takes the reference from the top of the stack and throws the exception represented by that reference, namely by triggering the $switchVM_E$ submachine. The *Jsr* instruction is used to implement finally clauses of Java. Its execution transfers the control to the

Fig. 12.2 Trustful execution of JVM$_\mathcal{E}$ instructions

---

$exec\,VM_E(instr) =$
$\quad exec\,VM_O(instr)$
$\quad$**case** $instr$ **of**
$\qquad Athrow \rightarrow$ **let** $[r] = take(opd, 1)$
$\qquad\qquad\qquad$ **if** $r \neq null$ **then** $switch := Throw(r)$
$\qquad\qquad\qquad\quad$ **else** $raise($ `"NullPointerException"` $)$
$\qquad Jsr(s) \rightarrow opd := opd \cdot [pc + 1]$
$\qquad\qquad\quad pc \;\; := s$
$\qquad Ret(x) \rightarrow pc := reg(x)$
$\qquad Prim(p) \rightarrow$ **let** $ws = take(opd, argSize(p))$
$\qquad\qquad\qquad$ **if** $p \in divMod \wedge sndArgIsZero(ws)$ **then**
$\qquad\qquad\qquad\quad raise($ `"ArithmeticException"` $)$
$\qquad GetField(\_, c/f) \rightarrow$ **let** $[r] = take(opd, 1)$
$\qquad\qquad\qquad\qquad$ **if** $r = null$ **then** $raise($ `"NullPointerException"` $)$
$\qquad PutField(\_, c/f) \rightarrow$ **let** $[r] \cdot ws = take(opd, 1 + size(c/f))$
$\qquad\qquad\qquad\qquad$ **if** $r = null$ **then** $raise($ `"NullPointerException"` $)$
$\qquad InvokeSpecial(\_, c/m) \rightarrow$
$\qquad\quad$ **let** $[r] \cdot ws = take(opd, 1 + argSize(c/m))$
$\qquad\quad$ **if** $r = null$ **then** $raise($ `"NullPointerException"` $)$
$\qquad InvokeVirtual(\_, c/m) \rightarrow$
$\qquad\quad$ **let** $[r] \cdot ws = take(opd, 1 + argSize(c/m))$
$\qquad\quad$ **if** $r = null$ **then** $raise($ `"NullPointerException"` $)$
$\qquad Checkcast(c) \rightarrow$ **let** $r = top(opd)$
$\qquad\qquad\qquad\qquad$ **if** $r \neq 0 \wedge \neg(classOf(r) \sqsubseteq c)$ **then**
$\qquad\qquad\qquad\qquad\quad raise($ `"ClassCastException"` $)$

---

given label and pushes the address of the next instruction on the operand stack. This address is typically used by *Ret* to return from the subroutine. Therefore from the top of the stack where this return address has been put by *Jsr*, it has to be stored in a register (using *Store*) to be found there by *Ret*, as one can see below in the compilation of finally statements.

JVM$_\mathcal{E}$ also extends in the expected way the rules where run-time exceptions might occur. A typical representative of this extension is the definition for *Prim*. The new rule throws an **ArithmeticException**, if the operator is an integer or long division or remainder operator and the right operand is 0. JVM$_\mathcal{E}$ throws a **NullPointerException** if the target reference of a *GetField*, *PutField*, *InvokeSpecial* or *InvokeVirtual* instruction is *null*, or if the reference of the *Athrow* instruction is *null*. The machine throws a **ClassCastException**, if for a *Checkcast* instruction the reference on top of stack is neither *null* nor assignment compatible with the required type.

12.2 Compilation of Java$_\mathcal{E}$

In this section we extend the compilation of Java$_\mathcal{O}$ statements to the new Java$_\mathcal{E}$ statements. We refine the compilation of the abruptions statements of Java$_\mathcal{I}$ and Java$_\mathcal{C}$ for the case that in Java$_\mathcal{E}$ they occur in the range of finally statements. We also define the exception tables for JVM$_\mathcal{E}$ programs, namely by an induction on JVM$_\mathcal{E}$ statements.

The JVM$_\mathcal{E}$-extension for statement compilation is defined in Fig. 12.3. For try-catch statements, the compilation of the try block *stm* is followed by a jump to the end of the compiled statement. The code for the exception handlers is generated in the order in which they appear in the statement. Each handler stores the exception from the top of the stack into its 'catch' parameter, followed first by the code of the catch clause, then by a jump to the end of the statement.

For try-finally statements, the compilation of the try-catch statement stm_1 is followed by a jump to the start fin of the subroutine stm_2 for the finally block. This is followed by a jump to the end of the compiled statement, to be executed upon returning from the finally statement. The subroutine first stores the return address into a fresh variable and then executes the code of stm_2, followed by a return to the stored address where in case it represents a pending abruption this abruption will be resumed.

For those exceptions that are thrown in the try-catch statement stm_1 but not caught by any of the catchers (if present), the exception table will point to the default label. Here the pending exception of class Throwable is stored from the operand into a fresh local variable, the subroutine is called, and upon return from there the pending exception is reloaded and rethrown. The compilation has to guarantee that the mentioned fresh variables are used only when an exception or return address is stored (and in particular not during execution of the finally block).

The compilation of break and continue statements to JVM$_\mathcal{I}$-code has to be extended for the case that they occur within a try block of a try-catch-finally statement and their corresponding target statement contains some try-catch-finally statement. In that case all finally blocks between the *jump* statement and its target have to be executed in innermost order (computed by the function *finallyLabsUntil(lab)*) before jumping to the target. Similarly for the sequence of fin labels (*finallyLabs*) appearing in the compilation of a return statement.

The exception tables are defined in Fig. 12.4. To guarantee that exceptions are searched in innermost order we make sure that inner try statements are concatenated before outer ones (see Lemma 14.2.1 for the properties of the exception table that are used to guarantee the correct execution of Java programs on the JVM).

Fig. 12.3 Compilation of Java$_\mathcal{E}$ abruption statements

$\mathcal{S}(\textbf{throw } exp;\,) = \mathcal{E}(exp) \cdot Athrow$
$\mathcal{S}(\textbf{try } stm \textbf{ catch } (c_1\,x_1)\,stm_1 \ldots \textbf{ catch } (c_n\,x_n)\,stm_n\,) =$
  $\text{try} \cdot \mathcal{S}(stm) \cdot \text{tryEnd} \cdot Goto(\text{end}) \cdot$
  $\text{handle}_1 \cdot Store(\textbf{addr}, \overline{x_1}) \cdot \mathcal{S}(stm_1) \cdot Goto(\text{end}) \cdot$
  $\vdots$
  $\text{handle}_n \cdot Store(\textbf{addr}, \overline{x_n}) \cdot \mathcal{S}(stm_n) \cdot Goto(\text{end}) \cdot$
  end
$\mathcal{S}(stm_1 \textbf{ finally } stm_2) =$
  $\text{try}_\text{f} \cdot \mathcal{S}(stm_1) \cdot Jsr(\text{fin}) \cdot Goto(\text{end}) \cdot$
  $\text{default} \cdot Store(\textbf{addr}, \overline{exc}) \cdot Jsr(\text{fin}) \cdot Load(\textbf{addr}, \overline{exc}) \cdot Athrow \cdot$
  $\text{fin} \cdot Store(\textbf{addr}, \overline{ret}) \cdot \mathcal{S}(stm_2) \cdot Ret(\overline{ret}) \cdot$
  end

$\mathcal{S}(\textbf{continue } lab;\,) = \textbf{let } [\text{fin}_1, \ldots, \text{fin}_n] = finallyLabsUntil(lab)$
                  $Jsr(\text{fin}_1) \cdot \ldots \cdot Jsr(\text{fin}_n) \cdot Goto(lab_c)$
$\mathcal{S}(\textbf{break } lab;\,) \;\;= \textbf{let } [\text{fin}_1, \ldots, \text{fin}_n] = finallyLabsUntil(lab)$
                  $Jsr(\text{fin}_1) \cdot \ldots \cdot Jsr(\text{fin}_n) \cdot Goto(lab_b)$

$\mathcal{S}(\textbf{return};\,) \;\;\;\; = \textbf{let } [\text{fin}_1, \ldots, \text{fin}_n] = finallyLabs$
                  $Jsr(\text{fin}_1) \cdot \ldots \cdot Jsr(\text{fin}_n) \cdot Return(\textbf{void})$
$\mathcal{S}(\textbf{return } exp;\,) =$
  $\textbf{if } finallyCodeToExec \textbf{ then}$
    $\mathcal{E}(exp) \cdot Store(\mathcal{T}(exp), \overline{var}) \cdot$
    $\textbf{let } [\text{fin}_1, \ldots, \text{fin}_n] = finallyLabs$
    $Jsr(\text{fin}_1) \cdot \ldots \cdot Jsr(\text{fin}_n) \cdot Load(\mathcal{T}(exp), \overline{var}) \cdot Return(\mathcal{T}(exp))$
  $\textbf{else}$
    $\mathcal{E}(exp) \cdot Return(\mathcal{T}(exp))$

Fig. 12.4 Definition of Java$_\mathcal{E}$ exception tables

$\mathcal{X}(\textbf{try } stm \textbf{ catch } (c_1\,x_1)\,stm_1 \ldots \textbf{ catch } (c_n\,x_n)\,stm_n\,) =$
  $\mathcal{X}(stm) \cdot$
  $\mathcal{X}(stm_1) \cdot Exc(\text{try}, \text{tryEnd}, \text{handle}_1, c_1) \cdot$
  $\vdots$
  $\mathcal{X}(stm_n) \cdot Exc(\text{try}, \text{tryEnd}, \text{handle}_n, c_n)$
$\mathcal{X}(stm_1 \textbf{ finally } stm_2) =$
  $\mathcal{X}(stm_1) \cdot Exc(\text{try}_\text{f}, \text{default}, \text{default}, \textbf{Throwable}) \cdot \mathcal{X}(stm_2)$
$\mathcal{X}(\{stm_1 \ldots stm_n\}) \;\;\;\;\;\;\;\; = \mathcal{X}(stm_1) \cdot \ldots \cdot \mathcal{X}(stm_n)$
$\mathcal{X}(\textbf{if } (exp)\,stm_1 \textbf{ else } stm_2) = \mathcal{X}(stm_1) \cdot \mathcal{X}(stm_2)$
$\mathcal{X}(\textbf{while } (exp)\,stm) \;\;\;\;\;\;\; = \mathcal{X}(stm)$
$\mathcal{X}(lab : stm) \;\;\;\;\;\;\;\;\;\;\;\;\;\;\; = \mathcal{X}(stm)$
$\mathcal{X}(\textbf{static } stm) \;\;\;\;\;\;\;\;\;\;\;\; = \mathcal{X}(stm)$
$\mathcal{X}(\_) \; = \epsilon$

13. Executing the JVM$_\mathcal{N}$

The specification of the Java Virtual Machine is not complete without the specification of all native methods which are used in the JDK libraries. Unfortunately, not all native methods are described in the official specifications. Therefore, one is constrained to using Sun's JVM if one wants to use Sun's JDK libraries.

Native methods do not have Java bytecode. Native methods are implemented in foreign programming languages. In our model, native methods are implemented via ASM rules. Therefore, a full specification of the JVM would consist of ASM rules for each native method which is used in the JDK libraries. In the $exec\,VM_N$ machine below, we describe—as examples—just two native methods, namely `Object/equals` and `Object/clone`. The executable version contains other native methods (see Appendix A).

The extension JVM$_\mathcal{N}$ of JVM$_\mathcal{E}$ consists in adding the execution of native methods to $exec\,VM_E$. In case there is no context switch and the method to execute is a native method, we execute the machine specified by $native\,VM$ which in this chapter is $exec\,VM_N$.

$trustfulScheme_N\,(native\,VM,\,switch\,VM) =$
  if $switch = Noswitch \wedge isNative(meth)$ **then**
    $native\,VM$
  else
    $trustfulScheme_C\,(exec\,VM_E,\,switch\,VM)$

$trustful\,VM_N = trustfulScheme_N\,(exec\,VM_N,\,switch\,VM_E)$

The method `Object/equals` tests whether the two argument references are equal. The method `Object/clone` creates an exact copy of the given reference if the class specified by the argument implements the `Cloneable` interface. Otherwise the exception `CloneNotSupportedException` is thrown.

$exec\,VM_N =$
  if $meth = \texttt{Object}/\,\texttt{equals}$ **then**
    $switch := Result(reg(0) = reg(1))$
  elseif $meth = \texttt{Object}/\,\texttt{clone}$ **then**
    let $r = reg(0)$
    if $classOf(r) \preceq_{\mathrm{h}} \texttt{Cloneable}$ **then**
      create r'
        $heap(r') := heap(r)$
        $switch \quad := Result(r')$
    else
      $raise(\,\texttt{"CloneNotSupportedException"}\,)$

14. Correctness of the compiler

In this chapter we formulate and prove the correctness of the compiler for Java$_\mathcal{E}$ programs. The goal of the chapter is to show that the run of the ASM for a Java$_\mathcal{E}$ program is equivalent to the corresponding run of the JVM$_\mathcal{E}$ for the compiled program, based upon a precise definition of the equivalence between a Java$_\mathcal{E}$ run and its implementation by a JVM$_\mathcal{E}$ run. For example, the run of the Java$_\mathcal{E}$ program is finite if and only if the run of the compiled JVM$_\mathcal{E}$ program is finite. The correspondence of states to be compared in the two runs will be made explicit by a mapping $n \mapsto \sigma(n)$ with the following properties:

1. If $m \leq n$, then $\sigma(m) \leq \sigma(n)$.
2. The nth state in the run of the Java$_\mathcal{E}$ program is equivalent to state $\sigma(n)$ in the run of the compiled JVM$_\mathcal{E}$ program.

The mapping from one run into the other will be constructed by induction on the number of steps of the first run. The mapping is not monotonic in the strict sense, since there are steps in the run of the ASM for Java$_\mathcal{E}$ which require zero steps on the JVM$_\mathcal{E}$.[1] There are also steps of Java$_\mathcal{E}$ which require more than one step on the JVM$_\mathcal{E}$. The equivalence of states will be explained in Sect. 14.1, where we identify how Java$_\mathcal{E}$ and the JVM$_\mathcal{E}$, upon navigation (via pos/pc) through their code, produce in corresponding method code segments the same values for (local, global, heap) variables and the same results of intermediate calculations (stored in $restbody/opd$), for the current method as well as for the method calls still to be completed (stored in $frames/stack$). Sect. 14.2 contains the correctness proof.

14.1 The correctness statement

In this section we make the notion of compilation correctness precise through which the runs of Java$_\mathcal{E}$ are related to their implementations by JVM$_\mathcal{E}$ runs. We have to identify the relevant locations in the states of the two machines, whose value evolution guarantees that the two runs yield the same result.

---

[1] In such cases we set $\sigma(n + 1) := \sigma(n)$, instead of explicitly introducing stutter steps as is usually done in the refinement literature. This also hides the abruption cycles introduced for the proof in [12].

We briefly summarize the dynamic states of $Java_{\mathcal{E}}$ and the $JVM_{\mathcal{E}}$. The dynamic state of $Java_{\mathcal{E}}$ is given by the following dynamic functions:

pos :	*Pos*
restbody :	*Phrase*
locals :	*MAP(Loc, Val)*
meth :	*Class/MSig*
frames :	*(Meth, Restbody, Pos, Locals)**
classState :	*Class* → *{Linked, Initialized, Unusable}*
globals :	*Class/Field* → *Val*
heap :	*Ref* → *Object(Class, MAP(Class/Field, Val))*

The dynamic state of the $JVM_{\mathcal{E}}$ is given by the following dynamic functions:

pc :	*Pc*
opd :	*Word**
reg :	*Map(RegNo, Word)*
meth :	*Class/MSig*
stack :	*(Pc, Reg, Opd, Meth)**
classState :	*Class* → *{Linked, Initialized, Unusable}*
globals :	*Class/Field* → *Val*
heap :	*Ref* → *Object(Class, MAP(Class/Field, Val))*
switch :	*Noswitch | Call(Meth, Args) | Result(Val) |*
	InitClass(Class) | Throw(Ref) | ThrowInit(Ref)

The dynamic functions *meth*, *classState*, *globals* and *heap* have the same name for $Java_{\mathcal{E}}$ and the $JVM_{\mathcal{E}}$. This identification is on purpose, since the two interpretations of these functions in $Java_{\mathcal{E}}$ and the $JVM_{\mathcal{E}}$ are the same. To be precise, we had to write $methJava_n = methVM_{\sigma(n)}$, etc. For the other dynamic functions—the only ones which remain to be investigated in this chapter—we have the following correspondence between the elements of the current frame, and the resulting correspondence between the elements of the method call stack:

$Java_{\mathcal{E}}$	$JVM_{\mathcal{E}}$
pos	*pc*
restbody	*opd*
locals	*reg*
frames	*stack*

We are now going to define, for each pair of these corresponding functions, in which sense they reflect equivalent descriptions for navigating through the code, for calculating intermediate values, and for computing the values of local variables.

14.1.1 The equivalence of *pos* and *pc*

What is the desired equivalence between the working positions *pos* and *pc* of Java$_\mathcal{E}$ and the JVM$_\mathcal{E}$?—We associate to each position α in the body of a method a code interval

$$[code(i) \mid \text{beg}_\alpha \leq i < \text{end}_\alpha].$$

The index beg_α is the index (label) of the first instruction which belongs to the compiled code for the phrase at position α. The index end_α is the index of the first instruction immediately following the code for the phrase at position α. If the statement at position α is not empty, then beg_α is less than end_α, otherwise beg_α is equal to end_α. The nesting of expressions and statements is preserved by the compiler. If a phrase is contained in another phrase, then the code interval of the phrase is contained in the code interval of the enclosing phrase.

Lemma 14.1.1. If β is a position inside $^\alpha phrase$, then $\text{beg}_\alpha \leq \text{beg}_\beta \leq \text{end}_\beta \leq \text{end}_\alpha$.

Proof. By induction on the size of $^\alpha phrase$. □

The equivalence for pos_n and $pc_{\sigma(n)}$ is defined in the invariants (**beg**)–(**exc**) of Theorem 14.1.1, stating one condition for each kind of phrases which may occur in *restbody* at pos_n, namely not yet computed expressions or statements, values of non-boolean or boolean or instance creation expressions, normal or abrupted termination results of statement execution. The equivalence conditions express that in each case, Java$_\mathcal{E}$ and the JVM$_\mathcal{E}$ are working on (representations of) the same phrase in the same computation phase of that phrase (entering or exiting). For example, if the current position *pos* of Java$_\mathcal{E}$ is α and the phrase at position α is not yet evaluated, then the *pc* of the JVM$_\mathcal{E}$ will be at index beg_α. If the phrase at position α is fully evaluated, then the *pc* will be at index end_α.

14.1.2 The equivalence of *restbody* and *opd*

We show here how to compute from *restbody* the operand stack *opd* of the JVM$_\mathcal{E}$ which is equivalent to it. The values are represented differently in Java$_\mathcal{E}$ and the JVM$_\mathcal{E}$. Values of Java$_\mathcal{E}$ are abstract values of the primitive types or references (elements of the universe *Val*), whereas values of the JVM$_\mathcal{E}$ are lists of one or two 32 bit words. We denote by $jvmVal(v)$ the list of words used in the JVM$_\mathcal{E}$ to represent a value v of Java$_\mathcal{E}$. We extend the data refinement function $jvmVal$ to finite sequences of values and arbitrary phrases. If *phrase* is not an element of the universe *Val*, then $jvmVal(phrase)$ is the empty list.

1. If the type of v is of size 1, then $jvmVal(v) = [w]$.

2. If the type of v is of size 2, then $jvmVal(v) = [w_1, w_2]$.
3. If $vals = (v_1, \ldots, v_n)$, then $jvmVal(vals) = jvmVal(v_1) \cdot \ldots \cdot jvmVal(v_n)$.
4. If φ is neither a value nor a sequence of values, then $jvmVal(\varphi) = [\,]$.

What is the desired equivalence between *restbody* and *opd*?—The operand stack *opd* of the $\text{JVM}_\mathcal{E}$ can be reconstructed from the *restbody* of $\text{Java}_\mathcal{E}$. Consider the evaluation of the following expression:

$$(3 * 5) + (2 * x)$$

If during the evaluation of the expression the current position is at the variable x, the *restbody* looks as follows:

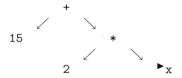

The corresponding operand stack of the $\text{JVM}_\mathcal{E}$ is the list $[15, 2]$. It is obtained by collecting into a list the $\text{Java}_\mathcal{E}$ values on the left-hand side of the path from the root of the expression to the current position and transforming them into the corresponding words of the $\text{JVM}_\mathcal{E}$ using the function $jvmVal$.

Conditional expressions and new instance creation expressions have to be treated with special care. For a conditional expression, the value of the boolean test expression exists in the *restbody* of $\text{Java}_\mathcal{E}$, but through the execution of the corresponding *Cond* instruction it is deleted from the operand stack of the $\text{JVM}_\mathcal{E}$. For an instance creation expression, the newly created reference has to be duplicated in the operand stack of the $\text{JVM}_\mathcal{E}$. (See the compilation of **new** c and note that in the abstract syntax tree the arguments of the instance initialization method are one level deeper than **new** c.)

Let α be a position in *restbody* of $\text{Java}_\mathcal{E}$. Then $javaOpd(restbody, \alpha)$ denotes the operand stack of the $\text{JVM}_\mathcal{E}$ when the evaluation of *restbody* is at position α. The function $javaOpd$ can be computed by recursion on the depth of the position α. We assume that positions are represented by finite lists of natural numbers. The root position *firstPos* is the empty list, and the ith successor of position α is obtained by appending the item i to the list α.

Definition 14.1.1 (javaOpd). Let α be a position in $body(meth)$.

1. $javaOpd(restbody, [\,]) := [\,]$.
2. If $body(meth)/\alpha$ is not an expression, then

$$javaOpd(restbody, \alpha \cdot [n]) := [\,].$$

3. If $body(meth)/\alpha = e_0 \mathbin{?} e_1 : e_2$, then

$$javaOpd(restbody, \alpha \cdot [n]) := javaOpd(restbody, \alpha).$$

4. If $body(meth)/\alpha = \texttt{new } c.c/m(exps)$, then

$$javaOpd(restbody, \alpha \cdot [1]) := javaOpd(restbody, \alpha) \cdot [v, v],$$

where $v = jvmVal(restbody/\alpha \cdot [0])$.
5. Otherwise,

$$javaOpd(restbody, \alpha \cdot [n]) := \\ javaOpd(restbody, \alpha) \cdot \\ jvmVal(restbody/\alpha \cdot [0]) \cdot \ldots \cdot jvmVal(restbody/\alpha \cdot [n-1])$$

As a special case, $javaOpd(restbody, \alpha \cdot [0]) = javaOpd(restbody, \alpha)$.

The definition of $javaOpd(restbody, \alpha)$ is by recursion on the length of α. If we reach a prefix β of α such that $body(meth)/\beta$ is a statement and not an expression, then the recursion stops with the empty list. If $body(meth)/\alpha$ is an equation $loc = exp$, then $javaOpd(restbody, \alpha \cdot [1]) = javaOpd(restbody, \alpha)$, since $jvmVal(loc) = [\,]$.

14.1.3 The equivalence of *locals* and *reg*

The correspondence between *locals* and *reg* is given by the function $x \mapsto \overline{x}$ used by the compiler to associate register numbers to local variables. The function depends on the method body. The equivalence condition holds modulo the refinement of Java values to JVM values.

Definition 14.1.2 (Equivalence of locals and reg). We write $locals \approx reg$, if for each variable x of type τ which is defined in *locals* the following is true:

1. If τ is of size 1, then $jvmVal(locals(x)) = [reg(\overline{x})]$.
2. If τ is of size 2, then $jvmVal(locals(x)) = [reg(\overline{x}), reg(\overline{x}+1)]$.

Note, that the relation $\approx$ depends on the current method and the class environment. For reasons of simplicity, however, we suppress these parameters.

14.1.4 The equivalence of *frames* and *stack*

At the beginning of the $\text{Java}_\mathcal{E}$ and $\text{JVM}_\mathcal{E}$ runs, *frames* and *stack* are both empty. This equivalence is preserved during the runs because each time a new frame is pushed on *frames*—namely in case of a class initialization or of a method or constructor invocation—the $\text{JVM}_\mathcal{E}$ is working on the same phrase, in the same computation phase, with equivalent operands (intermediate values) and local variables, and with correct return addresses from possibly nested subroutines in the registers. The most delicate part of this equivalence notion is the correctness of subroutine return addresses, which we are going to define now.

As a preparatory step for this definition, first we isolate the code segments in the compilation of abruption statements where the JVM will continue its execution upon the occurrence of an abruption. We define what it means that a code index i is a continuation for an abruption abr which is not an exception and which occurs during the execution of Java$_\mathcal{E}$ at a position α. The case of exceptions is special, as will become clear through Def. 14.1.7 and Theorem 14.1.1.

Definition 14.1.3 (Continuation for break). Code index i is a continuation for an abruption $Break(lab)$ at position α, if $finallyLabsUntil(\alpha, lab) = [\mathrm{fin}_1, \ldots, \mathrm{fin}_k]$ and

$$
\begin{aligned}
code(i) &= Jsr(\mathrm{fin}_1) \\
&\vdots \\
code(i+k-1) &= Jsr(\mathrm{fin}_k) \\
code(i+k) &= Goto(lab_b)
\end{aligned}
$$

or $k = 0$ and $i = lab_b$.[2]

Definition 14.1.4 (Continuation for continue). Code index i is a continuation for an abruption $Continue(lab)$ at position α, if $finallyLabsUntil(\alpha, lab) = [\mathrm{fin}_1, \ldots, \mathrm{fin}_k]$ and

$$
\begin{aligned}
code(i) &= Jsr(\mathrm{fin}_1) \\
&\vdots \\
code(i+k-1) &= Jsr(\mathrm{fin}_k) \\
code(i+k) &= Goto(lab_c)
\end{aligned}
$$

or $k = 0$ and $i = lab_c$.

Definition 14.1.5 (Continuation for return void). Code index i is a continuation for an abruption $Return$ at position α, if

$$
\begin{aligned}
code(i) &= Jsr(\mathrm{fin}_1) \\
&\vdots \\
code(i+k-1) &= Jsr(\mathrm{fin}_k) \\
code(i+k) &= Return(\texttt{void})
\end{aligned}
$$

where $[\mathrm{fin}_1, \ldots, \mathrm{fin}_k] = finallyLabs(\alpha)$.

---

[2] Note that the functions $finallyLabsUntil$ and $finallyLabs$, used for the compilation of Java$_\mathcal{E}$ abruption statements in Fig. 12.3 are implicitly parametrized by the position α of the compiled statement. This position parameter becomes explicit here to determine the **finally** blocks which remain to be executed, when the Java machine navigates through the code to reach the target statement of the abruption.

Definition 14.1.6 (Continuation for return value). Code index i is a continuation for an abruption $Return(val)$ at position α with respect to reg, if

1. $code(i) \qquad\quad = \quad Jsr(\text{fin}_1)$

$$\vdots \qquad\qquad\qquad \vdots$$

$$code(i + k - 1) \;=\; Jsr(\text{fin}_k)$$
$$code(i + k) \qquad=\quad Load(\tau, x)$$
$$code(i + k + 1) \;=\; Return(\tau)$$
where $[\text{fin}_1, \ldots, \text{fin}_k] = finallyLabs(\alpha)$,
2. if $size(\tau) = 1$, then $jvmVal(val) = [reg(x)]$,
3. if $size(\tau) = 2$, then $jvmVal(val) = [reg(x), reg(x + 1)]$,
4. if the position α is within a **try** block, then the code for the corresponding **finally** block does not use the local register(s) x (and $x + 1$).

When Java enters a **finally** block, the JVM jumps to the corresponding subroutine. After termination of the **finally** block Java moves to a position which depends on whether the **try-catch** statement has been terminated normally or abruptly. When the JVM returns from the subroutine, it jumps back to where it has been called from, namely the return address stored in reg upon entering the subroutine (either after execution of the compilation of a normally terminated **try-catch** statement or after having encountered an abruption during the execution of such a statement). The following definition makes this equivalence between Java$_\mathcal{E}$ and JVM$_\mathcal{E}$ returns from subroutines precise. It says what it means that during the execution of (possibly nested) subroutines, the registers of the JVM contain correct return addresses.

Definition 14.1.7 (Correct return address). We say that reg contains correct return addresses for position α in $restbody$, if the following conditions are satisfied:

(fin-norm) For each β, if $restbody/\beta = (Norm$ **finally** $s)$ and α is in s, then $code(reg(\overline{\text{ret}}_\beta)) = Goto(\text{end}_\beta)$.

(fin-abr) For each β, if $restbody/\beta = (abr$ **finally** $s)$, abr is not an exception and α is in s, then $reg(\overline{\text{ret}}_\beta)$ is a continuation for abr at position β with respect to reg.

(fin-exc) For each β, if $restbody/\beta = (Exc(r)$ **finally** $s)$ and α is in s, then $reg(\overline{\text{ret}}_\beta) = \text{default}_\beta + 2$ and $reg(\overline{\text{exc}}_\beta) = r$.

(**fin-norm**) defines the correct return address from **finally** code which was entered after normal execution of the corresponding **try-catch** statement. (**fin-abr**) does the same for **finally** code entered after occurrence of a *Break*, *Continue* or *Return* abruption. Returning from **finally** code to resume an exception, which has not been caught in the **try-catch** statement, is described in (**fin-exc**), where the exception has to be reloaded to be rethrown. The label $default_\beta$ is defined in the compilation scheme in Fig. 12.3. It is the label of the *Store* instruction at the beginning of the default handler for the `try-catch` statement, through which the exception was stored which now has to be reloaded.

We have now all the notions which are necessary to define the equivalence of *frames* and *stack*. When a new frame $(meth, restbody, pos, locals)$ is pushed on the stack, then, by Lemma 8.1.3, either $body(meth)/pos$ is a method or constructor invocation expression or *pos* is an initialization position (Def. 8.1.7). The following definition of the equivalence of *frames* and *stack* comprises these different possibilities.

Definition 14.1.8 (Equivalence of frames and stack). Inductive definition of $frames \approx stack$:

$$[] \approx [].$$

Assume that

1. $frames \approx stack$,
2. $locals \approx reg$,
3. reg contains correct return addresses for pos in $restbody$,
4. one of the following conditions is satisfied
   a) $body(meth)/pos$ is a method invocation and
      i. $pc = end_{pos} - 1$,
      ii. $opd = javaOpd(restbody, pos)$, or
   b) $body(meth)/pos$ is a constructor invocation and
      i. $pc = end_{pos} - 1$,
      ii. $restbody/pos = ref.c/m(\_)$,
      iii. $opd = javaOpd(restbody, pos) \cdot [ref]$, or
   c) $restbody/pos$ is an unevaluated expression or statement and
      i. $pc = beg_{pos}$,
      ii. $opd = javaOpd(restbody, pos)$, or
   d) $restbody/pos$ is a value v and
      i. $pc = end_{pos}$,
      ii. $opd = javaOpd(restbody, pos) \cdot jvmVal(v)$.

Then $frames \cdot (meth, restbody, pos, locals) \approx stack \cdot (pc, reg, opd, meth)$.

From the definition it immediately follows that, if $frames \approx stack$, then *frames* and *stack* have the same length.

14.1.5 Equivalence of states

Two more auxiliary definitions are needed before we can give a precise definition of the state invariants, which link together the above defined equivalences of pos/pc, $restbody/opd$, $locals/reg$ and $frames/stack$, thus yielding the needed definition of the equivalence of $Java_\mathcal{E}/JVM_\mathcal{E}$ runs started with $P/compile(P)$.

Positions in a method body are labeled as $\mathcal{E}$-positions, $\mathcal{S}$-positions, $\mathcal{B}_1(lab)$-positions or $\mathcal{B}_0(lab)$-positions depending on the kind of compilation function which has been used to compile the phrase at that position. For technical reasons, the position β in a method invocation statement $^\alpha(^\beta exp)$; is considered as an $\mathcal{S}$-position, too, if exp is an invocation of a method with return type void (cf. Case 54 in Theorem 14.1.1).

If α is an $\mathcal{S}$-position, then $\mathcal{X}(\alpha)$ denotes the subtable of the exception table of the method which corresponds to the statement at position α. If α is not an $\mathcal{S}$-position, then we set $\mathcal{X}(\alpha) := [\,]$.

In the rest of this chapter we take for granted, and consequently do not mention any more, that by the preceding definitions, in corresponding states n, $\sigma(n)$ both machines Java$_\mathcal{E}$ and the JVM$_\mathcal{E}$ work on the same method, with the same *classState*, with the same values of global variables, and with the same heap. Therefore for the correctness of the refinement, via the program compilation, of Java$_\mathcal{E}$ runs to JVM$_\mathcal{E}$ runs, four conditions remain to be guaranteed for each pair of corresponding frames, whether current or belonging to the frame stacks ($frames_n$, $stack_{\sigma(n)}$):

1. The values of corresponding local variables, which are stored in $locals_n$ and $reg_{\sigma(n)}$, must be the same. In view of the correctness of the implementation of finally code, it is also required that all the still relevant return addresses from subroutines, which are stored in the JVM$_\mathcal{E}$ in $reg_{\sigma(n)}$, are correct for the current position pos_n of Java$_\mathcal{E}$ in $restbody_n$ in the corresponding state n.
2. The same values must be computed for corresponding intermediate (still needed) results of expression evaluation or statement execution; these values are stored in $restbody_n$ and in $opd_{\sigma(n)}$.
3. Each machine must execute a code segment—described by pos_n and $pc_{\sigma(n)}$—which belongs to the same phrase of the original program, and both machines must work on it in the same phase (unevaluated, evaluated, normally terminated, or abrupted).
4. The current class initialization status in n is equivalent to the value of the *switch* location in $\sigma(n)$.

These four conditions constitute the integrity constraints formulated in the statement of Theorem 14.1.1 below. More precisely, the conditions are expressed for the inductive step by the frame stack equivalence property (**stack**). For the current method frame, which constitutes the basis of the induction, the condition on the equivalence of local variables is captured by (**reg**), the correctness of stored return addresses from finally code is formalized by (**fin**).

The condition on the equivalence of the still needed intermediate results is captured by the equations for $opd_{\sigma(n)}$ in the integrity constraints (**beg**)–(**abr**), using the refinement function *javaOpd* which translates the abstract Java$_\mathcal{E}$ values stored in $restbody_n$ to JVM$_\mathcal{E}$ operand stack values in $\sigma(n)$. For unevaluated phrases (**beg**) and for evaluated Boolean expressions (**bool1,bool2**) the exact condition is $opd_{\sigma(n)} = javaOpd(restbody_n, pos_n)$. The expression evaluation condition (**exp**) states that when Java$_\mathcal{E}$ has normally terminated computing the value (sequence) for the current expression (sequence) in state n, then in the corresponding state $\sigma(n)$ the JVM$_\mathcal{E}$ has finished executing the code compiled from that expression (sequence), and the $jvmVal$-refinements of the computed values are on top of the operand stack as it was when that expression computation was started. Condition (**new**) requires that when in state n a new object has been created in Java$_\mathcal{E}$, in the corresponding state $\sigma(n)$ two copies of the reference to that object appear on top of the JVM$_\mathcal{E}$ operand stack. Upon normal termination or non-exception abruption of a statement in Java$_\mathcal{E}$, in the corresponding state the JVM$_\mathcal{E}$ operand stack of intermediate values is empty, as formalized in (**stm**) and (**abr**).

The condition on the equivalence of the class initialization status is contained in the constraints (**clinit**) and (**exc-clinit**), the second one covering the special case of an exception which occurred upon executing class initialization code.

The condition on the equivalence of corresponding working positions pos_n and $pc_{\sigma(n)}$ of the two machines, namely "working on the same phrase in the same phase", splits into several integrity constraints, expressed in (**beg**)–(**exc**) and depending on whether the computation of the current phrase is just starting or whether it has been terminated (yielding a value, normal termination, an abruption or an exception). Roughly speaking, the integrity constraints express that except the special cases discussed below, when Java$_\mathcal{E}$ in state n starts respectively ends executing a phrase (at pos_n), then the JVM$_\mathcal{E}$ in the corresponding state $\sigma(n)$ starts (**beg**) respectively ends (**exp,bool1,bool2,new,stm**) (at position $pc_{\sigma(n)}$) the execution of the compiled code for that phrase.

More precisely, condition (**beg**) formalizes that when Java$_\mathcal{E}$ starts executing a not yet evaluated phrase (expression or statement), then in the corresponding state, the JVM$_\mathcal{E}$ starts executing the compiled code for that phrase—except for the special case of a while statement where the JVM$_\mathcal{E}$ may already have executed the initial *Goto* instruction of the compiled while statement (see Fig. 9.4 and Case 34 below).

The case of just terminated Java$_\mathcal{E}$-execution of phrases splits into subcases for expressions (**exp**)–(**new**) and for statements (**stm**)–(**exc**). For expressions it has to be distinguished whether the value (sequence) is non-Boolean (**exp,new**)—then the JVM$_\mathcal{E}$ terminates the compiled code for the current expression—or whether it is Boolean. In the Boolean case, depending on whether the tested condition is satisfied or not, $pc_{\sigma(n)}$ is the jump target (**bool1**) or the end of the compiled expression (**bool2**); note that in the Boolean case and differently from the case (**exp**) of non-Boolean expression values, through executing the test instruction, the $\text{JVM}_{\mathcal{E}}$ pops the computed Boolean value from its operand stack.

For the case that $\text{Java}_{\mathcal{E}}$ at pos_n yields an abruption statement which is not an exception, condition (**abr**) requires that $pc_{\sigma(n)}$ is a continuation for that abruption at pos_n with respect to $reg_{\sigma(n)}$ (and that the operand stack in $\sigma(n)$ is empty). For an exception at pos_n which is not within a class initialization method, condition (**exc**) implies that in $\sigma(n)$ the $switch\,VM_E$ submachine has been triggered by that exception, that $pc_{\sigma(n)}$ points within the compiled code for the phrase at pos_n (or within the immediately enclosing phrase in case of an expression), and that the exception is not caught by the subtable of exceptions corresponding to the statement at pos_n.

Theorem 14.1.1 (Correctness of the compiler). There exists a monotonic mapping σ from the run of the ASM for a $\text{Java}_{\mathcal{E}}$ program into the run of the ASM for the compiled $\text{JVM}_{\mathcal{E}}$ program such that the following invariants are satisfied for $\alpha = pos_n$:

(**reg**) $locals_n \approx reg_{\sigma(n)}$

(**stack**) $frames_n \approx stack_{\sigma(n)}$

(**beg**) If $restbody_n/\alpha$ is not evaluated, then
1. $pc_{\sigma(n)} = beg_\alpha$, or $beg_\alpha < end_\alpha$ and $code(beg_\alpha) = Goto(pc_{\sigma(n)})$,
2. $opd_{\sigma(n)} = javaOpd(restbody_n, \alpha)$.

(**exp**) If α is an $\mathcal{E}$-position, $restbody_n/\alpha = v$ and v is a value or a finite sequence of values, then
1. $pc_{\sigma(n)} = end_\alpha$,
2. $opd_{\sigma(n)} = javaOpd(restbody_n, \alpha) \cdot jvmVal(v)$.

(**bool1**) If α is a $\mathcal{B}_1(lab)$-position and $restbody_n/\alpha = True$, or if α is a $\mathcal{B}_0(lab)$-position and $restbody_n/\alpha = False$, then
1. $pc_{\sigma(n)} = lab$,
2. $opd_{\sigma(n)} = javaOpd(restbody_n, \alpha)$.

(**bool2**) If α is a $\mathcal{B}_1(lab)$-position and $restbody_n/\alpha = False$, or if α is a $\mathcal{B}_0(lab)$-position and $restbody_n/\alpha = True$, then
1. $pc_{\sigma(n)} = end_\alpha$,
2. $opd_{\sigma(n)} = javaOpd(restbody_n, \alpha)$.

(**new**) If $body(meth_n)/\alpha = \textbf{new }c$ and $restbody_n/\alpha = ref$, then
1. $pc_{\sigma(n)} = end_\alpha$,
2. $opd_{\sigma(n)} = javaOpd(restbody_n, \alpha) \cdot [ref, ref]$.

(**stm**) If α is an $\mathcal{S}$-position and $restbody_n/\alpha = Norm$, then
1. $pc_{\sigma(n)} = end_\alpha$,
2. $opd_{\sigma(n)} = [\,]$.

(**abr**) If $restbody_n/\alpha = abr$ and abr is not an exception, then
1. $opd_{\sigma(n)} = [\,]$,

2. $pc_{\sigma(n)}$ is a continuation for abr at position α with respect to $reg_{\sigma(n)}$.

(exc) If $restbody_n/\alpha = Exc(r)$ and $body(meth_n)/\alpha \neq \texttt{static}\_$, then
   1. $switch_{\sigma(n)} = Throw(r)$,
   2. $beg_\alpha \leq pc_{\sigma(n)}$,
   3. $pc_{\sigma(n)} < end_\alpha$, or α is an $\mathcal{E}$-position and $pc_{\sigma(n)} < end_{up(\alpha)}$,
   4. there is no $(f, u, \_, c) \in \mathcal{X}(\alpha)$ such that $f \leq pc_{\sigma(n)} < u$ and $classOf(r) \preceq_{\text{h}} c$.

(exc-clinit) If $restbody_n/\alpha = Exc(r)$ and $body(meth_n)/\alpha = \texttt{static}\_$, then $switch_{\sigma(n)} = ThrowInit(r)$.

(clinit) Assume that $restbody_n/\alpha = \texttt{static}\_$ and $c = classNm(meth_n)$. If $c \neq \texttt{Object}$ and not $initialized(super(c))$, then $switch_{\sigma(n)} = InitClass(super(c))$, otherwise $switch_{\sigma(n)} = Noswitch$.

(fin) $reg_{\sigma(n)}$ contains correct return addresses for α in $restbody_n$.

If nothing is said about $switch$, then $switch_{\sigma(n)} = Noswitch$. Moreover, the dynamic functions $meth$, $classState$, $globals$ and $heap$ are the same in state n of Java$_\mathcal{E}$ and in state $\sigma(n)$ of the JVM$_\mathcal{E}$.

14.2 The correctness proof

The reader who is more interested in the models for Java, the JVM and the Java-to-JVM compilation, as well as in the correctness conditions relating them, but not so much in the proof details, may skip this section. Be aware however that a detailed verification helps to become reasonably confident about the correctness and the completeness of the definitions. For example, only at the very last stage of writing out the relevant proof details we found out that the previous models we had worked with were incomplete, two cases related to special class initialization situations were missing and discovered through the attempt to complete the proof. They led us to refine the *initialize* rule and the *switchVM$_E$* machine. The ease and naturalness with which one can identify and incorporate such extensions of ASM models, even at a late state of the modeling process, is one of the reasons for the practicality of the ASM design method for large systems.

The following lemma lists some properties of the exception table which are used in the correctness proof of the compiler. Property 1 is used in Cases 73 and 78 of Theorem 14.1.1; Property 2 is used in Case 73; Property 3 is used in Cases 23, 75 and 80.

Lemma 14.2.1 (Exception table). The exception table has the following properties:

1. If $(f, u, \_, \_) \in \mathcal{X}(\alpha)$, then $beg_\alpha \leq f$ and $u \leq end_\alpha$.

2. If β is a position inside $^\alpha stm$ and h is a handler which occurs in the table $\mathcal{X}(\alpha)$ before the subtable $\mathcal{X}(\beta)$, then the interval protected by h is disjoint to the interval $\{i \mid \text{beg}_\beta \leq i < \text{end}_\beta\}$.
3. If β is a direct subposition of $^\alpha stm$ and β is not the position of a try Block, or a try-catch statement, then the intervals of handlers in $\mathcal{X}(\alpha)$ which do not belong to $\mathcal{X}(\beta)$ are disjoint to $\{i \mid \text{beg}_\beta \leq i < \text{end}_\beta\}$.

Proof. Statement 1 is proved by induction on the definition of $\mathcal{X}$ in Fig. 12.4. Statements 2 and 3 are proved by induction on the size of *stm*. Lemma 14.1.1 is used. □

Note that Theorem 8.4.1 (Java is type safe) and some of the Lemmata in Chapter 8 are used several times in the proof below.

Proof. (Theorem 14.1.1) The mapping σ is constructed by induction on n. $\sigma(0)$ is the initial JVM$_\mathcal{E}$-state defined by the compiled JVM$_\mathcal{E}$-program for the given Java$_\mathcal{E}$-program which defines the initial Java$_\mathcal{E}$-state 0. No local variable is defined yet, $frames_0$, $stack_{\sigma(0)}$, $opd_{\sigma(0)}$ are empty, no phrase is evaluated yet so that the invariants (**ref**)–(**fin**) are satisfied for $n = 0$. In the induction step from n to $n + 1$ we exploit our decomposition of the Java machine into a sequence of incrementally defined submachines Java$_\mathcal{I}$, Java$_\mathcal{C}$, Java$_\mathcal{O}$, Java$_\mathcal{E}$. It allows us to split the case distinction on $context(pos_n)$ into four groups, one for each submachine, and to isolate within each group the two subgroups corresponding to the submachines dealing with expression evaluation and statement execution respectively. In this way the stepwise refinement of the machines in Fig. 3.2, 3.3, 4.4, 4.5, 5.2, 6.2, 6.3, put together with the corresponding refinements of the JVM-submachines in Fig. 9.1, 10.1, 10.2, 11.1, 12.1, 12.2 and of the compilation functions, reveal the structure which underlies the local—instruction wise—checking of the run-time invariants, which imply the compiler correctness property. In particular it explains that for each type of phrase which occurs for elaboration, we will distinguish the cases whether that phrase is still unevaluated or whether its value has been computed, partially or completely, following exactly the cases appearing in our machine definitions. To simplify the task to check the completeness of our proof, in the case distinction below we follow the order in which the Java$_\mathcal{E}$-rules have been defined, although some cases are similar and could have been grouped into just one case. We assume that the proof is read in the order we present it, so that in later cases we may use shortcuts for reasonings which have been explained in full detail for earlier cases.

Java$_\mathcal{I}$-Expressions. Following Fig. 3.1 and Fig. 3.2, we have to consider the six cases for Java$_\mathcal{I}$-expressions: literals (Case 1), local variables (Case 2), terms built by unary or binary operators (Cases 3–7), assignment (Cases 8–9) and conditional expressions (Cases 10–13). Subcases appear where structural expressions can be partially evaluated.

Case 1. $context(pos_n) = {}^\alpha lit$: The run of Java$_\mathcal{E}$ proceeds with the rule $execJavaExp_I$ in Fig. 3.2 such that $pos_{n+1} = \alpha$ and $restbody_{n+1}/\alpha = v$, where $v = JLS(lit)$. We have to distinguish whether lit has been compiled with $\mathcal{E}$ or as a Boolean expression.

Assume that α is an $\mathcal{E}$-position. Due to the compilation according to Fig. 9.2, $code(\mathrm{beg}_\alpha)$ is the instruction $Prim(lit)$ and $\mathrm{end}_\alpha = \mathrm{beg}_\alpha + 1$. By the induction hypothesis (**beg**), it follows that $pc_{\sigma(n)} = \mathrm{beg}_\alpha$ and $opd_{\sigma(n)} = javaOpd(restbody_n, \alpha)$. We set $\sigma(n+1) := \sigma(n) + 1$. In state $\sigma(n)$, the JVM$_\mathcal{E}$ executes the instruction $Prim(lit)$ using the rule $execVM_I$ in Fig. 9.1. We obtain (using for the third equation also Def. 14.1.1 which guarantees $javaOpd(restbody_n, \alpha) = javaOpd(restbody_{n+1}, \alpha)$ if above and to the left of α, $restbody_{n+1}$ does not differ from $restbody_n$):

$$
\begin{aligned}
pc_{\sigma(n+1)} &= pc_{\sigma(n)} + 1 = \mathrm{beg}_\alpha + 1 = \mathrm{end}_\alpha, \\
opd_{\sigma(n+1)} &= opd_{\sigma(n)} \cdot JVMS(lit, [\,]) \\
&= javaOpd(restbody_{n+1}, \alpha) \cdot jvmVal(v).
\end{aligned}
$$

Hence, the invariant (**exp**) is satisfied in state $n + 1$. The other invariants remain true for $n + 1$, since the dynamic functions $locals_n$, $frames_n$, $reg_{\sigma(n)}$ and $stack_{\sigma(n)}$ are not changed from n to $n + 1$.

Assume that α is a $\mathcal{B}_1(lab)$-position. Then lit is either the literal **true** or the literal **false**. We first consider the case where lit is **true**. Then v is the value *True* by definition of *JLS*. Since α is a $\mathcal{B}_1(lab)$-position, $code(\mathrm{beg}_\alpha)$ is the instruction $Goto(lab)$ according to the compilation scheme in Fig. 9.3. By the induction hypothesis (**beg**), it follows that $pc_{\sigma(n)} = \mathrm{beg}_\alpha$ or $pc_{\sigma(n)} = lab$ and the operand stack $opd_{\sigma(n)}$ is $javaOpd(restbody_n, \alpha)$. If $pc_{\sigma(n)} = \mathrm{beg}_\alpha$, we set $\sigma(n+1) := \sigma(n) + 1$ and the JVM$_\mathcal{E}$ executes the $Goto(lab)$ instruction. If $pc_{\sigma(n)} = lab$, we set $\sigma(n+1) := \sigma(n)$ and the JVM$_\mathcal{E}$ does nothing (or one could say that the JVM$_\mathcal{E}$ executes a stutter step). In both cases we have $pc_{\sigma(n+1)} = lab$ and the invariant (**bool1**) is satisfied in state $n + 1$.

Now we consider the case where lit is the literal **false**. According to Fig. 9.3, $\mathrm{beg}_\alpha = \mathrm{end}_\alpha$, since $\mathcal{B}_1(\mathtt{false}, lab) = \epsilon$. By the induction hypothesis (**beg**), it follows that $pc_{\sigma(n)} = \mathrm{beg}_\alpha$ and $opd_{\sigma(n)} = javaOpd(restbody_n, \alpha)$. The literal **false** is evaluated to *False* in Java$_\mathcal{E}$. We set $\sigma(n+1) := \sigma(n)$ and see that the invariant (**bool2**) is satisfied.

The case where α is a $\mathcal{B}_0(lab)$-position is treated in a similar way.

Case 2. $context(pos_n) = {}^\alpha loc$: By (**def1**) and (**loc1**) of the Java type safety Theorem 8.4.1, it follows that $locals_n(loc)$ is a value. Let $v = locals_n(loc)$. Then $pos_{n+1} = \alpha$ and $restbody_{n+1}/\alpha = v$ (rule $execJavaExp_I$ in Fig. 3.2). By the induction hypothesis (**reg**), it follows that $locals_n \approx reg_{\sigma(n)}$. Assume that the size of the type of loc is 1. Then Def. 14.1.2 implies that $jvmVal(v) = [reg_{\sigma(n)}(\overline{loc})]$. (The case of size 2 is treated in a similar way.) Again we have to distinguish now whether loc has been compiled as Boolean expression or using $\mathcal{E}$.

Assume that α is an $\mathcal{E}$-position. According to Fig. 9.2, $code(\mathrm{beg}_\alpha)$ is the instruction $Load(\mathcal{T}(\alpha), \overline{loc})$ and $\mathrm{end}_\alpha = \mathrm{beg}_\alpha + 1$. By the induction hypothesis (**beg**), it follows that $pc_{\sigma(n)} = \mathrm{beg}_\alpha$ and $opd_{\sigma(n)} = javaOpd(restbody_n, \alpha)$. We set $\sigma(n+1) := \sigma(n) + 1$ and obtain (using Def. 14.1.1 as in Case 1)

$$
\begin{aligned}
pc_{\sigma(n+1)} &= pc_{\sigma(n)} + 1 = \mathrm{beg}_\alpha + 1 = \mathrm{end}_\alpha, \\
opd_{\sigma(n+1)} &= opd_{\sigma(n)} \cdot [reg_{\sigma(n)}(\overline{loc})] \\
&= javaOpd(restbody_{n+1}, \alpha) \cdot jvmVal(v).
\end{aligned}
$$

Hence, the invariant (**exp**) is satisfied for $n+1$.

Assume that α is a $\mathcal{B}_1(lab)$-position. Then, according to Fig. 9.3, $code(\mathrm{beg}_\alpha)$ is the instruction $Load(\mathcal{T}(loc), \overline{loc})$ followed by $Cond(\mathtt{ifne}, lab)$. Moreover, $\mathrm{end}_\alpha = \mathrm{beg}_\alpha + 2$. By the induction hypothesis (**beg**), it follows that $pc_{\sigma(n)}$ is beg_α and $opd_{\sigma(n)} = javaOpd(restbody_n, \alpha)$. We set $\sigma(n+1) := \sigma(n) + 2$. The $\mathrm{JVM}_\mathcal{E}$ executes the $Load$ instruction. If $v = True$, then the integer 1 is pushed on $opd_{\sigma(n)}$, since $jvmVal(True) = [1]$. At the $Cond$ instruction, the $\mathrm{JVM}_\mathcal{E}$ jumps to code index lab. Thus, $pc_{\sigma(n+1)} = lab$ and the invariant (**bool1**) is satisfied. If $v = False$, then the integer 0 is pushed on the operand stack and, at the $Cond$ instruction, the $\mathrm{JVM}_\mathcal{E}$ proceeds to the next instruction. Thus, $pc_{\sigma(n+1)} = pc_{\sigma(n)} + 2 = \mathrm{end}_\alpha$ and the invariant (**bool2**) is satisfied.

The case where α is a $\mathcal{B}_0(lab)$-position is treated in a similar way.

Case 3. $context(pos_n) = {}^\alpha({}^\beta exp_1 \, bop \, {}^\gamma exp_2)$ and $pos_n = \alpha$:

Then (**beg**) is satisfied (by the induction hypothesis). Also $pos_{n+1} = \beta$ (rule $execJavaExp_I$ in Fig. 3.2). In this case the $\mathrm{JVM}_\mathcal{E}$ does nothing, so that we set $\sigma(n+1) := \sigma(n)$. Since $\mathrm{beg}_\beta = \mathrm{beg}_\alpha$ and $javaOpd(restbody_n, \alpha) = javaOpd(restbody_{n+1}, \beta)$, the invariant (**beg**) is satisfied also in state $n+1$. Note, that exp_1 cannot be a value by Lemma 8.1.5.

Several cases are similar to this one. They have in common that the current position of $\mathrm{Java}_\mathcal{E}$ just moves from one unevaluated position to another unevaluated position and leaves $restbody$ unchanged, whereas the $\mathrm{JVM}_\mathcal{E}$ does nothing:

1. $restbody_n/pos_n$ as well as $restbody_{n+1}/pos_{n+1}$ are unevaluated,
2. the beginning of the code for pos_n is the same as the beginning of the code for pos_{n+1}, and
3. $javaOpd(restbody_n, pos_n) = javaOpd(restbody_{n+1}, pos_{n+1})$.

In all theses cases the invariant (**beg**) is satisfied also for $n+1$, if it was satisfied for n.

Case 4. $context(pos_n) = {}^\alpha({}^\beta val \, bop \, {}^\gamma exp)$ and $pos_n = \beta$:

Then $pos_{n+1} = \gamma$ (rule $execJavaExp_I$ in Fig. 3.2). Since β is an $\mathcal{E}$-position, by the induction hypothesis (**exp**), it follows that $pc_{\sigma(n)} = \mathrm{end}_\beta$ and $opd_{\sigma(n)}$ is $javaOpd(restbody_n, \beta) \cdot jvmVal(val)$. By Def. 14.1.1, it follows that

$$
\begin{aligned}
javaOpd(restbody_n, \gamma) &= javaOpd(restbody_n, \alpha) \cdot jvmVal(val) \\
&= javaOpd(restbody_n, \beta) \cdot jvmVal(val) \\
&= opd_{\sigma(n)} = opd_{\sigma(n+1)}.
\end{aligned}
$$

We set $\sigma(n+1) := \sigma(n)$. Since $beg_\gamma = end_\beta$ and $restbody_n = restbody_{n+1}$, the invariant (**beg**) is satisfied in state $n+1$.

Case 5. $context(pos_n) = {}^\alpha({}^\beta val_1 \ bop \ {}^\gamma val_2)$ and $pos_n = \gamma$:

By the induction hypothesis (**exp**), it follows that $pc_{\sigma(n)} = end_\gamma$ and $opd_{\sigma(n)} = javaOpd(restbody_n, \gamma) \cdot jvmVal(val_2)$. Note that by Def. 14.1.1

$$
javaOpd(restbody_n, \gamma) = javaOpd(restbody_n, \alpha) \cdot jvmVal(val_1).
$$

Thus we have

$$
opd_{\sigma(n)} = javaOpd(restbody_n, \alpha) \cdot jvmVal(val_1) \cdot jvmVal(val_2).
$$

We distinguish now whether the expression in α has been compiled using $\mathcal{E}$ or as a Boolean expression.

Assume that α is an $\mathcal{E}$-position. According to the compilation scheme in Fig. 9.2, $code(end_\gamma)$ is the instruction $Prim(bop)$ and $end_\alpha = end_\gamma + 1$.

Assume that the operation bop does not throw an exception. Then $pos_{n+1} = \alpha$ and $restbody_{n+1}/\alpha = v$, where $v = JLS(bop, val_1, val_2)$ (rule $execJavaExp_I$ in Fig. 3.2 yields up the computed value). We set $\sigma(n+1) := \sigma(n)+1$ and obtain, after the execution of the $Prim(bop)$ instruction (rule $execVM_I$ in Fig. 9.1), that $pc_{\sigma(n+1)} = end_\alpha$ and $opd_{\sigma(n+1)} = javaOpd(restbody_{n+1}, \alpha) \cdot jvmVal(v)$ using the fact that

$$
JVMS(bop, jvmVal(val_1) \cdot jvmVal(val_2)) = jvmVal(JLS(bop, val_1, val_2)).
$$

Thus, the invariant (**exp**) is satisfied in state $n+1$.

Assume that α is a $\mathcal{B}_1(lab)$-position. Then $code(end_\gamma + 1)$ is the instruction $Cond(\mathtt{ifne}, lab)$ and $end_\alpha = end_\gamma + 2$. Hence, we can proceed as in the second part of Case 2, which includes the case that α is a $\mathcal{B}_0(lab)$-position.

If the operation bop throws an **ArithmeticException** (rule $execJavaExp_E$ in Fig. 6.3), then $pos_{n+1} = \alpha$ and $restbody_{n+1}/\alpha = Exc(r)$, where r is a pointer to a newly created object of type **ArithmeticException**.[3] The JVM$_\mathcal{E}$ executes in state $\sigma(n)$ the instruction $Prim(bop)$ and throws the same exception as Java$_\mathcal{E}$ (rule $execVM_E$ in Fig. 12.2). We set $\sigma(n+1) := \sigma(n)+1$ and obtain $switch_{\sigma(n+1)} = Throw(r)$ (through the execution of $Athrow$, the last instruction of the code sequence defining $raise$ in Sect. 12.1). The invariant (**exc**) is satisfied in state $n+1$, since $beg_\alpha \leq end_\gamma = pc_{\sigma(n+1)} < end_\alpha$ and $\mathcal{X}(\alpha)$ is empty by definition.

---

[3] To simplify the proof, we assume that the execution of the macro $fail$ of Java$_\mathcal{E}$ as well as of the macro $raise$ of the JVM$_\mathcal{E}$ are counted in the given runs as one step.

Case 6. $context(pos_n) = {}^\alpha(uop \, {}^\beta exp)$ and $pos_n = \alpha$:

Similar to Case 3.

Case 7. $context(pos_n) = {}^\alpha(uop \, {}^\beta val)$ and $pos_n = \beta$:

Similar to Case 5. If uop is the negation operator and α is a $\mathcal{B}_1(lab)$-position, then according to the compilation scheme in Fig. 9.3, the position β is $\mathcal{B}_0(lab)$-position. We set $\sigma(n + 1) := \sigma(n)$ and the invariants (**bool1**) and (**bool2**) for β in state n can be carried over to α in state $n + 1$.

Case 8. $context(pos_n) = {}^\alpha(loc = {}^\beta exp)$ and $pos_n = \alpha$:

Similar to Case 3.

Case 9. $context(pos_n) = {}^\alpha(loc = {}^\beta val)$ and $pos_n = \beta$:

Assume that α is an $\mathcal{E}$-position and that the size of the type of the variable loc is 1. (The case of size 2 is treated in a similar way.) According to the compilation scheme in Fig. 9.2, $code(\text{end}_\beta)$ is the instruction $Dupx(0, 1)$ followed by $Store(1, \overline{loc})$. Moreover, $\text{end}_\alpha = \text{end}_\beta + 2$. By the induction hypothesis (**exp**), it follows that $pc_{\sigma(n)} = \text{end}_\beta$ and $opd_{\sigma(n)}$ is $javaOpd(restbody_n, \beta) \cdot jvmVal(val)$. We set $\sigma(n+1) := \sigma(n) + 2$. The JVM$_\mathcal{E}$ executes the $Dupx$ and the $Store$ instruction (using the rule $execVM_I$ in Fig. 9.1) such that

$$
\begin{aligned}
pc_{\sigma(n+1)} &= pc_{\sigma(n)} + 2 = \text{end}_\beta + 2 = \text{end}_\alpha, \\
opd_{\sigma(n+1)} &= javaOpd(restbody_{n+1}, \alpha) \cdot jvmVal(val).
\end{aligned}
$$

Hence, the invariant (**exp**) is satisfied in state $n + 1$. After the application of rule $execJavaExp_I$ in Fig. 3.2, we have $locals_{n+1}(loc) = val$ and after the execution of the $Store$ instruction, $reg_{\sigma(n+1)}(\overline{loc}) = jvmVal(val)$. Hence, the invariant (**reg**) is satisfied as well.

The invariant (**fin**) remains true, since the register $\overline{ret}_\beta$ for storing the return address of a **finally** block is not used as a register of a local variable in the **finally** block and is therefore different from $\overline{loc}$.

If α is a $\mathcal{B}_i(lab)$-position, then we can proceed as in the second part of Case 2.

Case 10. $context(pos_n) = {}^\alpha({}^\beta exp_0 \, ? \, {}^\gamma exp_1 \, : \, {}^\delta exp_2)$ and $pos_n = \alpha$:

Similar to Case 3.

Case 11. $context(pos_n) = {}^\alpha({}^\beta val \, ? \, {}^\gamma exp_1 \, : \, {}^\delta exp_2)$ and $pos_n = \beta$:

According to the compilation scheme in Fig. 9.2, β is a $\mathcal{B}_1(\text{beg}_\gamma)$-position. Since the test expression in a conditional expressions is of type **boolean**, by invariant (**val**) of Theorem 8.4.1, it follows that val is either *True* or *False*. Since in this case the JVM$_\mathcal{E}$ does nothing, we set $\sigma(n + 1) := \sigma(n)$.

If $val = True$, then by the induction hypothesis (**bool1**), it follows that $pc_{\sigma(n)} = \text{beg}_\gamma$ and $opd_{\sigma(n)} = javaOpd(restbody_n, \beta)$. Java$_\mathcal{E}$ proceeds with $pos_{n+1} = \gamma$. Since $javaOpd(restbody_n, \beta) = javaOpd(restbody_{n+1}, \gamma)$ (by $restbody_n = restbody_{n+1}$ and the third clause of Def. 14.1.1), the invariant (**beg**) is satisfied in state $n + 1$.

If $val = \mathit{False}$, then by the induction hypothesis (**bool2**), it follows that $pc_{\sigma(n)} = \mathrm{end}_\beta$ and $opd_{\sigma(n)} = javaOpd(restbody_n, \beta)$. Java$_\mathcal{E}$ proceeds with $pos_{n+1} = \delta$. The invariant (**beg**) is satisfied in state $n+1$, since $\mathrm{end}_\beta = \mathrm{beg}_\delta$ and $javaOpd(restbody_n, \beta) = javaOpd(restbody_{n+1}, \delta)$.

Case 12. $context(pos_n) = {}^\alpha({}^\beta \mathit{True}\,?\,^\gamma val\,:\,{}^\delta exp)$ and $pos_n = \gamma$:

Assume that α is an $\mathcal{E}$-position. By the induction hypothesis (**exp**), it follows that $pc_{\sigma(n)} = \mathrm{end}_\gamma$ and $opd_{\sigma(n)} = javaOpd(restbody_n, \gamma) \cdot jvmVal(val)$. Java$_\mathcal{E}$ executes the rule $execJavaExp_I$ in Fig. 3.2 such that $pos_{n+1} = \alpha$ and $restbody_{n+1}/\alpha = val$. According to the compilation scheme in Fig. 9.2, code index $\mathrm{end}_\gamma = \mathrm{end}_\alpha$, and the JVM$_\mathcal{E}$ does nothing in this case. We set $\sigma(n+1) := \sigma(n)$. Since $javaOpd(restbody_n, \gamma) = javaOpd(restbody_{n+1}, \alpha)$ (by Def. 14.1.1), the invariant (**exp**) is satisfied.

If α is a $\mathcal{B}_1(lab)$-position, then γ is a $\mathcal{B}_1(lab)$-position, too. If $val = \mathit{True}$, then we set $\sigma(n+1) := \sigma(n)$ and the invariant (**bool1**) remains true. If $val = \mathit{False}$, then we set $\sigma(n+1) := \sigma(n) + 1$, the JVM$_\mathcal{E}$ executes the $Goto(\mathrm{end}_\alpha)$ instruction at code index end_γ and the invariant (**bool2**) remains true. (Similarly if α is a $\mathcal{B}_0(lab)$-position.)

Case 13. $context(pos_n) = {}^\alpha({}^\beta \mathit{False}\,?\,^\gamma exp\,:\,{}^\delta val)$ and $pos_n = \delta$:

Assume that α is an $\mathcal{E}$-position. By the induction hypothesis (**exp**), it follows that $pc_{\sigma(n)} = \mathrm{end}_\delta$ and $opd_{\sigma(n)} = javaOpd(restbody_n, \delta) \cdot jvmVal(val)$. Java$_\mathcal{E}$ executes rule $execJavaExp_I$ in Fig. 3.2 such that $pos_{n+1} = \alpha$ and $restbody_{n+1}/\alpha = val$. According to the compilation scheme in Fig. 9.2, $code(\mathrm{end}_\delta)$ is the instruction $Goto(\mathrm{end}_\alpha)$. We set $\sigma(n+1) := \sigma(n) + 1$. The JVM$_\mathcal{E}$ executes the $Goto$ instruction and the invariant (**exp**) is satisfied, since $javaOpd(restbody_n, \delta) = javaOpd(restbody_{n+1}, \alpha)$ (by Def. 14.1.1).

In case α is a $\mathcal{B}_i(lab)$-position, we proceed as in Case 12.

Java$_\mathcal{I}$-Statements. Following Fig. 3.1 and Fig. 3.3, we have to consider the eight cases for Java$_\mathcal{I}$-statements: empty statement (Case 14), expression statements (Cases 15–16), jump and labeled statements (Cases 17–18, 19–22), propagation of abruptions (Case 23), blocks (Cases 24–27), if-then-else (Cases 28–31) and while statements (Cases 32–34), and type declarations (Case 35). Subcases appear for evaluating subterms.

Case 14. $context(pos_n) = {}^\alpha;$

Then $pos_{n+1} = pos_n = \alpha$ and $restbody_{n+1}/\alpha = \mathit{Norm}$ (rule $execJavaStm_I$ in Fig. 3.3). By the induction hypothesis (**beg**), it follows that $pc_{\sigma(n)} = \mathrm{beg}_\alpha$ and $opd_{\sigma(n)} = javaOpd(restbody_n, \alpha) = [\,]$ (by clauses 1 and 2 of Def. 14.1.1). Since the code for the empty statement is empty (Fig. 9.4), $\mathrm{beg}_\alpha = \mathrm{end}_\alpha$. We set $\sigma(n+1) := \sigma(n)$ and the invariant (**stm**) is satisfied in state $n+1$.

Case 15. $context(pos_n) = {}^\alpha({}^\beta exp);$ and $pos_n = \alpha$:

Similar to case 3.

Case 16. $context(pos_n) = {}^\alpha({}^\beta val);$ and $pos_n = \beta$:

Then $pos_{n+1} = \alpha$ and $restbody_{n+1}/\alpha = Norm$ (rule $execJavaStm_I$ in Fig. 3.3). Since β is an $\mathcal{E}$-position (Fig. 9.2), by the induction hypothesis **(exp)**, it follows that $pc_{\sigma(n)} = end_\beta$ and $opd_{\sigma(n)} = javaOpd(restbody_n, \beta) \cdot jvmVal(val)$. Since $javaOpd(restbody_n, \beta)$ is empty, the operand stack $opd_{\sigma(n)}$ is equal to $jvmVal(val)$. The expression statement is compiled such that $code(end_\beta)$ is the instruction $Pop(size(\mathcal{T}(\beta)))$ and $end_\alpha = end_\beta + 1$ (Fig. 9.4). We set $\sigma(n+1) := \sigma(n) + 1$ and after the execution of the Pop instruction (rule $execVM_I$ in Fig. 9.1), we have $pc_{\sigma(n+1)} = end_\alpha$ and $opd_{\sigma(n+1)} = [\,]$ and the invariant **(stm)** is satisfied in state $n + 1$.

Case 17. $context(pos_n) = {}^\alpha\texttt{break}\ lab$;

Then $pos_{n+1} = \alpha$ and $restbody_{n+1}/\alpha = Break(lab)$ (rule $execJavaStm_I$ in Fig. 3.3). By the induction hypothesis **(beg)**, it follows that $pc_{\sigma(n)} = beg_\alpha$ or $code(beg_\alpha) = Goto(pc_{\sigma(n)})$ and $opd_{\sigma(n)} = [\,]$. The **break**-statement is compiled in Fig. 12.3 such that beg_α is a continuation for a $Break(lab)$ at position α in the sense of Def. 14.1.3. If the position α is not enclosed by **try** blocks, then $code(beg_\alpha) = Goto(lab_b)$ and lab_b is a continuation for a $Break(lab)$ at position α, too. We set $\sigma(n+1) := \sigma(n)$ and the invariant **(abr)** is satisfied in state $n + 1$.

Case 18. $context(pos_n) = {}^\alpha\texttt{continue}\ lab$;

Similar to Case 17.

Case 19. $context(pos_n) = {}^\alpha lab : {}^\beta stm$ and $pos_n = \alpha$:

Similar to Case 3.

Case 20. $context(pos_n) = {}^\alpha lab : {}^\beta Norm$ and $pos_n = \beta$:

Then $pos_{n+1} = \alpha$ and $restbody_{n+1}/\alpha = Norm$ (rule $execJavaStm_I$ in Fig. 3.3). We set $\sigma(n+1) := \sigma(n)$. Since $end_\beta = end_\alpha$ (Fig. 9.4), the invariant **(stm)** is still satisfied in state $n + 1$.

Case 21. $context(pos_n) = {}^\alpha lab : {}^\beta Break(l)$ and $pos_n = \beta$:

By the induction hypothesis **(abr)**, it follows that $opd_{\sigma(n)} = [\,]$ and $pc_{\sigma(n)}$ is a continuation for a $Break(l)$ at position β in the sense of Def. 14.1.3.

Assume that $lab = l$. Then $pos_{n+1} = \alpha$ and $restbody_{n+1}/\alpha = Norm$ (rule $execJavaStm_I$ in Fig. 3.3). Since $pc_{\sigma(n)}$ is a continuation for a $Break(l)$ at position β and $finallyLabsUntil(\beta, lab) = [\,]$, Def. 14.1.3 implies that either $code(pc_{\sigma(n)})$ is the instruction $Goto(lab_b)$ or $pc_{\sigma(n)} = lab_b$. In the first case we set $\sigma(n+1) := \sigma(n) + 1$ and the $JVM_\mathcal{E}$ executes the $Goto$ instruction. In the second case we set $\sigma(n+1) := \sigma(n)$ and the $JVM_\mathcal{E}$ does nothing. Since $lab_b = end_\alpha$, the invariant **(stm)** is satisfied in state $n + 1$.

Assume that $lab \neq l$. Then $pos_{n+1} = \alpha$ and $restbody_{n+1}/\alpha = Break(l)$. We set $\sigma(n+1) := \sigma(n)$. The invariant **(abr)** is still satisfied, since in this case $finallyLabsUntil(\beta, lab) = finallyLabs(\alpha, lab)$ and $pc_{\sigma(n)}$ is also a continuation for a $Break(l)$ at position α.

Case 22. $context(pos_n) = {}^\alpha lab : {}^\beta Continue(l)$ and $pos_n = \beta$:

By the induction hypothesis (**abr**), it follows that $opd_{\sigma(n)} = [\,]$ and $pc_{\sigma(n)}$ is a continuation for a $Continue(l)$ at position β in the sense of Def. 14.1.4.

Assume that $lab = l$. Then $pos_{n+1} = \beta$ and $restbody_{n+1}/\beta = body(meth_n)/\beta$ (rule $execJavaStm_I$ in Fig. 3.3). Since $pc_{\sigma(n)}$ is a continuation for the abruption $Continue(l)$ at position β, Def. 14.1.4 implies that either $code(pc_{\sigma(n)})$ is the instruction $Goto(lab_c)$ or $pc_{\sigma(n)} = lab_c$. In the first case we set $\sigma(n+1) := \sigma(n) + 1$ and the JVM$_\mathcal{E}$ executes the $Goto$ instruction. In the second case we set $\sigma(n+1) := \sigma(n)$ and the JVM$_\mathcal{E}$ does nothing. Since $lab_c = beg_\alpha$ and $beg_\alpha = beg_\beta$, the invariant (**beg**) is satisfied in state $n+1$.

Assume that $lab \neq l$. Then $pos_{n+1} = \alpha$ and $restbody_{n+1}/\alpha = Continue(l)$. We set $\sigma(n+1) := \sigma(n)$. The invariant (**abr**) is still satisfied, since $pc_{\sigma(n)}$ is also a continuation for a $Continue(l)$ at position α.

Case 23. $context(pos_n) = {}^\alpha phrase({}^\beta abr)$, $pos_n \neq firstPos$, $pos_n = \beta$ and $propagatesAbr(restbody_n/\alpha)$:

Then Java$_\mathcal{E}$ propagates the abruption upwards such that $pos_{n+1} = \alpha$ and $restbody_{n+1}/\alpha = abr$ (rule $execJavaStm_I$ in Fig. 3.3). We set $\sigma(n+1) := \sigma(n)$.

Assume that abr is not an exception. By the induction hypothesis (**abr**), it follows, that $pc_{\sigma(n)}$ is a continuation for abr at position β. Since the assumption $propagatesAbr(restbody_n/\alpha)$ implies that $body(meth_n)/\alpha$ is neither a labeled statement nor a `try-finally` statement, $pc_{\sigma(n)}$ is also a continuation for abr at position α. Hence, the invariant (**abr**) is satisfied in state $n+1$.

Assume that $abr = Exc(r)$. By the induction hypothesis (**exc**) (which applies because $pos_n \neq firstPos$ and $body(meth_n)/\beta \neq$ `static_`), it follows that

1. $switch_{\sigma(n)} = Throw(r)$,

2. $beg_\beta \leq pc_{\sigma(n)}$,

3. $pc_{\sigma(n)} < end_\beta$, or β is an $\mathcal{E}$-position and $pc_{\sigma(n)} < end_{up(\beta)}$,

4. there is no $(f, u, \_, c) \in \mathcal{X}(\beta)$ with $f \leq pc_{\sigma(n)} < u$ and $classOf(r) \preceq_h c$.

Since the nesting of expressions and statements is preserved by the compiler, we have $beg_\alpha \leq beg_\beta$ and $end_\beta \leq end_\alpha$ (Lemma 14.1.1). It follows that $beg_\alpha \leq pc_{\sigma(n)} < end_\alpha$. Since $propagatesAbr(restbody_n, \alpha)$ implies that $body(meth_n)/\beta$ is neither a `try` block in a `try-catch` statement nor a `try-catch` statement in a `try-finally` statement, by clause 3 of Lemma 14.2.1 it follows that there is no $(f, u, \_, c)$ in $\mathcal{X}(\alpha)$ such that $f \leq pc_{\sigma(n)} < u$ and $classOf(r) \preceq_h c$. Hence, the invariant (**exc**) is satisfied in state $n+1$.

Case 24. $context(pos_n) = {}^\alpha\{\,\}$:

Similar to Case 14.

Case 25. $context(pos_n) = {}^\alpha\{{}^{\beta_1} stm_1 \ldots {}^{\beta_n} stm_n\}$ and $pos_n = \alpha$:

Similar to Case 3.

Case 26. $context(pos_n) = {}^\alpha\{{}^{\beta_1} Norm \ldots {}^{\beta_n} Norm\}$ and $pos_n = \beta_n$:

Then $pos_{n+1} = \alpha$ and $restbody_{n+1}/\alpha = Norm$ (rule $execJavaStm_I$ in Fig. 3.3). By the induction hypothesis (**stm**), it follows that $pc_{\sigma(n)} = end_{\beta_n}$ and $opd_{\sigma(n)} = [\,]$. We set $\sigma(n+1) := \sigma(n)$. Since $end_\alpha = end_{\beta_n}$ (Fig. 9.4), the invariant (**stm**) is satisfied in state $n+1$.

Case 27. $context(pos_n) = {}^\alpha\{{}^{\beta_1} Norm \ldots {}^{\beta_i} Norm^{\beta_{i+1}} stm_{i+1} \ldots {}^{\beta_n} stm_n\}$ and $pos_n = \beta_n$:

Then $pos_{n+1} = \beta_{i+1}$ (rule $execJavaStm_I$ in Fig. 3.3). By the induction hypothesis (**stm**), it follows that $pc_{\sigma(n)} = end_{\beta_i}$ and $opd_{\sigma(n)} = [\,]$. We set $\sigma(n+1) := \sigma(n)$. By Lemma 8.1.2, 8.1.4 and 8.1.5, it follows that stm_{i+1} is not evaluated. Since $end_{\beta_i} = beg_{\beta_{i+1}}$ (Fig. 9.4), the invariant (**beg**) is satisfied in state $n+1$.

Case 28. $context(pos_n) = {}^\alpha\texttt{if}\,({}^\beta exp)\,{}^\gamma stm_1$ else ${}^\delta stm_2$ and $pos_n = \alpha$:

Similar to Case 3.

Case 29. $context(pos_n) = {}^\alpha\texttt{if}\,({}^\beta val)\,{}^\gamma stm_1$ else ${}^\delta stm_2$ and $pos_n = \beta$:

Similar to Case 11.

Case 30. $context(pos_n) = {}^\alpha\texttt{if}\,({}^\beta True)\,{}^\gamma Norm$ else ${}^\delta stm$ and $pos_n = \gamma$:

Similar to Case 12.

Case 31. $context(pos_n) = {}^\alpha\texttt{if}\,({}^\beta False)\,{}^\gamma stm$ else ${}^\delta Norm$ and $pos_n = \gamma$:

Similar to Case 13.

Case 32. $context(pos_n) = {}^\alpha\texttt{while}\,({}^\beta exp)^\gamma stm$ and $pos_n = \alpha$:

Similar to Case 3.

Case 33. $context(pos_n) = {}^\alpha\texttt{while}\,({}^\beta val)^\gamma stm$ and $pos_n = \beta$:

The position β is a $\mathcal{B}_1(beg_\gamma)$-position (Fig. 9.4). Since the test expression in a while-statement is of type boolean, by invariant (**val**) of Theorem 8.4.1, it follows that val is either $True$ or $False$. We set $\sigma(n+1) := \sigma(n)$.

Assume that $val = True$. Then $pos_{n+1} = \gamma$ (Fig. 3.3). By the induction hypothesis (**bool1**), it follows that $pc_{\sigma(n)} = beg_\gamma$ and $opd_{\sigma(n)} = [\,]$. Since stm is not evaluated, the invariant (**beg**) is satisfied in state $n+1$.

Assume that $val = False$. Then $pos_{n+1} = \alpha$ and $restbody_n/\alpha = Norm$ (Fig. 3.3). By the induction hypothesis (**bool2**), it follows that $pc_{\sigma(n)} = end_\beta$ and $opd_{\sigma(n)} = [\,]$. Since $end_\beta = end_\alpha$ (Fig. 9.4), the invariant (**stm**) is satisfied in state $n+1$.

Case 34. $context(pos_n) = {}^\alpha\texttt{while}\,({}^\beta True)^\gamma Norm$ and $pos_n = \gamma$:

Then $pos_{n+1} = \alpha$ and $restbody_{n+1}/\alpha = body(meth_n)/\alpha$ (Fig. 3.3). By the induction hypothesis (**stm**), it follows that $pc_{\sigma(n)} = end_\gamma$ and $opd_{\sigma(n)} = [\,]$. We set $\sigma(n+1) := \sigma(n)$. Since $code(beg_\alpha)$ is the instruction $Goto(end_\gamma)$ (Fig. 9.4), the invariant (**beg**) is satisfied in state $n+1$.

Remark: This case is the reason that the invariant (**beg**) does not just say $pc_{\sigma(n)} = beg_\alpha$ but allows also that $code(beg_\alpha) = Goto(pc_{\sigma(n)})$.

Case 35. $context(pos_n) = {}^\alpha Type\; x;$

Similar to Case 14.

Java$_C$-Expressions. Following Fig. 4.3 and Fig. 4.4, we have to consider the four cases for Java$_C$-expressions, namely for static fields (Case 36) and assignments to them (Cases 37–38), for static method invocations (Cases 39–40), and for the left-to-right evaluation of expression sequences (Cases 41–44).

Case 36. $context(pos_n) = {}^\alpha c.f$:

According to Fig. 10.3, the access to the static field f of class c is compiled as the instruction $GetStatic(\mathcal{T}(\alpha), c/f)$. By the induction hypothesis (**beg**), it follows that $pc_{\sigma(n)} = beg_\alpha$ and $opd_{\sigma(n)} = javaOpd(restbody_n, \alpha)$.

Assume that the class c is initialized. Then, by rule $execJavaExp_C$ in Fig. 4.4, $pos_{n+1} = \alpha$ and $restbody_{n+1}/\alpha = globals_n(c/f)$.

Assume that α is an $\mathcal{E}$-position. We set $\sigma(n+1) := \sigma(n)+1$. The JVM$_\mathcal{E}$ executes the $GetStatic$ instruction (rule $execVM_C$ in Fig. 10.1). Since $pc_{\sigma(n+1)} = end_\alpha$ and $opd_{\sigma(n+1)} = opd_{\sigma(n)} \cdot globals_n(c/f)$, the invariant (**exp**) is satisfied in state $n+1$. Note, that $globals_n(c/f)$ is a value by invariant (**global**) of Theorem 8.4.1.

The cases where α is a $\mathcal{B}_i(lab)$-position are treated as in Case 2.

Assume that the class c is not initialized. Assume that $classState_n(c) = Linked$. Then Java$_\mathcal{E}$ has to initialize the class c:

$$
\begin{aligned}
frames_{n+1} &= frames_n \cdot (meth_n, restbody_n, \alpha, locals_n),\\
meth_{n+1} &= c/\texttt{<clinit>},\\
restbody_{n+1} &= body(c/\texttt{<clinit>}),\\
pos_{n+1} &= firstPos,\\
locals_{n+1} &= \emptyset,\\
classState_{n+1}(c) &= Initialized.
\end{aligned}
$$

We set $\sigma(n+1) := \sigma(n)+2$. In state $\sigma(n)$, the JVM$_\mathcal{E}$ executes the $GetStatic$ instruction such that $switch_{n+1} = InitClass(c)$. In state $\sigma(n)+1$, it executes the $switchVM_C$ rule in Fig. 10.2 such that

$$
\begin{aligned}
stack_{\sigma(n+1)} &= stack_{\sigma(n)} \cdot (pc_{\sigma(n)}, reg_{\sigma(n)}, opd_{\sigma(n)}, meth_{\sigma(n)}),\\
meth_{\sigma(n+1)} &= c/\texttt{<clinit>},\\
pc_{\sigma(n+1)} &= 0,\\
opd_{\sigma(n+1)} &= [\,],\\
reg_{\sigma(n+1)} &= \emptyset,\\
classState_{n+1}(c) &= Initialized.
\end{aligned}
$$

Since $locals_{n+1}$ and $reg_{\sigma(n+1)}$ are both empty, the invariant (**reg**) is satisfied. We have

$$
\begin{aligned}
frames_n &\approx stack_{\sigma(n)}, \\
locals_n &\approx reg_{\sigma(n)}, \\
pc_{\sigma(n)} &= beg_\alpha, \\
opd_{\sigma(n)} &= javaOpd(restbody_n, \alpha).
\end{aligned}
$$

Therefore by the induction hypothesis (**fin**), $frames_{n+1} \approx stack_{\sigma(n+1)}$ in the sense of Def. 14.1.8 and the invariant (**stack**) is satisfied. Since by Def. 14.1.1 $javaOpd(restbody_{n+1}, pos_{n+1}) = [\,]$, the invariant (**beg**) is satisfied. If c is the class `Object` or the direct super class of c is initialized, then $switch_{\sigma(n+1)}$ is $Noswitch$; otherwise $switch_{\sigma(n+1)}$ is $InitClass(super(c))$ (Fig. 10.2). Hence, the invariant (**clinit**) is satisfied as well.

Assume that $classState_n(c) = Unusable$. We set $\sigma(n + 1) := \sigma(n) + 2$. $Java_\mathcal{E}$ throws a `NoClassDefFoundError` (by the refinement of $initialize(c)$ in Sect. 6.2). Since after having executed the $GetStatic$ instruction, the $JVM_\mathcal{E}$ does the same (rule $switchVM_E$ in Fig. 12.1), the invariant (**exc**) is satisfied (by Fig. 12.4, $\mathcal{X}(\alpha) = [\,]$).

Case 37. $context(pos_n) = {}^\alpha(c.f = {}^\beta exp)$ and $pos_n = \alpha$:

Similar to Case 3.

Case 38. $context(pos_n) = {}^\alpha(c.f = {}^\beta val)$ and $pos_n = \beta$:

If the class c is not yet initialized in state n, then we proceed as in Case 36. Otherwise, the proof is similar to Case 9.

Case 39. $context(pos_n) = {}^\alpha c.m^\beta(exps)$ and $pos_n = \alpha$:

Similar to Case 3.

Case 40. $context(pos_n) = {}^\alpha c.m^\beta(vals)$ and $pos_n = \beta$:

If the class c is not yet initialized in state n, then we proceed as in Case 36. Otherwise, $Java_\mathcal{E}$ executes an $invokeMethod(\alpha, c/m, vals)$ such that

$$
\begin{aligned}
frames_{n+1} &= frames_n \cdot (meth_n, restbody_n, \alpha, locals_n), \\
meth_{n+1} &= c/m, \\
restbody_{n+1} &= body(c/m), \\
pos_{n+1} &= firstPos, \\
locals_{n+1} &= zip(argNames(c/m), vals).
\end{aligned}
$$

By the induction hypothesis (**exp**), it follows that $pc_{\sigma(n)} = end_\beta$ and $opd_{\sigma(n)} = javaOpd(restbody_n, \beta) \cdot jvmVal(vals)$. We set $\sigma(n+1) := \sigma(n)+2$. According to the compilation scheme in Fig. 10.3, $code(end_\beta)$ is the instruction $InvokeStatic(\mathcal{T}(\alpha), c/m)$ and $end_\alpha = end_\beta + 1$. In state $\sigma(n)$, the $JVM_\mathcal{E}$ executes the $InvokeStatic$ instruction (rule $execVM_C$ in Fig. 10.1) such that

$$
\begin{aligned}
opd_{\sigma(n)+1} &= javaOpd(restbody_n, \beta), \\
switch_{\sigma(n)+1} &= Call(c/m, jvmVal(vals)).
\end{aligned}
$$

In state $\sigma(n) + 1$, the $JVM_\mathcal{E}$ executes the $switchVM_C$ rule in Fig. 10.2 and, since a static method cannot be abstract by Constraint 4.1.6, performs a $pushFrame(c/m, jvmVal(vals))$ such that

$$
\begin{aligned}
stack_{\sigma(n+1)} &= stack_{\sigma(n)} \cdot (pc_{\sigma(n)}, reg_{\sigma(n)}, opd_{\sigma(n)+1}, meth_{\sigma(n)}), \\
meth_{\sigma(n+1)} &= c/m, \\
pc_{\sigma(n+1)} &= 0, \\
opd_{\sigma(n+1)} &= [], \\
reg_{\sigma(n+1)} &= makeReg(jvmVal(vals)).
\end{aligned}
$$

Since $zip(argNames(c/m), vals) \approx makeReg(jvmVal(vals))$, the invariant (**reg**) is satisfied for $n + 1$. We have $meth_n = meth_{\sigma(n)}$ and

$$
\begin{aligned}
frames_n &\approx stack_{\sigma(n)}, \\
locals_n &\approx reg_{\sigma(n)}, \\
pc_{\sigma(n)} &= end_\alpha - 1, \\
opd_{\sigma(n)+1} &= javaOpd(restbody_n, \alpha).
\end{aligned}
$$

Therefore, the induction hypothesis (**fin**) implies $frames_{n+1} \approx stack_{\sigma(n+1)}$ (Def. 14.1.8) and the invariant (**stack**) is satisfied for $n + 1$. Since by Def. 14.1.1 $javaOpd(restbody_{n+1}, pos_{n+1}) = []$, the invariant (**beg**) for $n + 1$ is satisfied as well.

Case 41. $context(pos_n) = {}^\alpha()$:

Then $pos_{n+1} = \alpha$ and $restbody_{n+1}/\alpha = []$ (Fig. 4.4). By the induction hypothesis (**beg**), it follows that $pc_{\sigma(n)} = beg_\alpha$ and $opd_{\sigma(n)} = javaOpd(restbody_n, \alpha)$. We set $\sigma(n + 1) := \sigma(n)$. Since $end_\alpha = beg_\alpha$, the invariant (**exp**) is satisfied in state $n + 1$.

Case 42. $context(pos_n) = {}^\alpha({}^{\beta_1} exp_1, \dots, {}^{\beta_n} exp_n)$ and $pos_n = \alpha$:

Similar to Case 3.

Case 43. $context(pos_n) = {}^\alpha({}^{\beta_1} val_1, \dots, {}^{\beta_n} val_n)$ and $pos_n = \beta_n$:

Then $pos_{n+1} = \alpha$ (Fig. 4.4). By the induction hypothesis (**exp**), it follows that

$$
\begin{aligned}
pc_{\sigma(n)} &= end_{\beta_n}, \\
opd_{\sigma(n)} &= javaOpd(restbody_n, \beta_n) \cdot jvmVal(val_n).
\end{aligned}
$$

We set $\sigma(n + 1) := \sigma(n)$. Since $end_{\beta_n} = end_\alpha$ and, by Def. 14.1.1,

$$
\begin{aligned}
javaOpd(restbody_n, \beta_n) \cdot jvmVal(val_n) = \\
javaOpd(restbody_n, \alpha) \cdot jvmVal(val_1) \cdot \dots jvmVal(val_n),
\end{aligned}
$$

and since in this case $javaOpd(restbody_n, \alpha) = javaOpd(restbody_{n+1}, \alpha)$, the invariant (**exp**) is satisfied in state $n + 1$.

Case 44. $context(pos_n) = {}^\alpha({}^{\beta_1} val_1, \dots, {}^{\beta_i} val_i, {}^{\beta_{i+1}} exp_{i+1}, \dots, {}^{\beta_n} exp_n)$ and $pos_n = \beta_i$:

Then $pos_{n+1} = \beta_{i+1}$ (Fig. 4.4). By the induction hypothesis (**exp**), it follows that

$$
\begin{aligned}
pc_{\sigma(n)} &= end_{\beta_i}, \\
opd_{\sigma(n)} &= javaOpd(restbody_n, \beta_i) \cdot jvmVal(val_i).
\end{aligned}
$$

We set $\sigma(n+1) := \sigma(n)$. Since $\mathrm{end}_{\beta_i} = \mathrm{beg}_{\beta_{i+1}}$ and, by Def. 14.1.1,

$$javaOpd(restbody_n, \beta_{i+1}) = javaOpd(restbody_n, \beta_i) \cdot jvmVal(val_i),$$

and since $restbody_n = restbody_{n+1}$, the invariant (**beg**) is satisfied in state $n+1$.

Java$_C$-Statements. Following Fig. 4.3 and Fig. 4.5, we have to consider the three new cases which appear for statement execution in Java$_C$, namely start of and return from static initialization code (Cases 45–46), method return and its propagation through labeled statements to the beginning of the method body (Cases 47–53), and normal completion of expression statements for methods returning `void` (Case 54).

Case 45. $context(pos_n) = {}^\alpha\mathtt{static}\,{}^\beta stm$ and $pos_n = \alpha$:

Let c be the class of $meth_n$. Assume that c is the class `Object` or the direct super class of c is initialized. Then $pos_{n+1} = \beta$ (rule $execJavaStm_E$ in Fig. 4.5). We set $\sigma(n+1) := \sigma(n)$. Since $\mathrm{beg}_\alpha = \mathrm{beg}_\beta$ (Fig. 10.3) and $restbody_n = restbody_{n+1}$, the invariant (**beg**) is still satisfied.

Otherwise, c is not `Object` and the direct super class of c is not initialized. Java$_\mathcal{E}$ has to initialize $super(c)$. By the induction hypothesis (**clinit**), it follows that $switch_{\sigma(n)}$ is $InitClass(super(c))$. We set $\sigma(n+1) := \sigma(n)+1$, since the JVM$_\mathcal{E}$ does one step of $switchVM_E$, and proceed as in Case 36.

Case 46. $context(pos_n) = {}^\alpha\mathtt{static}\,{}^\beta Return$ and $pos_n = \beta$:

Similar to Case 23.

Case 47. $context(pos_n) = {}^\alpha\mathtt{return}\,{}^\beta exp;$ and $pos_n = \alpha$:

Similar to Case 3.

Case 48. $context(pos_n) = {}^\alpha\mathtt{return}\,{}^\beta val;$ and $pos_n = \beta$:

Then $pos_{n+1} = \alpha$ and $restbody_{n+1}/\alpha = Return(val)$ (Fig. 4.5). By the induction hypothesis (**exp**), it follows that $pc_{\sigma(n)} = \mathrm{end}_\beta$ and $opd_{\sigma(n)}$ is $jvmVal(val)$. Let $[\mathrm{fin}_1, \ldots, \mathrm{fin}_k] = finallyLabs(\alpha)$. Then according to the compilation scheme in Fig. 12.3 we have:

$$
\begin{aligned}
code(pc_{\sigma(n)}) &= Store(\mathcal{T}(\beta), \overline{var}) \\
code(pc_{\sigma(n)}+1) &= Jsr(\mathrm{fin}_1) \\
\vdots\quad\quad & \qquad\quad \vdots \\
code(pc_{\sigma(n)}+k) &= Jsr(\mathrm{fin}_k) \\
code(pc_{\sigma(n)}+k+1) &= Load(\mathcal{T}(\beta), \overline{var}) \\
code(pc_{\sigma(n)}+k+2) &= Return(\mathcal{T}(\beta))
\end{aligned}
$$

We set $\sigma(n+1) := \sigma(n)+1$. The JVM executes the store instruction such that $opd_{\sigma(n+1)} = [\,]$ and $pc_{\sigma(n+1)} = pc_{\sigma(n)} + 1$. Since $pc_{\sigma(n)} + 1$ is a continuation for $Return(val)$ at position α in the sense of Def. 14.1.6, the invariant (**abr**) is satisfied in state $n+1$.

Case 49. $context(pos_n) = {}^\alpha\texttt{return}$;

Similar to Case 48.

Case 50. $context(pos_n) = {}^\alpha lab : {}^\beta Return$ and $pos_n = \beta$:

Similar to Case 23.

Case 51. $context(pos_n) = {}^\alpha lab : {}^\beta Return(val)$ and $pos_n = \beta$:

Similar to Case 23.

Case 52. $context(pos_n) = {}^\alpha Return(val)$, $pos_n = firstPos$ and $frames_n \neq [\,]$:

Then Java$_\mathcal{E}$ executes an $exitMethod(val)$ such that

$$
\begin{aligned}
frames_n &= frames_{n+1} \cdot (meth_{n+1}, rest, pos_{n+1}, locals_{n+1}), \\
restbody_{n+1} &= rest[val/pos_{n+1}].
\end{aligned}
$$

By the induction hypothesis (**abr**), it follows that $pc_{\sigma(n)}$ is a continuation for $Return(val)$ at position α with respect to $reg_{\sigma(n)}$. Since $finallyLabs(\alpha) = [\,]$ (due to $pos_n = firstPos$), Def. 14.1.6 implies that

$$
\begin{aligned}
code(pc_{\sigma(n)}) &= Load(\tau, x), \\
code(pc_{\sigma(n)} + 1) &= Return(\tau), \\
jvmVal(val) &= [reg_{\sigma(n)}(x)].
\end{aligned}
$$

We set $\sigma(n+1) := \sigma(n) + 3$. In state $\sigma(n)$, the JVM$_\mathcal{E}$ executes the $Load$ instruction such that $opd_{\sigma(n)+1} = jvmVal(val)$. In state $\sigma(n)+1$, the JVM$_\mathcal{E}$ executes the $Return$ instruction such that $switch_{\sigma(n)+2} = Result(jvmVal(val))$. In state $\sigma(n) + 2$, the JVM$_\mathcal{E}$ executes rule $switchVM_C$ in Fig. 10.2 and performs a $popFrame(1, jvmVal(val))$, since $meth_n$ has a return type different from $\texttt{void}$ (by invariant (**abr4**) of Theorem 8.4.1) and is therefore not an implicitly called $\texttt{<clinit>}$ method. We obtain:

$$
\begin{aligned}
stack_{\sigma(n)} &= stack_{\sigma(n+1)} \cdot (pc', reg_{\sigma(n+1)}, opd', meth_{\sigma(n+1)}), \\
pc_{\sigma(n+1)} &= pc' + 1, \\
opd_{\sigma(n+1)} &= opd' \cdot jvmVal(val).
\end{aligned}
$$

By the induction hypothesis (**stack**), Def. 14.1.8 and Lemma 8.1.3 it follows that

$$
\begin{aligned}
frames_{n+1} &\approx stack_{\sigma(n+1)}, \\
locals_{n+1} &\approx reg_{\sigma(n+1)}, \\
pc' &= end_{pos_{n+1}} - 1, \\
opd' &= javaOpd(rest, pos_{n+1}).
\end{aligned}
$$

Hence, the invariants (**reg**) and (**stack**) are satisfied in state $n + 1$. Since $pc_{\sigma(n+1)} = end_{pos_{n+1}}$, $restbody_{n+1}/pos_{n+1} = val$ and

$$
\begin{aligned}
opd_{\sigma(n+1)} &= javaOpd(rest, pos_{n+1}) \cdot jvmVal(val) \\
&= javaOpd(restbody_{n+1}, pos_{n+1}) \cdot jvmVal(val),
\end{aligned}
$$

the invariant (**exp**) is satisfied as well. Def. 14.1.8 implies that $reg_{\sigma(n+1)}$ contains correct return addresses for pos_{n+1} in $rest$. Since $restbody_{n+1}$ is obtained from $rest$ just by substituting val for pos_{n+1}, it also contains correct return addresses for pos_{n+1} in $restbody_{n+1}$ and the invariant (**fin**) is satisfied in state $n+1$.

Case 53. $context(pos_n) = {}^{\alpha}Return$, $pos_n = firstPos$ and $frames_n \neq []$:

Then Java$_{\mathcal{E}}$ executes an $exitMethod(Norm)$ such that

$$frames_n = frames_{n+1} \cdot (meth_{n+1}, rest, pos_{n+1}, locals_{n+1}).$$

$$restbody_{n+1} = \begin{cases} rest, & \text{if } meth_n = \_/\texttt{<clinit>}; \\ rest[locals_n(\texttt{this})/pos_{n+1}], & \text{if } meth_n = \_/\texttt{<init>}(\_); \\ rest[Norm/pos_{n+1}], & \text{otherwise.} \end{cases}$$

By the induction hypothesis (**abr**), it follows that $pc_{\sigma(n)}$ is a continuation for a $Return$ at position α with respect to $reg_{\sigma(n)}$. Since $finallyLabs(\alpha) = []$ (due to $pos_n = firstPos$), Def. 14.1.5 implies that $code(pc_{\sigma(n)})$ is the instruction $Return(\texttt{void})$. We set $\sigma(n+1) := \sigma(n)+2$. In state $\sigma(n)$, the JVM$_{\mathcal{E}}$ executes the $Return(\texttt{void})$ instruction such that $switch_{\sigma(n)+1} = Result([])$. In state $\sigma(n)+1$, the JVM$_{\mathcal{E}}$ executes a $popFrame(0, [])$, if $meth_n$ is a class initialization method, and a $popFrame(1, [])$, otherwise. We thus obtain:

$$stack_{\sigma(n)} = stack_{\sigma(n+1)} \cdot (pc', reg_{\sigma(n+1)}, opd_{\sigma(n+1)}, meth_{\sigma(n+1)}),$$
$$pc_{\sigma(n+1)} = \begin{cases} pc', & \text{if } meth_n = \_/\texttt{<clinit>}; \\ pc' + 1, & \text{otherwise.} \end{cases}$$

By the induction hypothesis (**stack**) and Def. 14.1.8, it follows that

1. $frames_{n+1} \approx stack_{\sigma(n+1)}$,
2. $locals_{n+1} \approx reg_{\sigma(n+1)}$,
3. $reg_{\sigma(n+1)}$ contains correct return addresses for pos_{n+1} in $rest$.

Hence, the invariants (**reg**) and (**stack**) are satisfied in state $n+1$. The invariant (**fin**) is satisfied, since $reg_{\sigma(n+1)}$ contains also correct return addresses for pos_{n+1} in $restbody_{n+1}$.

Assume that $meth_n$ is a class initialization method. Then $restbody_{n+1} = rest$ and $pc_{\sigma(n+1)} = pc'$. Def. 14.1.8 and Lemma 8.1.3 imply that the invariants (**beg**) or (**exp**) are still satisfied.

Assume that $meth_n$ is an instance initialization method. Then $restbody_{n+1}$ is obtained from $rest$ by substituting $locals_n(\texttt{this})$ at position pos_{n+1} and $pc_{\sigma(n+1)} = pc' + 1$. Def. 14.1.8 and the induction hypothesis (**stack**) imply that

1. $pc' = end_{pos_{n+1}} - 1$,
2. $rest/pos_{n+1} = ref.meth_n(\_)$,
3. $opd_{\sigma(n+1)} = javaOpd(rest, pos_{n+1}) \cdot [ref]$.

From invariant (**chain3**) of Theorem 8.4.1 it follows that $locals_n(\texttt{this})$ is the reference ref. Since $pc_{\sigma(n+1)} = end_{pos_{n+1}}$ and $restbody_{n+1}/pos_{n+1} = ref$, the invariant (**exp**) is satisfied.

Otherwise, $meth_n$ is a class or instance method with return type $\texttt{void}$ (invariant (**abr3**) of Theorem 8.4.1). Def. 14.1.8 implies that

1. $pc' = end_{pos_{n+1}} - 1$,
2. $opd_{\sigma(n+1)} = javaOpd(rest, pos_{n+1})$.

Since $pc_{\sigma(n+1)} = pc' + 1$ and $restbody_{n+1} = rest[Norm/pos_{n+1}]$, the invariant (**stm**) is satisfied.

Case 54. $context(pos_n) = {}^\alpha({}^\beta Norm)$; and $pos_n = \beta$:

Similar to Case 16, exploiting that we consider such positions β of method invocations with return type $\texttt{void}$ as $\mathcal{S}$-positions.

Java$_\mathcal{O}$-Expressions. Following Fig. 5.1 and Fig. 5.2, we have to consider the seven new kinds of expressions occurring in Java$_\mathcal{O}$, namely $\texttt{this}$ (Case 55), $\texttt{new } c$ (Case 56), instance fields (Cases 57–58) and assignment to them (Cases 59–61), $\texttt{instanceof}$ (Cases 62–63) and type cast expressions (Cases 64–65), and instance method invocations (Cases 66–68).

Case 55. $context(pos_n) = {}^\alpha\texttt{this}$:

Similar to Case 2.

Case 56. $context(pos_n) = {}^\alpha\texttt{new } c$:

By the induction hypothesis (**beg**), it follows that $pc_{\sigma(n)} = beg_\alpha$ and $opd_{\sigma(n)} = javaOpd(restbody_n, \alpha)$. According to the compilation scheme in Fig. 11.2, $code(beg_\alpha)$ is the instruction $New(c)$ followed by the instruction $Dupx(0,1)$ and $end_\alpha = beg_\alpha + 2$.

Assume that the class c is initialized in state n. Then $pos_{n+1} = \alpha$ and $restbody_{n+1}/\alpha = ref$, where ref is a reference to a newly created object of type c on the heap (rule $execJavaExp_O$ in Fig. 5.2). We set $\sigma(n+1) := \sigma(n) + 2$. In state $\sigma(n)$, the JVM$_\mathcal{E}$ executes the instruction $New(c)$, such that $opd_{\sigma(n)+1} = opd_{\sigma(n)} \cdot [ref]$. Then, the JVM$_\mathcal{E}$ executes the instruction $Dupx(0,1)$. Since $pc_{\sigma(n+1)} = end_\alpha$ and $opd_{\sigma(n+1)} = opd_{\sigma(n)} \cdot [ref, ref]$, the invariant (**new**) is satisfied.

If the class c is not initialized in state n, we proceed as in Case 36.

Case 57. $context(pos_n) = {}^\alpha({}^\beta exp.c/f)$ and $pos_n = \alpha$:

Similar to Case 3.

Case 58. $context(pos_n) = {}^\alpha({}^\beta ref.c/f)$ and $pos_n = \beta$:

By the induction hypothesis (**exp**), it follows that $pc_{\sigma(n)} = end_\beta$ and $opd_{\sigma(n)} = javaOpd(restbody_n, \beta) \cdot [ref]$. According to the compilation scheme in Fig. 11.2, $code(end_\beta)$ is the instruction $GetField(\mathcal{T}(\alpha), c/f)$. We set $\sigma(n+1) := \sigma(n) + 1$. If $ref = null$, then Java$_\mathcal{E}$ (Fig. 6.3) as well as the JVM$_\mathcal{E}$ (Fig. 12.2) throw a new $\texttt{NullPointerException}$ and the invariant (**exc**) is satisfied in state $n+1$, since $\mathcal{X}(\alpha) = [\,]$. Otherwise, $pos_{n+1} = \alpha$

and $restbody_{n+1}/\alpha = v$, where $v = getField_n(ref, c/f)$ (Fig. 5.2). The $\text{JVM}_{\mathcal{E}}$ executes the instruction $GetField$ in rule $execVM_O$ in Fig. 11.1. Since $pc_{\sigma(n+1)} = pc_{\sigma(n)} + 1 = end_\alpha$ and $opd_{\sigma(n+1)} = opd_{\sigma(n)} \cdot jvmVal(v)$, the invariant (**exp**) is satisfied in state $n + 1$.

Case 59. $context(pos_n) = {}^\alpha({}^\beta exp_1.c/f = {}^\gamma exp_2)$ and $pos_n = \alpha$:

Similar to Case 3.

Case 60. $context(pos_n) = {}^\alpha({}^\beta ref.c/f = {}^\gamma exp)$ and $pos_n = \beta$:

Similar to Case 4.

Case 61. $context(pos_n) = {}^\alpha({}^\beta ref.c/f = {}^\gamma val)$ and $pos_n = \gamma$:

By the induction hypothesis (**exp**), it follows that $pc_{\sigma(n)} = end_\gamma$ and $opd_{\sigma(n)} = javaOpd(restbody_n, \gamma) \cdot jvmVal(val)$. By Def. 14.1.1, it follows that

$$opd_{\sigma(n)} = javaOpd(restbody_n, \alpha) \cdot [ref] \cdot jvmVal(val).$$

According to the compilation scheme in Fig. 11.2, $code(end_\gamma)$ is the instruction $Dupx(1, size(\mathcal{T}(\alpha)))$ followed by the instruction $PutField(\mathcal{T}(\alpha), c/f)$ and $end_\alpha = end_\gamma + 2$. We set $\sigma(n+1) := \sigma(n) + 2$. In state $\sigma(n)$, the $\text{JVM}_{\mathcal{E}}$ executes the $Dupx$ instruction such that

$$opd_{\sigma(n)+1} = javaOpd(restbody_n, \alpha) \cdot jvmVal(val) \cdot [ref] \cdot jvmVal(val).$$

If $ref = null$, then $\text{Java}_{\mathcal{E}}$ (Fig. 6.3) as well as the $\text{JVM}_{\mathcal{E}}$ (Fig. 12.2) throw a NullPointerException and the invariant (**exc**) is satisfied for $n + 1$. Otherwise, $pos_{n+1} = \alpha$, $restbody_{n+1}/\alpha = val$ and the field c/f of the object $heap_n(ref)$ is updated to val in both machines. In state $\sigma(n) + 1$, the $\text{JVM}_{\mathcal{E}}$ executes the $PutField$ instruction (Fig. 11.1). Since $pc_{\sigma(n+1)} = end_\alpha$ and $opd_{\sigma(n+1)} = javaOpd(restbody_n, \alpha) \cdot jvmVal(val)$, the invariant (**exp**) is satisfied in state $n + 1$. Moreover, the heap of $\text{Java}_{\mathcal{E}}$ and the heap of the $\text{JVM}_{\mathcal{E}}$ are still identical.

Case 62. $context(pos_n) = {}^\alpha({}^\beta exp \text{ instanceof } c)$ and $pos_n = \alpha$:

Similar to Case 3.

Case 63. $context(pos_n) = {}^\alpha({}^\beta ref \text{ instanceof } c)$ and $pos_n = \beta$:

Then $pos_{n+1} = \alpha$ and $restbody_{n+1}/\alpha = v$, where v is the value of the boolean expression $ref \neq null \wedge classOf(ref) \preceq c$ (rule $execJavaExp_O$ in Fig. 5.2).

Assume that α is an $\mathcal{E}$-position. By the induction hypothesis (**exp**), it follows that $pc_{\sigma(n)} = end_\beta$ and $opd_{\sigma(n)} = javaOpd(restbody_n, \alpha) \cdot [ref]$. According to the compilation scheme in Fig. 11.2, $code(end_\beta)$ is the instruction $InstanceOf(c)$. We set $\sigma(n+1) := \sigma(n) + 1$. The $\text{JVM}_{\mathcal{E}}$ (Fig. 11.1) replaces ref on top of the operand stack with the result of the boolean expression $ref \neq null \wedge classOf(ref) \sqsubseteq c$ (represented as an integer). Since the relations $\preceq$ and $\sqsubseteq$ agree on reference types (see Def. 8.4.1), we obtain $opd_{\sigma(n+1)} = javaOpd(restbody_{n+1}, \alpha) \cdot jvmVal(v)$ and the invariant (**exp**) is satisfied.

If α is a $\mathcal{B}_i(lab)$-position, we proceed as in the second part of Case 2.

Case 64. $context(pos_n) = {}^\alpha(c)^\beta exp$ and $pos_n = \alpha$:

Similar to Case 3.

Case 65. $context(pos_n) = {}^\alpha(c)^\beta ref$ and $pos_n = \beta$:

By the induction hypothesis (**exp**), it follows that $pc_{\sigma(n)} = \text{end}_\beta$ and $opd_{\sigma(n)} = javaOpd(restbody_n, \alpha) \cdot [ref]$. We set $\sigma(n+1) := \sigma(n) + 1$. Since $code(\text{end}_\beta)$ is the instruction $Checkcast(c)$ (Fig. 11.2), the JVM$_\mathcal{E}$ executes in state $\sigma(n)$ the $Checkcast$ instruction.

Assume that $ref = null$ or $classOf(ref) \preceq c$. Then $pos_{n+1} = \alpha$ and $restbody_{n+1}/\alpha = ref$ (Fig. 5.2). The JVM$_\mathcal{E}$ leaves the operand stack as it is and increments the program counter such that $pc_{\sigma(n+1)} = \text{end}_\alpha$ (Fig. 11.1) and the invariant (**exp**) is still satisfied.

If $ref \neq null$ and $classOf(ref) \not\preceq c$, then Java$_\mathcal{E}$ as well as the JVM$_\mathcal{E}$ throw a `ClassCastException` and the invariant (**exc**) is satisfied in state $n + 1$.

Case 66. $context(pos_n) = {}^\alpha({}^\beta exp.c/m^\gamma(exps))$ and $pos_n = \alpha$:

Similar to Case 3.

Case 67. $context(pos_n) = {}^\alpha({}^\beta ref.c/m^\gamma(exps))$ and $pos_n = \beta$:

Then $pos_{n+1} = \gamma$. Since by Fig. 11.2 in this case the JVM$_\mathcal{E}$ does nothing, we set $\sigma(n+1) := \sigma(n)$.

Assume that c/m is a constructor. Then by the induction hypothesis (**new**), it follows that $pc_{\sigma(n)} = \text{end}_\beta$ and

$$\begin{aligned} opd_{\sigma(n)} &= javaOpd(restbody_n, \beta) \cdot [ref, ref] \\ &= javaOpd(restbody_n, \alpha) \cdot [ref, ref] \quad \text{(Clause 5 of Def. 14.1.1)} \end{aligned}$$

By Clause 4 of Def. 14.1.1, we have

$$javaOpd(restbody_n, \gamma) = javaOpd(restbody_n, \alpha) \cdot [ref, ref].$$

Since $\text{end}_\beta = \text{beg}_\gamma$ (Fig. 11.2), the invariant (**beg**) is satisfied for $n + 1$.

If c/m is an instance method, then the invariant (**beg**) in state $n + 1$ follows similarly from the induction hypothesis (**exp**) and Clause 5 of Def. 14.1.1.

Case 68. $context(pos_n) = {}^\alpha({}^\beta ref.c/m^\gamma(vals))$ and $pos_n = \gamma$:

By the induction hypothesis (**exp**), it follows that $pc_{\sigma(n)} = \text{end}_\gamma = \text{end}_\alpha - 1$ (Fig. 11.2). If c/m is an instance method, then

$$opd_{\sigma(n)} = javaOpd(restbody_n, \alpha) \cdot [ref] \cdot jvmVal(vals).$$

If c/m is a constructor, then

$$opd_{\sigma(n)} = javaOpd(restbody_n, \alpha) \cdot [ref, ref] \cdot jvmVal(vals).$$

If $ref \neq null$, then Java$_\mathcal{E}$ executes $invokeMethod(\alpha, c'/m, [ref] \cdot vals)$, where class c' is determined as follows and $d = classNm(meth_n)$ (Fig. 5.2):

$callKind(\alpha)$	c'	$code(\text{end}_\gamma)$
Virtual	$lookup(classOf(ref), c/m)$	$InvokeVirtual(\mathcal{T}(\alpha), c/m)$
Super	$lookup(super(d), c/m)$	$InvokeSpecial(\mathcal{T}(\alpha), c/m)$
Special	c	$InvokeSpecial(\mathcal{T}(\alpha), c/m)$

In state $n + 1$ we have:

$$\begin{aligned}
frames_{n+1} &= frames_n \cdot (meth_n, restbody_n, \alpha, locals_n), \\
meth_{n+1} &= c'/m, \\
restbody_{n+1} &= body(c'/m), \\
pos_{n+1} &= firstPos, \\
locals_{n+1} &= zip(argNames(c'/m), [ref] \cdot vals).
\end{aligned}$$

We set $\sigma(n+1) := \sigma(n) + 2$, one step for the *invoke* instruction and one step for executing the *pushFrame* in the submachine $switchVM_C$.

Assume that $callKind(\alpha) = Virtual$. In state $\sigma(n)$, the $\text{JVM}_\mathcal{E}$ executes the *InvokeVirtual* instruction such that $opd_{\sigma(n)+1} = javaOpd(restbody_n, \alpha)$ and $switch_{\sigma(n)+1} = Call(c'/m, [ref] \cdot jvmVal(vals))$. In state $\sigma(n) + 1$, the $\text{JVM}_\mathcal{E}$ executes a $pushFrame(c'/m, [ref] \cdot jvmVal(vals))$ (Fig. 10.2), since by Theorem 8.4.1 and the Lookup Lemma 8.4.1 the method c'/m is not abstract. Thus we have

$$\begin{aligned}
stack_{\sigma(n+1)} &= stack_{\sigma(n)} \cdot (pc_{\sigma(n)}, reg_{\sigma(n)}, opd_{\sigma(n)+1}, meth_{\sigma(n)}), \\
meth_{\sigma(n+1)} &= c'/m, \\
pc_{\sigma(n+1)} &= 0, \\
opd_{\sigma(n+1)} &= [], \\
reg_{\sigma(n+1)} &= makeReg([ref] \cdot jvmVal(vals)).
\end{aligned}$$

As in Case 40 we can conclude that the invariants (**reg**), (**stack**), (**beg**) and (**fin**) are satisfied.

Assume that $callKind(\alpha) = Super$. From Sect. 5.1.5 it follows that m is not abstract in c and $super(d) \preceq_h c$. Hence, $lookup(super(d), c/m) = c$ and $c' = c$. (One could as well assign the call kind *Special* to α.) In state $\sigma(n)$, the $\text{JVM}_\mathcal{E}$ executes the instruction $InvokeSpecial(\mathcal{T}(\alpha), c/m)$ and in state $\sigma(n) + 1$ a $pushFrame(c/m, [ref] \cdot jvmVal(vals))$. The rest goes as above.

Assume that $callKind(\alpha) = Special$ and c/m is a constructor. Then the difference to the other cases is that $opd_{\sigma(n)+1} = javaOpd(restbody_n, \alpha) \cdot [ref]$. Since the case of a constructor is treated separately in Def. 14.1.8, we still can conclude that $frames_{n+1} \approx stack_{\sigma(n+1)}$. If c/m is an instance method, we proceed as above.

If $ref = null$, then $\text{Java}_\mathcal{E}$ as well as the $\text{JVM}_\mathcal{E}$ throw a `NullPointerException` and the invariant (**exc**) is satisfied.

$\text{Java}_\mathcal{E}$-Statements. Following Fig. 6.1 and Fig. 6.2, we have to consider the six new cases which appear for statement execution in $\text{Java}_\mathcal{E}$, namely `throw` (Cases 69–70), `try-catch` (Cases 71–75) and `try-catch-finally` statements

(Cases 76–80), exception propagation through labeled statements (Case 81), uncaught exceptions in class initialization (Case 82) and propagation of uncaught exceptions to the invoker (Case 83).

Case 69. $context(pos_n) = {}^\alpha\mathtt{throw}\,{}^\beta exp$ and $pos_n = \alpha$:

Similar to Case 3.

Case 70. $context(pos_n) = {}^\alpha\mathtt{throw}\,{}^\beta ref$ and $pos_n = \beta$:

Since β is an $\mathcal{E}$-position, by the induction hypothesis (**exp**), it follows that $pc_{\sigma(n)} = end_\beta$ and $opd_{\sigma(n)} = [ref]$. According to Fig. 12.3, $code(end_\beta)$ is the instruction $Athrow$ and $end_\alpha = end_\beta + 1$. We set $\sigma(n+1) := \sigma(n) + 1$.

Assume that $ref \neq null$. Then $pos_{n+1} = \alpha$ and $restbody_{n+1}/\alpha = Exc(ref)$ (rule $execJavaStm_E$ in Fig. 6.2). The JVM$_\mathcal{E}$ executes the $Athrow$ instruction (rule $execVM_E$ in Fig. 12.2) such that $switch_{\sigma(n+1)} = Throw(ref)$ and $pc_{\sigma(n+1)} = pc_{\sigma(n)}$. Since $beg_\alpha \leq end_\beta$, $end_\beta < end_\alpha$, $end_\beta = pc_{\sigma(n+1)}$ and $\mathcal{X}(\alpha) = [\,]$, the invariant (**exc**) is satisfied in state $n+1$.

Assume that $ref = null$. Then $pos_{n+1} = \alpha$ and $restbody_{n+1}/\alpha = Exc(r)$, where r is a reference to a new object of type `NullPointerException`. The JVM$_\mathcal{E}$ raises the same exception when it executes the $Athrow$ instruction. Thus, $switch_{n+1} = Throw(r)$ and the invariant (**exc**) is satisfied in state $n+1$.

Case 71. $context(pos_n) = {}^\alpha\mathtt{try}\,{}^\beta stm$ `catch` $\ldots$ and $pos_n = \alpha$:

Similar to Case 3.

Case 72. $context(pos_n) = {}^\alpha\mathtt{try}\,{}^\beta Norm$ `catch` $\ldots$ and $pos_n = \beta$:

Then $pos_{n+1} = \alpha$ and $restbody_{n+1}/\alpha = Norm$ (Fig. 6.2). By the induction hypothesis (**stm**), it follows that $pc_{\sigma(n)} = end_\beta$ and $opd_{\sigma(n)} = [\,]$. According to the compilation scheme in Fig. 12.3, $code(end_\beta)$ is the instruction $Goto(end_\alpha)$. We set $\sigma(n+1) := \sigma(n) + 1$. The JVM$_\mathcal{E}$ executes the $Goto$ instruction and the invariant (**stm**) is satisfied in state $n+1$.

Case 73. $context(pos_n) = {}^\alpha\mathtt{try}^\beta abr$ `catch` $(c_1\,x_1)^{\gamma_1}\,s_1 \ldots$ `catch` $(c_n\,x_n)^{\gamma_n}\,s_n$ and $pos_n = \beta$:

Assume that abr is not an exception. Then $pos_{n+1} = \alpha$ and $restbody_{n+1}/\alpha$ is abr (rule $execJavaStm_E$ in Fig. 6.2). By the induction hypothesis (**abr**), it follows that $opd_{\sigma(n)} = [\,]$ and $pc_{\sigma(n)}$ is a continuation for abr at position β. We set $\sigma(n+1) := \sigma(n)$. Since $pc_{\sigma(n)}$ is also a continuation for abr at position α, the invariant (**abr**) is satisfied in state $n+1$.

Assume that $abr = Exc(r)$. By the induction hypothesis (**exc**), it follows that

1. $switch_{\sigma(n)} = Throw(r)$,
2. $beg_\beta \leq pc_{\sigma(n)} < end_\beta$ (β is not an $\mathcal{E}$-position),
3. there is no $(f, u, \_, c) \in \mathcal{X}(\beta)$ with $f \leq pc_{\sigma(n)} < u$ and $classOf(r) \preceq_{\mathrm{h}} c$.

The definition of the exception table in Fig. 12.4 says that

$$\begin{aligned}
\mathcal{X}(\alpha) \;=\; & \mathcal{X}(\beta) \cdot \\
& \mathcal{X}(\gamma_1) \cdot Exc(\mathrm{beg}_\alpha, \mathrm{end}_\beta, \mathrm{beg}_{\gamma_1} - 1, c_1) \cdot \\
& \;\;\vdots \\
& \mathcal{X}(\gamma_n) \cdot Exc(\mathrm{beg}_\alpha, \mathrm{end}_\beta, \mathrm{beg}_{\gamma_n} - 1, c_n)
\end{aligned}$$

Assume that there exists an i such that $1 \le i \le n$ and $classOf(r) \preceq_h c_i$. Let $j := \min\{i \mid classOf(ref) \preceq_h c_i\}$. Then $pos_{n+1} = \gamma_j$ and $locals_{n+1}$ is $locals_n \oplus \{(x_j, r)\}$ (rule $execJavaStm_E$ in Fig. 6.2). We set $\sigma(n+1) := \sigma(n)+2$. In state $\sigma(n)$, the $\mathrm{JVM}_\mathcal{E}$ executes the rule $switchVM_E$ in Fig. 12.1. It looks for the first handler (f, u, h, c) in the exception table of the method such that $f \le pc_{\sigma(n)} < u$ and $classOf(r) \preceq_h c$. The intervals protected by handlers in the table before $\mathcal{X}(\alpha)$ are disjoint to $\{k \mid \mathrm{beg}_\alpha \le k < \mathrm{end}_\alpha\}$ (Lemma 14.2.1) and cannot be used, since $\mathrm{beg}_\alpha \le pc_{\sigma(n)} < \mathrm{end}_\beta$. The handlers in $\mathcal{X}(\beta)$ cannot be used by the induction hypothesis (**exc**). The handlers in $\mathcal{X}(\gamma_i)$ cannot be used by Lemma 14.2.1, since the code interval of γ_i is disjoint from the code interval of β and $\mathrm{beg}_\beta \le pc_{\sigma(n)} < \mathrm{end}_\beta$. Hence, the first handler found by the $\mathrm{JVM}_\mathcal{E}$ is $(\mathrm{beg}_\alpha, \mathrm{end}_\beta, \mathrm{beg}_{\gamma_j} - 1, c_j)$ and by Fig. 12.1

1. $pc_{\sigma(n)+1} = \mathrm{beg}_{\gamma_j} - 1$,
2. $opd_{\sigma(n)+1} = [r]$,
3. $switch_{\sigma(n)+1} = Noswitch$.

In state $\sigma(n) + 1$, it executes the $Store(\mathtt{addr}, \overline{x_j})$ instruction which is at $\mathrm{beg}_{\gamma_j} - 1$ (Fig. 12.3). Hence, in state $n + 1$ the invariants (**reg**) and (**beg**) are satisfied.

Assume that there is no j such that $1 \le j \le n$ and $classOf(r) \preceq_h c_j$. Then $pos_{n+1} = \alpha$ and $restbody_{n+1}/\alpha = Exc(r)$. We set $\sigma(n + 1) := \sigma(n)$. Since the intervals $\{j \mid \mathrm{beg}_{\gamma_i} \le j < \mathrm{end}_{\gamma_i}\}$ do not contain $pc_{\sigma(n)}$, by Lemma 14.2.1 it follows that there is no $(f, u, \_, c) \in \mathcal{X}(\alpha)$ with $f \le pc_{\sigma(n)} < u$ and $classOf(r) \preceq_h c$. Hence, the invariant (**exc**) is satisfied in state $n + 1$.

Case 74. $context(pos_n) = {}^\alpha\mathtt{try}\, {}^\beta Exc(r) \ldots \mathtt{catch}\;\; (c_i\, x_i)\, {}^{\gamma_i} Norm \ldots$ and $pos_n = \gamma_i$:

Then $pos_{n+1} = \alpha$ and $restbody_{n+1}/\alpha = Norm$ (rule $execJavaStm_E$ in Fig. 6.2). By the induction hypothesis (**stm**), it follows that $pc_{\sigma(n)} = \mathrm{end}_{\gamma_i}$ and $opd_{\sigma(n)} = []$. We set $\sigma(n + 1) := \sigma(n) + 1$. According to the compilation scheme in Fig. 12.3, the instruction $code(\mathrm{end}_{\gamma_i})$ is $Goto(\mathrm{end}_\alpha)$. The $\mathrm{JVM}_\mathcal{E}$ executes the $Goto$ instruction and $pc_{\sigma(n+1)} = \mathrm{end}_\alpha$. Hence, the invariant (**stm**) is satisfied in state $n + 1$.

Case 75. $context(pos_n) = {}^\alpha\mathtt{try}\, {}^\beta Exc(r) \ldots \mathtt{catch}\;\; (c_i\, x_i)\, {}^{\gamma_i} abr \ldots$ and $pos_n = \gamma_i$:

Similar to Case 23. If $abr = Exc(\_)$, one has to look at the exception table $\mathcal{X}(\alpha)$ in Case 73 and use Lemma 14.2.1.

Case 76. $context(pos_n) = {}^\alpha({}^\beta stm_1\, \mathtt{finally}\; {}^\gamma stm_2)$ and $pos_n = \alpha$:

Similar to Case 3.

Case 77. $context(pos_n) = {}^\alpha({}^\beta Norm \text{ finally } {}^\gamma stm)$ and $pos_n = \beta$:

Then $pos_{n+1} = \gamma$ (rule $execJavaStm_E$ in Fig. 6.2). By the induction hypothesis (**stm**), it follows that $pc_{\sigma(n)} = end_\beta$ and $opd_{\sigma(n)} = [\,]$. We set $\sigma(n+1) := \sigma(n) + 2$. According to the compilation scheme in Fig. 12.3, $code(end_\beta)$ is the instruction $Jsr(beg_\gamma - 1)$ followed by a $Goto(end_\alpha)$. In state $\sigma(n)$, the $\text{JVM}_\mathcal{E}$ executes the Jsr instruction such that $pc_{\sigma(n)+1} = beg_\gamma - 1$ and $opd_{\sigma(n)+1} = [end_\beta + 1]$ (Fig. 12.2). In state $\sigma(n) + 1$, it executes the instruction $Store(\text{addr}, \overline{\text{ret}}_\alpha)$. Hence, $reg_{\sigma(n+1)}(\overline{\text{ret}}_\alpha) = end_\beta + 1$. Since $code(end_\beta + 1)$ is $Goto(end_\alpha)$, $reg_{\sigma(n+1)}$ contains correct return addresses for γ in $restbody_{n+1}$ and the invariant (**fin**) is satisfied in state $n + 1$. Since $pc_{\sigma(n+1)} = beg_\gamma$ and $opd_{\sigma(n+1)} = [\,]$, the invariant (**beg**) is satisfied as well.

Case 78. $context(pos_n) = {}^\alpha({}^\beta abr \text{ finally } {}^\gamma stm)$ and $pos_n = \beta$:

Then $pos_{n+1} = \gamma$ (rule $execJavaStm_E$ in Fig. 6.2).

Assume that abr is not an exception. By the induction hypothesis (**abr**), it follows that $opd_{\sigma(n)} = [\,]$ and $pc_{\sigma(n)}$ is a continuation for abr at position β with respect to $reg_{\sigma(n)}$. By Def. 14.1.3, 14.1.4, 14.1.5 and 14.1.6, it follows that

1. $code(pc_{\sigma(n)}) = Jsr(beg_\gamma - 1)$ and

2. $pc_{\sigma(n)} + 1$ is a continuation for abr at position α with respect to $reg_{\sigma(n)}$.

We set $\sigma(n + 1) := \sigma(n) + 2$. In state $\sigma(n)$, the $\text{JVM}_\mathcal{E}$ executes the Jsr instruction such that $pc_{\sigma(n)+1} = beg_\gamma - 1$ and $opd_{\sigma(n)+1} = [pc_{\sigma(n)} + 1]$. In state $\sigma(n) + 1$, it executes the instruction $Store(\text{addr}, \overline{\text{ret}}_\alpha)$. Hence, $reg_{\sigma(n+1)}(\overline{\text{ret}}_\alpha) = pc_{\sigma(n)} + 1$. Since $pc_{\sigma(n)} + 1$ is a continuation for abr at position α with respect to $reg_{\sigma(n+1)}$, $reg_{\sigma(n+1)}$ contains correct return addresses for γ in $restbody_{n+1}$ and the invariant (**fin**) is satisfied in state $n + 1$. Since $pc_{\sigma(n+1)} = beg_\gamma$ and $opd_{\sigma(n+1)} = [\,]$, the invariant (**beg**) is satisfied as well.

Assume that $abr = Exc(r)$. By the induction hypothesis (**exc**), it follows that

1. $switch_{\sigma(n)} = Throw(r)$,

2. $beg_\beta \leq pc_{\sigma(n)} < end_\beta$ (β is not an $\mathcal{E}$-position),

3. there is no $(f, u, \_, c) \in \mathcal{X}(\beta)$ with $f \leq pc_{\sigma(n)} < u$ and $classOf(r) \preceq_{\text{h}} c$.

The definition of the exception table in Fig. 12.4 says that

$$\mathcal{X}(\alpha) = \mathcal{X}(\beta) \cdot Exc(beg_\alpha, \text{default}_\alpha, \text{default}_\alpha, \text{Throwable}) \cdot \mathcal{X}(\gamma).$$

We set $\sigma(n + 1) := \sigma(n) + 4$. In state $\sigma(n)$, the $\text{JVM}_\mathcal{E}$ executes rule $switchVM_E$ in Fig. 12.1. By Lemma 14.2.1 and consequence 3 above of (**exc**), the first handler in the exception table that catches the exception r is $(beg_\alpha, \text{default}_\alpha, \text{default}_\alpha, \text{Throwable})$ and

1. $pc_{\sigma(n)+1} = \text{default}_\alpha$,

2. $opd_{\sigma(n)+1} = [r]$,

3. $switch_{\sigma(n)+1} = Noswitch$.

The compilation scheme in Fig. 12.3 says that

$$
\begin{aligned}
code(\text{default}_\alpha) &= Store(\texttt{addr}, \overline{\text{exc}}_\alpha) \\
code(\text{default}_\alpha + 1) &= Jsr(\text{beg}_\gamma - 1)
\end{aligned}
$$

In state $\sigma(n)+1$, the JVM$_\mathcal{E}$ stores the exception r in register $\overline{\text{exc}}_\alpha$. In state $\sigma(n)+2$, it jumps to the subroutine and, in state $\sigma(n)+3$, it stores the return address default$_\alpha$+2 in register $\overline{\text{ret}}_\alpha$ such that $reg_{\sigma(n+1)}$ contains correct return addresses for γ in $restbody_{n+1}$ and the invariant (**fin**) is satisfied in state $n+1$. Since $pc_{\sigma(n+1)} = \text{beg}_\gamma$ and $opd_{\sigma(n+1)} = [\,]$, the invariant (**beg**) is satisfied as well.

Case 79. $context(pos_n) = {}^\alpha(^\beta s \texttt{ finally } {}^\gamma Norm)$ and $pos_n = \gamma$:

Then $pos_{n+1} = \alpha$ and $restbody_{n+1}/\alpha = s$ (Fig. 6.2). By the induction hypothesis (**stm**), it follows that $pc_{\sigma(n)} = \text{end}_\gamma$ and $opd_{\sigma(n)} = [\,]$. The instruction $code(\text{end}_\gamma)$ is $Ret(\overline{\text{ret}}_\alpha)$ (Fig. 12.3). In state $\sigma(n)$, the JVM$_\mathcal{E}$ executes the Ret instruction and $pc_{\sigma(n)+1} = reg_{\sigma(n)}(\overline{\text{ret}}_\alpha)$.

Assume that $s = Norm$. We set $\sigma(n+1) := \sigma(n) + 2$. By the induction hypothesis (**fin**) and (**fin-norm**) of Def. 14.1.7, it follows that $code(pc_{\sigma(n)+1})$ is the instruction $Goto(\text{end}_\alpha)$. Therefore, in state $\sigma(n)+1$, the JVM$_\mathcal{E}$ executes the $Goto$ instruction such that $pc_{\sigma(n+1)} = \text{end}_\alpha$ and the invariant (**stm**) is still satisfied.

Assume that $s = abr$ and abr is not an exception. By the induction hypothesis (**fin**) and (**fin-abr**) of Def. 14.1.7, it follows that $pc_{\sigma(n)+1}$ is a continuation for abr at position α with respect to $reg_{\sigma(n)}$. We set $\sigma(n+1) := \sigma(n) + 1$ and the invariant (**abr**) is satisfied in state $n+1$.

Assume that $s = Exc(r)$. By the induction hypothesis (**fin**) and (**fin-exc**) of Def. 14.1.7, it follows that $reg_{\sigma(n)}(\overline{\text{ret}}_\alpha) = \text{default}_\alpha + 2$ and $reg_{\sigma(n)}(\overline{\text{exc}}_\alpha) = r$. The compilation scheme in Fig. 12.3 says that

$$
\begin{aligned}
code(\text{default}_\alpha + 2) &= Load(\texttt{addr}, \overline{\text{exc}}_\alpha) \\
code(\text{default}_\alpha + 3) &= Athrow
\end{aligned}
$$

We set $\sigma(n+1) := \sigma(n) + 3$. Since $pc_{\sigma(n)+1} = \text{default}_\alpha + 2$, in state $\sigma(n)+1$, the JVM$_\mathcal{E}$ loads the reference r on the operand stack and, in state $\sigma(n)+2$, it executes the $Athrow$ instruction. Hence,

1. $switch_{\sigma(n+1)} = Throw(r)$,
2. $\text{beg}_\alpha \leq \text{default}_\alpha + 3 = pc_{\sigma(n+1)} < \text{end}_\alpha$,
3. there is no $(f, u, \_, c) \in \mathcal{X}(\alpha)$ such that $f \leq pc_{\sigma(n+1)} < u$ and $classOf(r) \preceq_h c$,

and the invariant (**exc**) is satisfied in state $n+1$.

Case 80. $context(pos_n) = {}^\alpha(^\beta s \texttt{ finally } {}^\gamma abr)$ and $pos_n = \gamma$:

Then $pos_{n+1} = \alpha$ and $restbody_{n+1}/\alpha = abr$ (rule $execJavaStm_E$ in Fig. 6.2). The rest is similar to Case 23.

Case 81. $context(pos_n) = {}^\alpha lab : {}^\beta Exc(r)$ and $pos_n = \beta$:

Similar to Case 23.

Case 82. $context(pos_n) = {}^\alpha\texttt{static}\,{}^\beta Exc(r)$ and $pos_n = \beta$:

Then $pos_{n+1} = \alpha$. If $classOf(r) \preceq_\text{h} \texttt{Error}$, then $restbody_{n+1}/\alpha = Exc(r)$. Otherwise, $restbody_{n+1}/\alpha = Exc(ref)$, where ref is a newly created object of type $\texttt{ExceptionInInitializerError}$ (rule $execJavaStm_E$ in Fig. 6.2). By the induction hypothesis (**exc**), it follows that $switch_{\sigma(n)} = Throw(r)$ and that the exception r is not caught in the $\texttt{<clinit>}$ method. We set $\sigma(n + 1) := \sigma(n) + 1$. The $\text{JVM}_\mathcal{E}$ executes rule $switchVM_E$ in Fig. 12.1. If $classOf(r) \preceq_\text{h} \texttt{Error}$, then $switch_{\sigma(n+1)} = ThrowInit(r)$. Otherwise, $switch_{\sigma(n+1)} = ThrowInit(ref)$, where ref is the newly created object of type $\texttt{ExceptionInInitializerError}$. In both cases the invariant (**exc-clinit**) is satisfied in state $n + 1$.

Case 83. $context(pos_n) = Exc(r)$, $pos_n = firstPos$ and $frames_n \neq [\,]$:

Assume that $meth_n$ is not a class initialization method. Then $\text{Java}_\mathcal{E}$ executes $exitMethod(Exc(r))$ such that

$$\begin{aligned} frames_n &= frames_{n+1} \cdot (meth_{n+1}, rest, pos_{n+1}, locals_{n+1}), \\ restbody_{n+1} &= rest[Exc(r)/pos_{n+1}]. \end{aligned}$$

By the induction hypothesis (**exc**), it follows that $switch_{\sigma(n)} = Throw(r)$ and that there is no handler in the exception table which catches the exception r. We set $\sigma(n + 1) := \sigma(n) + 1$. The $\text{JVM}_\mathcal{E}$ executes the rule $switchVM_E$ in Fig. 12.1 and performs a $popFrame(0, [\,])$ such that

$$stack_{\sigma(n)} = stack_{\sigma(n+1)} \cdot (pc_{\sigma(n+1)}, reg_{\sigma(n+1)}, opd_{\sigma(n+1)}, meth_{\sigma(n+1)}).$$

Since $frames_n \approx stack_{\sigma(n)}$, Def. 14.1.8 and Lemma 8.1.3 imply that

1. $frames_{n+1} \approx stack_{\sigma(n+1)}$,
2. $locals_{n+1} \approx reg_{\sigma(n+1)}$,
3. $reg_{\sigma(n+1)}$ contains correct return addresses for pos_{n+1} in $rest$,
4. $\text{beg}_{pos_{n+1}} \leq pc_{\sigma(n+1)} < \text{end}_{pos_{n+1}}$.

Since $\mathcal{X}(pos_{n+1}) = [\,]$, the invariant (**exc**) is satisfied. Since $restbody_{n+1}$ is obtained from $rest$ by inserting $Exc(r)$ at pos_{n+1}, $reg_{\sigma(n+1)}$ contains also correct return addresses for pos_{n+1} in $restbody_{n+1}$ and the invariant (**fin**) is satisfied as well.

Assume that $meth_n$ is the $\texttt{<clinit>}$ method of class c. Then $\text{Java}_\mathcal{E}$ marks the class c as $Unusable$ and makes an $exitMethod(Exc(r))$. Since pos_n is the first position in the body of the $\texttt{<clinit>}$ method, $body(meth_n)/pos_n$ is a static initializer $\texttt{static}\_$. By the induction hypothesis (**exc-clinit**), it follows that $switch_{\sigma(n)} = ThrowInit(r)$. We set $\sigma(n+1) := \sigma(n)+1$. The $\text{JVM}_\mathcal{E}$ marks the initialization state of class c as $Unusable$, too, and makes a $popFrame(0, [\,])$ (rule $switchVM_E$ in Fig. 12.1). By Lemma 8.1.3, it follows that pos_{n+1} is a class initialization position (Def. 8.1.7).

If $body(meth_{n+1})/pos_{n+1} = \texttt{static\_}$, then the class c is the direct super class of the class of $meth_{n+1}$. Therefore, $switch_{\sigma(n+1)}$ is still $ThrowInit(r)$ and the invariant (**exc-clinit**) is satisfied in state $n + 1$.

Otherwise, pos_{n+1} is an $\mathcal{E}$-position and $\mathcal{X}(pos_{n+1}) = [\,]$. Then the class c cannot be the direct super class of the class of $meth_{n+1}$ and therefore, $switch_{\sigma(n+1)} = Throw(r)$. Note, that if $pos_{n+1} = \beta$ in $^{\alpha}c/f = {}^{\beta}val$, then $pc_{\sigma(n+1)} = \mathrm{end}_\beta$, $up(\beta) = \alpha$, $\mathrm{end}_\beta < \mathrm{end}_\alpha$ and therefore $pc_{\sigma(n+1)} < \mathrm{end}_{up(\beta)}$. Hence, the invariant (**exc**) is satisfied.

This concludes the proof. $\qquad\qquad\qquad\qquad\qquad\qquad\qquad\qquad\qquad\qquad$ $\square$

Part III

Bytecode Verification: The Secure JVM

In Part III we extend the trustfully executing JVM of Part II by the verifier and loading components which load and verify bytecode before it may be executed by the trustful VM. We analyze the ambiguities and inconsistencies encountered in the official description in [23], and resolve them by an appropriate new bytecode verifier (Chapter 16).

First we define a diligent VM (Chapter 17) which adds a bytecode verifying submachine to the trustful VM of Part II. We prove the soundness (Theorem 17.1.1) and the completeness (Theorem 17.1.2) of this bytecode verifier. Then we refine the diligent VM to the dynamic VM (Chapter 18) which at run-time loads and references classes when they are needed, before they are passed to the verifier.

The bytecode verifier simulates at link-time, i.e., on type frames instead of value frames, all possible run-time paths through the submitted program, trying to verify certain type conditions which will guarantee the safety of the trustful execution at run-time. We extract these link-time checkable conditions—bytecode type assignments (Chapter 16)—from natural run-time type checks of a defensive VM (Chapter 15). We show that these checks are monotonic, i.e., are preserved when type frames get more specific. In run-time terms, the checking component of the defensive VM can be defined in a modular way by successively refined submachines $check_I$, $check_C$, $check_O$, $check_E$, $check_N$.

In the bytecode verifier the checking machines are coupled to machines $propagate VM_I$ and $propagate VM_E$ (Chapter 17), which propagate checked type frames to possible successor frames (Sect. 16.2), resulting in a link-time simulation of the trustful VM of Part II.

We prove that bytecode type assignments guarantee the desired run-time safety (Theorem 16.4.1), that the compiler of Part II generates code with bytecode type assignments (Theorem 16.5.1), and that our bytecode verifier computes most specific bytecode type assignments (Theorem 17.1.2), thus establishing the Main Theorem of this book. For the completeness proof we refine the compiler to generate code with type information, which is then used in the inductive steps of the proof.

15. The defensive virtual machine

In this chapter we lift the trustfully executing machine of Part II to a defensive machine which checks each instruction before its execution to satisfy certain constraints about types, resource bounds, etc., guaranteeing correct execution in such a way that if the defensive VM executes bytecode successfully, then also the trustful VM does so with the same semantical effect. Our goal here is to prepare the description of the bytecode verifier, to be given in the next chapters, by a transparent definition of the verification functionality, namely in terms of run-time checks of the safe executability of single instructions. We formulate these checking conditions in terms of the types of values instead of values themselves so that they can be adapted in the next two chapters to link-time verifiable properties.

The JVM defines a set of constraints on JVM code to guarantee that its execution cannot go wrong (cf. [23, §4.8]). Static constraints define the well-formedness of the bytecode in Java class files, for example, that branch targets are within the method where the branch occurs or that any access to registers is within the domain of the register environment. Structural constraints specify constraints between JVM instructions and run-time data, for instance that the operand stack does not underflow or overflow, or that methods are called with the right number and types of arguments, or that the JVM does not jump out of the code by executing a *Ret* instruction with an invalid address.

Since static constraints do not change at run-time, these constraints need be checked only once, for example at link-time. In the sequel, we will assume that all static constraints hold (see Appendix C.6). Structural constraints are defined as restrictions on run-time data structures. As preparation for their definition for the bytecode verification in the next chapters, we develop in this chapter a defensive VM that augments the trustful VM of Part II with additional run-time checks to assure that for each instruction all structural constraints, in particular typing constraints, hold upon execution. The checking component can be defined by stepwise refinement, analogously to the layering of the execution component, thus leading to a series of conservatively extended defensive machines for $\text{JVM}_{\mathcal{I}}$, $\text{JVM}_{\mathcal{C}}$, $\text{JVM}_{\mathcal{O}}$, $\text{JVM}_{\mathcal{E}}$, $\text{JVM}_{\mathcal{N}}$. We conclude the chapter with a proof that the checking mechanism is monotonic with respect to type refinements.

Fig. 15.1 Defensive JVM interpreter

$defensiveScheme_I(check, trustfulVM) =$
   if $\neg validCodeIndex(code, pc) \vee$
      $\neg check(instr, maxOpd, pc, type(reg), type(opd))$ **then**
         $halt :=$ `"Runtime check failed"`
   else
      $trustfulVM$

$validCodeIndex(code, pc) = (0 \leq pc \wedge pc < length(code))$

15.1 Construction of the defensive JVM

The defensive JVM extends (and refines) the trustful JVM with a checking component: before an instruction is executed the types of the current state are checked. Fig. 15.1 defines the scheme for the defensive VM which will be instantiated in the following sections for the JVM submachines. If checking fails, the machine reports failure. The *execVM* rules are lifted forms of those introduced in Part II; *check* and *type* denote functions defined below in this section expressing that the execution of the current instruction will not violate the conditions which are required to hold for the stack size and the types of the values the instruction operates on. The above *defensiveScheme_I* will be refined in Sect. 15.3 to the *defensiveScheme_C* by introducing switching, similarly to the extension of the trustful JVM_I to the trustful JVM_C, and in Sect. 15.6 to a scheme which takes into account also native methods.

15.2 Checking JVM_I

In this section we define the defensive VM as an instantiation of the scheme in Fig. 15.1, namely by

   $defensiveVM_I = defensiveScheme_I(check_I, trustfulVM_I)$

The checking function $check_I$ of this defensive JVM_I guarantees the following safety properties, which can be made precise and be proved once we have defined the machine.

1. Primitive operations are executed with the right number and types of the arguments.
2. Local variables are used consistently and correctly, that is, the machine does not operate individually on words of double words; double words are not swapped, and local variables are assigned before they are accessed.
3. The operand stack does not overflow or underflow.

Types. The first two conditions require the introduction of a type system. The JVM is weakly typed: at different times the same register can hold an integer, a float, or a low or high word of a long or double. The same is true for the operand stack. Hence we trace the types of words in the registers and on the operand stack and check the types before executing an instruction.

```
data WordType = int
              | lowLong
              | highLong
              | float
              | lowDouble
              | highDouble
```

The universe *WordType* denotes the types of words. The JVM specification, on purpose, does not specify which part of a double word is its high or low word. This is up to the implementation.[1] In JVM$_\mathcal{I}$ two types are compatible (denoted by $\sqsubseteq$) if they are syntactically equal. The relation $\sqsubseteq$ is refined to a subsort relation in JVM$_\mathcal{O}$. The relation $\sqsubseteq_{\text{suf}}$ takes as its arguments two sequences of types. It checks whether a suffix of the first argument is compatible to the second argument.

State. We keep track of the types of words in registers and on the operand stack tagging words with types.

type $Word = (Int,\ WordType)$

As a consequence, all dynamic functions that operate on words are refined to include type information. The function *type* selects the type component of the dynamic functions *reg* and *opd*, that is *type* applied on a type extended operand stack of the form $[(w_1, t_1), \ldots, (w_n, t_n)]$ returns $[t_1, \ldots, t_n]$; *type* applied to a local environment $\{(x_1, (w_1, t_1)), \ldots, (x_n, (w_n, t_n))\}$ returns $\{(x_1, t_1), \ldots, (x_n, t_n)\}$. The pair $(regT, opdT)$ of the type components *type*(*reg*) and *type*(*opd*) is called a *type frame*.

Environment. The third of the above conditions requires the introduction of a constant *maxOpd* denoting the maximum number of words the operand stack can hold.

Rules. Lifting the execution rules of JVM$_\mathcal{I}$ onto the new state representation is easily described: the semantic functions $JVMS(p, ws)$ now take (and return) sequences of word/type pairs instead of sequences of words only. The other operations work on the components of the new representation in the standard way, like application, indexing or concatenation. Hence, it remains to specify the boolean valued function *check$_I$* for checking JVM$_\mathcal{I}$'s dynamic constraints, see Fig. 15.2.

---

[1] The real JVM also supports *Boolean*, *Byte*, *Short* and *Char*, but since the JVM supports them only in a very limited way, we identify these types with *Int*.

Fig. 15.2 Checking JVM$_\mathcal{I}$ instructions

$check_I(instr, maxOpd, pc, regT, opdT) =$
   case $instr$ **of**
     $Prim(p) \rightarrow opdT \sqsubseteq_{\mathrm{suf}} argTypes(p) \wedge$
                   $\neg overflow(maxOpd, opdT, retSize(p) - argSize(p))$
     $Dupx(s_1, s_2) \rightarrow \mathbf{let}\ [ts_1, ts_2] = tops(opdT, [s_1, s_2])$
                  $length(opdT) \geq s_1 + s_2 \wedge$
                  $\neg overflow(maxOpd, opdT, s_2) \wedge$
                  $validTypeSeq(ts_1) \wedge validTypeSeq(ts_2)$
     $Pop(s) \rightarrow length(opdT) \geq s$
     $Load(t, x) \rightarrow$
        if $size(t) = 1$ **then** $[regT(x)] \sqsubseteq_{\mathrm{mv}} t \wedge \neg overflow(maxOpd, opdT, 1)$
        else $[regT(x), regT(x+1)] \sqsubseteq_{\mathrm{mv}} t \wedge \neg overflow(maxOpd, opdT, 2)$
     $Store(t, \_) \rightarrow opdT \sqsubseteq_{\mathrm{suf}} t$
     $Goto(o) \quad\rightarrow True$
     $Cond(p, o) \rightarrow opdT \sqsubseteq_{\mathrm{suf}} argTypes(p)$
     $Halt \quad\quad \rightarrow True$

Checking a *Prim* instruction requires that the appropriate argument types appear on top of the stack and that the result type can be pushed on the operand stack without overflow.

$$overflow(maxOpd, opdT, s) = length(opdT) + s > maxOpd$$

The function *argTypes* returns the sequence of argument types of a primitive operation with the low type listed before the high type. For example,

$$argTypes(\mathtt{dadd}) = [\mathtt{lowDouble}, \mathtt{highDouble}, \mathtt{lowDouble}, \mathtt{highDouble}].$$

Dupx and *Pop* are polymorphic. They do not require a particular type on the stack. Rather any type can be provided as long as its size equals the required size and it is a well-formed JVM type. For this purpose we define the function *validTypeSeq*.[2]

$$
\begin{aligned}
validTypeSeq([\,]) \quad &= True \\
validTypeSeq([t]) \quad &= \neg isHigh(t) \\
validTypeSeq([t, \_]) &= \neg isHigh(t)
\end{aligned}
$$

$$isHigh(t) = (t = \mathtt{highLong} \vee t = \mathtt{highDouble})$$

Following this definition also the sequence $[\mathtt{int}, \mathtt{float}]$ is a valid type sequence of size 2.

    A *Load* instruction loads the run types stored under the location(s) x (and possibly $x + 1$) onto the operand stack only if they match the move type and if enough space is left. The rule implicitly checks that registers are not accessed before they are assigned. Indeed for a register x to which no

---

[2] The definition of the predicate *isHigh* is refined in Sect. 15.4.

value has been assigned, $regT(x)$ yields *undef* which is not compatible to any defined type. Likewise, the rule checks that for double words the types stored under locations x and $x+1$ have the correct low and high types, otherwise the representation of the move type would not match the runtime-type according to the following definition of the compatibility relation between sequences of word types and move types:

`[int]`	$\sqsubseteq_{\text{mv}}$ `int`	$= \textit{True}$
`[float]`	$\sqsubseteq_{\text{mv}}$ `float`	$= \textit{True}$
`[lowLong, highLong]`	$\sqsubseteq_{\text{mv}}$ `long`	$= \textit{True}$
`[lowDouble, highDouble]`	$\sqsubseteq_{\text{mv}}$ `double`	$= \textit{True}$

Store and *Cond* require appropriate argument types on the stack. For *Goto* and *Halt* nothing has to be checked.

15.3 Checking JVM$_C$

In this section we refine the *defensiveScheme$_I$* to the *defensiveScheme$_C$* which incorporates the switching machine, and then instantiate this scheme with the new checking function *check$_C$* to the defensive JVM$_C$:

$$\textit{defensiveVM}_C = \textit{defensiveScheme}_C(\textit{check}_C, \textit{trustfulVM}_C)$$

Since JVM$_C$ introduces class fields and class methods, the defensive JVM$_C$ adds a check constraint for each of the new instructions to guarantee the following security properties:

1. The type of every value stored in a class field is compatible with its declared type.
2. The actual arguments to each class method invocation are compatible with the corresponding formal parameters.
3. The type of every returned result is compatible with the declared result type.

Environment. Every method has its own maximum operand stack size so that we refine *maxOpd* by an additional method parameter. For this reason *maxOpd* appears in the class file component of method declarations (see Sect. 10.1).

$$\textit{maxOpd}: \textit{Class}/\textit{MSig} \to \textit{Nat}$$

Similarly, we refine *check* = *check*(*meth*), etc.

Rules. Fig. 15.3 extends the *defensiveScheme$_I$* by the switching submachine and by checking constraints on class fields and methods. A *GetStatic* instruction can be executed provided the operand stack has sufficient space to push the stored value. The *PutStatic* instruction requires the popped value to be

---

Fig. 15.3 Checking JVM$_C$ instructions

$defensiveScheme_C(check, trustfulVM) =$
  if $switch = Noswitch$ **then**
    $defensiveScheme_I(check(meth), trustfulVM)$
  else
    $trustfulVM$

$check_C(meth)(instr, maxOpd, pc, regT, opdT) =$
  $check_I(instr, maxOpd, pc, regT, opdT) \lor$
  case $instr$ **of**
    $GetStatic(t, c/f)$ $\rightarrow \neg overflow(maxOpd, opdT, size(t))$
    $PutStatic(t, c/f)$ $\rightarrow opdT \sqsubseteq_{suf} t$
    $InvokeStatic(t, c/m) \rightarrow opdT \sqsubseteq_{suf} argTypes(c/m) \land$
                   $\neg overflow(maxOpd, opdT, size(t) -$
                                    $argSize(c/m))$
    $Return(t)$ $\rightarrow opdT \sqsubseteq_{suf} returnType(meth) \land$
                      $returnType(meth) \sqsubseteq_{mv} t$

---

compatible with the field type. The *InvokeStatic* instruction requires that the actual argument types are compatible to the types of the formal parameters of the method. If the method returns a result, enough space must be left to push the result onto the operand stack.[3] Executing a *Return* instruction requires that the actual type on top of the stack is compatible with the result type of the method and this type must be compatible with the move type as specified by the instruction parameter. In case of a *Return* without return value, the constraint is satisfied. (The condition will be sharpened in Sect. 15.4 by the clause *endinit* for returns from instance initialization methods.) Of course, the run-time dependent length of the method call invocation stack is and cannot be checked for overflow.

$[] \sqsubseteq_{mv}$ **void** $= True$

15.4 Checking JVM$_\mathcal{O}$

In this section we extend the defensive machine to handle also constraints for object-oriented language features. The extension adds the checking counterpart to the extension of the trustful $execVM_C$ to the trustful $execVM_O$: new rules are added for checking each of the object-oriented instructions executed by $execVM_O$. Therefore we define the defensive JVM$_\mathcal{O}$ as an instantiation of the $defensiveScheme_C$.

$defensiveVM_O = defensiveScheme_C(check_O, trustfulVM_O)$

---

[3] The overflow check can be suspended until the method returns. However, this would complicate the formulation.

For checking JVM$_\mathcal{O}$ instructions, the compatibility notion must be refined, to take the inheritance hierarchy into account, and it must be guaranteed that only fields of initialized instances may be accessed and only methods of initialized instances may be called. The defensive JVM$_\mathcal{O}$ guarantees the following safety properties, in addition to the ones of the JVM$_\mathcal{C}$:

1. The type of every target of an object access or of a method call is compatible with the required type.
2. The argument of any *InstanceOf* or *Checkcast* operation is compatible with `Object`.

With respect to object creation and initialization the defensive JVM guarantees the following security properties:

1. A newly created object is regarded as *un-initialized*. An object becomes *fully initialized* when the constructor of class `Object` is invoked. The invocation of another constructor makes an object *partially initialized*.
2. Constructors are invoked on un-initialized or partially initialized objects only. If an object is un-initialized, then the invoked constructor is in the class of the object. If an object is partially initialized, then the invoked constructor is in the same class as the invoking constructor or in the direct superclass.
3. When a constructor returns, it has invoked a constructor either in the same class or in the superclass.
4. Field accesses are performed on fully initialized objects only.
5. Instance methods are invoked on fully initialized objects only.
6. References to not fully initialized objects are neither stored in class fields, nor in instance fields, nor in array elements. References to not fully initialized objects cannot be passed as arguments to methods and are not returned by methods.
7. References to not fully initialized objects, however, can be moved from the operand stack to local registers and vice versa. They can also be compared with other references using the operator '=='. The *Checkcast* and *Instanceof* instructions are applied to fully initialized objects only.

What does it mean that an object is fully initialized? It means that there is a sequence of constructor calls for the object, starting with a constructor of the class of the object, such that each constructor in the sequence, except for the constructor of class `Object`, calls either another constructor of the same class or a constructor of its direct superclass before the instance members of the object are accessed. Fully initialized, however, does not mean that all constructor calls in the sequence do terminate normally. In a deviate program, it may happen that a constructor stores the value of `this` in a global variable and throws an exception afterwards. The exception can be caught and later the object can be used from the global class variable in its insecure state. Nevertheless, the object is regarded as fully initialized because all constructors of the type hierarchy have been called.

The JLS does not allow direct or indirect recursive constructor invocations (see [18, §8.6.5]), because cycles through explicit constructor invocations can easily be detected in Java source code. On the bytecode level, however, such cycles are not so obvious, because an argument expression of a constructor can contain a subexpression which creates a new instance of the same class and hence uses the same constructor. Therefore recursive constructor calls are allowed in bytecode programs (although this is not explicitly mentioned in [23]).

Types. The above listed constraints require the introduction of new type descriptors. Since the new types are later also used in the bytecode verifier, we call them *verify types*.

```
data VerifyType
  = int
  | lowLong
  | highLong
  | float
  | lowDouble
  | highDouble
  | Null
  | Class
  | Interface
  | Array
  | (Class, Pc)_new
  | InInit
  | unusable
```

The primitive verify types are identical with the corresponding word types. The descriptor `Null` represents its only value *null* and is compatible with any reference types.[4] Reference types are class types, interface types, array types and `Null`. Initialized instances of a class c are denoted simply by the name itself. The type descriptor $(c, pc)_{new}$ is the type of an un-initialized object created at code index pc. Partially initialized objects are of type *InInit*. The types $(c, pc)_{new}$ and *InInit* are not considered as reference types. The type descriptor `unusable` is added in order to have a topmost element in the set of verify types. Every value can be of type `unusable`. The compatibility relation is defined on verify types σ, τ as follows:

Definition 15.4.1. For verify types σ and τ the relation $\sigma \sqsubseteq \tau$ is true, iff one of the following conditions is true:

1. $\sigma = \tau$, or
2. σ and τ are reference types and $\sigma \preceq \tau$ (see Def. 5.1.2), or
3. $\tau = $ `unusable`.

---

[4] `Null` has a special status: it can only be generated by *Prim*(`null`); afterwards `Null` can be propagated like any other type.

Since the types $(c, pc)_{new}$ and *InInit* are not reference types, they are compatible with themselves and **unusable** only.

The *Load*, *Store* and *Return* instructions are allowed to move class references and *null*. The instructions *Load* and *Store* are even allowed to move uninitialized objects, the *Return* instruction not. Therefore the notion of compatibility between verifier types and move types is extended as follows. Let c be any reference type:

$$[c] \qquad \sqsubseteq_{mv} \mathbf{addr} = \mathit{True}$$
$$[(\_,\_)_{new}] \sqsubseteq_{mv} \mathbf{addr} = \mathit{True}$$
$$[\mathit{InInit}] \quad \sqsubseteq_{mv} \mathbf{addr} = \mathit{True}$$

The definition of the predicate *isHigh* is refined to include also the type **unusable**. Hence a valid type sequence is not allowed to begin with the type **unusable**.

$$isHigh(t) = (t = \mathtt{highLong} \vee t = \mathtt{highDouble} \vee t = \mathtt{unusable})$$

State. We have to distinguish un-initialized object, partially initialized objects and initialized objects. Therefore we introduce a new type *InitState*:

data $\mathit{InitState} = \mathit{New}(Pc) \mid \mathit{InInit} \mid \mathit{Complete}$

We keep track of the initialization status of a reference in the dynamic function *initState*:

$initState\colon \mathit{Ref} \to \mathit{InitState}$

A newly created un-initialized object of class c with reference r has initialization state $\mathit{New}(pc)$, where pc is the code index of the instruction *New*. If an initializer method declared in class c is called on r, the value of $\mathit{initState}(r)$ is updated to *InInit*. When the initialization method of class **Object** is called, the partially initialized object r gets fully initialized and we update $\mathit{initState}(r)$ to *Complete* (see Fig. 15.5).

References in the stack and in the registers are tagged with **reference**. The universe *WordType* is extended by **reference**.

data $WordType = \ldots$
$\qquad\qquad\quad \mid$ reference

The heap contains the type information about references. Thus we have to extend our definition for *type* on words:

$type(r, \mathbf{reference}) = typeOf(r)$
$type(\_, t) = t$

$typeOf(r) =$
  if $(r = null)$ **then** Null
  else case $heap(r)$ **of**
        $Object(c, \mathit{fields}) \to$ **case** $initState(r)$ **of**
                $New(pc) \to (c, pc)_{new}$
                $InInit \quad \to InInit$
                $Complete \to c$

Fig. 15.4 Checking JVM$_{\mathcal{O}}$ instructions

$check_{\mathcal{O}}(meth)(instr, maxOpd, pc, regT, opdT) =$
$\quad check_{\mathcal{C}}(meth)(instr, maxOpd, pc, regT, opdT) \wedge endinit(meth, instr, regT) \vee$
case $instr$ **of**
$\quad New(c) \rightarrow \neg overflow(maxOpd, opdT, 1)$
$\quad GetField(t, c/f) \rightarrow opdT \sqsubseteq_{\text{suf}} c \wedge \neg overflow(maxOpd, opdT, size(t) - 1)$
$\quad PutField(t, c/f) \rightarrow opdT \sqsubseteq_{\text{suf}} c \cdot t$
$\quad InvokeSpecial(\_, c/m) \rightarrow$
$\qquad$ **let** $[c'] \cdot \_ = take(opdT, 1 + argSize(c/m))$
$\qquad length(opdT) > argSize(c/m) \wedge$
$\qquad opdT \sqsubseteq_{\text{suf}} argTypes(c/m) \wedge$
$\qquad \neg overflow(maxOpd, opdT, retSize(c/m) - argSize(c/m) - 1) \wedge$
$\qquad$ **if** $methNm(m) =$ `"<init>"` **then**
$\qquad\quad initCompatible(meth, c', c)$
$\qquad$ **else** $c' \sqsubseteq c$
$\quad InvokeVirtual(\_, c/m) \rightarrow$
$\qquad opdT \sqsubseteq_{\text{suf}} c \cdot argTypes(c/m) \wedge$
$\qquad \neg overflow(maxOpd, opdT, retSize(c/m) - argSize(c/m) - 1)$
$\quad InstanceOf(c) \rightarrow opdT \sqsubseteq_{\text{suf}}$ `Object`
$\quad Checkcast(c) \;\; \rightarrow opdT \sqsubseteq_{\text{suf}}$ `Object`

Rules. The *execVM$_O$* rules are lifted for *GetField*, *PutField*, *InvokeSpecial* and *InvokeVirtual* onto the new state representation. Fig. 15.4 extends the *check* function of JVM$_C$ for these instructions. The conditions are similar to the ones for the class counterparts in the object-based language, additionally the type of the target reference must be an initialized subtype of the instruction parameter. The instructions *InstanceOf* and *Checkcast* both check whether the top of the stack denotes an initialized reference type. The instruction *New(c)* requires that there is still space on the type operand stack for the type $(c, pc)_{new}$ of a newly created un-initialized object of class c. When *execVM$_O$* executes an instruction *New(c)* and creates a new reference r, then the initialization state of r has to be set in the following way:

$$initState(r) := New(pc)$$

It remains to explain the conditions for calling and for returning from instance initialization methods. To initialize objects an `<init>` method has to be called. The target object must be un-initialized. The actual argument types must be compatible with the formal parameters.

If the target object is typed by $(c, pc)_{new}$ (the initialization method is called the first time for the target object), then the called method must be declared in the class c. Otherwise—the target object is typed by *InInit*—the machine executes initialization code. Then, the called method must either be declared in the same class or in the immediate super class. This is captured by the predicate *initCompatible* that is specified as follows:

Fig. 15.5 Pushing a new JVM$_\mathcal{O}$ frame

$pushFrame(c/m, args) =$
  $stack := stack \cdot [(pc, reg, opd, meth)]$
  $meth := c/m$
  $pc \quad := 0$
  $opd \quad := []$
  $reg \quad := makeRegs(args)$
  if $methNm(m) = $ `"<init>"` **then**
    let $[r] \cdot \_ = args$
    if $c = $ `Object` **then**
      $initState(r) := Complete$
    else
      $initState(r) := InInit$

$initCompatible(\_, (c, \_)_{new}, c') \ = (c = c')$
$initCompatible(c/m, InInit, c') = (c = c' \vee super(c) = c')$

Whenever an initialization method is called, the dynamic function *initState* will be updated. This updating is performed in the *switchVM*, namely as follows. An object becomes initialized, when the initialization method of the root of the inheritance tree is called. Fig. 15.5 refines the definition of pushing the type frame on the type stack. If an `Object`/`<init>` frame is pushed, *initState* is updated to *Complete*. If a c/`<init>` frame is pushed with $c \neq$ `Object`, then the function *initState* is updated to *InInit*. Note that this update changes the *initState* of the reference—from *New(pc)*, assigned to it when the reference has been created—only at the first constructor call.

Each `<init>` method should invoke another `<init>` method of the same class or of its direct superclass. Therefore, we assume that an `<init>` method keeps its target object in register 0. We forbid that it uses the instruction *Store*(_, 0) to store a different value in register 0. Hence, at the end, when an `<init>` method returns and register 0 has a type different from *InInit*, we know that it has called another `<init>` method. Therefore the check for the *Return* instruction is refined in *check$_O$* by the following condition:

$endinit(c/m, instr, regT) =$
  if $instr = Return(_) \wedge methNm(m) = $ `"<init>"` $\wedge c \neq$ `Object` **then**
    $0 \in dom(regT) \wedge regT(0) \neq InInit$
  else *True*

15.5 Checking JVM$_\mathcal{E}$

This section adds the checking counterpart to the extension of the trustful *execVM$_O$* to the trustful *execVM$_E$*, namely by checking each of the error handling instructions.

Fig. 15.6 Checking JVM$_\mathcal{E}$ instructions

$check_E(meth)(instr, maxOpd, pc, regT, opdT) =$
$\quad check_O(meth)(instr, maxOpd, pc, regT, opdT) \vee$
$\quad$**case** $instr$ **of**
$\qquad Store(\mathbf{addr}, x) \rightarrow length(opdT) > 0 \wedge isRetAddr(top(opdT))$
$\qquad Athrow \qquad\quad \rightarrow opdT \sqsubseteq_{\text{suf}}$ **Throwable**
$\qquad Jsr(o) \qquad\quad\; \rightarrow \neg overflow(maxOpd, opdT, 1)$
$\qquad Ret(x) \qquad\quad\; \rightarrow isRetAddr(regT(x))$

$isRetAddr(\mathbf{retAddr}(\_)) = True$
$isRetAddr(\_) \qquad\quad\;\, = False$

$defensiveVM_E = defensiveScheme_C(check_E, trustfulVM_E)$

The defensive JVM$_\mathcal{E}$ assures the following security properties:

1. *Athrow* is only applied on throwable objects.
2. Program counters denote always valid addresses.

These aspect can be guaranteed if we keep track of the use of references and program counters in the store.

Types. The instructions *Jsr* and *Ret* push program counters on the stack and load program counters from local variables, respectively. We add the new variant $\mathbf{retAddr}$ to our type system.

data *WordType* $= \ldots$
$\qquad\qquad\quad | \; \mathbf{retAddr}(Pc)$

data *VerifyType* $= \ldots$
$\qquad\qquad\quad | \; \mathbf{retAddr}(Pc)$

In the JVM only the *Store* operation is allowed to move return addresses from the stack into a register. Therefore, we have to extend the corresponding *check* definition for *Store*.

Rules. The extension of the *check* function for JVM$_\mathcal{E}$ instructions is given in Fig. 15.6. The *Athrow* instruction requires that the reference on top of the operand stack is an instance of type **Throwable**. The *Jsr* instruction pushes $\mathbf{retAddr}$ on the type operand stack, provided enough space is left on the stack. The *Ret* instruction checks whether a $\mathbf{retAddr}$ is stored in the accessed location.

$\quad$ *Jsr* and *Ret* require to lift the $execVM_E$. The $Jsr(s)$ instruction pushes the value $(pc + 1, \mathbf{retAddr}(s))$ on the operand stack indicating that $pc + 1$ is a return address for subroutine s.

$$Jsr(s) \rightarrow opd := opd \cdot [(pc + 1, \mathbf{retAddr}(s))]$$
$$\qquad\quad pc \;\; := s$$

The $Ret(x)$ instruction only takes the first component of the register x as its next program counter.

The defensive JVM$_\mathcal{E}$ does not allow computed gotos: only *Jsr* generates return addresses and pushes them on the stack, only *Store* can move a return address into a register. The condition on *Ret* guarantees that only program generated return addresses can be used.

15.6 Checking JVM$_\mathcal{N}$

Native methods do not have Java bytecode. Native methods are implemented in foreign programming languages. In our model, native methods are implemented via ASM rules, hence they cannot be checked in the ASM model itself. We have to check from outside that the implementation of each native method is correct and does not change the state of the JVM in an unsafe way.

$$defensiveScheme_N(check, trustfulVM) =$$
$$\quad \textbf{if } isNative(meth) \textbf{ then}$$
$$\quad\quad \textbf{if } check(meth) \textbf{ then } trustfulVM$$
$$\quad\quad \textbf{else } halt := \texttt{"unknown native method"}$$
$$\quad \textbf{else}$$
$$\quad\quad defensiveScheme_C(check_E, trustfulVM)$$

The check for a native method ensures that the virtual machine has native code for the method and knows what to do when the method is called. Since the only native methods which are implemented in Chapter 13 are `clone` and `equal`, only those two methods are accepted as native.[5]

$$check_N(c/m) =$$
$$\quad c/m = \texttt{Object}/\,\texttt{equals} \ \vee$$
$$\quad c/m = \texttt{Object}/\,\texttt{clone}$$

$$defensiveVM_N = defensiveScheme_N(check_N, trustfulVM_N)$$

We could check at run-time that the return value of a native method is of the return type of the method. However, such a check cannot be performed by the bytecode verifier in the next chapters. The implementor of a native method is responsible that the method returns always values of the right type. For example, the implementor of the native method `clone` of class `Object` must ensure that this method returns a valid reference and not a value of a primitive type.

_____
[5] The executable AsmGofer model in Appendix A contains further native methods.

15.7 Checks are monotonic

The run-time checks do not operate on the values directly, they operate on the types of the values. In this way it is possible to reuse the same checks in the next chapter for the definition of bytecode type assignments and in Chapter 17 for the diligent VM. The checks depend on the type frame $(regT, opdT)$ and are monotonic in these types. To make this statement more precise we need two predicates $\sqsubseteq_{reg}$ and $\sqsubseteq_{seq}$ for comparing types of registers and types of operand stacks.

$$regS \sqsubseteq_{reg} regT = \forall\, x \in dom(regT) : regS(x) \sqsubseteq regT(x)$$

$$xs \sqsubseteq_{seq} ys = (length(xs) = length(ys)) \wedge \forall\, (x, y) \in zip(xs, ys) : x \sqsubseteq y$$

If $regS \sqsubseteq_{reg} regT$, then we say that $regS$ is *more specific* than $regT$. Similarly, if $opdS \sqsubseteq_{seq} opdT$, then $opdS$ is also *more specific* than $opdT$. Note, that if $regS$ is more specific than $regT$, then $regS$ may assign types to more local registers than $regT$. This is in contrast to types of operand stacks. If $opdS$ is more specific than $opdT$, then $opdS$ and $opdT$ have the same length and assign types to exactly the same stack positions.

The following lemma says that a check remains true if the type frame is replaced by a more specific one. The lemma is used in the next chapter in the proof of the soundness of bytecode type assignments. It is also used in Chapter 17 for showing that the bytecode verifier computes principal (most specific) type assignments. Hence, monotonicity is an important property of the structural checks. We write $check(meth, pc, regT, opdT)$ for $check_E(meth)(code(meth)(pc), maxOpd(meth), pc, regT, opdT)$.

Lemma 15.7.1 (Checks are monotonic). Assume that $(regS, opdS)$ and $(regT, opdT)$ are type frames with $regS \sqsubseteq_{reg} regT$ and $opdS \sqsubseteq_{seq} opdT$. If $check(meth, pc, regT, opdT)$ returns true, then $check(meth, pc, regS, opdS)$ returns true as well.

Proof. The lemma is proved by a case distinction over the different instructions of the JVM. It uses the fact that the compatibility relation $\sqsubseteq$ of Def. 15.4.1 is transitive. □

16. Bytecode type assignments

In this chapter we analyze the dynamic constraints, which are checked at run-time by the defensive VM, to extract from them link-time checkable conditions on bytecode which, if satisfied, imply that the defensive VM executes the code without violating any run-time check (Soundness Theorem 16.4.1 for bytecode type assignments). We refine the compilation function of Part II by an appropriate type frame, which is associated to every instruction, and show that code, if generated from a correct Java program and following this certifying compilation scheme, does satisfy these link-time checkable bytecode conditions (Compiler Completeness Theorem 16.5.2 for bytecode type assignments). In the next chapter we will show that for a large class of programs bytecode type assignments can be computed using a fixed point computation.

The defensive VM checks dynamic constraints at run-time, at the price of slowing down the performance of the system. The slow down can be avoided if checks are performed only once, namely before running the fast but trustful machine. This is the task of the Java bytecode verifier.

At link-time, run-time data are not available. For example, the verifier does not know which reference value will be created by a *New* instruction or which path the execution will take and, usually, it is impossible to check all possible paths. To compensate this, the Java bytecode verifier imposes certain restrictions on the bytecode. For example, the verifier verifies every *independent* execution path through the code to ensure that for the verification all reachable instructions in the code are verified at least once. Similarly the verifier abstracts from the concrete reference generated by a *New* instruction and restricts the form of the program in such a way that link-time information is sufficient to keep track of un-initialized instances.

In this chapter we formulate such conditions by the notion of a bytecode type assignment. A bytecode type assignment assigns type frames to the code indices of method bodies and must satisfy several constraints. Our notion of bytecode type assignments differs from similar notions in the literature; for example it does not use the so-called subroutine call stacks of Stata and Abadi [34] or the modification histories of Qian [27]. Our typing rules for return addresses are simpler than O'Callahan's type system in [26].

In Sect. 16.1 we explain the problems with bytecode verification and with current bytecode verifiers. In particular we show that SUN's treatment of subroutines is inconsistent. In Sect. 16.2 we define by stepwise refinement the possible successors of (certifying) type frames, which are used in Sect. 16.3 for the definition of bytecode type assignments. Sect. 16.4 contains the proof of the soundness of bytecode type assignments, and Sect. 16.5 the proof that bytecode generated by the compiler of Part II is typeable.

16.1 Problems of bytecode verification

Bytecode verification is complicated because of the instructions $Jsr(s)$ and $Ret(x)$. Without these instructions bytecode verification would be much simpler. In this section we explain the general problems of bytecode verification, and show the particular problems and inconsistencies encountered in current bytecode verifier implementations.

16.1.1 Why are subroutines problematic?

The instructions $Jsr(s)$ and $Ret(x)$ are used to implement the **finally** block of Java **try** statements. The **finally** block is called with the instruction $Jsr(s)$ and the bytecode starting at code index s is called a *subroutine*. The instruction $Ret(x)$ is used to return from the subroutine. Control jumps to the address stored in the local variable x. Since the same **finally** block may be called from different positions, a subroutine is executed in different environments. The subroutine must be *polymorphic* in the variables which are not modified by the subroutine.

In Fig. 16.1, the **finally** block is called from several positions: (1) Before the expression i * i is returned, its value is saved in a new local variable x, and then the **finally** block is executed. Afterwards the saved value of x is returned. (2) The **finally** block is called at the end of the **try** block, where the variable j has a value. (3) Because of errors which could occur in the **try** block, the compiler inserts a default handler which does the following: the value of a possible error or exception is saved in a temporary variable y and then the **finally** block is executed. After termination of the **finally** block, the saved value of y is thrown again.

In Fig. 16.1, the subroutine S is called from three different positions.[1] Each time exactly one of the variables j, x, y has a value, whereas the other two variables are undefined. When S is called from block A, the variable x contains an **int**. When S is called at label C, the variable j contains an **int**. When S is called in the exception handler H, the variable y contains a pointer which is compatible with **Throwable**.

Polymorphism is one of the problems with subroutines. Another problem is that subroutines are not always left via a $Ret(x)$ instruction. Subroutines

---

[1] We write the examples in terms of real bytecode. See Appendix C.8 for real and abstract bytecode instructions.

Fig. 16.1 A polymorphic subroutine ($\leadsto$ CD)

```
static int m(int i) {        A: iload i        C: jsr S
  int j;                        ifne B            goto E
  try {                         iload i        H: astore y
    if (i == 0)                 iload i           jsr S
      return i * i;             imul              aload y
    j = i + i;                  istore x          athrow
  } finally { i = 0; }          jsr S          S: astore 4
  return j + i;                 iload x           iconst_0
}                               ireturn           istore i
                                                  ret 4
                             B: iload i        E: iload j
                                iload i           iload i
                                iadd              iadd
                                istore j          ireturn

                        catch Throwable from A to C using H
```

Fig. 16.2 Breaking out of a subroutine to the top level ($\leadsto$ CD)

```
static void m(boolean b) {        goto W
  while (b) {                  A: jsr S
    try {                         return
      return;                  S: astore r
    } finally {                   iload b
      if (b) break;               ifne R
    }                             ret r
  }                           W: iload b
}                                ifne A
                             R: return
```

Fig. 16.3 Breaking out of a subroutine to an enclosing subroutine ($\leadsto$ CD)

```
static void m(boolean b) {        jsr S1
  try {                           return
    return;                   S1: astore r1
  } finally {                     goto W
    while (b) {                A: jsr S2
      try {                       return
        return;               S2: astore r2
      } finally {                 iload b
        if (b) break;             ifne R1
      }                           ret r2
    }                         W: iload b
  }                              ifne A
}                             R1: ret r1
```

Fig. 16.4 Jumping out of a subroutine with an exception handler ($\leadsto$ CD)

```
static void m(boolean b) {      A:  jsr S
  try {                             return
    try {                       S:  astore r
      return;                       iload b
    } finally {                     ifeq B
      if (b)                        new E
        throw new E();              athrow
    }                           B:  ret r
  } catch (E x) {               H:  pop
    return;                         return
  }
}                               catch E from A to H using H
```

Fig. 16.5 Which variables are modified by the subroutine? ($\leadsto$ CD)

```
static void m(boolean b) {      A:  iload b
  while (true) {                    ifeq B
    try {                           jsr S
      if (b) return;                return
    } finally {                 B:  jsr S
      if (b) break;                 goto A
    }                           S:  astore r
  }                                 iload b
  b = true;                         ifne E
}                                   ret r
                                E:  iconst_1
                                    istore b
                                    return
```

Fig. 16.6 Inconsistencies in Sun's JDK 1.2 verifier ($\leadsto$ CD)

```
    jsr S                       A:  jsr S
    return                          return
S:  astore_1                    S:  astore_1
    jsr S      // rejected          goto A      // accepted
    return
```

Fig. 16.7 A valid Java program rejected by Sun's JDK 1.2 verifier ($\leadsto$ CD)

```
class Test {
  static void m(boolean b) {
    try {
      try { if (b) return; }
      finally {
        try { if (b) return; }
        finally { if (b) return; }
      }
    } finally { if (b) return; }
  }
}
```

Fig. 16.8 A valid Java program rejected by all known verifiers ($\leadsto$ CD)

```
class Test {
  static int m(boolean b) {
    int i;
    try {
      if (b) return 1;
      i = 2;
    } finally { if (b) i = 3; }
    return i;
  }
}
```

Fig. 16.9 Another Java program rejected by all known verifiers ($\leadsto$ CD)

```
class Test {
  int m(boolean b) {
  int i;
  L: {
      try {
        if (b) return 1;
        i = 2;
        if (b) break L;
      } finally { if (b) i = 3; }
      i = 4;
    }
    return i;
  }
}
```

can also be left via a $Cond(p, j)$ instruction or via a *Throw*. Unfortunately, it is not obvious from the bytecode where exactly a subroutine is left. It is also not obvious to which subroutine an instruction belongs. For example, in Fig. 16.2, the `finally` block can be left via a `break` statement. This fact is reflected in the bytecode: the instruction 'ifne R' jumps out of the subroutine S to the label R which belongs to the top-level. It is also possible to jump out of a subroutine to an enclosing subroutine. In Fig. 16.3, the instruction 'ifne R1' jumps out of the subroutine S2 to the enclosing subroutine S1. Moreover, a subroutine can be left via an exception handler. In Fig. 16.4, the subroutine S throws an exception of type E. This exception is then caught by the top-level handler H.

In some cases it is not so clear which variables are modified by a subroutine just by looking at the bytecode. In Fig. 16.5 we see in the Java program on the left-hand side that the variable b is not modified in the `finally` block. In the bytecode on the right-hand side, however, the only way to reach the instruction 'istore b' is via the subroutine S. Therefore, why should the variable b not be considered as modified by the subroutine S?

Sun's treatment of subroutines is inconsistent. For example, the JVM specification requires that subroutines are not recursive. Sun's JDK 1.2 verifier, however, accepts some recursive subroutines and rejects others. The bytecode on the left-hand side in Fig. 16.6 is rejected with the error 'Recursive call to jsr entry'. The bytecode on the right-hand side in Fig. 16.6, however, is accepted by Sun's verifier although it is as recursive as the rejected bytecode.

It turns out that recursive subroutines are harmless, because return addresses can be stored in local variables only (see Fig. 15.6). They cannot be stored in an array. They cannot be loaded on the operand stack. The only operations which are allowed with return addresses are duplication or deletion. Therefore, our notion of bytecode type assignment is focused on polymorphism and allows trivial forms of recursion.

Fig. 16.7 shows an example of a valid Java program which is rejected by Sun's JDK 1.2 verifier[14, bug no. 4268120]. This should not happen, since a verifier should at least accept all bytecode that has been generated by a correct compiler from valid Java programs.

The program in Fig. 16.8 suggests that bytecode verification is not possible at all, because it is rejected by any bytecode verifier we have tried including JDK 1.2, JDK 1.3, Netscape 4.73-4.76, Microsoft VM for Java 5.0 and 5.5 and the Kimera Verifier (http://kimera.cs.washington.edu/). The problem is that in the eyes of the verifier the variable i is unusable at the end of the method at the `return i` instruction, whereas according to the JLS [19, §16.2.14] the variable i is definitely assigned after the `try` statement [14, bug no. 4381996]. Our rules of definite assignment for the `try` statement in Table 8.6 are stronger and therefore the program is already rejected by our

Fig. 16.10 What is the type of variable x in the bytecode? ($\rightsquigarrow$ CD)

```
void m1(Integer i, String s) {          aload i
  Comparable x;                         ifnull A
  if (i != null)                        aload i
    x = i;                              astore x
  else                                  goto B
    x = s;                      A:      aload s
  m2(x);                                astore x
}                               B:      aload_0
                                        aload x
void m2(Comparable x) {}                invokevirtual m2(Comparable)
                                        return
```

compiler (see Remark 8.3.1). Fig. 16.9 shows a similar problem for labeled statements.

16.1.2 Why sets of reference types?

One of the main tasks of bytecode verification is to infer the types of local variables in method bodies. Only the types of the arguments of a method are known because they are contained in the method signature in the class file. The types of the other local variables are not known and must be inferred. Fig. 16.10 contains an example with a local variable x of type Comparable (see Fig. 16.11 for the type hierarchy). Since the class Integer as well as class String implement the interface Comparable, both arguments i and s of the method can be assigned to the variable x in the body.

In the corresponding bytecode in Fig. 16.10, the type of x is not known. When the verifier reaches label B during its static analysis, the variable x can contain an Integer or a String. Since both types are reference types, the verifier tries to merge the two types. The JVM specification says in [23] that 'the merged type of two references is the first common superclass of the two types and that such a reference type always exists because the type Object is a superclass of all class and interface types.' In our example the first common superclass of Integer and String is the class Object as can be seen in Fig. 16.11. Hence, the type assigned to variable x at label B is Object. The method invocation at the next instruction, however, requires an argument of type Comparable and so the verification process fails.

Sun's JDK 1.2 verifier does not reject the bytecode. Instead it inserts an additional run-time check for methods with arguments of interface type. Hence, the compatibility of method arguments has to be checked at run-time in contradiction to the JVM specification [23]. A better solution is to allow *sets of reference types* in the bytecode verification process. The type of variable x at label B in Fig. 16.10 is then the set {Integer, String}. The meaning of this type is 'either Integer or String'. At the method invocation

Fig. 16.11 A piece of the Java type hierarchy

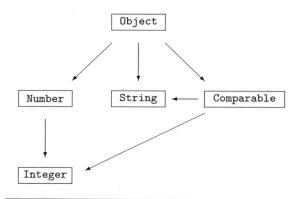

in the next instruction, the verifier has just to check that each element of the set of reference types assigned to x is a subtype of Comparable. No additional run-time checks are needed.

Therefore we extend the universe of verify types to include also finite sets of reference types. Remember that reference types are class types, interface types, array types and the special type Null which is used as the type of the null pointer.

> **data** *VerifyType* = . . .
> | *Powerset*(Null | *Class* | *Interface* | *Array*)

A single reference type R is often identified with the singleton set $\{R\}$. Examples of sets of reference types are:

> {Integer, String}, {Comparable}, {int[], float[]}

The compatibility relation $\sqsubseteq$ has to be extended to such sets. Therefore we need the notion of an *upper bound* of a set of reference types.

Definition 16.1.1 (Upper bound). A type A is an *upper bound* of a set τ of reference types, if $B \preceq A$ for every $B \in \tau$.

For example, the upper bounds of the verify type {Float, Integer} are the following types:

> Number, Object, Comparable.

The classes Integer, Float and Double are direct subclasses of Number and implement the interface Comparable. The class Number is a direct subclass of Object and does not implement Comparable.

Definition 16.1.2 (Compatibility). Let σ and τ be finite sets of reference types. We define $\sigma \sqsubseteq \tau$ iff each upper bound of τ is an upper bound of σ.

For example, the following compatibility relations are true:

$$\{\texttt{Integer}, \texttt{String}\} \sqsubseteq \{\texttt{Comparable}\}$$

Reason: `Integer` and `String` implement the interface `Comparable`.

$$\{\texttt{Double}\} \sqsubseteq \{\texttt{Integer}, \texttt{Float}\}$$

Reason: The upper bounds of $\{\texttt{Integer}, \texttt{Float}\}$ are `Number`, `Comparable`, `Object`.

Definition 16.1.3 (Array type). A set τ of reference types is called an *array type*, if there exists a type A such that $A[\,]$ is an upper bound of τ.

For example, the verify type $\{\texttt{int}[\,], \texttt{float}[\,]\}$ is not an array type, because its only upper bounds are `Object`, `Cloneable` and `Serializable` (see Def. 5.1.2). The verify type $\{\texttt{Integer}[\,], \texttt{Float}[\,]\}$, is an array type, because $\texttt{Object}[\,]$ is an upper bound. The verify type $\{\texttt{Null}\}$ is an array type, too.

In the soundness and completeness proof for the bytecode verifier the following properties of the extended compatibility relation are relevant:

Lemma 16.1.1 (Properties of sets of reference types).

V1. $\tau \sqsubseteq \tau$.
V2. $\rho \sqsubseteq \sigma$ and $\sigma \sqsubseteq \tau \implies \rho \sqsubseteq \tau$.
V3. $\tau \sqsubseteq \{A\} \iff A$ is an upper bound of τ.
V4. If $\sigma \sqsubseteq \tau$ and $\tau \sqsubseteq \{\texttt{Object}[\,]\}$, then $\{A \mid A[\,] \in \sigma\} \sqsubseteq \{A \mid A[\,] \in \tau\}$.

Proof. The properties can be derived using the subtype relation for reference types in Def. 5.1.2. Property V4 is used for the array instructions which are listed in Appendix C.7. □

Remark 16.1.1. We could replace Def. 16.1.2 and define $\sigma \sqsubseteq \tau$ iff for each $A \in \sigma$ there exists a $B \in \tau$ such that $A \preceq B$. This version of compatibility satisfies the properties V1–V4, too.

16.2 Successors of bytecode instructions

Since the verifier works at link-time, it operates only on the type components of the items stored in registers and on the operand stack, as introduced for the defensive VM. These type components constitute a type frame. For each instruction, the verifier tries to simulate the effect for all possible successors. To determine the successor type frame, in this section a function *succ* is defined by stepwise refinement for each of the submachines.

Fig. 16.12 Successors for $JVM_{\mathcal{I}}$ instructions

$succ_I(instr, pc, regT, opdT) =$
  case $instr$ **of**
    $Prim(p) \rightarrow \{(pc + 1, regT, drop(opdT, argSize(p)) \cdot returnType(p))\}$
    $Dupx(s_1, s_2) \rightarrow$
      $\{(pc + 1, regT, drop(opdT, s_1 + s_2) \cdot$
                      $take(opdT, s_2) \cdot take(opdT, s_1 + s_2))\}$
    $Pop(s) \rightarrow \{(pc + 1, regT, drop(opdT, s))\}$
    $Load(t, x) \rightarrow$
      if $size(t) = 1$ **then**
        $\{(pc + 1, regT, opdT \cdot [regT(x)])\}$
      else
        $\{(pc + 1, regT, opdT \cdot [regT(x), regT(x + 1)])\}$
    $Store(t, x) \rightarrow$
      if $size(t) = 1$ **then**
        $\{(pc + 1, regT \oplus \{(x, top(opdT))\}, drop(opdT, 1))\}$
      else
        $\{(pc + 1, regT \oplus \{(x, t_0), (x + 1, t_1)\}, drop(opdT, 2))\}$
      where $[t_0, t_1] = take(opdT, 2)$
    $Goto(o) \quad \rightarrow \{(o, regT, opdT)\}$
    $Cond(p, o) \rightarrow \{(pc + 1, regT, drop(opdT, argSize(p))),$
                    $(o, regT, drop(opdT, argSize(p)))\}$

16.2.1 Successors for $JVM_{\mathcal{I}}$ instructions

Fig. 16.12 defines the $succ_I$ function which computes for every $JVM_{\mathcal{I}}$ instruction and given type frame the set of instructions together with the corresponding type frames which are possible successors of the given instruction and type frame in the given method. It simulates on the type frame all transitions an instruction can make (see Chapter 9 for the definition of the effect of the instructions). Successors which can be reached via an exception are listed below in the function $succ_E$. The argument $instr$ of the function $succ_I$ is the instruction at code index pc.

16.2.2 Successors for $JVM_{\mathcal{C}}$ instructions

Fig. 16.13 defines the extension of $succ_I$ to the function $succ_C$. In contrast to the registers and to the operand stack that are weakly typed, class fields in $JVM_{\mathcal{C}}$ are strongly typed: every field always holds a single type. In contrast to the defensive VM, the verifier therefore uses the declared type of the global field which is stored as first parameter in *GetStatic* and *PutStatic* instructions. Similarly, for method invocations the declared return type is propagated to the successor type frame. Since the effect of a return instruction is to leave the given method, such instructions generate no successors in that method.

Fig. 16.13 Successors for JVM_C instructions

$succ_C(meth)(instr, pc, regT, opdT) =$
$\quad succ_I(instr, pc, regT, opdT) \cup$
$\quad \textbf{case } instr \textbf{ of}$
$\quad\quad GetStatic(t, c/f) \quad\quad \rightarrow \{(pc+1, regT, opdT \cdot t)\}$
$\quad\quad PutStatic(t, c/f) \quad\quad \rightarrow \{(pc+1, regT, drop(opdT, size(t)))\}$
$\quad\quad InvokeStatic(t, c/m) \rightarrow \{(pc+1, regT, drop(opdT, argSize(c/m)) \cdot t)\}$
$\quad\quad Return(mt) \quad\quad\quad\quad \rightarrow \emptyset$

16.2.3 Successors for $JVM_\mathcal{O}$ instructions

Successors of $JVM_\mathcal{O}$ instructions with given type frame are defined in Fig. 16.14. For instructions which do not relate to object initialization, the successors are computed similarly to those for JVM_C instructions in Fig. 16.13, taking into account also the type of the target object. The link-time checkable requirements on object initialization pose several new problems. The defensive VM keeps track of the initialization status of objects by adding information to the generated run-time reference via the dynamic function *initState*. For link-time verification this run-time information has to be simulated in the type system.

At link-time, different *New* instructions can be distinguished by their instruction index. However, this information does not denote uninitialized objects uniquely. For instance, it does not suffice to distinguish different run-time instances of *New* which is part of a loop body. But if we require that the uninitialized type that we generate when we simulate a *New* instruction is neither in any of the type registers nor in the type operand stack, then this assures uniqueness of the type description. The successor of *New* in Fig. 16.14 replaces the uninitialized type on the operand stack with the verify type **unusable** and filters out all registers with the uninitialized type such that they are not available at the successor code index. We do not add this as a check to the function $check_\mathcal{O}$ in Fig. 15.4, because that would violate the monotonicity property of Lemma 15.7.1.

By construction any execution of an instance initialization method initializes only a single object. As a consequence in any type frame of an initialization method there is the type descriptor *InInit* for only this object. By definition, an object is regarded as fully initialized after execution of an instance initialized method. Hence in the successor of an *InvokeSpecial* instruction which invokes an initialization method, the uninitialized type of the object has to be replaced by the initialized type. In case of *InInit* the initialized type is equal to the class of the current initialization method.

Fig. 16.14 Successors for $JVM_{\mathcal{O}}$ instructions

$succ_O(meth)(instr, pc, regT, opdT) =$
$\quad succ_C(meth)(instr, pc, regT, opdT) \cup$
$\quad$ **case** $instr$ **of**
$\qquad New(c) \rightarrow \{(pc + 1, regS, opdS \cdot [(c, pc)_{new}])\}$
$\qquad\quad$ **where** $regS = \{(x, t) \mid (x, t) \in regT, t \neq (c, pc)_{new}\}$
$\qquad\qquad opdS = [\textbf{if } t = (c, pc)_{new} \textbf{ then unusable else } t \mid t \in opdT]$
$\qquad GetField(t, c/f) \rightarrow \{(pc + 1, regT, drop(opdT, 1) \cdot t)\}$
$\qquad PutField(t, c/f) \rightarrow \{(pc + 1, regT, drop(opdT, 1 + size(t)))\}$
$\qquad InvokeSpecial(t, c/m) \rightarrow$
$\qquad\quad$ **let** $opdT' = drop(opdT, 1 + argSize(c/m)) \cdot t$
$\qquad\quad$ **if** $methNm(m) = \texttt{"<init>"}$ **then**
$\qquad\qquad$ **case** $top(drop(opdT, argSize(c/m)))$ **of**
$\qquad\qquad\quad (c, o)_{new} \rightarrow \{(pc + 1, regT[c/(c, o)_{new}], opdT'[c/(c, o)_{new}])\}$
$\qquad\qquad\quad InInit \quad \rightarrow$ **let** $c/\_ = meth$
$\qquad\qquad\qquad\qquad\qquad \{(pc + 1, regT[c/InInit], opdT'[c/InInit])\}$
$\qquad\quad$ **else**
$\qquad\qquad \{(pc + 1, regT, opdT')\}$
$\qquad InvokeVirtual(t, c/m) \rightarrow$
$\qquad\quad$ **let** $opdT' = drop(opdT, 1 + argSize(c/m)) \cdot t$
$\qquad\quad \{(pc + 1, regT, opdT')\}$
$\qquad InstanceOf(c) \rightarrow \{(pc + 1, regT, drop(opdT, 1) \cdot [\texttt{int}])\}$
$\qquad Checkcast(t) \rightarrow \{(pc + 1, regT, drop(opdT, 1) \cdot t)\}$

16.2.4 Successors for $JVM_{\mathcal{E}}$ instructions

The function $succ_E$ in Fig. 16.15 reflects the consequences of exception handling and embedded subroutines. We first consider which handler frames have to be included as possible successors of $JVM_{\mathcal{E}}$ instructions. For *Athrow* instructions the control proceeds according to the exception table of the method. Therefore every possible handler of the thrown exception provides a candidate for a successor instruction. It would be wrong to restrict the successors of the *Athrow* instruction to those handlers *(from, upto, handle, τ)* for which $c \sqsubseteq \tau$, where c is the topmost type on the operand stack. At run-time the topmost reference on the operand stack will be of a subtype of c and could be caught by a different handler.

Several instructions might throw run-time exceptions. Therefore, the handlers which catch run-time exceptions have to be included in the successors, too. Moreover, the VM might throw a `VirtualMachinError` almost at any position in the bytecode. Therefore, for each code index and each instruction, except for *Jsr*, *Goto*, *Return* and *Load*, we include into the set of possible successors all handlers which protect the code index.

Fig. 16.15 Successors for JVM$_\mathcal{E}$ instructions

$succ_E(meth)(instr, pc, regT, opdT) =$
 $\quad succ_O(meth)(instr, pc, regT, opdT) \cup allhandlers(instr, meth, pc, regT) \cup$
 case $instr$ **of**
 $\quad Athrow \rightarrow \emptyset$
 $\quad Jsr(s) \rightarrow \{(s, regT, opdT \cdot [\mathtt{retAddr}(s)])\}$
 $\quad Ret(x) \rightarrow \emptyset$

Fig. 16.16 Some instructions do not throw exceptions ($\rightsquigarrow$ CD)

```
class Test {
  boolean m(boolean b) {
    try {
      try { if (b) return b; }
      finally {
        try { if (b) return b; }
        catch (Throwable x) { if (b) return b; }
      }
    } finally { if (b) return b; }
    return b;
  }
}
```

Fig. 16.17 Successors are monotonic

	$regV$	$\sqsubseteq_{reg}$	$regT$	
	$opdV$	$\sqsubseteq_{seq}$	$opdT$	
for each successor				there exists a successor
$(s, regS, opdS)$ of	$\downarrow$		$\downarrow$	$(s, regU, opdU)$ of
$(pc, regV, opdV)$				$(pc, regT, opdT)$
	$regS$	$\sqsubseteq_{reg}$	$regU$	
	$opdS$	$\sqsubseteq_{seq}$	$opdU$	

$$allhandlers(Jsr(\_), m, pc, regT) = \{\}$$
$$allhandlers(Goto(\_), m, pc, regT) = \{\}$$
$$allhandlers(Return(\_), m, pc, regT) = \{\}$$
$$allhandlers(Load(\_,\_), m, pc, regT) = \{\}$$
$$allhandlers(instr, m, pc, regT) =$$
$$\{(h, regT, [t]) \mid (f, u, h, t) \in excs(m) \wedge f \le pc < u\}$$

It seems that this simple definition is good enough for bytecode generated by a Java compiler (see Sect. 16.5). We assume that the instructions *Jsr*, *Goto*, *Return* and *Load* wich are used for the compilation of the `continue`, `break` and `return` statements in Fig. 12.3 do not throw exceptions. Therefore they do not have successors via the exception table. Otherwise, programs like the one in Fig. 16.16 would be rejected by our verifier.

The instruction $Jsr(s)$ pushes the type `retAddr(s)` on top of the operand stack indicating that this is a return address to a caller which has called subroutine s. The successor of a *Ret* instruction is not defined in the function $succ_E$. Instead, it is treated as a special case in the definition of bytecode type assignments in the next section, and also in the definition of type propagation in the bytecode verifier in Sect. 17.5. The reason for this is that a *Ret* instruction does not return all local registers, but only the registers the corresponding subroutine has modified. The types of the other registers have to be propagated from the caller of the subroutine.

The following lemma says that the successors of an instruction with respect to a more specific type frame are more specific than some successors with respect to the more general type frame. The lemma is needed in the next chapter in the proof that the bytecode verifier computes principal type assignments if there exist any at all. We write $succ(meth, pc, regT, opdT)$ for

$$succ_E(meth)(code(meth)(pc), pc, regT, opdT),$$

similarly $check(meth, pc, regT, opdT)$ for

$$check_E(meth)(code(meth)(pc), maxOpd(meth), pc, regT, opdT).$$

Lemma 16.2.1 (Successors are monotonic). Assume that $(regV, opdV)$ and $(regT, opdT)$ are type frames with $regV \sqsubseteq_{reg} regT$ and $opdV \sqsubseteq_{seq} opdT$. If $check(meth, pc, regT, opdT)$ is true and $(s, regS, opdS)$ is a successor in $succ(meth, pc, regV, opdV)$, then there exists a successor $(s, regU, opdU)$ in $succ(meth, pc, regT, opdT)$ such that $regS \sqsubseteq_{reg} regU$ and $opdS \sqsubseteq_{seq} opdU$ (see Fig. 16.17).

Proof. The lemma follows by a case distinction along the JVM instructions from the transitivity of the compatibility relation $\sqsubseteq$ (see Def. 15.4.1). □

16.3 Type assignments without subroutine call stacks

In this section we show how one can resolve the inconsistencies pointed out in Sect. 16.1, and obtain a sound and sufficiently complete notion of bytecode type assignment. This notion combines the type frame successor function of the previous section with the checking function of the defensive VM.

Based on the examples in Sect. 16.1 we make the following assumptions about subroutines. We assume that the first instruction of a subroutine is a $Store(\text{addr}, x)$ instruction which stores the return address in a variable x. This assumption is reasonable, since if a subroutine ever returns, it has to take its return address from a local variable in the Ret instruction. The return address is on top of the operand stack, when the subroutine is called. It has to be stored in the local variable somewhere in the subroutine. We assume that this is at the beginning.

Our second assumption is that the code generated by a Java compiler for a **finally** block is connected. The code may contain several Ret instructions, but the code indices for the block must form an interval. Both assumptions are implicit in the notion of bytecode type assignment below.

We divide the instruction set of the Java VM into normal instructions and control transfer instructions.

Definition 16.3.1 (Control transfer instructions). Control transfer instructions are: $Goto(i)$, $Cond(p, i)$, $Return(\tau)$, $Throw$, $Jsr(i)$, $Ret(x)$.

Each code index has a (possibly empty) set of successor indices which can be reached in the next step of the execution of the Java VM without applying a return instruction ($Return(t)$ or $Ret(x)$).

Definition 16.3.2 (Successor index). A code index j is called a *successor index* of i (with respect to a given method), if one of the following conditions is true:

- The ith instruction is not a control transfer instruction and $j = i + 1$
- The ith instruction is $Goto(j)$
- The ith instruction is $Cond(p, k)$ or $Jsr(k)$ and $j \in \{i + 1, k\}$
- There exists a handler $(f, u, j, \_)$ in the exception table of the method such that $f \leq i < u$ and the ith instruction is not Jsr, $Goto$, $Return$ or $Load$

Note that the index of a Jsr instruction has two possible successors unlike the type frame associated to a successor instruction in Fig. 16.15 which has only one (except for type frames of possible exception handlers). This is because in the intended "pairing" of $Jsr(s)$ and $Ret(x)$ instructions, the subroutine called by Jsr returns to the instruction immediately following Jsr, similarly to the association between the index i of a method invocation instruction and its successor index $i + 1$ which is reached by executing the corresponding $Return$ instruction from the invoked method. In the following definition of reachability it is important that both successor indices of Jsr are included.

Definition 16.3.3 (Reachable). A code index j is called *reachable from i* if there exists a finite (possibly empty) sequence of successor steps from i to j. A code index is called *reachable*, if it is reachable from 0.

Since the treatment of subroutines is rather complicated we have to define precisely what we mean by a subroutine.

Definition 16.3.4 (Subroutine). If i is reachable from 0 and the ith instruction is $Jsr(s)$, then the code index s is called a *subroutine* of the method.

Since we assume that the first instruction of a subroutine stores the return address in a local variable, the possible returns from the subroutine are easy to identify.

Definition 16.3.5 (Return from subroutine). A code index r is a possible return from subroutine s, if $code(s) = Store(\texttt{addr}, x)$, $code(r) = Ret(x)$ and r is reachable from $s + 1$ on a path that does not use any $Store(\_, x)$ instruction.

The instructions which belong to a subroutine are simply those which are in the interval between the first instruction of the subroutine and any possible return from the subroutine (there could be several).

Definition 16.3.6 (Belongs to a subroutine). A code index i *belongs* to subroutine s, if there exists a possible return r from s such that $s \le i \le r$.

For the treatment of polymorphic subroutines a function *mod* is used which assigns to each subroutine the set of local variables modified by the subroutine. This set includes also the variables which are used in other subroutines called by this subroutine as well as the variables which are used in implicitly called exception handlers, as long as they belong to the subroutine.

Definition 16.3.7 (Modified variables). Let s be a subroutine. A variable x belongs to $mod(s)$, if there exists a code index i which belongs to s such that $code(i) = Store(t, y)$ and one of the following conditions is satisfied:

1. $size(t) = 1$ and $x = y$, or
2. $size(t) = 2$ and $x = y$ or $x = y + 1$.

The set $mod(s)$ of variables which are modified by a subroutine is used to restrict the type assignment to local variables when a subroutine returns with a $Ret(x)$ instruction. At this time, the variable x must be of type $\texttt{retAddr}(s)$ for some subroutine s. The types of the variables modified by s have to be returned to the callers of s. For this purpose we use the notion of the restriction of type assignments to a given set of variables (see Sect. 2.3). Since instructions $Ret(x)$ have no successor type frames, they have to be treated in a special way in the following definition.

Definition 16.3.8 (Bytecode type assignment). A bytecode type assignment with domain $\mathcal{D}$ for a method μ is a family $(regT_i, opdT_i)_{i \in \mathcal{D}}$ of type frames satisfying the following conditions:

T1. $\mathcal{D}$ is a set of valid code indices of the method μ.

T2. Code index 0 belongs to $\mathcal{D}$.

T3. Let $[\tau_1, \ldots, \tau_n] = argTypes(\mu)$ and $c = classNm(\mu)$. If μ is a
   a) class initialization method: $regT_0 = \emptyset$.
   b) class method: $\{0 \mapsto \tau_1, \ldots, n-1 \mapsto \tau_n\} \sqsubseteq_{\mathrm{reg}} regT_0$.
   c) instance method: $\{0 \mapsto c, 1 \mapsto \tau_1, \ldots, n \mapsto \tau_n\} \sqsubseteq_{\mathrm{reg}} regT_0$.
   d) constructor: $\{0 \mapsto InInit, 1 \mapsto \tau_1, \ldots, n \mapsto \tau_n\} \sqsubseteq_{\mathrm{reg}} regT_0$.

T4. The list $opdT_0$ is empty.

T5. If $i \in \mathcal{D}$, then $check(\mu, i, regT_i, opdT_i)$ is true.

T6. If $i \in \mathcal{D}$ and $(j, regS, opdS) \in succ(\mu, i, regT_i, opdT_i)$, then
   $j \in \mathcal{D}$, $regS \sqsubseteq_{\mathrm{reg}} regT_j$ and $opdS \sqsubseteq_{\mathrm{seq}} opdT_j$.

T7. If $i \in \mathcal{D}$, $code(i) = Ret(x)$ and $regT_i(x) = \mathtt{retAddr}(s)$, then for all
   reachable $j \in \mathcal{D}$ with $code(j) = Jsr(s)$:
   a) $j + 1 \in \mathcal{D}$,
   b) $regT_i \sqsubseteq_{\mathrm{reg}} mod(s) \lhd regT_{j+1}$,
   c) $opdT_i \sqsubseteq_{\mathrm{seq}} opdT_{j+1}$,
   d) $regT_j \sqsubseteq_{\mathrm{reg}} mod(s) \lhd regT_{j+1}$,
   e) if $\mathtt{retAddr}(\ell)$ occurs in $mod(s) \lhd regT_{j+1}$, then each code index
      which belongs to s belongs to l,
   f) neither $(c, k)_{new}$ nor $InInit$ occur in $mod(s) \lhd regT_{j+1}$.

T8. If $i \in \mathcal{D}$ and $\mathtt{retAddr}(s)$ occurs in $regT_i$, then i belongs to s.
   If $i \in \mathcal{D}$ and $\mathtt{retAddr}(s)$ occurs in $opdT_i$, then $i = s$.

The verify type $\mathtt{unusable}$ is allowed on the operand stack but not as the type
of a register.

   T1 says that the domain $\mathcal{D}$ of a bytecode type assignment must be a
set of valid code indices. A bytecode type assignment does not necessarily
assign type frames to all code indices which are reachable from 0 according
to Def. 16.3.3. For example, if the bytecode jumps at index i to subroutine s
and s does never return, then $i + 1$ does not necessarily belong to $\mathcal{D}$. We will
see in the soundness proof that at run-time the program counter pc always
belongs to $\mathcal{D}$. This is certainly true at the beginning, because T2 ensures that
code index 0 is in $\mathcal{D}$.
   T3 and T4 are conditions for the type frame at code index 0. The operand
stack must be empty at the beginning. The declared types of the arguments
of the method must be more specific than the types assigned in $regT_0$. An
instance method assigns the value of $\mathtt{this}$ to register 0, hence the type of 0
must be the class in which the method is defined. When a constructor is called,
the $\mathtt{this}$ object becomes partially initialized, hence the type of register 0
must be $InInit$ except in class $\mathtt{Object}$ where the $\mathtt{this}$ object becomes fully
initialized. Therefore, the constructor of class $\mathtt{Object}$ is treated as an instance
method in T3. We do not require that the types of the arguments are equal
to the ones in $regT_0$, because it may happen that the code later jumps back

to 0 when some of the registers have more general types or are not even used any longer.

In T5, we use the check functions of the defensive VM in the previous chapter to ensure the correct applicability of an instruction. Since the check functions operate on the type frame and not on the raw values, we can apply them to $regT_i$ and $opdT_i$ for each code index i in the domain $\mathcal{D}$ of the bytecode assignment. We write $check(meth, pc, regT, opdT)$ for $check_E(meth)(code(meth)(pc), maxOpd(meth), pc, regT, opdT)$.

T6 says that a successor type frame has to be more specific than the type frame assigned to the successor index. T6 requires that the successor index j of i belongs to the domain $\mathcal{D}$. Since $\mathcal{D}$ consists of valid code indices only, T6 ensures that successor code indices are valid code indices. T6 therefore makes it impossible to drop off the end of a method body. The length of the operand stack of the computed successor type frame for the instruction with index j must be the same as the length of the operand stack which is assigned to j and the types must be compatible. For type registers the condition is weakened. For each register in the computed successor either the type is compatible with the one assigned at index j or it cannot be used at successor index j.

T7 deals with subroutines. If the ith instruction is $Ret(x)$, a return from a subroutine, then by T5 the local variable x has type $\texttt{retAddr}(s)$ in $regT_i$ for some subroutine s. This means that the value of x at run-time will be a return address to a caller of the subroutine s. Let j be any code index which calls s, i.e., $code(j) = Jsr(s)$. Then the code index $j + 1$ must be valid (a). For local variables which are used at index $j + 1$ and are modified by the subroutine s, the type at i must be more specific than at $j + 1$ (b). For local variables not modified by s, the type at j, from where the subroutine s was called, has to be more specific than the type at index $j + 1$ to which subroutine s is returning (d). The types assigned to the operand stack at index i must be more specific than the types at index $j + 1$ (c).

Condition T7 (e) ensures that subroutines are properly nested. If a type $\texttt{retAddr}(\ell)$ is used at code index $j + 1$ for a register which is not modified by the subroutine s, then the subroutine l must enclose s in the sense of Def. 16.3.6. In Fig. 16.18 all conditions are satisfied except of T7 (e). Although the subroutine s is called by the subroutine l, the variables x and r_2 which are modified by s are not in $mod(l)$. We have $mod(s) = \{r_2, x\}$ and $mod(l) = \{r_1\}$. Because x is not in $mod(l)$, the type $\texttt{String}$ is propagated at the $Jsr(l)$ instruction and not the type $\texttt{int}$. At run-time there would be a type violation there. Condition T7 (e) is violated, because the second $Jsr(s)$ belongs to subroutine l but subroutine s is not contained in l. Condition T7 (e) is used below in the proof of the Coincidence Lemma 16.4.1.

Instead of condition T7 (e) we could also use the following inductive definition of the sets $mod(s)$:

Fig. 16.18 Violation of T7 (e): subroutine s is not contained in l ($\rightsquigarrow$ CD)

	$opdT_i$	$regT_i$
$Jsr(s)$	[]	{}
$Prim(\texttt{"abc"})$	[]	$\{x \mapsto \texttt{int}\}$
$Store(\texttt{addr}, x)$	[String]	$\{x \mapsto \texttt{int}\}$
$Jsr(l)$	[]	$\{x \mapsto \texttt{String}\}$
// at run-time x is an $\texttt{int}$ and not a $\texttt{String}$!		
$Load(\texttt{addr}, x)$	[]	$\{x \mapsto \texttt{String}\}$
$InvokeVirtual(\texttt{String/length()})$	[int]	{}
$Return(\texttt{int})$	[int]	{}
$l : Store(\texttt{addr}, r_1)$	[rA(l)]	{}
$Jsr(s)$	[]	$\{r_1 \mapsto \texttt{rA}(l)\}$
$Ret(r_1)$	[]	$\{x \mapsto \texttt{int}, r_1 \mapsto \texttt{rA}(l)\}$
$s : Store(\texttt{addr}, r_2)$	[rA(s)]	{}
$Prim(7)$	[]	$\{r_2 \mapsto \texttt{rA}(s)\}$
$Store(\texttt{int}, x)$	[int]	$\{r_2 \mapsto \texttt{rA}(s)\}$
$Ret(r_2)$	[]	$\{x \mapsto \texttt{int}, r_2 \mapsto \texttt{rA}(s)\}$

Fig. 16.19 Violation of T7 (f): $(c, k)_{new}$ occurs in $mod(s) \triangleleft regT_{j+1}$ ($\rightsquigarrow$ CD)

	$opdT_i$	$regT_i$
$Jsr(s)$	[]	{}
$Store(\texttt{addr}, x)$	$[(c, k)_{new}]$	{}
$j : Jsr(s)$	[]	$\{x \mapsto (c, k)_{new}\}$
$InvokeSpecial(c/\texttt{<init>})$	$[(c, k)_{new}]$	$\{x \mapsto (c, k)_{new}\}$
$Load(\texttt{addr}, x)$	[c]	$\{x \mapsto c\}$
// use uninitialized object!		
$Return(\texttt{addr})$	[c]	$\{x \mapsto c\}$
$s : Store(\texttt{addr}, r)$	[retAddr(s)]	{}
$k : New(c)$	[]	$\{r \mapsto \texttt{retAddr}(s)\}$
$Ret(r)$	$[(c, k)_{new}]$	$\{r \mapsto \texttt{retAddr}(s)\}$

1. If i belongs to s and $code(i) = Store(t, x)$, then $x \in mod(s)$ and, if $size(t) = 2$, then $x + 1 \in mod(s)$.
2. If i belongs to l, $code(i) = Jsr(s)$ and $x \in mod(s)$, then $x \in mod(l)$.

With this extended definition of mod, more bytecode programs would have type assignments. A compiler for Java, however, had to use more local registers for storing return values and for storing exceptions in default handlers.

Condition T7 (f) is similar to a condition proposed by Freund and Mitchell in [17]. Without T7 (f) a subroutine may create new objects which can later be used without being fully initialized. This behavior is shown in Fig. 16.19 (example from [17]). When the second object which has been created in the subroutine is initialized, the type $(c, k)_{new}$ is replaced by c everywhere in the type frame. The variable x gets type c, although the value of x at run-time is an uninitialized object. Hence a bytecode type assignment must ensure that there is always at most one object of type $(c, k)_{new}$. Without T7 (f) (or a similar condition) this is not possible.

In a similar way T7 (f) prevents code from initializing an object twice. Fig. 16.20 shows an example of what could happen without T7 (f). Since the variable x is not modified by the subroutine s, it does not belong to $mod(s)$. Therefore type $(c, k)_{new}$ is propagated from j to $j + 1$ and type c remains at index i. The object can be initialized a second time.

In Fig. 16.21 conditions T1–T7 are satisfied but condition T8 is violated. According to Def. 16.3.5 the last instruction $Ret(r_1)$ is a possible return from subroutine s_1. Therefore $mod(s_1) = \{r_1, r_2\}$. The instruction $Ret(r_2)$ is a possible return from subroutine s_1. Since the instruction $Ret(r_2)$ is before s_1, the set $mod(s_2)$ is empty although subroutine s_1 stores at run-time an integer in register x. Condition T8 is violated, since the type $\texttt{retAddr}(s_2)$ is used several times for register r_2, but there are no instructions that belong to subroutine s_2.

16.4 Soundness of bytecode type assignments

For the rest of this chapter we assume that each method in each class of the current class environment has a bytecode type assignment.

What does it mean that the type assignment is sound? It means that the bytecode does not violate any checks when it runs on the defensive VM. One can show that at run-time the values of the operands and the values stored in local variables belong to the assigned types. If there is a verify type assigned to a local variable, then at run-time the local variable contains a value which belongs to that verify type. If the type is a primitive type, then the value is of exactly that type. If the type is a reference type, then the value is a pointer to an object or array which is compatible with that type. The same is true for the verify types assigned to the operand stack. Moreover, at run-time the

Fig. 16.20 Violation of T7 (f): $(c, k)_{new}$ occurs in $mod(s) \triangleleft regT_{j+1}$ ($\rightsquigarrow$ CD)

	$opdT_i$	$regT_i$
$k : New(c)$	$[]$	$\{\}$
$\quad Store(\mathtt{addr}, x)$	$[(c, k)_{new}]$	$\{\}$
$j : Jsr(s)$	$[]$	$\{x \mapsto (c, k)_{new}\}$
$\quad Load(\mathtt{addr}, x)$	$[]$	$\{x \mapsto (c, k)_{new}\}$
$\quad InvokeSpecial(c/\mathtt{<init>})$	$[(c, k)_{new}]$	$\{x \mapsto (c, k)_{new}\}$
$\quad$ // the object is initialized twice!		
$\quad Return$	$[]$	$\{x \mapsto c\}$
$s : Store(\mathtt{addr}, r)$	$[\mathtt{retAddr}(s)]$	$\{x \mapsto (c, k)_{new}\}$
$\quad Load(\mathtt{addr}, x)$	$[]$	$\{r \mapsto \mathtt{retAddr}(s), x \mapsto (c, k)_{new}\}$
$\quad InvokeSpecial(c/\mathtt{<init>})$	$[(c, k)_{new}]$	$\{r \mapsto \mathtt{retAddr}(s), x \mapsto (c, k)_{new}\}$
$i : Ret(r)$	$[]$	$\{r \mapsto \mathtt{retAddr}(s), x \mapsto c\}$

Fig. 16.21 Violation of T8 ($\rightsquigarrow$ CD)

	$opdT_i$	$regT_i$
$\quad Prim(\mathtt{"abc"})$	$[]$	$\{\}$
$\quad Store(\mathtt{addr}, x)$	$[\mathtt{String}]$	$\{\}$
$j : Jsr(s_1)$	$[]$	$\{x \mapsto \mathtt{String}\}$
$\quad Prim(7)$	$[]$	$\{r_2 \mapsto \mathtt{rA}(s_2)\}$
$\quad Store(\mathtt{int}, x)$	$[\mathtt{int}]$	$\{r_2 \mapsto \mathtt{rA}(s_2)\}$
$l : Ret(r_2)$	$[]$	$\{r_2 \mapsto \mathtt{rA}(s_2)\}$
$s_1 : Store(\mathtt{addr}, r_1)$	$[\mathtt{rA}(s_1)]$	$\{x \mapsto \mathtt{String}\}$
$\quad Jsr(s_2)$	$[]$	$\{x \mapsto \mathtt{String}, r_1 \mapsto \mathtt{rA}(s_1)\}$
$\quad Load(\mathtt{addr}, x)$	$[]$	$\{x \mapsto \mathtt{String}\}$
$\quad$ // at run-time x is an $\mathtt{int}$ and not a $\mathtt{String}$!		
$\quad InvokeVirtual(\mathtt{String/length()})$	$[\mathtt{int}]$	$\{\}$
$\quad Return(\mathtt{int})$	$[\mathtt{int}]$	$\{\}$
$s_2 : Store(\mathtt{addr}, r_2)$	$[\mathtt{rA}(s_2)]$	$\{r_1 \mapsto \mathtt{rA}(s_1)\}$
$\quad Prim(1)$	$[]$	$\{r_1 \mapsto \mathtt{rA}(s_1), r_2 \mapsto \mathtt{rA}(s_2)\}$
$\quad Cond(\mathtt{ifeq}, l)$	$[\mathtt{int}]$	$\{r_1 \mapsto \mathtt{rA}(s_1), r_2 \mapsto \mathtt{rA}(s_2)\}$
$\quad Ret(r_1)$	$[]$	$\{r_1 \mapsto \mathtt{rA}(s_1), r_2 \mapsto \mathtt{rA}(s_2)\}$

operand stack has exactly the same length as the list of verify types which
are assigned to the operand stack.

The crucial point is how to define what it means that a return address
belongs to the type $\texttt{retAddr}(s)$. The idea is that $j + 1$ belongs to the type
$\texttt{retAddr}(s)$, if $code(j) = Jsr(s)$ and, for all variables x which are not modified
by the subroutine s, the value of x in the local environment belongs to the
type assigned to x at index $j+1$, i.e., $reg(x)$ belongs to $regT_{j+1}(x)$. Therefore
a return address has to be typed with respect to the local environment reg.
Moreover, the type of a reference depends on the class of the reference, which
is stored in the *heap*, and on the initialization status of the reference, which
is stored in the functions $initState$ (see the definition of the function $type$ in
Sect. 15.4).

Definition 16.4.1 (Typing rules). Let $(regT_i, opdT_i)_{i \in \mathcal{D}}$ be a type assignment for a method μ. Let reg be a local environment for μ, v be a value and
τ be a verify type. The typing judgment $reg \vdash v{:}\tau$ is defined by the following
rules:

$$\frac{\begin{array}{l} type(v) \sqsubseteq \tau \\ \tau \neq \texttt{retAddr}(\_) \end{array}}{reg \vdash v{:}\tau}$$

$$\frac{j \in \mathcal{D},\ code(j) = Jsr(s),\ s \text{ does not return}}{reg \vdash (j+1, \texttt{retAddr}(s)){:}\,\texttt{retAddr}(s)}$$

$$\frac{\begin{array}{l} j \in \mathcal{D},\ code(j) = Jsr(s),\ s \text{ returns} \\ reg \vdash reg(x){:}\,regT_{j+1}(x) \text{ for each } x \in \mathrm{dom}(clean(mod(s) \lhd regT_{j+1})) \end{array}}{reg \vdash (j+1, \texttt{retAddr}(s)){:}\,\texttt{retAddr}(s)}$$

The function *clean* filters out all not fully initialized types:

$$clean(regT) = \{(x,t) \in regT \mid t \neq (\_,\_)_{new},\ t \neq InInit\}$$

A subroutine s returns, if there exists an $i \in \mathcal{D}$ such that $code(i) = Ret(x)$
and $regT_i(x) = \texttt{retAddr}(s)$.

The typing rules for return addresses depend on the local environment
reg, the function *heap* and the type assignment to the method. Since a *Store*
instruction changes the local environment, a return address could possibly
loose its type. The following coincidence lemma therefore states a convenient
condition under which a return address keeps its type. The typing of a return
address from a subroutine depends only on the local variables which are not
modified by the subroutine. In the following we often omit the tag $\texttt{retAddr}(s)$
in values which represent return addresses.

Lemma 16.4.1 (Coincidence). If $reg \vdash j + 1{:}\,\texttt{retAddr}(s)$ and
$mod(s) \lhd reg = mod(s) \lhd reg'$, then $reg' \vdash j + 1{:}\,\texttt{retAddr}(s)$.

Proof. By induction on the length of a derivation of $reg \vdash v{:}\,\tau$. Assume that

$$reg \vdash j + 1{:}\,\mathtt{retAddr}(s) \text{ and } mod(s) \lhd reg = mod(s) \lhd reg'.$$

From the typing rules we obtain that $j \in \mathcal{D}$ and $code(j) = Jsr(s)$.

If s does not return, we obtain $reg' \vdash j + 1{:}\,\mathtt{retAddr}(s)$ by the second typing rule. Otherwise, by the third typing rule we have

1. $j \in \mathcal{D}$, $code(j) = Jsr(s)$, s returns,
2. $reg \vdash reg(x){:}\,regT_{j+1}(x)$ for each $x \in dom(clean(mod(s) \lhd regT_{j+1}))$.

Let x be a local variable which is defined in $regT_{j+1}$ but does not belong to $mod(s)$. Since reg' is equal to reg outside of $mod(s)$, it follows by (2) that $reg \vdash reg'(x){:}\,regT_{j+1}(x)$. If $regT_{j+1}(x)$ is not a return address type, then, by the first typing rule, we immediately obtain $reg' \vdash reg'(x){:}\,regT_{j+1}(x)$. Otherwise there is an ℓ such that $regT_{j+1}(x) = \mathtt{retAddr}(\ell)$. By T7 (e) and Def. 16.3.7, it follows that $mod(s) \subseteq mod(\ell)$. Hence,

$$mod(\ell) \lhd reg = mod(\ell) \lhd reg'.$$

By the induction hypothesis, we obtain that $reg' \vdash reg'(x){:}\,\mathtt{retAddr}(\ell)$.

Hence, the three premises of the third typing rule are satisfied and we can conclude that $reg' \vdash j + 1{:}\,\mathtt{retAddr}(s)$. $\square$

Because of object initialization the types of references may change at run-time. When the initialization state of an object *ref* changes from *InInit* to *Complete*, its type given by the function *typeOf*(*ref*) changes from *InInit* to *classOf*(*ref*), too. Once the initialization state is *Complete*, the reference keeps its type forever. Since un-initialized types and partially initialized types are excluded in the typing rules for return addresses via the function *clean*, the initialization of objects causes no problems for typing judgments.

A bytecode type assignment ensures by T6 that if the instruction at code index i is a call to an instance initialization method invoked on a reference of type $(c, k)_{new}$, this type is replaced by the type c everywhere in the type frame at code index $i+1$. When the instance initialization method is executed at run-time, we know that the reference on which it is invoked is of that type. In the soundness proof below, we have to prove that in the future, after the instance initialization method has returned and the object has been initialized, the invariants are still true. At code index i, however, we do not know what the heap will be after the completion of the initialization method. Hence we have to prove the invariants for all possible continuations of the current heap. A possible continuation of the current heap with respect to a frame on the stack, is a heap in the state of the computation when the frame again becomes the current frame.

Definition 16.4.2 (Active reference). Let $(pc^*, reg^*, opd^*, meth^*)$ be a frame and $(regT_i, opdT_i)_{i \in \mathcal{D}}$ be the bytecode type assignment for $meth^*$. We say that the frame *contains an active reference r with assigned type τ*, if one of the following two conditions is satisfied:

1. there exists a local register x with $regT_{pc^*}(x) = \tau$ and $reg^*(x) = r$, or
2. there exists a stack position i with $opdT_{pc^*}(i) = \tau$ and $opd^*(i) = r$.

We say that a reference r is *active* in the frame, if the frame contains r with some assigned type.

Definition 16.4.3 (Continuation of the heap). Let f be a frame on the stack. A *continuation of the heap* for f is a function $heap^*$ with the following properties:

1. $dom(heap) \subseteq dom(heap^*)$,
2. $classOf(p) = classOf^*(p)$ for each $p \in dom(heap)$.

If the frame f is followed by a constructor invocation frame with **this** object ref, then

3. $initState(p) = initState^*(p)$ for each active p of f with $p \neq ref$,
4. $initState^*(ref) = Complete$.

If the frame f is not followed by a constructor invocation frame, then

3. $initState(p) = initState^*(p)$ for each active p in f.

Definition 16.4.4 (Continuation of a frame). Assume that the frame $(pc^*, reg^*, opd^*, meth^*)$ is a frame on the stack of the JVM. Let μ be the method of the next frame (the called frame). Let *vals* be a sequence of possible return values compatible with the return type of μ with respect to a continuation of $heap$ for the frame. If the return type is **void**, then *vals* is the empty sequence. Then $(pc^*+1, reg^*, opd^* \cdot vals, meth^*)$ is called a *continuation* of the frame.

Definition 16.4.5 (Init sequence). An *init sequence* on the stack is a maximal sequence of consecutive frames on the stack with the following properties:

1. Each frame in the sequence is a constructor invocation frame.
2. For each frame in the sequence except for the first frame, the constructor belongs to the same class as the constructor of the parent frame or is in its direct superclass.
3. The value of register 0 is the same in all frames of the sequence.

The value of register 0 is called the *init object* of the init sequence.

Theorem 16.4.1 (Soundness of type assignments).
Assume that in the given run, the frame $(pc^*, reg^*, opd^*, meth^*)$

1. is the current frame $(pc, reg, opd, meth)$ and $heap^*$ is the current heap *heap*, or

2. is a frame on the stack waiting for a `<clinit>` method to return and $heap^*$ is a continuation of $heap$ for the frame, or

3. is a continuation of a frame f on the stack and $heap^*$ is a continuation of $heap$ for the frame f.

Let $(regT_i, opdT_i)_{i \in \mathcal{D}}$ be the type assignment for $meth^*$. Then the following invariants are satisfied at run-time for the frame $(pc^*, reg^*, opd^*, meth^*)$:

(pc) $pc^* \in \mathcal{D}$ (hence pc^* is a valid code index for $meth^*$).

(check) $check(meth^*, pc^*, types(reg^*), types(opd^*))$ is true.

(reg1) $\mathrm{dom}(regT_{pc^*}) \subseteq \mathrm{dom}(reg^*)$.

(reg2) $reg^* \vdash reg^*(x) \colon regT_{pc^*}(x)$ for every $x \in \mathrm{dom}(regT_{pc^*})$.

(reg64) If $reg^*(x) = (w_1, \texttt{low}t)$ and $reg^*(x+1) = (w_2, \texttt{high}t)$, then the pair (w_1, w_2) is a correct 64-bit value of type t.

(opd1) $\mathrm{dom}(opdT_{pc^*}) = \mathrm{dom}(opd^*)$.

(opd2) $reg^* \vdash opd^*(i) \colon opdT_{pc^*}(i)$ for each $i \in \mathrm{dom}(opdT_{pc^*})$.

(opd3) $length(opdT_{pc^*}) < maxOpd$.

(opd64) If $opd^*(k) = (w_1, \texttt{low}t)$ and $opd^*(k+1) = (w_2, \texttt{high}t)$, then the pair (w_1, w_2) is a correct 64-bit value of type t.

(init1) If the frame contains an active reference r with assigned type $InInit$, then $meth^*$ is an `<init>` method (not of class `Object`), $r = reg^*(0)$ and $classOf(r) \sqsubseteq classNm(meth^*)$. Conversely, if $meth^*$ is an `<init>` method, then $reg^*(0)$ contains a reference r with $initState(r) = InInit$ or $initState(r) = Complete$.

(init2) For each c and i, the frame contains at most one active reference r with assigned type $(c, i)_{new}$.

(init3) If the frame contains an active reference r with assigned type $(c, i)_{new}$, then r is not the init object of an init sequence of $stack$ and r is not active in any other frame.

The following global invariants are true at run-time:

(global) If the `static` field c/f of declared type A is used in the program, then $type(globals(c/f)) \sqsubseteq A$.

(ref) If a reference r is used in the current state of the JVM, then r points to an existing object or array on the heap; $classOf(r)$ is a non-`abstract` class or an array type.

(object) If $classOf(r)$ is a class c and d/f is an instance field of c of declared type A, then $type(getField(r, d/f)) \sqsubseteq A$.

(array) If $classOf(r)$ is an array type $A[\,]$, then $type(arrayElem(r,i)) \sqsubseteq A$ for each $i < arraySize(r)$.

(initseq) There are not two different init sequences on *stack* with the same init object.

Proof. We show first that the invariant (check) follows from the other invariants:

The type assignment ensures that $check(meth^*, pc^*, regT_{pc^*}, opdT_{pc^*})$ is true. Let $regS = types(reg^*)$ and $opdS = types(opd^*)$ be the type assignments associated to the local environment reg^* and the operand stack opd^*. From (reg1), (reg2), (opd1) and (opd2) we can deduce that $regS \sqsubseteq_{\mathrm{reg}} regT_{pc^*}$ and $opdS \sqsubseteq_{\mathrm{seq}} opdT_{pc^*}$. Since the structural constraints are monotonic (Lemma 15.7.1), it follows that $check(meth^*, pc^*, regS, opdS)$ is true as well.

The remaining invariants are proved by an induction on the run of the defensive VM. We show here the critical cases for subroutines, object initialization and the current frame.

Case 1. $code(pc) = Jsr(s)$: The new pc is s and the new operand stack is $opd \cdot [pc + 1]$. The type assignment condition T6 ensures that

$- \; regT_{pc} \sqsubseteq_{\mathrm{reg}} regT_s$

$- \; opdT_{pc} \cdot [\mathtt{retAddr}(s)] \sqsubseteq_{\mathrm{seq}} opdT_s$

This implies (by the transitivity of $\sqsubseteq$ and the induction hypothesis) invariants (reg1), (reg2), (reg64), (opd1), (opd2), (opd3) (using T5 and the check in Fig. 15.6) and (opd64) at s, except for $reg \vdash pc+1 : \mathtt{retAddr}(s)$. The induction hypothesis says that $reg \vdash reg(x) : regT_{pc}(x)$ for every $x \in \mathrm{dom}(regT_{pc})$. If s does not return, then by the second typing rule of Def. 16.4.1,

$\qquad reg \vdash pc + 1 : \mathtt{retAddr}(s).$

Otherwise, if s returns, then by T7 (d), $regT_{pc} \sqsubseteq_{\mathrm{reg}} mod(s) \lhd regT_{pc+1}$ and, by the third typing rule of Def. 16.4.1, it follows that $reg \vdash pc+1 : \mathtt{retAddr}(s)$. The invariants (init1)–(init3) and the global invariants can be moved from pc to s.

Case 2. $code(pc) = Ret(x)$: Condition T5 and the check in Fig. 15.6 ensure that there exists a subroutine s such that $regT_{pc}(x) = \mathtt{retAddr}(s)$ and therefore s returns. The induction hypothesis (reg2) for x implies that $reg \vdash reg(x) : \mathtt{retAddr}(s)$. Let $reg(x) = j + 1$. By the third typing rule in Def. 16.4.1 it follows that

$\qquad reg \vdash reg(x) : regT_{j+1}(x)$ for every $x \in \mathrm{dom}(clean(mod(s) \lhd regT_{j+1}))$.

The new pc is $j+1$. The typing rules in Def. 16.4.1 also yield that $j \in \mathcal{D}$ and $code(j) = Jsr(s)$. The type assignment condition T7 ensures that

$- \; j + 1 \in \mathcal{D}$ (hence $j + 1$ is a valid code index for $meth$)

- $regT_{pc} \sqsubseteq_{\mathrm{reg}} mod(s) \lhd regT_{j+1}$
- $opdT_{pc} \sqsubseteq_{\mathrm{seq}} opdT_{j+1}$
- $regT_j \sqsubseteq_{\mathrm{reg}} mod(s) \lhd regT_{j+1}$
- Neither $(c,k)_{new}$ nor $InInit$ occur in $mod(s) \lhd regT_{j+1}$

Invariants (reg1), (reg2) and (reg64) follow from the induction hypothesis at pc. Namely $regT_j \sqsubseteq_{\mathrm{reg}} mod(s) \lhd regT_{j+1}$, the fact that neither $(c,k)_{new}$ nor $InInit$ occur in $mod(s) \lhd regT_{j+1}$ and the typing rules for the return address $j+1$ imply that

$$reg \vdash reg(x) \colon regT_{j+1}(x) \quad \text{for every } x \in \mathrm{dom}(regT_{j+1}) \setminus mod(s).$$

Moreover, $regT_{pc} \sqsubseteq_{\mathrm{reg}} mod(s) \lhd regT_{j+1}$ implies that

$$reg \vdash reg(x) \colon regT_{j+1}(x) \quad \text{for every } x \in \mathrm{dom}(regT_{j+1}) \cap mod(s).$$

Invariants (opd1)–(opd64) follow immediately from the induction hypothesis, since the operand stack is propagated to $j+1$ without modifications. The global invariants and the invariants (init1)–(init3) can be moved from pc to $j+1$, since by condition T7 (f) we know that $mod(s) \lhd regT_{j+1}$ is free of $(\_,\_)_{new}$ and $InInit$.

Case 3. $code(pc) = Store(t,x)$: Assume that $size(t) = 1$ (the argument for the case $size(t) = 2$ is similar). The type assignment condition T6 ensures that there exist $opdS$ and τ such that

- $opdT_{pc} = opdS \cdot [\tau]$
- $opdS \sqsubseteq_{\mathrm{seq}} opdT_{pc+1}$
- $regT_{pc}[x \mapsto \tau] \sqsubseteq_{\mathrm{reg}} regT_{pc+1}$

Hence, $opd = opd' \cdot [v]$. Let $reg' = reg[x \mapsto v]$. The new pc is $pc+1$, the new operand stack is opd' and the new local environment is reg'. Invariants (pc), (reg1), (reg64), (opd1), (opd3), (opd64) for $pc+1$ follow from the induction hypothesis. The same holds for invariants (reg2) and (opd2), using part 1 of Def. 16.4.1, except for operands and local variables of return address type. Assume that $\mathtt{retAddr}(\ell)$ occurs in $regT_{pc+1}$ or $opdT_{pc+1}$. Then $\mathtt{retAddr}(\ell)$ already occurs in $regT_{pc}$ or $opdT_{pc}$ and, by T8, pc belongs to subroutine ℓ. Therefore $x \in mod(\ell)$ and $mod(\ell) \lhd reg = mod(\ell) \lhd reg'$. We can apply the Coincidence Lemma 16.4.1 and see that, if $reg \vdash j+1 \colon \mathtt{retAddr}(\ell)$, then $reg' \vdash j+1 \colon \mathtt{retAddr}(\ell)$. Hence, the invariants are also satisfied for return addresses at code index $pc+1$. The global invariants and the invariants (init1)–(init3) can be moved from pc to $pc+1$ without problems.

Case 4. $code(pc) = New(c)$: The type assignment condition T6 for the successor frame (see Fig. 16.14) ensures that

- $opdS \cdot [(c,pc)_{new}] \sqsubseteq_{\mathrm{seq}} opdT_{pc+1}$, where
  $opdS = [\textbf{if } t = (c,pc)_{new} \textbf{ then } \mathtt{unusable} \textbf{ else } t \mid t \in opdT_{pc}]$
- $\{(x,t) \in regT_{pc} \mid t \neq (c,pc)_{new}\} \sqsubseteq_{\mathrm{reg}} regT_{pc+1}$

Hence the only occurrence of the type $(c, pc)_{new}$ in the type frame at $pc + 1$ is the topmost position in $opdT_{pc+1}$. Since there is only one occurrence of this type, invariant (init2) can be carried over from pc to $pc + 1$. The other invariants follow with similar arguments as in the previous cases.

The VM creates a new reference r on *heap* with $classOf(r) = c$. Hence, each continuation of the new heap for a frame f on *stack* is also a continuation of the current *heap* for f. Therefore the invariants for continuations of other frames on the stack remain true.

Case 5. $code(pc) = InvokeSpecial(\texttt{void}, c/\texttt{<init>})$: We consider the invocation of a nullary constructor only. The general case is similar. For a nullary constructor the type assignment condition T5 yields with Fig. 15.4 that

– $opdT_{pc} = opdS \cdot [\tau]$ and $initCompatible(meth, \tau, c)$.

The predicate *initCompatible* implies that one of the following statements is true:

– $\tau = (c, k)_{new}$ for some k

– $\tau = InInit$ and $c = classNm(meth)$ or c is the direct superclass of $classNm(meth)$

Let r be the topmost value on the operand stack *opd*.

Invariants (opd1) and (opd2) yield $reg \vdash r : \tau$ and thus $type(r) = \tau$.

The defensive VM deletes r from *opd*, pushes the current frame onto the stack (Fig. 15.5) and sets $initState(r)$ to *Complete* if c is class $\texttt{Object}$ and to *InInit* otherwise. Hence $type(r)$ might change and we have to think about the possibility that the invariants for the continuations of other frames on the stack might be violated. Fortunately this is not the case because of invariants (init3) and (initseq).

We have to show the invariants for the new frame for the method $c/\texttt{<init>}$:

If $\tau = (c, k)_{new}$, then by invariant (init3), the reference r is not the init object of any init sequence on *stack*. This fact is needed, because r is the init object of the new frame created for the method $c/\texttt{<init>}$. Hence all init sequences have different init objects and invariant (initseq) is true. Invariant (init1) is true in the new frame, since $classOf(r) = c$. The other invariants are trivially true for the new frame.

If $\tau = InInit$, then by invariant (init1) we are already in an init sequence with init object r. This init sequence is extended by the new frame. By the induction hypothesis (init1), we obtain that $classOf(r) \sqsubseteq classNm(meth)$. Since $classNm(meth) \sqsubseteq c$, it follows that $classOf(r) \sqsubseteq c$. The other invariants are trivially true for the new frame.

It is not enough to show the invariants for the new frame for method $c/\texttt{<init>}$. We have to show them also for every continuation of the current frame which is pushed on *stack* and for every continuation of the current *heap*. In such a continuation we are at code index $pc + 1$ and we can assume that $initState(r) = Complete$ (Def. 16.4.3 and 16.4.4).

If $\tau = (c, k)_{new}$, then in the successor type frame of pc the type τ is replaced by c (Fig. 16.14). Because $initState(r) = Complete$ in the continuation of the frame, we have $type(r) = c$ and hence $reg \vdash r : c$. Note, that if the successor frame contains an active occurrence of r, then its assigned type in the current frame must be τ.

If $\tau = InInit$, then in the successor type frame of pc the type τ is replaced by $classNm(meth)$ (Fig. 16.14). By the induction hypothesis (init1) it follows that $classOf(r) \sqsubseteq classNm(meth)$. Since $type(r) = classOf(r)$ in the continuation, we obtain $reg \vdash r : type(r)$.

Case 6. $code(pc) = Return(t)$: The checks in Fig. 15.3 and 15.4 (including the clause $endinit$) ensure that

– $opdT_{pc} \sqsubseteq_{\text{suf}} returnType(meth)$

– $returnType(meth) \sqsubseteq_{\text{mv}} t$

– If $meth$ is an `<init>` method not in class `Object`, then $0 \in dom(regT_{pc})$ and $regT_{pc}(0) \neq InInit$

The VM pops the topmost frame from the stack and makes it again the current frame. The returned value is appended to the operand stack and the program counter is incremented, if necessary. Hence we obtain exactly a continuation of the frame according to Def. 16.4.4. Moreover, the current heap is a continuation of itself for the topmost frame according to Def. 16.4.3. The induction hypothesis yields the invariants for the new state.

Case 7. $code(pc) = Dupx(s_1, s_2)$: The check in Fig. 15.2 ensures that

– $opdT_{pc} = opdS \cdot ts_1 \cdot ts_2$

– $length(ts_i) = s_i$ and $validTypeSeq(ts_i)$ for $i = 1, 2$

Hence, $opd = opd' \cdot ws_1 \cdot ws_2$, where $length(ws_i) = s_i$ and the new operand stack at $pc + 1$ is $opd' \cdot ws_2 \cdot ws_1 \cdot ws_2$.

By the definition of the predicate $validTypeSeq$, the type sequences ts_1 and ts_2 do not start with a type $hight$. Hence, by invariant $(opd2)$, the first words in the sequences ws_1 and ws_2 do not have the type tag $hight$. Therefore we see that the instruction $Dupx$ cannot be used to construct an invalid 64-bit value be permuting single words on the operand stack and the invariant (opd64) remains true.

The cases for the other instructions are treated in a similar way.   □

The entanglement of embedded subroutines and object initialization is rather delicate. In our approach we forbid that a caller of a subroutine uses later an un-initialized or partially initialized object stored in a register not modified by the subroutine. This prevents that a subroutine can mislead the caller in believing that an object has already been initialized by the subroutine although it is not (Fig. 16.19). It prevents also the reverse direction that a caller of a subroutine believes an object is still un-initialized although the subroutine already did that (Fig. 16.20). We could achieve the same by other conditions on subroutines. We could forbid that

1. a caller passes not fully initialized objects to a subroutine and
2. a subroutine returns not fully initialized objects to a caller.

The first condition can be implemented by defining the successor set of a $Jsr(s)$ instruction at type frame $(regT, opdT)$ as follows:

$$\{(s, clean(regT), clean(opdT) \cdot [\texttt{retAddr}(s)])\}$$

Here the function *clean* filters out all $(\_,\_)_{new}$ and *InInit* types in $regT$ and replaces them by $\texttt{unusable}$ in $opdT$. The second condition can be implemented by changing T7 (f) in the definition of bytecode type assignment to the following condition:

f') Neither $(c_{-},\_)_{new}$ nor *InInit* occur in $mod(s) \lhd regT_{j+1}$ or in $opdT_{j+1}$.

The above soundness proof, however, becomes much more complicated because invariants (init1)–(init3) have to be included into the typing rules for return addresses and the function *clean* has to be removed. Moreover, the type of a return address depends then on the initialization status of the objects and a new coincidence lemma has to be proved.

16.5 Certifying compilation

In this section we prove that bytecode generated by the compiler of Part II is typeable. For this purpose we extend the functions $\mathcal{E}$, $\mathcal{B}_1$, $\mathcal{B}_0$ and $\mathcal{S}$ for the compilation of expressions, boolean expressions and statements such that they generate also type frames for the instructions. Hence, the result of the extended compilation is not only a sequence of bytecode instructions but a sequence of triples $(instr, regT, opdT)$, where $(regT, opdT)$ is a type frame for the instruction *instr*. We then prove that the so generated type frames satisfy the conditions T1–T8 of Def. 16.3.8 for bytecode type assignments.

The extended compiler is a *certifying compiler* which generates *type carrying code*. What it does is similar to the so-called *off-device pre-verification* in [25]. Type frames are called *stack maps* in [25]. Our extended compiler, however, does not inline subroutines as it is done in [25].

When compiling Java methods one has to make sure that "execution never falls off the bottom of the code array" [23, §4.8.2]. On the Java language level, this property follows from the reachability analysis of Sect. 8.2. For each method body the predicate *normal* must return *False*, hence the body cannot complete normally (invariant (norm) in Theorem 8.4.1); the result of the execution of a method body is a *Return*, *Return(val)* or *Exc(ref)*. So the obvious conjecture is, that if a statement $^{\alpha}stm$ cannot complete normally, i.e., if $normal(\alpha)$ is false, then execution cannot fall off the bottom of the compiled code for the statement, i.e., code index end_{α} is not reachable from beg_{α}. Unfortunately the conjecture is not true for our compiler.

Example (⤳ CD) 16.5.1. Consider the following method:

```
int m() α{
   int i;
   try { i = 7;}
   finally { return 3; }
}
```

According to Table 8.3 the predicate $normal(\alpha)$ is false. Hence the method body is legal. When we compile the method using the compiler of Part II, we obtain the following code:

$$\begin{aligned}
&\text{beg}_\alpha : Prim(7) && \text{fin} : Store(\texttt{addr}, r) \\
&\qquad\quad Store(\texttt{int}, i) && \qquad\ Prim(3) \\
&\qquad\quad Jsr(\text{fin}) && \qquad\ Return(\texttt{int}) \\
&\qquad\quad Goto(\text{end}_\alpha) && \qquad\ Ret(r) \\
&\text{default} : Store(\texttt{addr}, e) && \text{end}_\alpha : Nop \\
&\qquad\quad Jsr(\text{fin}) \\
&\qquad\quad Load(\texttt{addr}, e) \\
&\qquad\quad Athrow
\end{aligned}$$

In this code fragment, index end_α is reachable (Def. 16.3.3) from beg_α. Nevertheless, the bytecode is accepted by the verifier, since, due to the $Return(\texttt{int})$ instruction (see Fig. 16.13), the verifier does not reach the instruction $Ret(r)$ and therefore $Goto(\text{end}_\alpha)$ is dead code for the verifier. The Nop instruction at the end of the method body is automatically inserted by the compiler to ensure that the target labels of jump instructions are within the body of the method (see static constraints in Appendix C.6).

Also the converse of the conjecture is not true for the compiler of Part II. If $normal(\alpha)$ is true for a position α, then code index end_α is not necessarily reachable from beg_α.

Example (⤳ CD) 16.5.2. Consider the following statement:

```
αif (true)
   return;
else
   i = 2;
```

From the equations in Table 8.3 it follows that $normal(\alpha)$ is true. When we compile the statement using the compiler of Part II, we obtain the following code:

$$\begin{aligned}
&\text{beg}_\alpha : Goto(\text{if}_\alpha) \\
&\qquad\quad Prim(2) \\
&\qquad\quad Store(\texttt{int}, i) \\
&\qquad\quad Goto(\text{end}_\alpha) \\
&\quad\ \text{if}_\alpha : Return(\texttt{void}) \\
&\quad \text{end}_\alpha :
\end{aligned}$$

In this code fragment, label end_α is not reachable from beg_α.

Example (↝ CD) 16.5.3. Assume that b is variable of type `boolean`. Consider the following statement:

$^{\alpha}$`while (b ? true : true);`

From the equations in Table 8.3 it follows that $normal(\alpha)$ is true, since the expression 'b ? `true`: `true`' is not a constant expression. When we compile the statement using the compiler of Part II, then index end_α is not reachable from beg_α.

Example (↝ CD) 16.5.4. This example shows that it is impossible to write a compiler such that Java's notion of reachability (Sect. 8.2) coincides with the bytecode reachability relation of Def. 16.3.3. Consider the following method:

```
void m(boolean b) {
  boolean z;
  while (b ? true: true);
  b = z;
}
```

According to Table 8.3 the statement 'b = z' is reachable, since the boolean expression 'b ? `true`: `true`' is not a constant expression with value true and the `while` statement can complete normally in the eyes of the static analysis of Sect. 8.2. Moreover, according to the rules of definite assignment, the variable z is definitely assigned after the `while` statement, since $false(\alpha) = vars(\alpha)$ for $^{\alpha}$`true` and $z \in vars(\alpha)$. Hence the method is a legal Java method which should be accepted by any Java compiler. For the bytecode verifier, however, the $Load(\texttt{int}, \texttt{z})$ instruction which corresponds to the access to z in 'b = z' should not be reachable, because the bytecode verifier cannot infer that the variable z has been initialized.

The example shows a not so obvious inconsistency in the design of the Java programming language. In the rules of definite assignment (Sect. 8.3), the expression 'b ? `true`: `true`' is treated like the constant 'true'. In the reachability analysis of Sect. 8.2, however, the expression 'b ? `true`: `true`' is treated like an arbitrary boolean expression which can also have the value false.

What is the domain $\mathcal{D}$ of a bytecode type assignment generated by the extended compiler? Assume that the code array generated for a method μ is the list

$$[code(0), \ldots, code(codeLength(\mu) - 1)]$$

and the corresponding type frames generated by the extended compiler are

$$(reg T_i, opd T_i)_{0 \leq i < codeLength(\mu)}.$$

Assume that for each position α in the body of the method, the code generated for the phrase at position α is the sublist

$[code(i) \mid \text{beg}_\alpha \le i < \text{end}_\alpha]$.

Note that the code for the method μ cannot be the empty sequence, because the body of the method is not *normal*.

Definition 16.5.1 (Domain of the generated type assignment). The domain $\mathcal{D}$ for the type assignment generated by the certifying compiler is the least (w.r.t. set inclusion) set of natural numbers with the following properties:

1. $0 \in \mathcal{D}$.
2. If $i \in \mathcal{D}$ and $code(i)$ is not a control transfer instruction (Def. 16.3.1), then $i + 1 \in \mathcal{D}$.
3. If $i \in \mathcal{D}$ and $code(i) = Goto(j)$, then $j \in \mathcal{D}$.
4. If $i \in \mathcal{D}$ and $code(i) = Cond(p, j)$, then $i + 1 \in \mathcal{D}$ and $j \in \mathcal{D}$.
5. If $i \in \mathcal{D}$ and $code(i) = Jsr(j)$, then $j \in \mathcal{D}$.
6. If $i \in \mathcal{D}$, $(f, u, h, \_) \in excs(\mu)$ and $f \le i < u$, then $h \in \mathcal{D}$.
7. If $^\alpha(^\beta stm\ \texttt{finally}\ ^\gamma block)$ is a substatement in the body of μ, $i \in \mathcal{D}$, $code(i) = Jsr(\text{fin}_\alpha)$ and $\text{end}_\gamma \in \mathcal{D}$, then $i + 1 \in \mathcal{D}$.

The extended compiler generates a type frame for each instruction in the code for a method. The assignment of types to local registers is based on the static analysis for the Java source code of the method described in Sect. 8.3.

Definition 16.5.2 (Types of local registers). Let α be a position in the body of the method μ to be compiled. For a subset X of $vars(\alpha)$, the set of variables, formal parameters and $\texttt{catch}$ parameters which are in the scope of a declaration at position α, we denote by $\mathcal{R}(\alpha, X)$ the assignment of the declared types to the (variable numbers of) variables in the set X. More precisely, let x be an identifier in X of declared type t.

1. If t is of size 1, then $(\overline{x}, t)$ belongs to $\mathcal{R}(\alpha, X)$.
2. If t is of size 2, then $(\overline{x}, \texttt{low}t)$ and $(\overline{x} + 1, \texttt{high}t)$ belong to $\mathcal{R}(\alpha, X)$.
3. If μ is an instance method of class c, then $(0, c)$ belongs to $\mathcal{R}(\alpha, X)$, too.
4. If μ is a constructor in class c (different from $\texttt{Object}$) and α is *firstPos* or a position in an argument of an explicit constructor invocation $\texttt{this}(exps)$ or $\texttt{super}(exps)$ at the beginning of the body of the constructor, then $(0, InInit)$ belongs to $\mathcal{R}(\alpha, X)$; if α is another position in the body of the constructor, then $(0, c)$ belongs to $\mathcal{R}(\alpha, X)$.
5. If α is a position in $^\delta block$ in $^\beta(^\gamma stm\ \texttt{finally}\ ^\delta block)$ with $\text{end}_\delta \in \mathcal{D}$, then $(\overline{ret}_\beta, \texttt{retAddr}(\text{fin}_\beta))$ belongs to $\mathcal{R}(\alpha, X)$ (we assume that $\overline{ret}_\beta$ is different from $\overline{x}$ and $\overline{x} + 1$ for all $x \in vars(\beta)$ and different from $\overline{ret}_\xi$, if the position β is in a $\texttt{finally}$ block of a $\texttt{try-finally}$ statement at position ξ, cf. Fig. 16.27).

We use the following abbreviations:

$$\mathcal{P}(\alpha) := \mathcal{R}(\alpha, before(\alpha)), \quad \mathcal{A}_1(\alpha) := \mathcal{R}(\alpha, true(\alpha)),$$
$$\mathcal{A}(\alpha) := \mathcal{R}(\alpha, after(\alpha)), \quad \mathcal{A}_0(\alpha) := \mathcal{R}(\alpha, false(\alpha)).$$

The functions *before*, *after*, *true* and *false* are the static functions defined in Sect. 8.3.

Let α be a position in an expression. Then $\mathcal{T}(\alpha)$ is the Java type of the subexpression at position α. By $\mathcal{V}(\alpha)$ we denote the corresponding list of verify types. For example, if $\mathcal{T}(\alpha)$ is double, then $\mathcal{V}(\alpha)$ is the list [lowDouble, highDouble]; if $\mathcal{T}(\alpha)$ is byte, then $\mathcal{V}(\alpha)$ is the list [int]. There is one case which has to be treated in a different way. If α is the position of this in an explicit constructor invocation at the beginning of the body of a constructor, then $\mathcal{V}(\alpha) = InInit$. Note that after parsing and elaboration, an explicit constructor invocation this(*exps*) or super(*exps*) is replaced by this.*c*/<init>(*ts*)(*exps*). It is not allowed that this occurs in the arguments *exps* (see Sect. 5.1.3).

Fig. 16.22–16.28 define the extended compiler. We call the extended compiler a *certifying* compiler, because the type frames it generates can be understood as a certificate that the generated bytecode behaves in a well-defined manner on the virtual machine. The first components of the triples generated by the certifying compiler are exactly the instructions generated by the compiler of Part II.

In Fig. 16.28 we use the pseudo instructions *Continue*(l) and *Break*(l). These instructions are just alternative names for the *Goto*(l) instruction used by the original compiler in Fig. 12.3. We use *Continue*(l) and *Break*(l) to simplify notations in the proofs below.

Since condition 7 in Def. 16.5.1 is more restrictive than the corresponding definition for the successor indices of a *Jsr* instruction in Def. 16.3.2, it is obvious that $\mathcal{D}$ is a subset of the reachable code indices of method μ. The converse is not true as Example 16.5.1 shows.

Lemma 16.5.1. If $i \in \mathcal{D}$, then i is reachable from code index 0 via a path with elements from $\mathcal{D}$.

Proof. By induction on the generation of the set $\mathcal{D}$.   □

The successor code indices of a bytecode instruction are defined in Def. 16.3.2. The code generated by our compiler has the property that the $i + 1$ successor of a *Jsr* instruction at index i cannot be reached on a path avoiding index i, for example via a *Goto*($i + 1$). Therefore, if $i + 1$ belongs to $\mathcal{D}$, then the *Ret* instruction of the corresponding subroutine belongs to $\mathcal{D}$, too.

Lemma 16.5.2. If, in code generated by our compiler, $code(j) = Jsr(\_)$ and $j + 1$ is a successor (Def. 16.3.2) of i, then $i = j$.

Proof. The following facts are used:

1. The compilation of expressions and test expressions is free of *Jsr*.

Fig. 16.22 Certifying compilation of Java$_\mathcal{I}$ expressions

$$\mathcal{E}(^\alpha lit, opdT) = (Prim(lit), \mathcal{A}(\alpha), opdT)$$
$$\mathcal{E}(^\alpha loc, opdT) = (Load(\mathcal{T}(\alpha), \overline{loc}), \mathcal{A}(\alpha), opdT)$$
$$\mathcal{E}(^\alpha(loc = {}^\beta exp), opdT) =$$
$$\qquad \mathcal{E}(^\beta exp, opdT) \cdot (Dupx(0, size(\mathcal{T}(\beta))), \mathcal{A}(\beta), opdT \cdot \mathcal{V}(\beta)) \cdot$$
$$\qquad (Store(\mathcal{T}(\beta), \overline{loc}), \mathcal{A}(\beta), opdT \cdot \mathcal{V}(\beta) \cdot \mathcal{V}(\beta))$$
$$\mathcal{E}(^\alpha(uop\,{}^\beta exp), opdT) =$$
$$\qquad \mathcal{E}(^\beta exp, opdT) \cdot (Prim(uop), \mathcal{A}(\beta), opdT \cdot \mathcal{V}(\beta))$$
$$\mathcal{E}(^\alpha(!\,{}^\beta exp), opdT) =$$
$$\qquad \mathcal{B}_1(^\beta exp, una_\alpha) \cdot (Prim(\mathbf{1}), \mathcal{A}(\beta), opdT) \cdot$$
$$\qquad (Goto(\mathrm{end}_\alpha), \mathcal{A}(\beta), opdT \cdot [\texttt{int}]) \cdot$$
$$\qquad una_\alpha \cdot (Prim(\mathbf{0}), \mathcal{A}(\beta), opdT) \cdot \mathrm{end}_\alpha$$
$$\mathcal{E}(^\alpha(^\beta exp_1 \, bop \, {}^\gamma exp_2), opdT) =$$
$$\qquad \mathcal{E}(^\beta exp_1, opdT) \cdot \mathcal{E}(^\gamma exp_1, opdT \cdot \mathcal{V}(\beta)) \cdot$$
$$\qquad (Prim(bop), \mathcal{A}(\gamma), opdT \cdot \mathcal{V}(\beta) \cdot \mathcal{V}(\gamma))$$
$$\mathcal{E}(^\alpha(^\beta exp_0 \, ? \, {}^\gamma exp_1 : {}^\delta exp_2), opdT) =$$
$$\qquad \mathcal{B}_1(^\beta exp_0, \mathrm{if}_\alpha, opdT) \cdot \mathcal{E}(^\delta exp_2, opdT) \cdot$$
$$\qquad (Goto(\mathrm{end}_\alpha), \mathcal{A}(\delta), opdT \cdot \mathcal{V}(\delta)) \cdot \mathrm{if}_\alpha \cdot \mathcal{E}(^\gamma exp_1, opdT) \cdot \mathrm{end}_\alpha$$

Fig. 16.23 Certifying compilation of Java$_\mathcal{I}$ statements

$$\mathcal{S}(;) = \epsilon$$
$$\mathcal{S}(^\alpha(^\beta exp);) = \mathcal{E}(^\beta exp, []) \cdot (Pop(size(\mathcal{T}(\beta))), \mathcal{A}(\beta), [\mathcal{V}(\beta)])$$
$$\mathcal{S}(^\alpha\{^{\beta_1} stm_1 \ldots {}^{\beta_n} stm_n\}) = \mathcal{S}(^{\beta_1} stm_1) \cdot \ldots \cdot \mathcal{S}(^{\beta_n} stm_n)$$
$$\mathcal{S}(^\alpha \texttt{if}\ (^\beta exp)\,{}^\gamma stm_1\ \texttt{else}\ {}^\delta stm_2) =$$
$$\qquad \mathcal{B}_1(^\beta exp, \mathrm{if}_\alpha, []) \cdot \mathcal{S}(^\delta stm_2) \cdot$$
$$\qquad (Goto(\mathrm{end}_\alpha), \mathcal{A}(\delta), []) \cdot$$
$$\qquad \mathrm{if}_\alpha \cdot \mathcal{S}(^\gamma stm_1) \cdot \mathrm{end}_\alpha$$
$$\mathcal{S}(^\alpha\texttt{while}\ (^\beta exp)\,{}^\gamma stm) =$$
$$\qquad (Goto(\mathrm{test}_\alpha), \mathcal{P}(\alpha), []) \cdot \mathrm{while}_\alpha \cdot \mathcal{S}(^\gamma stm) \cdot$$
$$\qquad \mathrm{test}_\alpha \cdot \mathcal{B}_1(^\beta exp, \mathrm{while}_\alpha, [])$$
$$\mathcal{S}(^\alpha lab: {}^\beta stm) = lab_c \cdot \mathcal{S}(^\beta stm) \cdot lab_b$$

Fig. 16.24 Certifying compilation of Java$_\mathcal{I}$ expressions for control flow

$$\mathcal{B}_1(^\alpha\mathtt{true}, lab, opdT) = (Goto(lab), \mathcal{A}_1(\alpha), opdT)$$
$$\mathcal{B}_1(^\alpha\mathtt{false}, lab, opdT) = \epsilon$$
$$\mathcal{B}_1(^\alpha(!\ ^\beta exp), lab, opdT) = \mathcal{B}_0(^\beta exp, lab, opdT)$$
$$\mathcal{B}_1(^\alpha(^\beta exp_0\ ?\ ^\gamma exp_1 : {}^\delta exp_2), lab, opdT) =$$
$$\quad \mathcal{B}_1(^\beta exp_0, \mathrm{if}_\alpha, opdT) \cdot \mathcal{B}_1(^\delta exp_2, lab, opdT) \cdot$$
$$\quad (Goto(\mathrm{end}_\alpha), \mathcal{A}_0(\delta), opdT) \cdot \mathrm{if}_\alpha \cdot \mathcal{B}_1(^\gamma exp_1, lab, opdT) \cdot \mathrm{end}_\alpha$$
$$\mathcal{B}_1(^\alpha exp, lab, opdT) =$$
$$\quad \mathcal{E}(^\alpha exp, opdT) \cdot (Cond(\mathtt{ifne}, lab), \mathcal{A}(\alpha), opdT \cdot [\mathtt{int}])$$

$$\mathcal{B}_0(^\alpha\mathtt{true}, lab, opdT) = \epsilon$$
$$\mathcal{B}_0(^\alpha\mathtt{false}, lab, opdT) = (Goto(lab), \mathcal{A}_0(\alpha), opdT)$$
$$\mathcal{B}_0(^\alpha(!\ ^\beta exp), lab, opdT) = \mathcal{B}_1(^\beta exp, lab, opdT)$$
$$\mathcal{B}_0(^\alpha(^\beta exp_0\ ?\ ^\gamma exp_1 : {}^\delta exp_2), lab, opdT) =$$
$$\quad \mathcal{B}_1(^\beta exp_0, \mathrm{if}_\alpha, opdT) \cdot \mathcal{B}_0(^\delta exp_2, lab, opdT) \cdot$$
$$\quad (Goto(\mathrm{end}_\alpha), \mathcal{A}_1(\delta), opdT) \cdot \mathrm{if}_\alpha \cdot \mathcal{B}_0(^\gamma exp_1, lab, opdT) \cdot \mathrm{end}_\alpha \ .$$
$$\mathcal{B}_1(^\alpha exp, lab, opdT) =$$
$$\quad \mathcal{E}(^\alpha exp, opdT) \cdot (Cond(\mathtt{ifeq}, lab), \mathcal{A}(\alpha), opdT \cdot [\mathtt{int}])$$

Fig. 16.25 Certifying compilation of Java$_\mathcal{C}$ expressions/statements

$$\mathcal{E}(^\alpha c.f, opdT) = (GetStatic(\mathcal{T}(\alpha), c/f), \mathcal{A}(\alpha), opdT)$$
$$\mathcal{E}(^\alpha c.f = {}^\beta exp, opdT) =$$
$$\quad \mathcal{E}(^\beta exp, opdT) \cdot (Dupx(0, size(\mathcal{T}(\beta))), \mathcal{A}(\beta), opdT \cdot \mathcal{V}(\beta)) \cdot$$
$$\quad (PutStatic(\mathcal{T}(\alpha), c/f), \mathcal{A}(\beta), opdT \cdot \mathcal{V}(\beta) \cdot \mathcal{V}(\beta))$$
$$\mathcal{E}(^\alpha c.m^\beta(exps), opdT) =$$
$$\quad \mathcal{E}(^\beta(exps), opdT) \cdot (InvokeStatic(\mathcal{T}(\alpha), c/m), \mathcal{A}(\beta), opdT \cdot \mathcal{V}(\beta))$$
$$\mathcal{E}(^\alpha(^{\beta_1} exp, \ldots, {}^{\beta_n} exp_n), opdT) =$$
$$\quad \mathcal{E}(^{\beta_1} exp_1, opdT) \cdot \mathcal{E}(^{\beta_2} exp_2, opdT \cdot \mathcal{V}(\beta_1)) \cdot$$
$$\quad \vdots$$
$$\quad \mathcal{E}(^{\beta_n} exp_n, opdT \cdot \mathcal{V}(\beta_1) \cdot \ldots \cdot \mathcal{V}(\beta_{n-1}))$$
$$\mathcal{S}(^\alpha\mathtt{static}\ ^\beta stm) = \mathcal{S}(^\beta stm)$$

Fig. 16.26 Certifying compilation of $\text{Java}_{\mathcal{O}}$ expressions

---

$\mathcal{E}(^{\alpha}\texttt{this}, opdT) = (Load(\texttt{addr}, 0), \mathcal{A}(\alpha), opdT)$
$\mathcal{E}(^{\alpha}\texttt{new } c/m^{\beta}(exps), opdT) =$
$\quad \textbf{let } \tau = (c, \text{beg}_{\alpha})_{new} \textbf{ in}$
$\quad \text{beg}_{\alpha} \cdot (New(c), \mathcal{P}(\alpha), opdT) \cdot (Dupx(0,1), \mathcal{P}(\alpha), opdT \cdot \tau) \cdot$
$\quad \mathcal{E}(^{\beta}(exps), opdT \cdot \tau \cdot \tau) \cdot$
$\quad (InvokeSpecial(\texttt{void}, c/m), \mathcal{A}(\beta), opdT \cdot [\tau, \tau] \cdot \mathcal{V}(\beta))$
$\mathcal{E}(^{\alpha}(^{\beta}exp.c/f), opdT) =$
$\quad \mathcal{E}(^{\beta}exp, opdT) \cdot (GetField(\mathcal{T}(\alpha), c/f), \mathcal{A}(\beta), opdT \cdot \mathcal{V}(\beta))$
$\mathcal{E}(^{\alpha}(^{\beta}exp_1.c/f = {}^{\gamma}exp_2), opdT) =$
$\quad \mathcal{E}(^{\beta}exp_1, opdT) \cdot \mathcal{E}(^{\gamma}exp_2, opdT \cdot \mathcal{V}(\beta)) \cdot$
$\quad (Dupx(1, size(\mathcal{T}(\alpha))), \mathcal{A}(\gamma), opdT \cdot \mathcal{V}(\beta) \cdot \mathcal{V}(\gamma)) \cdot$
$\quad (PutField(\mathcal{T}(\alpha), c/f), \mathcal{A}(\gamma), opdT \cdot \mathcal{V}(\gamma) \cdot \mathcal{V}(\beta) \cdot \mathcal{V}(\gamma))$
$\mathcal{E}(^{\alpha}(^{\beta}exp.c/m^{\gamma}(exps)), opdT) =$
$\quad \mathcal{E}(^{\beta}exp, opdT) \cdot \mathcal{E}(^{\gamma}(exps), opdT \cdot \mathcal{V}(\beta)) \cdot$
$\quad (Invoke[callKind(\alpha)](\mathcal{T}(\alpha), c/m), \mathcal{A}(\gamma), opdT \cdot \mathcal{V}(\beta) \cdot \mathcal{V}(\gamma))$
$\mathcal{E}(^{\alpha}(^{\beta}exp \texttt{ instanceof } c), opdT) =$
$\quad \mathcal{E}(^{\beta}exp, opdT) \cdot (InstanceOf(c), \mathcal{A}(\beta), opdT \cdot \mathcal{V}(\beta))$
$\mathcal{E}(^{\alpha}((c)^{\beta}exp), opdT) =$
$\quad \mathcal{E}(^{\beta}exp, opdT) \cdot (CheckCast(c), \mathcal{A}(\beta), opdT \cdot \mathcal{V}(\beta))$

Fig. 16.27 Certifying compilation of $\text{Java}_{\mathcal{E}}$ statements

---

$\mathcal{S}(^{\alpha}\texttt{throw } ^{\beta}exp) = \mathcal{E}(^{\beta}exp, [\,]) \cdot (Athrow, \mathcal{A}(\beta), [\mathcal{V}(\beta)])$
$\mathcal{S}(^{\alpha}\texttt{try } ^{\beta}block \texttt{ catch } (c_1\, x_1)\, ^{\gamma_1}block_1 \ldots \texttt{ catch } (c_n\, x_n)\, ^{\gamma_n}block_n) =$
$\quad \text{beg}_{\beta} \cdot \mathcal{S}(^{\beta}block) \cdot \text{end}_{\beta} \cdot$
$\quad (Goto(\text{end}_{\alpha}), \mathcal{A}(\beta), [\,]) \cdot$
$\quad \text{handle}_{\gamma_1} \cdot (Store(\texttt{addr}, \overline{x_1}), \mathcal{P}(\beta), [c_1]) \cdot \mathcal{S}(^{\gamma_1}block_1) \cdot$
$\quad (Goto(\text{end}_{\alpha}), \mathcal{A}(\gamma_1), [\,]) \cdot$
$\qquad \vdots$
$\quad \text{handle}_{\gamma_n} \cdot (Store(\texttt{addr}, \overline{x_n}), \mathcal{P}(\beta), [c_n]) \cdot \mathcal{S}(^{\gamma_n}block_n) \cdot \text{end}_{\alpha}$
$\mathcal{S}(^{\alpha}(^{\beta}stm \texttt{ finally } ^{\gamma}block)) =$
$\quad \text{beg}_{\alpha} \cdot \mathcal{S}(^{\beta}stm) \cdot (Jsr(\text{fin}_{\alpha}), \mathcal{A}(\beta), [\,]) \cdot$
$\quad (Goto(\text{end}_{\alpha}), \mathcal{A}(\alpha), [\,]) \cdot$
$\quad \text{default}_{\alpha} \cdot (Store(\texttt{addr}, \overline{exc}), \mathcal{P}(\beta), [\texttt{Throwable}]) \cdot$
$\quad (Jsr(\text{fin}_{\alpha}), \mathcal{P}(\beta) \oplus \{(\overline{exc}, \texttt{Throwable})\}, [\,]) \cdot$
$\quad (Load(\texttt{addr}, \overline{exc}), \mathcal{P}(\beta) \oplus \{(\overline{exc}, \texttt{Throwable})\}, [\,]) \cdot$
$\quad (Athrow, \mathcal{P}(\beta), [\texttt{Throwable}]) \cdot$
$\quad \text{fin}_{\alpha} \cdot (Store(\texttt{addr}, \overline{ret}_{\alpha}), \mathcal{P}(\gamma), [\texttt{retAddr}(\text{fin}_{\alpha})]) \cdot \mathcal{S}(^{\gamma}block) \cdot$
$\quad (Ret(\overline{ret}_{\alpha}), \mathcal{A}(\gamma), [\,]) \cdot \text{end}_{\alpha}$

Fig. 16.28 Certifying compilation of Java$_\mathcal{E}$ abruptions statements

$\mathcal{S}(^\alpha \mathtt{continue}\ lab;) =$
  let $[\mathrm{fin}_{\beta_1}, \ldots, \mathrm{fin}_{\beta_n}] = finallyLabsUntil(\alpha, lab)$
  $(Jsr(\mathrm{fin}_{\beta_1}), \mathcal{P}(\beta_1), []) \cdot \ldots \cdot (Jsr(\mathrm{fin}_{\beta_n}), \mathcal{P}(\beta_n), []) \cdot$
  $(Continue(lab_c), \mathcal{P}(\beta_n), [])$
$\mathcal{S}(^\alpha \mathtt{break}\ lab;) =$
  let $[\mathrm{fin}_{\beta_1}, \ldots, \mathrm{fin}_{\beta_n}] = finallyLabsUntil(\alpha, lab)$
  $(Jsr(\mathrm{fin}_{\beta_1}), regB \oplus \mathcal{P}(\beta_1), []) \cdot \ldots \cdot (Jsr(\mathrm{fin}_{\beta_n}), regB \oplus \mathcal{P}(\beta_n), []) \cdot$
  $(Break(lab_b), regB, [])$
  where $^\gamma(lab\colon stm)$ encloses α **and**
  where $regB = $ **if** $Break(lab_b) \in \mathcal{D}$ **then** $\mathcal{A}(\gamma)$ **else** $\emptyset$
$\mathcal{S}(^\alpha \mathtt{return};) =$
  let $[\mathrm{fin}_{\beta_1}, \ldots, \mathrm{fin}_{\beta_n}] = finallyLabs(\alpha)$
  $(Jsr(\mathrm{fin}_{\beta_1}), \mathcal{P}(\beta_1), []) \cdot \ldots \cdot (Jsr(\mathrm{fin}_{\beta_n}), \mathcal{P}(\beta_n), []) \cdot$
  $(Return(\mathtt{void}), \emptyset, [])$
$\mathcal{S}(^\alpha \mathtt{return}\ ^\beta exp;) =$
  let $[\mathrm{fin}_{\gamma_1}, \ldots, \mathrm{fin}_{\gamma_n}] = finallyLabs(\alpha)$
  $\mathcal{E}(^\beta exp) \cdot (Store(\mathcal{T}(\beta), \overline{var}), \mathcal{A}(\beta), \mathcal{V}(\beta)) \cdot$
  $(Jsr(\mathrm{fin}_{\gamma_1}), \mathcal{P}(\gamma_1) \oplus \{(\overline{var}, \mathcal{V}(\beta))\}, []) \cdot$
  $\vdots$
  $(Jsr(\mathrm{fin}_{\gamma_n}), \mathcal{P}(\gamma_n) \oplus \{(\overline{var}, \mathcal{V}(\beta))\}, []) \cdot$
  $(Load(\mathcal{T}(\beta), \overline{var}), \{(\overline{var}, \mathcal{V}(\beta))\}, []) \cdot$
  $(Return(\mathcal{T}(\beta)), \emptyset, [\mathcal{V}(\beta)])$

Fig. 16.29 The general pattern for abruptions statements

```
γlab: {
    β2try {
        εtry { ... }
        finally {
            β1try { αbreak lab; }
                finally δ1{ ... }
        }
    } finally δ2{ ... }
}
```

2. The compilation of statements does not end in a *Jsr* instruction.

3. The compilation of statements does not start after a *Jsr* instruction.

4. Targets i of $Goto(i)$, $Cond(\_, i)$ and $\mathcal{B}_z(exp, i)$ are not after a *Jsr*.

5. No exception handler starts after a *Jsr* instruction.

6. No subroutine starts after a *Jsr* instruction.

Therefore, if $code(j) = Jsr(\_)$, then the only possible way to reach $j+1$ is via j. $\square$

In the compiled code of an expression, the end of the code is reachable from the beginning of the code. For statements this is not true. In an infinite loop or in a return statement, the end of the code is not reachable from the beginning.

Lemma 16.5.3. Let α be a position in the body of μ.

1. In $\mathcal{E}(^{\alpha}exp)$, code index end_α is reachable from beg_α.
2. In $\mathcal{B}_i(^{\alpha}exp, lab)$, at least one of lab or end_α is reachable from beg_α.

Proof. By induction on the size of $^{\alpha}exp$. $\square$

The label used in the compilation of a boolean test expression cannot jump inside the code of the expression. It can jump to the beginning of the test expression, for example in `while (true) {}`.

Lemma 16.5.4. In $\mathcal{B}_z(^{\alpha}exp, lab, opdT)$, either $lab \le beg_\alpha$ or $end_\alpha < lab$.

Proof. Top down, starting at the *firstPos* of the body of μ. $\square$

A successor of an instruction in the bytecode for a phrase is either also an instruction in the code for the phrase, or the next instruction immediately following the code for the phrase, or the target of an exception handler which protects the instruction, or a jump to a subroutine of an enclosing `finally` statement, or a jump to the beginning or the end of an enclosing labeled statement.

Lemma 16.5.5. If $beg_\alpha \le i < end_\alpha$ in $\mathcal{E}(^{\alpha}exp, opdT)$ and j is a successor (Def. 16.3.2) of i, then one of the following is true:

1. $beg_\alpha \le j \le end_\alpha$, or
2. there exists a handler $(f, u, j\_) \in excs(\mu)$ with $f \le i < u$.

Lemma 16.5.6. If $beg_\alpha \le i < end_\alpha$ in $\mathcal{B}_z(^{\alpha}exp, lab, opdT)$ and j is a successor (Def. 16.3.2) of i, then one of the following is true:

1. $beg_\alpha \le j \le end_\alpha$, or
2. $j = lab$, or
3. there exists a handler $(f, u, j\_) \in excs(\mu)$ with $f \le i < u$.

Lemma 16.5.7. If $\mathrm{beg}_\alpha \leq i < \mathrm{end}_\alpha$ in $\mathcal{S}(^\alpha stm)$ and j is a successor (Def. 16.3.2) of i, then one of the following is true:

1. $\mathrm{beg}_\alpha \leq j \leq \mathrm{end}_\alpha$, or
2. there exists a handler $(f, u, j_-) \in excs(\mu) \setminus \mathcal{X}(^\alpha stm)$ with $f \leq i < u$, or
3. there exists a statement $^\beta(^\gamma stm \ \mathtt{finally} \ ^\delta block)$ in the body of μ such that α is a position in $^\gamma stm$, $code(i) = Jsr(j)$ and $j = \mathrm{fin}_\beta$,
4. there exists a statement $lab{:}\,^\beta stm$ in the body of μ such that α is a position in $^\beta stm$ and
   a) $code(i) = Continue(j)$ and $j = lab_c = \mathrm{beg}_\beta$ or
   b) $code(i) = Break(j)$ and $j = lab_b = \mathrm{end}_\beta$.

Proof. By induction on the size of $^\alpha stm$. □

The code for a phrase has entry points. Each path entering the code must go to one of these entry points. In the code generated by the compiler of Part II, each phrase has exactly one entry point, the first instruction of the code for the phrase.

Lemma 16.5.8. If α is a position in the body of μ and j is a successor (Def. 16.3.2) of i with $\mathrm{beg}_\alpha < j < \mathrm{end}_\alpha$, then $\mathrm{beg}_\alpha \leq i < \mathrm{end}_\alpha$.

Proof. Top down, starting at the *firstPos* of the body of μ. □

Lemma 16.5.1 can be strengthened to subphrases of the body of μ. If a code index in the code interval of a subphrase of the body of μ belongs to $\mathcal{D}$, then the code index is reachable from the beginning of the interval via a path in $\mathcal{D}$. It follows that the first instruction of the code of the subphrase belongs to $\mathcal{D}$, too.

Lemma 16.5.9. If α is a position in the body of μ and if i is a code index in $\mathcal{D}$ with $\mathrm{beg}_\alpha \leq i < \mathrm{end}_\alpha$, then i is reachable from beg_α via a path in $\{j \mid \mathrm{beg}_\alpha \leq j < \mathrm{end}_\alpha\} \cap \mathcal{D}$.

Proof. By Lemma 16.5.1, there exists a path from code index 0 to i with elements from $\mathcal{D}$. If $\mathrm{beg}_\alpha = i$, we are done. Otherwise, consider the last element on the path which is not in $\{j \mid \mathrm{beg}_\alpha < j < \mathrm{end}_\alpha\} \cap \mathcal{D}$. By Lemma 16.5.8, it follows that this last element must be beg_α. □

If the *Ret* instruction at the end of a finally block in Fig. 16.27 belongs to $\mathcal{D}$, then the instruction is reachable from the beginning of the block. Hence, the $Ret(\overline{ret}_\alpha)$ instruction is a possible return from the subroutine in the sense of Def. 16.3.5, since in the code of the finally block no $Store(\_, \overline{ret}_\alpha)$ is used.

Lemma 16.5.10. Let $^\alpha(^\beta stm \ \mathtt{finally} \ ^\gamma block)$ be a substatement in the body of μ. If $\mathrm{end}_\gamma \in \mathcal{D}$, then end_γ is reachable from beg_γ via a path in $\{i \mid \mathrm{beg}_\gamma \leq i \leq \mathrm{end}_\gamma\} \cap \mathcal{D}$.

Proof. If end_γ is in $\mathcal{D}$, then by Lemma 16.5.9 there exists a path from beg_α to end_γ in $\{j \mid \text{beg}_\alpha \leq j < \text{end}_\alpha\} \cap \mathcal{D}$. Since the path has to leave the code of $^\beta stm$, it must reach fin_α via $Jsr(\text{fin}_\alpha)$ and hence also beg_γ. If the path leaves the code of $^\gamma block$ again before reaching end_γ, then it loops back to beg_α and reaches beg_γ later again. The end piece of the path is in $\{j \mid \text{beg}_\gamma \leq j \leq \text{end}_\gamma\} \cap \mathcal{D}$ and connects beg_γ with end_γ. $\qquad\square$

Corollary 16.5.1. *Let $^\alpha(^\beta stm$ `finally` $^\gamma block)$ be a substatement in the body of μ. If $\text{end}_\gamma \in \mathcal{D}$, then end_γ is a possible return from subroutine fin_α in the sense of Def. 16.3.5.*

Proof. By Fig. 16.27 we have

$$code(\text{fin}_\alpha) = Store(\texttt{addr}, \overline{ret}_\alpha) \quad \text{and} \quad code(\text{end}_\gamma) = Ret(\overline{ret}_\alpha).$$

By Lemma 16.5.10, end_γ is reachable from end_γ via a path which is entirely in the code for $^\gamma block$. Since the code for $^\gamma block$ does not use any $Store(\_, \overline{ret}_\alpha)$ instruction, end_γ is a possible return from subroutine fin_α, in the sense of Def. 16.3.5. $\qquad\square$

As we have seen in Example 16.5.1, it is not true that, if code index end_α is reachable from beg_α, then $normal(\alpha)$ is true. Therefore, in Lemma 16.5.11 below, we need a stronger assumption than simple reachability. We assume that end_α is reachable from beg_α via a path which is entirely in the set $\mathcal{D}$. Exercise 16.5.1 below provides an example, why `break` statements have to be treated as a special case.

Definition 16.5.3 (Critical path). A path from beg_α to end_α is a *critical path for $^\alpha stm$*, if the last step in the path is a $Break(lab)$ and the position α is in the scope of the label lab in the body of μ.

Note, that the path in Lemma 16.5.10 which connects the end of a subroutine with the beginning is not critical for the `finally` block.

Lemma 16.5.11. *Let $^\alpha stm$ be a statement in the body of μ.*

1. If code index end_α is reachable from code index beg_α via a path in the set $\{j \mid \text{beg}_\alpha \leq j \leq \text{end}_\alpha\} \cap \mathcal{D}$ which is not critical for $^\alpha stm$, then $normal(\alpha)$ is true.
2. If $\text{beg}_\alpha \leq i < \text{end}_\alpha$, $i \in \mathcal{D}$, $code(i) = Break(lab)$ and $\text{end}_\alpha \leq lab$, then the corresponding `break` lab can exit $^\alpha stm$ (Def. 8.2.2).

Proof. By induction on the size of $^\alpha stm$. We consider the case of a statement $^\alpha(^\beta stm$ `finally` $^\gamma block)$ in Fig. 16.27.

Consider a path from beg_α to end_α in $\{j \mid \text{beg}_\alpha \leq j \leq \text{end}_\alpha\} \cap \mathcal{D}$ which is not critical for α. We can assume that the path does not loop back to beg_α.

By Lemma 16.5.7, the different possibilities for the path to leave the code of $^\beta stm$ are via end_β, default_α, $Jsr(\text{fin}_\alpha)$, or $Break(\text{end}_\alpha)$.

If the path leaves $^\beta stm$ via $Break(\text{end}_\alpha)$, then it would be critical for α.

Suppose that the path reaches fin_α. From fin_α the path proceeds to beg_γ. Then, again by Lemma 16.5.7, it can leave the code of $^\gamma block$ via end_γ or $Break(\text{end}_\alpha)$. If the path reaches end_γ, then it gets stuck at the following $Ret(\overline{ret}_\alpha)$ instruction contradicting the assumption that it reaches end_α. If the path leaves the code of $^\gamma block$ via $Break(\text{end}_\alpha)$, then the path would be critical for α. Hence, the path cannot reach fin_α.

Suppose that the path reaches default_α. Then the path must reach fin_α because otherwise it gets stuck at the *Athrow* instruction. Contradiction.

The only possibility that remains to leave the code of $^\beta stm$ is via end_β. The part of the path from beg_β to end_β is not critical for β, since a $Break(lab_b)$ at the end of a critical path would jump below end_α. Hence we can apply the induction hypothesis 1 to β and obtain that $normal(\beta)$ is true.

At the instruction $Jsr(\text{fin}_\alpha)$ at end_β the path proceeds to $Goto(\text{end}_\alpha)$. Otherwise, it would go through fin_α. Since the path is in $\mathcal{D}$, the instruction $Goto(\text{end}_\alpha)$ belongs to $\mathcal{D}$. By Def. 16.5.1 and Lemma 16.5.2 it follows that end_γ is in $\mathcal{D}$.

Since end_γ is in $\mathcal{D}$, by Lemma 16.5.10 there exists a path from beg_γ to end_γ in $\{j \mid \text{beg}_\gamma \leq j \leq \text{end}_\gamma\} \cap \mathcal{D}$ which is not critical for γ. Hence we can apply the induction hypothesis 1 to $^\gamma block$ and obtain that $normal(\gamma)$ is true.

From Table 8.3 it follows that $normal(\alpha)$ is true.

The second part of the lemma is shown in a similar way. The difficult case is a $Break(lab)$ instruction in the code of $^\beta stm$. By the induction hypothesis 2 for β, it follows that the corresponding **break** *lab* statement can exit β. In order to conclude that it can also exit α, we have to show that $normal(\gamma)$ is true. According to Fig. 16.28 the $Break(lab)$ is preceded by a cascade of Jsr instructions. One of them is $Jsr(\text{fin}_\alpha)$. Since the $Break(lab)$ is in $\mathcal{D}$, by Def. 16.5.1 and Lemma 16.5.2 it follows that end_γ is in $\mathcal{D}$. As in the proof of the first part of the lemma it follows that $normal(\gamma)$ is true. Hence, the **break** *lab* statement can exit α.   □

In Def. 16.3.7, the set of register numbers modified by a subroutine is defined. We extend the notion and define the set of variables modified by an arbitrary subphrase of the body of μ.

Definition 16.5.4 (Modified variables). Let α be a position in the body of μ. A variable x belongs to $mod(\alpha)$, if there exists a code index i with $\text{beg}_\alpha \leq i < \text{end}_\alpha$, i is reachable from beg_α and $code(i) = Store(\_, \overline{x})$.

For subroutines the two definitions are related in the following sense.

Lemma 16.5.12. Let $^\alpha(^\beta stm$ `finally` $^\gamma block)$ be a substatement in the body of μ with $end_\gamma \in \mathcal{D}$. If $x \in mod(\gamma)$, then $\overline{x} \in mod(\mathrm{fin}_\alpha)$. If the size of the type of x is 2, then $\overline{x} + 1 \in mod(\mathrm{fin}_\alpha)$.

Proof. Consider the code for the statement in Fig. 16.27. Let $x \in mod(\gamma)$. This means that there exists a reachable code index i with $beg_\gamma \leq i < end_\gamma$ and $code(i) = Store(\_, \overline{x})$. By Corollary 16.5.1, end_γ is a possible return from subroutine fin_α. Hence $\overline{x} \in mod(\mathrm{fin}_\alpha)$. □

An obvious conjecture is that variables which are definitely assigned after a phrase but not before the phrase occur in *Store* instructions in the code interval for the phrase. For expressions and boolean test expressions, this fact is true and can be proved by a simple induction on the size of the expression.

Lemma 16.5.13. Let α be a position in the body of μ.

1. In $\mathcal{E}(^\alpha exp, opdT)$ we have: $after(\alpha) \setminus before(\alpha) \subseteq mod(\alpha)$.
2. In $\mathcal{B}_1(^\alpha exp, lab, opdT)$ we have:
   a) If lab is reachable from beg_α, then $true(\alpha) \setminus before(\alpha) \subseteq mod(\alpha)$.
   b) If end_α is reachable from beg_α, then $false(\alpha) \setminus before(\alpha) \subseteq mod(\alpha)$.
3. In $\mathcal{B}_0(^\alpha exp, lab, opdT)$ we have:
   a) If lab is reachable from beg_α, then $false(\alpha) \setminus before(\alpha) \subseteq mod(\alpha)$.
   b) If end_α is reachable from beg_α, then $true(\alpha) \setminus before(\alpha) \subseteq mod(\alpha)$.

Proof. By induction on the size of $^\alpha exp$. □

For statements the fact has to be formulated in a slightly different way. The reason is shown in the following example.

Example (↝ CD) 16.5.5. Consider the following code fragment (which hopefully will never be written by a Java programmer):

```
L: α{
    if (true)
        break L;
    else
        i = 3;
}
```

This piece of code is compiled by the compiler of Part II as follows (remember that $Break(end_\alpha)$ is just an alias for $Goto(end_\alpha)$):

$$
\begin{aligned}
beg_\alpha &: Goto(\mathrm{if}_\alpha) \\
&\quad Prim(3) \\
&\quad Store(\texttt{int}, \texttt{i}) \\
&\quad Goto(end_\alpha) \\
\mathrm{if}_\alpha &: Break(end_\alpha) \\
end_\alpha &:
\end{aligned}
$$

Although the variable i belongs to $after(\alpha) \setminus before(\alpha)$ and end_α is reachable from beg_α, the variable i does not belong to $mod(\alpha)$, since the $Store(\texttt{int}, \texttt{i})$ instruction is not reachable from the beginning. The example does not contradict the following lemma, since the path from beg_α to end_α is critical for α.

Lemma 16.5.14. Let $^\alpha stm$ be a statement in the body of μ.

1. If code index end_α is reachable from code index beg_α via a path in the set $\{j \mid beg_\alpha \leq j \leq end_\alpha\} \cap \mathcal{D}$ which is not critical for $^\alpha stm$, then $after(\alpha) \setminus before(\alpha) \subseteq mod(\alpha)$.
2. If an instruction $Break(lab_b)$ is reachable from code index beg_α via a path in $\{j \mid beg_\alpha \leq j < end_\alpha\} \cap \mathcal{D}$ and α is in the scope of the label lab in the body of μ, then $break(\alpha, lab) \setminus before(\alpha) \subseteq mod(\alpha)$.

Proof. By induction on the size of $^\alpha stm$. We consider the case of a statement $^\alpha(^\beta stm \; \texttt{finally} \; ^\gamma block)$ in Fig. 16.27.

According to Table 8.6, $before(\alpha) = before(\beta) = before(\gamma)$ and

$$after(\alpha) \setminus before(\alpha) \subseteq (after(\beta) \setminus before(\beta)) \cup (after(\gamma) \setminus before(\gamma)).$$

Consider a path from beg_α to end_α in $\{j \mid beg_\alpha \leq j \leq end_\alpha\} \cap \mathcal{D}$ which is not critical for α.

As in the proof of Lemma 16.5.11 it follows that the first part of the path goes from beg_β to end_β and is not critical for β. Hence we can apply the induction hypothesis 1 to β and obtain that

$$after(\beta) \setminus before(\beta) \subseteq mod(\beta) \subseteq mod(\alpha).$$

Following further the proof of Lemma 16.5.11 we see that end_γ is in $\mathcal{D}$ and that there exists a path from beg_γ to end_γ in $\{j \mid beg_\gamma \leq j \leq end_\gamma\} \cap \mathcal{D}$ which is not critical for γ. Hence we can apply the induction hypothesis 1 to $^\gamma block$ and obtain that

$$after(\gamma) \setminus before(\gamma) \subseteq mod(\gamma) \subseteq mod(\alpha).$$

Hence, statement 1 of the lemma is shown for α.

Statement 2 is proved in a similar way. $\square$

In the main theorem we prove that the type frames computed by the extended compiler restricted to the domain $\mathcal{D}$ of Def. 16.5.1 is a bytecode type assignment in the sense of Def. 16.3.8.

Theorem 16.5.1. The family $(regT_i, opdT_i)_{i \in \mathcal{D}}$ of type frames generated by the certifying compiler for the body of method μ is a bytecode type assignment for μ.

Proof. We have to show that conditions T1–T8 of Def. 16.3.8 are satisfied.

T1 says that $\mathcal{D}$ must be a set of valid code indices. So we have to show that, if $i \in \mathcal{D}$, then $0 \leq i < codeLength(\mu)$.

Obviously, each index $i \in \mathcal{D}$ is less than or equal to $codeLength(\mu)$. Suppose that $codeLength(\mu)$ belongs to $\mathcal{D}$. By Lemma 16.5.1, it follows that $codeLength(\mu)$ is reachable from code index 0 via a path in $\mathcal{D}$. Since the body of μ is not contained in an enclosing labeled statement, Lemma 16.5.11 yields that the body of μ is *normal*. This is a contradiction, since the body of a method cannot be *normal* (Sect. 8.2). Hence $codeLength(\mu) \notin \mathcal{D}$ and T1 is satisfied.

T2 is satisfied, since 0 belongs to $\mathcal{D}$ according to Def. 16.5.1.

Next we prove that the triples generated by the certifying compiler for expressions, test expressions and statements have the following properties.

If $\mathcal{E}(^{\alpha}exp, opdT) = [code(i) \mid m \leq i < n]$ and there is no code index i with $m \leq i < n$ such that a type $(\_, i)_{new}$ occurs in $opdT$ and, $opdT$ is free of *InInit* or α is a position in an argument of an explicit constructor invocation at the beginning of a constructor, then the following is true:

E1. $\mathcal{P}(\alpha) \sqsubseteq_{reg} regT_m$ and $opdT = opdT_m$.

E2. If $m \leq i < n$ and $i \in \mathcal{D}$, then $check(\mu, i, regT_i, opdT_i)$ is true.

E3. If $m \leq i < n$, $i \in \mathcal{D}$ and $(j, regS, opdS) \in succs(\mu, i, regT_i, opdT_i)$, then $j \in \mathcal{D}$ and one of the following is true:

   a) $m \leq j < n$, $regS \sqsubseteq_{reg} regT_j$ and $opdS \sqsubseteq_{seq} opdT_j$, or

   b) $j = n$, $regS \sqsubseteq_{reg} \mathcal{A}(\alpha)$ and $opdS \sqsubseteq_{seq} opdT \cdot \mathcal{V}(\alpha)$, or

   c) there exists an entry (f, u, j, t) in $excs(\mu)$ such that $f \leq i < u$, $regS \sqsubseteq_{reg} \mathcal{P}(\alpha)$ and $opdS = [t]$.

E4. If $m \leq i < n$, $i \in \mathcal{D}$ and $regT_i(x) = \texttt{retAddr}(s)$, then i belongs to s.

If $\mathcal{B}_z(^{\alpha}exp, lab, opdT) = [code(i) \mid m \leq i < n]$ and there is no code index i with $m \leq i < n$ such that a type $(\_, i)_{new}$ occurs in $opdT$, and $opdT$ is free of *InInit* or α is a position in an argument of an explicit constructor invocation at the beginning of a constructor, then the following is true:

B1. If $m < n$, then $\mathcal{P}(\alpha) \sqsubseteq_{reg} regT_m$ and $opdT = opdT_m$.

B2. If $m \leq i < n$ and $i \in \mathcal{D}$, then $check(\mu, i, regT_i, opdT_i)$ is true.

B3. If $m \leq i < n$, $i \in \mathcal{D}$ and $(j, regS, opdS) \in succs(\mu, i, regT_i, opdT_i)$, then $j \in \mathcal{D}$ and one of the following is true:

   a) $m \leq j < n$, $regS \sqsubseteq_{reg} regT_j$ and $opdS \sqsubseteq_{seq} opdT_j$, or

   b) $j = n$, $regS \sqsubseteq_{reg} \mathcal{A}_{1-z}(\alpha)$ and $opdS \sqsubseteq_{seq} opdT$, or

   c) $j = lab$, $regS \sqsubseteq_{reg} \mathcal{A}_z(\alpha)$ and $opdS \sqsubseteq_{seq} opdT$, or

   d) there exists an entry (f, u, j, t) in $excs(\mu)$ such that $f \leq i < u$, $regS \sqsubseteq_{reg} \mathcal{P}(\alpha)$ and $opdS = [t]$.

B4. If $m \leq i < n$, $i \in \mathcal{D}$ and $regT_i(x) = \mathtt{retAddr}(s)$, then i belongs to s.

For $\mathcal{S}(^{\alpha}stm) = [code(i) \mid m \leq i < n]$ the following is true:

S1. If $m \leq n$, then $\mathcal{P}(\alpha) \sqsubseteq_{\mathrm{reg}} regT_m$ and $opdT_m = [\,]$.

S2. If $m \leq i < n$ and $i \in \mathcal{D}$, then $check(\mu, i, regT_i, opdT_i)$ is true.

S3. If $m \leq i < n$, $i \in \mathcal{D}$ and $(j, regS, opdS) \in succs(\mu, i, regT_i, opdT_i)$, then $j \in \mathcal{D}$ and one of the following is true:

    a) $m \leq j < n$, $regS \sqsubseteq_{\mathrm{reg}} regT_j$ and $opdS \sqsubseteq_{\mathrm{seq}} opdT_j$, or

    b) $j = n$, $regS \sqsubseteq_{\mathrm{reg}} \mathcal{A}(\alpha)$ and $opdS = [\,]$, or

    c) there exists an entry (f, u, j, t) in $excs(\mu) \setminus \mathcal{X}(^{\alpha}stm)$ such that $f \leq i < u$, $regS \sqsubseteq_{\mathrm{reg}} \mathcal{P}(\alpha)$ and $opdS = [t]$, or

    d) there exists a statement $^{\beta}(lab\colon s)$ in the body of μ such that α is in s, $j = lab_c$, $regS \sqsubseteq_{\mathrm{reg}} \mathcal{P}(\beta)$ and $opdS = [\,]$, or

    e) there exists a statement $^{\beta}(lab\colon s)$ in the body of μ such that α is in s, $j = lab_b$, $regS \sqsubseteq_{\mathrm{reg}} \mathcal{A}(\beta)$ and $opdS = [\,]$, or

    f) there exists a statement $^{\beta}(s\ \mathtt{finally}\ b)$ in the body of μ such that α is in s, $j = \mathrm{fin}_\beta$, $regS \sqsubseteq_{\mathrm{reg}} \mathcal{P}(\beta)$ and $opdS = [\mathtt{retAddr}(\mathrm{fin}_\beta)]$.

S4. If $m \leq i < n$, $i \in \mathcal{D}$ and $regT_i(x) = \mathtt{retAddr}(s)$, then i belongs to s.

Properties E1–E4, B1–B4, S1–S4 are proved by induction on the size of $^{\alpha}exp$ and $^{\alpha}stm$. The following facts are used in the proof:

1. If $\mathcal{B}_1(^{\alpha}exp, lab, opdT) = \epsilon$, then $false(\alpha) = before(\alpha)$.
2. If $\mathcal{B}_0(^{\alpha}exp, lab, opdT) = \epsilon$, then $true(\alpha) = before(\alpha)$.
3. If $\mathcal{S}(^{\alpha}stm) = \epsilon$, then $after(\alpha) = before(\alpha)$.

Consider now the body $body_\mu$ of the method μ with

$$\mathcal{S}(body_\mu) = [code(i) \mid 0 \leq i < codeLength(\mu)].$$

The properties S1–S3 are true for the body.

From S1 we obtain that $\mathcal{P}(firstPos) \sqsubseteq_{\mathrm{reg}} regT_0$ and $opdT_0 = [\,]$, hence T3 and T4 are satisfied.

From S2 it follows that the checks are true for every code index $i \in \mathcal{D}$, hence T5 is satisfied.

Condition T6 follows from S3, since the cases (b)–(f) are not possible for a successor j of an index $i \in \mathcal{D}$. Case (b) is not possible, since $codeLength(\mu) \notin \mathcal{D}$ as we have seen above. Case (c) is not possible because the exception table $excs(\mu)$ is defined to be $\mathcal{X}(body_\mu)$. Cases (d)–(f) are not possible, since $body_\mu$ cannot be contained in another statement in the body of μ.

The second part of condition T8 follows directly from Fig. 16.27. The first part of condition T8 follows from S4. If $\mathtt{retAddr}(s)$ occurs in a $regT_i$, then, by Def. 16.5.2 (5), there exists a substatement $^\alpha(^\beta stm$ `finally` $^\gamma block)$ of the body of μ such that $s = \text{fin}_\alpha$ and $\text{end}_\gamma \in \mathcal{D}$. The code index i belongs to the code of a subphrase of $^\gamma block$. By Corollary 16.5.1 it follows that end_γ is a possible return from subroutine fin_α. Therefore i belongs to fin_α in the sense of Def. 16.3.6.

It remains to show that (a)–(f) of T7 are satisfied.

Assume that $i \in \mathcal{D}$, $code(i) = Ret(x)$, $regT_i(x) = \texttt{retAddr}(s)$, $j \in \mathcal{D}$ and $code(j) = Jsr(s)$. The Ret instruction occurs in Fig. 16.27 only, therefore there exists a position α in the body of μ such that $x = \overline{ret}_\alpha$ and $s = \text{fin}_\alpha$. Since i and j are in $\mathcal{D}$, by Def. 16.5.1 (7), it follows that $j + 1$ is in $\mathcal{D}$, hence T7 (a) is shown. For T7 (b)–(f) we have to consider the $Jsr(s)$ instructions which occur in Fig. 16.27 and Fig. 16.28.

Consider the first $Jsr(\text{fin}_\alpha)$ instruction in Fig. 16.27 in the code of the statement $^\alpha(^\beta stm$ `finally` $^\gamma block)$. Then $i = \text{end}_\gamma$, $j = \text{end}_\beta$, $regT_i = \mathcal{A}(\gamma)$, $regT_j = \mathcal{A}(\beta)$ and $regT_{j+1} = \mathcal{A}(\alpha)$.

For T7 (b) we have to show that $\mathcal{A}(\gamma) \sqsubseteq_{\text{reg}} mod(\text{fin}_\alpha) \lhd \mathcal{A}(\alpha)$.

Let x be a variable in $after(\alpha)$ such that $\overline{x} \in mod(\text{fin}_\alpha)$. If x is in $after(\gamma)$, then $\mathcal{A}(\gamma)(x) = \mathcal{A}(\alpha)(x)$ and we are done. Otherwise, x is in $after(\beta)$ and, by definition of $after(\alpha)$, there is no subexpression $x = exp$ in $^\gamma block$. Hence, there is no instruction $Store(\_, \overline{x})$ in between beg_γ and end_γ and, since $\overline{x}$ is different from $\overline{ret}_\alpha$, $\overline{x}$ does not belong to $mod(\text{fin}_\alpha)$. Contradiction.

T7 (c) is satisfied, since $opdT_i$ as well as $opdT_{j+1}$ are empty.

For T7 (d) we have to show that $\mathcal{A}(\beta) \sqsubseteq_{\text{reg}} mod(\text{fin}_\alpha) \lhd \mathcal{A}(\alpha)$.

Let x be a variable in $after(\alpha)$ such that $\overline{x} \notin mod(\text{fin}_\alpha)$. If x is in $after(\beta)$, then $\mathcal{A}(\beta)(x) = \mathcal{A}(\alpha)(x)$ and we are done. Otherwise, x is in $after(\gamma)$ and not in $before(\gamma)$. By Lemma 16.5.10 (which is applicable because $\text{end}_\gamma = i \in \mathcal{D}$), Lemma 16.5.14, the remark preceding Lemma 16.5.14 and Lemma 16.5.12, it follows, that $\overline{x} \in mod(\text{fin}_\alpha)$. Contradiction.

For T7 (e) assume that $\texttt{retAddr}(l)$ occurs in $mod(\text{fin}_\alpha) \lhd \mathcal{A}(\alpha)$. By item (5) of Def. 16.5.2, it follows that α is a position in a `finally` block with subroutine l. Hence, using Corollary 16.5.1 to guarantee the existence of a possible return from subroutine l, the code for subroutine fin_α belongs to l in the sense of Def. 16.3.6.

T7 (f) is satisfied, since a type $(c, k)_{new}$ is never used as the type of a local register in the type frames generated by the certifying compiler; furthermore, by Def. 16.5.2 (4), $InInit$ is used only as the type of register 0 in the code for explicit constructor invocations at the beginning of the body of a constructor, but in our case α is not such a position. Hence, neither $(c, k)_{new}$ nor $InInit$ occur in $mod(s) \lhd regT_{j+1}$.

Let us now consider the Jsr instruction in the default handler in Fig. 16.27. For T7 (b) we have to show that

$$\mathcal{A}(\gamma) \sqsubseteq_{\text{reg}} mod(\text{fin}_\alpha) \lhd (\mathcal{P}(\beta) \oplus \{(\overline{exc}, \texttt{Throwable})\})$$

This is true, since $before(\beta) = before(\gamma) \subseteq after(\gamma)$, by Table 8.6, and the variable $\overline{exc}$ has been chosen by the compiler to be sufficiently fresh (see Sect. 12.2) so that there is no $Store(\_, \overline{exc})$ instruction between beg_γ and end_γ. Hence, $\overline{exc}$ does not belong to $mod(\mathrm{fin}_\alpha)$. T7 (c)–(f) follow as above.

Finally we move to the Jsr instructions in $\mathcal{S}(^\alpha\texttt{break } lab;)$ in Fig. 16.28. The difficult case is when the instruction $Break(lab_b)$ is in the domain $\mathcal{D}$ and $regB = \mathcal{A}(\gamma)$ in Fig. 16.28. If $Break(lab_b)$ is in $\mathcal{D}$, then by Lemma 16.5.9 and 16.5.11, it follows that $^\alpha\texttt{break } lab$ can exit (Def. 8.2.2) the labeled statement $^\gamma(lab : stm)$ enclosing α.

The general situation is pictured in Fig. 16.29.

Consider the instruction $Jsr(\mathrm{fin}_{\beta_1})$. For T7 (b) we have to show that

$$\mathcal{A}(\delta_1) \sqsubseteq_{\mathrm{reg}} mod(\mathrm{fin}_{\beta_1}) \lhd (\mathcal{A}(\gamma) \oplus \mathcal{P}(\beta_2)).$$

By the nesting of the $\texttt{try-finally}$ statements,

$$\mathcal{P}(\beta_2) \subseteq \mathcal{P}(\beta_1) = \mathcal{P}(\delta_1) \subseteq \mathcal{A}(\delta_1).$$

Let x be a variable in $after(\gamma) \cap mod(\mathrm{fin}_{\beta_1})$. By Table 8.6 and Def. 8.3.1, x is in $after(\beta_1)$ because the $^\alpha\texttt{break } lab$ can exit γ. Moreover, there is a $Store(\_, x)$ instruction in the code for the block at position δ_1. This can only be, if there is an assignment $x = exp$ in the block at δ_1. By Table 8.6, it follows that $x \in after(\delta_1)$.

For T7 (d) we have to show that

$$\mathcal{A}(\gamma) \oplus \mathcal{P}(\beta_1) \sqsubseteq_{\mathrm{reg}} mod(\mathrm{fin}_{\beta_1}) \lhd (\mathcal{A}(\gamma) \oplus \mathcal{P}(\beta_2)).$$

This is true because $\mathcal{P}(\beta_2) \subseteq \mathcal{P}(\beta_1)$. T7 (c)–(f) follow as above.

The remaining cases from Fig. 16.28 are shown in a similar way.   □

Remark 16.5.1. The examples in Fig. 16.8 and 16.9 were found during a first attempt to prove the preceding theorem for the previous version of our bytecode verifier. After we detected the counter examples, we decided to restrict the rules of definite assignment for $\texttt{finally}$ statements and labeled statements in such a way that the above proof goes through. Hence, in our view the programs in Fig. 16.8 and 16.9 are no longer valid Java programs (see also Remark 8.3.1).

Theorem 16.5.2 (Completeness of the compiler). Bytecode generated by the compiler of Part II from a correct Java program does have type assignments.

Proof. Follows from the previous theorem, since the certifying compiler is a conservative extension of the compiler of Part II.   □

Exercise ($\leadsto$ CD) 16.5.1. Show that in the code generated by the certifying compiler for the following method, code index end_α is reachable from beg_α via a path in $\mathcal{D}$.

```
void m(boolean b) {
lab:
  ᵅtry { if (b) break lab; }
    finally { break lab; }
}
```

This example shows why Lemma 16.5.11 is rather tricky. Note, that $normal(\alpha)$ is false.

Exercise 16.5.2. In the proof of Theorem 16.5.1, we assume that the length of the list $regT_i$ for $i \in \mathcal{D}$ is less than $maxOpd$. Show that the function $maxOpd$ of Appendix D.2 has the property, too.

17. The diligent virtual machine

In this chapter we distill from the incrementally defined defensive machine the analogously stepwise refined *diligent* virtual machine. It combines the trustful machine of Part II with a link-time bytecode verifier. We prove (Theorem 17.1.1) that this verifier is sound, i.e., that for each method in the class environment, the verifier either computes a bytecode type assignment in the sense of Chapter 16 or terminates with a `VerifyError`. We also prove (Theorem 17.1.2) the completeness of the verifier, i.e., that a) if there exists a bytecode type assignment for the body of a method, then the bytecode verifier computes a principal (most specific) type assignment; b) if the body of a method is not typeable, then the bytecode verifier returns a `VerifyError`. By the soundness of bytecode type assignments (Theorem 16.4.1) it follows that, if the bytecode verifier is successful, then the run-time checks of the defensive VM of Chapter 15 are always satisfied thus establishing the Main Theorem of this book.

17.1 Principal bytecode type assignments

Bytecode type assignments can be compared in the obvious way. We say that a type assignment $(reg\,V_i, opd\,V_i)_{i \in \mathcal{V}}$ is *more specific* than the type assignment $(reg\,T_i, opd\,T_i)_{i \in \mathcal{D}}$, if the following three conditions are satisfied:

1. $\mathcal{V} \subseteq \mathcal{D}$,
2. $reg\,V_i \sqsubseteq_{reg} reg\,T_i$ for each $i \in \mathcal{V}$,
3. $opd\,V_i \sqsubseteq_{seq} opd\,T_i$ for each $i \in \mathcal{V}$.

Hence a more specific type assignment assigns type frames to less code indices. It assigns more specific types to more local variables and it assigns more specific types to an operand stack of the same size. A most specific type assignment to bytecode is called a *principal type assignment*.

Let μ be the method which has to be verified. The bytecode verifier attempts to compute a bytecode type assignment $(reg\,V_i, opd\,V_i)_{i \in \mathcal{V}}$ for the method. At the beginning the set $\mathcal{V}$ consists of code index zero only. More indices are added to $\mathcal{V}$ whenever they can be reached by the computation which tries to propagate the already computed type frames to the possible successor indices. It can happen that during this process an index is revisited and the type frame for the index has to be changed. In this case the index is added to a set $\mathcal{C}$ of changed indices whereby it becomes subject to yet another verification step, namely the attempt to propagate its new type frame. The bytecode verifier proceeds until the set $\mathcal{C}$ is empty. It can be shown that the verifier always terminates. During the verification the following invariants are satisfied which correspond exactly to the seven conditions for bytecode type assignments in Def. 16.3.8. We formulate the invariants as a theorem which will be proved later.

Theorem 17.1.1 (Soundness of the verifier). Let μ be the method to be verified. During the verification process the following invariants are satisfied where $\mathcal{C} = dom(changed)$ and $\mathcal{V} = dom(visited)$:

I1. $\mathcal{C} \subseteq \mathcal{V}$ and $\mathcal{V}$ is a set of valid code indices of the method μ.

I2. Code index 0 belongs to $\mathcal{V}$.

I3. Let $[\tau_1, \ldots, \tau_n] = argTypes(\mu)$ and $c = classNm(\mu)$. If μ is a
    a) class initialization method: $regV_0 = \emptyset$.
    b) class method: $\{0 \mapsto \tau_1, \ldots, n-1 \mapsto \tau_n\} \sqsubseteq_{reg} regV_0$.
    c) instance method: $\{0 \mapsto c, 1 \mapsto \tau_1, \ldots, n \mapsto \tau_n\} \sqsubseteq_{reg} regV_0$.
    d) constructor: $\{0 \mapsto InInit, 1 \mapsto \tau_1, \ldots, n \mapsto \tau_n\} \sqsubseteq_{reg} regV_0$.
    (The constructor of class `Object` is treated as an instance method.)

I4. The list $opdV_0$ is empty.

I5. If $i \in \mathcal{V} \setminus \mathcal{C}$, then $check(\mu, i, regV_i, opdV_i)$ is true.

I6. If $i \in \mathcal{V} \setminus \mathcal{C}$ and $(j, regS, opdS) \in succ(\mu, i, regV_i, opdV_i)$, then
    $j \in \mathcal{V}$, $regS \sqsubseteq_{reg} regV_j$ and $opdS \sqsubseteq_{seq} opdV_j$.

I7. If $i \in \mathcal{V} \setminus \mathcal{C}$, $code(i) = Ret(x)$ and $regV_i(x) = \texttt{retAddr}(s)$, then for all reachable $j \in \mathcal{V} \setminus \mathcal{C}$ with $code(j) = Jsr(s)$:
    a) $j + 1 \in \mathcal{V}$,
    b) $regV_i \sqsubseteq_{reg} mod(s) \lhd regV_{j+1}$,
    c) $opdV_i \sqsubseteq_{seq} opdV_{j+1}$,
    d) $regV_j \sqsubseteq_{reg} mod(s) \lhd regV_{j+1}$,
    e) if $\texttt{retAddr}(\ell)$ occurs in $mod(s) \lhd regV_{j+1}$, then each code index which belongs to s belongs to l,
    f) neither $(c, k)_{new}$ nor $InInit$ occur in $mod(s) \lhd regV_{j+1}$.

I8. If $i \in \mathcal{V}$ and $\texttt{retAddr}(s)$ occurs in $regV_i$, then i belongs to s.
    If $i \in \mathcal{V}$ and $\texttt{retAddr}(s)$ occurs in $opdV_i$, then $i = s$.

If the set $\mathcal{C}$ of changed code indices is empty, then I1–I8 are equivalent to the conditions T1–T8 of Def. 16.3.8 and the verifier has computed a bytecode type assignment. Conversely, if the method to be verified has a bytecode type assignment, then the bytecode type assignment computed by the verifier will be more specific. In other words, the verifier is complete.

Theorem 17.1.2 (Completeness of the verifier). If the method μ has a bytecode type assignment $(regT_i, opdT_i)_{i \in \mathcal{D}}$, then during the verification process $(regV_i, opdV_i)_{i \in \mathcal{V}}$ will always be more specific than $(regT_i, opdT_i)_{i \in \mathcal{D}}$ and no `VerifyError` will occur.

We are going now to define a sequence of four *diligent* virtual machines and to prove soundness and completeness for their verifier.

17.2 Verifying JVM$_\mathcal{I}$

In this section we define the verifier component for JVM$_\mathcal{I}$. In each step, if no verification failure did occur yet, the verifier chooses an instruction pc to be verified and (if possible) propagates the so far computed type frame to each of the possible successor instructions of pc. It checks the applicability of an instruction using the *check* function of the *defensive VM* in Chapter 15. To determine the successor type-frame, the function *succ* of Chapter 16 is used.

State. To simulate the type state we introduce type registers and a type operand stack. Since the verifier simulates the effect for all possible (immediate) successors of an instruction (within a single frame), two dynamic functions $regV$ and $opdV$ store the type registers and the type stack for each instruction. They are the verifier analogue of the type component functions $regT$ and $opdT$ of the defensive VM in Chapter 15 and are initially undefined for every $i \neq 0$; $opdV_0$ is initialized by the empty stack and $regV_0$ by the types of the method arguments and of the target reference. The other functions $opdV_i$ and $regV_i$ ($i \neq 0$) are initially undefined. Additionally, we need two dynamic functions *changed* and *visited* which control the way the verification runs through the code.

$$
\begin{array}{ll}
regV & : Nat \rightarrow Map(RegNo, VerifyType) \\
opdV & : Nat \rightarrow VerifyType^* \\
visited & : Nat \rightarrow Bool \\
changed & : Nat \rightarrow Bool
\end{array}
$$

The *visited* function represents those code indices that already have a type frame assigned by the functions $regV$ and $opdV$. The *changed* function always holds those instruction indices that are not verified yet, meaning that the type frame associated to them has still to be checked for a possible propagation to the successor indices. Initially $changed(0) = True = visited(0)$ and $changed(i) = undef = visited(i)$ for $i \neq 0$.

Rules. Verification always starts with the first instruction at index 0. In JVM$_\mathcal{I}$ the verification has successfully finished if the domain of *changed* (i.e., where the function takes a value which is different from *undef*) is empty so that the trustful VM can be executed.

$$diligentVM_I =$$
$$\textbf{if } dom(changed) \neq \emptyset \textbf{ then}$$
$$verifyScheme_I(code, maxOpd, propagateVM_I, succ_I, check_I)$$
$$\textbf{else}$$
$$trustfulVM_I$$

We define a verification scheme for reuse in the following sections. The *verifyScheme$_I$* chooses an arbitrary instruction that needs to be verified. The type frame associated to this instruction is checked and, if in the current state *check* (see Chapter 15) yields *False*, the machine stops (reporting failure). Otherwise the current type frame is propagated and the instruction is marked as verified.

$$verifyScheme_I(code, maxOpd, propagateVM, succ, check) =$$
$$\textbf{choose } pc \in dom(changed)$$
$$\textbf{if } check(code(pc), maxOpd, pc, regV_{pc}, opdV_{pc}) \textbf{ then}$$
$$changed(pc) := undef$$
$$propagateVM(code, succ, pc)$$
$$\textbf{else}$$
$$halt := \texttt{"Verification failed"}$$

In *propagateVM$_I$* the type registers and the type operand stack resulting from the type simulation step are propagated to every successor whereby these successor indices become subject to verification. Successor type frames are computed in *diligentVM$_I$* by the function *succ$_I$* of Fig. 16.12.

$$propagateVM_I(code, succ, pc) =$$
$$\textbf{forall } (s, regS, opdS) \in succ(code(pc), pc, regV_{pc}, opdV_{pc})$$
$$propagateSucc(code, s, regS, opdS)$$

The *propagateSucc* rule works as follows: If the index s of the successor instruction has not been seen previously by the verifier and if it is a valid index in the method to be verified, the result of the simulation is copied to the successor instruction and the instruction is marked as visited but not yet verified. The assignment is restricted for retAddr-types to satisfy condition I8. If the successor instruction has been seen before and the two type stacks are compatible ($\sqsubseteq_{seq}$) and the newly computed type registers are a superset of and compatible with those registers that are already stored at the instruction ($\sqsubseteq_{reg}$), then the destination needs no further checking and the type state of the successor instruction remains unchanged.

$$validReg(\texttt{retAddr}(l), pc) = pc \in belongsTo(l)$$
$$validReg(t, pc) \qquad\quad = True$$

$$validOpd(\texttt{retAddr}(l), pc) = (l = pc)$$
$$validOpd(t, pc) \qquad\quad = True$$

$propagateSucc(code, s, regS, opdS) =$
   if $s \notin dom(visited)$ **then**
      if $validCodeIndex(code, s)$ **then**
        $regV_s$ $:= \{(x, t) \mid (x, t) \in regS, validReg(t, s)\}$
        $opdV_s$ $:= [\textbf{if } validOpd(t, s) \textbf{ then } t \textbf{ else } \textbf{unusable} \mid t \in opdS]$
        $visited(s)$ $:= True$
        $changed(s) := True$
      else
        $halt :=$ `"Verification failed (invalid code index)"`
   elseif $regS \sqsubseteq_{\mathrm{reg}} regV_s \wedge opdS \sqsubseteq_{\mathrm{seq}} opdV_s$ **then**
      $skip$
   elseif $length(opdS) = length(opdV_s)$ **then**
      $regV_s$ $:= regV_s \sqcup_{\mathrm{reg}} regS$
      $opdV_s$ $:= opdV_s \sqcup_{\mathrm{opd}} opdS$
      $changed(s) := True$
   else
      $halt :=$ `"Propagate failed"`

Otherwise if the operand stacks have the same length, we merge the stacks and the registers. If the lengths of the stacks differ, then propagation is not possible. For primitive types t_1 and t_2 we denote by $t_1 \sqcup t_2$ the least upper bound of the two types according to Def. 15.4.1.

$$t_1 \sqcup t_2 = \textbf{if } t_1 = t_2 \textbf{ then } t_1 \textbf{ else } \textbf{unusable}$$

$$opdS \sqcup_{\mathrm{opd}} opdV = [s \sqcup v \mid (s, v) \in zip(opdS, opdV)]$$

$$regS \sqcup_{\mathrm{reg}} regT = \{(x, t) \mid (x, t) \in regs, t \neq \textbf{unusable}\}$$
$$\textbf{where } regs = \{(x, regS(x) \sqcup regT(x)) \mid x \in dom(regS) \cap dom(regT)\}$$

The merging of verify types has the following properties:

1. $t_1 \sqsubseteq t_1 \sqcup t_2$,
2. $t_2 \sqsubseteq t_1 \sqcup t_2$,
3. if $t_1 \sqsubseteq s$ and $t_2 \sqsubseteq s$, then $t_1 \sqcup t_2 \sqsubseteq s$.

Similar properties hold for the merging of operand stacks ($\sqcup_{\mathrm{opd}}$ with respect to $\sqsubseteq_{\mathrm{seq}}$) and the merging of registers ($\sqcup_{\mathrm{reg}}$ with respect to $\sqsubseteq_{\mathrm{reg}}$). (We assume that the type **unusable** is not used in register types. It is allowed on the operand stacks only.)

The verification process in the $diligentVM_I$ terminates. Each instruction is checked only a finite number of times. Each merge introduces at least one new occurrence of the type **unusable** or reduces the domain of the type register function whose domain is finite. Therefore either the rules are not applicable (in which case it terminates because of failure detection) or $dom(changed)$ eventually becomes empty so that the trustful VM will be executed.

We have to show that the verifier is sound and complete. For the soundness we have to check that the invariants I1–I6 are satisfied during the verification process (I7 is empty for the $diligentVM_I$).

Proof. (Theorem 17.1.1) Let $\mathcal{V} = dom(visited)$ and $\mathcal{C} = dom(changed)$. The set $\mathcal{C}$ is always a subset of $\mathcal{V}$, since a new code index is added to $\mathcal{C}$ only in the *propagateSucc* rule. $\mathcal{V}$ contains only valid code indices. In fact either the index is visited for the first time and is added to $\mathcal{V}$ because it is a valid code index of the verified method, or, in case of a merge, we know that the index has already been visited. Hence invariant I1 is satisfied.

The verification starts at code index 0 with empty operand stack type assignment (I4) and register type assignment reflecting the argument types of the method and possibly the type of the target reference (I3). Hence in particular 0 belongs to $\mathcal{V}$ (I2).

At the beginning of the verification process I5 holds because by initialization $\mathcal{V} \setminus \mathcal{C}$ is empty. A code index is removed from $\mathcal{C}$ in *verifyScheme$_I$* only if its type frame satisfies the *check* predicate, so that I5 is satisfied also during the verification process.

If a code index is removed from $\mathcal{C}$, then the *propagate VM$_I$* rule enforces the invariant I6 about the successor indices.

Invariant I8 remains true, since in *propagateSucc* invalid types are deleted or replaced by `unusable`, when a new code index is added to $\mathcal{V}$.   □

What remains to be shown is that if the bytecode has a type assignment $(regT_i, opdT_i)_{i \in \mathcal{D}}$, then the verification process does not fail and the so far computed $(regV_i, opdV_i)_{i \in \mathcal{V}}$ is always more specific (as defined at the beginning of Sect. 17.1).

Proof. (Theorem 17.1.2) The initial assignment $(regV_0, opdV_0)$ with which the verifier starts satisfies the completeness condition, namely by properties T1–T4 of bytecode type assignments.

We prove now that the condition is preserved under each verification step (induction on the choose steps). Assume that *verifyScheme$_I$* chooses a code index $pc \in \mathcal{C}$ and let $instr = code(pc)$. Since $\mathcal{C}$ is a subset of $\mathcal{V}$ and $\mathcal{V}$ is by the induction hypothesis a subset of $\mathcal{D}$, we know by T5 that the function $check(instr, maxOpd, pc, regT_{pc}, opdT_{pc})$ returns true. By the induction hypothesis $regV_{pc}$ and $opdV_{pc}$ are more specific than $regT_{pc}$ and $opdT_{pc}$ so that by the monotonicity of the check functions (Lemma 15.7.1), it follows that the function $check(instr, maxOpd, pc, regV_{pc}, opdV_{pc})$ returns true as well and the verifier proceeds and propagates the successors.

Assume that $(s, regS, opdS)$ is one of the successors with respect to $regV_{pc}$ and $opdV_{pc}$. By the monotonicity of successors (Lemma 16.2.1), we know that there exists also a successor $(s, regU, opdU)$ of pc with respect to the less specific type frame $(regT_{pc}, opdT_{pc})$ such that

$$regS \sqsubseteq_{\text{reg}} regU \text{ and } opdS \sqsubseteq_{\text{seq}} opdU.$$

By T6 in Def. 16.3.8, we have that $s \in \mathcal{D}$ and

$regU \sqsubseteq_{\mathrm{reg}} regT_s$ and $opdU \sqsubseteq_{\mathrm{seq}} opdT_s$.

By the transitivity of $\sqsubseteq_{\mathrm{reg}}$ and $\sqsubseteq_{\mathrm{seq}}$, it follows that

$regS \sqsubseteq_{\mathrm{reg}} regT_s$ and $opdS \sqsubseteq_{\mathrm{seq}} opdT_s$.

By T1, $s \in \mathcal{D}$ implies that s is a valid code index in the given method.

If the index s is visited for the first time in $propagateSucc$, then $regV_s$ is set to $regS'$ and $opdV_s$ to $opdS'$, where $regS'$ is obtained from $regS$ by deleting all invalid return addresses and $opdS'$ is replaced from $opdS$ by replacing all invalid return addresses by unusable. A return address retAddr(l) for a register is valid, if s belongs to the subroutine l (Def. 16.3.6). A return address retAddr(l) is valid on the operand stack only if $s = l$. We have to show that

$regS' \sqsubseteq_{\mathrm{reg}} regT_s$ and $opdS' \sqsubseteq_{\mathrm{seq}} opdT_s$.

Assume that the register x is defined in $regT_s$. Then x is defined in $regS$ and $regS(x) \sqsubseteq regT_s(x)$. If $reg(S) = $ retAddr(l), then $regT_s(x) = $ retAddr(l), since the type unusable does not occur in $regT_s$. By T8, s belongs to l. Therefore x is defined in $regS'$ and $regS'(x) = regS(x) \sqsubseteq regT_s(x)$.

Assume that k is a location on the operand stack. Then $opdS(k) \sqsubseteq opdT_s(k)$. Assume that $opdS(k) = $ retAddr(l) and $s \neq l$. Then $opdT_s(k) = $ unusable or $opdT_s(k) = $ retAddr(l). In the first case we have $opdS'(k) \sqsubseteq opdT_s(k)$. The second case is not possible by T8.

If the successor index has been seen before we know by the induction hypothesis that

$regV_s \sqsubseteq_{\mathrm{reg}} regT_s$ and $opdV_s \sqsubseteq_{\mathrm{seq}} opdT_s$.

If ($regS, opdS$) is more specific than ($regV_s, opdV_s$), then the verifier does not change the so far computed type assignment. Otherwise, since

$opdS \sqsubseteq_{\mathrm{seq}} opdT_s$ and $opdV_s \sqsubseteq_{\mathrm{seq}} opdT_s$,

both stacks have the same length and can be merged. By the properties of least upper bounds, we can conclude that

$regV_s \sqcup_{\mathrm{reg}} regS \sqsubseteq_{\mathrm{reg}} regT_s$ and $opdV_s \sqcup_{\mathrm{opd}} opdS \sqsubseteq_{\mathrm{seq}} opdT_s$,

and the new type assignment remains more specific.   □

17.3 Verifying JVM$_C$

In this section we apply the $verifyScheme_I$ to all methods of a given class or interface and instantiate the resulting $diligentScheme$ with the $trustfulVM_C$ and with the successor and check functions $succ_C$, $check_C$.

In JVM$_C$ a class or interface must be successfully verified before it is initialized. The verifier has to verify every method of a class. If each method invocation and return can be guaranteed to be type correct, the verifier can check each method individually. The type correctness of method invocation is taken care of by starting the verification of the method with the types of its formal parameters; the type correctness of returning from a method is verified by checking for return instructions the top of the operand type frame against the return type of the method. In this way the *diligentVM$_C$* can be obtained from the *diligentVM$_I$* by applying the bytecode verification to all methods of the class to be verified.

State. In order to make our model close to an executable model, instead of checking all methods in parallel we choose a not furthermore specified but fixed order for method verification. This requires the following extension of the state of *diligentVM$_I$*. A new dynamic function *verifyClass* contains the class to be verified. The dynamic function *verifyMeths* holds all methods of the class to be verified.

> *verifyClass*: *Class*
> *verifyMeths*: *Class* / *MSig**
> *meth$_v$* = *top*(*verifyMeths*)

Verification starts with the first method of *verifyMeths*, abbreviated as *meth$_v$*. We leave the particular ordering of *verifyMeths* unspecified, as well as the corresponding functions *top*, *drop*, *null* which are used to walk through *verifyMeths* in an attempt to exhaust it. Verification succeeds, if all instructions of all methods are verified.

Rules. We define a scheme for the diligent JVM$_C$ which iterates a refinement of the verifier of the diligent JVM$_I$. As long as a class is not verified (and the verification did not fail) the verification process proceeds. After the class has been verified, the VM continues with the trustful code execution.

> *diligentScheme*(*verifyVM*, *execVM*) =
>   **if** ¬*isChecked* **then**
>   *verifyVM*
>   **else**
>   *execVM*

The top level guard *isChecked* tests whether there is still some instruction in some method of the class to verify.

> *isChecked* = (*null*(*verifyMeths*) ∧ *dom*(*changed*) = ∅)

The diligent JVM$_C$ is obtained by instantiating the scheme:

> *diligentVM$_C$* = *diligentScheme*(*verifyVM*, *trustfulVM$_C$*)
>   **where** *verifyVM* = *verifyScheme$_C$*(*propagateVM$_I$*, *succ$_C$*, *check$_C$*)

The *verifyScheme$_C$* is the *verifyScheme$_I$* extended by resetting the verifier, once a method of the class has been successfully verified, for the verification of the next method to verify, and by updating the verification status of the class to *Linked* once all its methods have been verified successfully.

$verifyScheme_C(propagate VM, succ, check) =$
  if $dom(changed) \neq \emptyset$ **then**
    $verifyScheme_I(code(meth_v), maxOpd(meth_v), propagate VM,$
              $succ(meth_v), check(meth_v))$
  else
    let $verifyMeths' = drop(verifyMeths, 1)$
    $verifyMeths := verifyMeths'$
    if $length(verifyMeths') > 0$ **then**
      $initVerify(top(verifyMeths'))$
    else
      $classState(verifyClass) := Linked$

Whenever a method is verified, the verifier drops it from the still to be verified methods in *verifyMeths* and resets its dynamic functions to their initial state for the next method to be verified using the following *initVerify* rule. This rule formalizes the assumptions made for the initial verifier state in *diligentVM$_I$*.

$initVerify(meth) =$
  $visited(0)$ $:= True$
  $changed(0) := True$
  $regV_0$ $:= formals(meth)$
  $opdV_0$ $:= []$
  forall $i \in dom(visited), i \neq 0$
    $visited(i)$ $:= undef$
    $changed(i) := undef$
    $regV_i$ $:= undef$
    $opdV_i$ $:= undef$

The type correctness of method invocation is guaranteed by using the argument types of the method as initial assignments for the type registers, described by a static function *formals*, to be refined for instance methods and constructors in Sect. 17.4:

$formals(c/m) = $ **if** $isStatic(c/m)$ **then** $makeRegs(argTypes(c/m))$

We have to extend the *switchVM$_C$* of the *trustfulVM* in Fig. 10.2 in order to support verifying of classes before class initialization. When the trustful VM switches to the initialization of a class which has not yet been linked, the diligent VM triggers a submachine to link this class. For this purpose the universe *ClassState* is extended.

data $ClassState = \dots \mid Referenced$

A class can be in one of the states *Referenced*, *Linked*, *Initialized* or *Unusable*. We assume in this chapter that at the beginning all classes are referenced.

$switchVM_C =$
  $\dots$
  case $switch$ **of**
    $InitClass(c) \rightarrow$ **if** $classState(c) = Referenced$ **then**
              $linkClass(c)$

Linking a class or interface c involves linking (i.e., verifying and preparing) c, its direct superclass and its direct superinterfaces. If the superclass of c and all its direct superinterfaces are already linked or if c is `Object`, the verification of c is started. Otherwise the linking submachine is triggered for one of the still to be linked superinterfaces or the superclass of c—unless a class circularity error is detected. Due to the finiteness of the class inheritance, the recursive calls of the submachine *linkClass* terminate. If any of the superclasses or superinterfaces of c is c itself, then the class hierarchy is cyclic and the VM stops with an error.[1]

> $linkClass(c) =$
>   **let** $classes = \{super(c)\} \cup implements(c)$
>   **if** $c = $ `Object` $\vee\ \forall\ c' \in classes : classState(c') \geq Linked$ **then**
> $prepareVerify(c)$
>   **elseif** $\neg cyclicInheritance(c)$ **then**
>   **choose** $c' \in classes, classState(c') = Referenced$
> $linkClass(c')$
>   **else**
> $halt := $ `"Cyclic Inheritance: "` $\cdot\ classNm(c)$

There is a preparatory test for starting the verification, namely checking the format of the class file and the static constraints for the method bodies (see Appendix C.6 for a definition of the predicate *constraintViolation*).

> $prepareVerify(c) =$
>   **if** $constraintViolation(c)$ **then**
> $halt := violationMsg(classNm(c))$
>   **else**
>   **let** $verifyMeths' = [(c/m) \mid m \in dom(methods(cEnv(c))),$
> $\neg null(code(c/m))]$
> $verifyMeths := verifyMeths'$
> $verifyClass := c$
> $initVerify(top(verifyMeths'))$
> $prepareClass(c)$

Preparing the class involves creating its static fields and initializing those fields to their standard values.

> $prepareClass(c) =$
>   **forall** $f \in staticFields(c)$
> $globals(c/f) := defaultVal(type(c/f))$

In the diligent VM, only after a class has been successfully verified and prepared for initialization, it is initialized by executing its `<clinit>` method (see Fig. 10.2).

---

[1] The real JVM throws a `ClassCircularityError`.

17.4 Verifying JVM$_\mathcal{O}$

In this section we instantiate the *diligentScheme* by the *trustfulVM$_O$* and the extension of the *verifyScheme$_C$* by *succ$_O$* and *check$_O$*.

Verification of JVM$_\mathcal{O}$ code has to consider, in a run-time independent way, the impact of instance methods and instance fields, of subtypes, and of object initialization. Checking instance methods and instance fields raises no new problem but requires slight modifications. The most obvious is, that the initialization of the verifier must be adapted to prepend the target reference of instance methods and constructors before the parameter types. For a constructor not in class `Object` the target reference has type *InInit*. In all other cases the type of the target reference is the class of the method. The derived function *formals* is therefore refined by:

$formals(c/m) =$
  if *isStatic*(c/m) **then** *makeRegs*$(argTypes(c/m))$
  elseif *methNm*$(m) =$ "`<init>`" $\wedge\ c \neq$ `Object` **then**
    makeRegs$([InInit] \cdot argTypes(c/m))$
  else
    makeRegs$([c] \cdot argTypes(c/m))$

Because of the subtype relation two different class types can be merged to a common ancestor in the class tree and not to the type `unusable` as in the case of primitive types. A common ancestor of two class types, however, can also be an interface type. In general, two reference types can have several least ancestor types. Therefore we work with sets of reference types (see Sect. 16.1.2). The least upper bound $\sqcup$ of two sets of reference types with respect to the compatibility relation $\sqsubseteq$ in Def. 16.1.2 is simply their union.

$rs_1 \sqcup rs_2 = rs_1 \cup rs_2$

The least upper bound of a set of reference types and a verify type which is not a set of reference types is the type `unusable`.

The *diligentVM$_O$* is obtained by instantiating the *diligentScheme* with the check function *check$_O$*, the successor function *succ$_O$* and the *trustfulVM$_O$*.

$diligentVM_O = diligentScheme(verifyVM, trustfulVM_O)$
  where *verifyVM* $= verifyScheme_C(propagateVM_I, succ_O, check_O)$

Reference types require that instructions might be checked several times. Nevertheless, the verification process terminates. The type states can be merged only a finite number of times: the domains of the type state functions are finite and the number of reference types in a program is finite.

17.5 Verifying JVM$_\mathcal{E}$

This section extends the verifier for the object-oriented machine to verify also the constraints which are related to exceptions and embedded subroutines. The *diligentVM$_E$* is obtained by instantiating the *diligentScheme* with a refinement $propagate VM_E$ of $propagate VM_I$ by rules for Jsr and Ret instructions, and with $succ_E$, $check_E$ and $trustful VM_E$ instead of $succ_O$, $check_O$ and $trustful VM_O$.

$$diligent VM_E = diligentScheme(verify VM, trustful VM_E)$$
$$\textbf{where } verify VM = verifyScheme_C(propagate VM_E, succ_E, check_E)$$

The extended rule $propagate VM_E$ completes the definition of the function $succ_E$ in Fig. 16.15 by propagating type frames also to the successors of Ret instructions, namely to the direct successors $j + 1$ of all code indices j from where the corresponding subroutine may possibly have been called. As we will prove below, this is done in such a way that the invariant I7 from Theorem 17.1.1 is satisfied for indices in $\mathcal{V} \setminus \mathcal{C}$, where $\mathcal{V} = dom(visited)$ and $\mathcal{C} = dom(changed)$.

$$propagate VM_E(code, succ, pc) =$$
$$propagate VM_I(code, succ, pc)$$
$$\textbf{case } code(pc) \textbf{ of}$$
$$\quad Jsr(s) \rightarrow enterJsr(s) := \{pc\} \cup enterJsr(s)$$
$$\quad\quad \textbf{forall } (i, x) \in leaveJsr(s), i \notin dom(changed)$$
$$\quad\quad\quad \textbf{if } reg V_i(x) = \texttt{retAddr}(s) \textbf{ then}$$
$$\quad\quad\quad\quad propagateJsr(code, pc, s, i)$$
$$\quad Ret(x) \rightarrow \textbf{let } \texttt{retAddr}(s) = reg V_{pc}(x)$$
$$\quad\quad\quad leaveJsr(s) := \{(pc, x)\} \cup leaveJsr(s)$$
$$\quad\quad\quad \textbf{forall } j \in enterJsr(s), j \notin dom(changed)$$
$$\quad\quad\quad\quad propagateJsr(code, j, s, pc)$$

The rule $propagate VM_E$ takes also care that during the verification process, the set $enterJsr(s)$ contains exactly the code indices of visited instructions $Jsr(s)$, i.e.,

$$enterJsr(s) = \{j \in \mathcal{V} \mid code(j) = Jsr(s)\}.$$

Similarly $propagate VM_E$ computes the set $leaveJsr(s)$, a superset of the following set:

$$\{(i, x) \mid i \in \mathcal{V}, \ code(i) = Ret(x), \ reg V_i(x) = \texttt{retAddr}(s)\}.$$

The equality does not hold, because the type of a local register can disappear in a merge.

$$propagateJsr(code, j, s, i) =$$
$$propagateSucc(code, j + 1, regJ \oplus mod(s) \lhd reg V_i, opd V_i) \textbf{ where}$$
$$\quad regJ = \{(x, t) \mid (x, t) \in mod(s) \lhd reg V_j,$$
$$\quad\quad\quad validJump(t, s) \wedge t \neq (\_, \_)_{new} \wedge t \neq InInit\}$$

$$validJump(\texttt{retAddr}(l), s) = belongsTo(s) \subseteq belongsTo(l)$$
$$validJump(t, s) \qquad\qquad = True$$

Except for the initialization of the new functions when the verification of a method starts, which will be given below, this completes the definition of the $diligent VM_E$. It remains to show that the additional propagation rule $propagate VM_E$ is sound and complete.

Proof. (Theorem 17.1.1, continued) Assume the rule *propagateJsr*(*code*, j, s, i) has been applied without producing a failure. Then we know that i and j are in $\mathcal{V} \setminus \mathcal{C}$ and

- $code(j) = Jsr(s)$
- $code(i) = Ret(x)$
- $regV_i(x) = \mathtt{retAddr}(s)$

We have to show that the type frame propagation to the successor $j + 1$ satisfies conditions (a)–(f) of I7.

$j + 1 \in \mathcal{V}$ holds because the *validCodeIndex* test was passed successfully.

PropagateJsr propagates the new stack from i to $j + 1$, simulating a possible return from the subroutine. In this way we ensure condition (c) of invariant I7.

The types for the registers which are propagated to $j + 1$ are a combination of the types at j where the subroutine has been called and the types at i where the subroutine returns.

Let us call a type *invalid*, if it is a return address type $\mathtt{retAddr}(\ell)$ such that the subroutine s is not contained in ℓ.

If a register is modified by the subroutine, then its type from i is propagated. Otherwise the register disappears at $j + 1$. This implies condition (b) of invariant I7. If a register is not modified by the subroutine, then its type from j is propagated if this type is valid and different from $(\_, \_)_{new}$ and *InInit*. Otherwise the register disappears at $j+1$. This implies conditions (d)–(f) of invariant I7.   □

Proof. (Theorem 17.1.2, continued) Assume that the method we are verifying has a bytecode type assignment $(regT_i, opdT_i)_{i \in \mathcal{D}}$.

When *propagateJsr*(*code*, j, s, i) is called we know by the induction hypothesis that

$$regV_j \sqsubseteq_{\mathrm{reg}} regT_j \text{ and } opdV_j \sqsubseteq_{\mathrm{seq}} opdT_j,$$

$$regV_i \sqsubseteq_{\mathrm{reg}} regT_i \text{ and } opdV_i \sqsubseteq_{\mathrm{seq}} opdT_i.$$

We have to show that in the next step of the verification, after the successors have been propagated to $j + 1$, the following holds:

$$regV_{j+1} \sqsubseteq_{\mathrm{reg}} regT_{j+1} \text{ and } opdV_{j+1} \sqsubseteq_{\mathrm{seq}} opdT_{j+1}.$$

It is enough to show that

$$regJ \oplus (mod(s) \lhd regV_i) \sqsubseteq_{\mathrm{reg}} regT_{j+1} \text{ and } opdV_i \sqsubseteq_{\mathrm{seq}} opdT_{j+1}.$$

By T7 (b), we know that $regT_i \sqsubseteq_{\mathrm{reg}} mod(s) \lhd regT_{j+1}$ and then we use that $regV_i \sqsubseteq_{\mathrm{reg}} regT_i$.

By T7 (c), we know that $opdT_i \sqsubseteq_{\mathrm{seq}} opdT_{j+1}$.

By T7 (d), we know that $regT_j \sqsubseteq_{\mathrm{reg}} mod(s) \lhd regT_{j+1}$ and then we use that $regV_j \sqsubseteq_{\mathrm{reg}} regT_j$.

What remains to be shown is that $regJ(x) \sqsubseteq regT_{j+1}(x)$, if x is defined in $regT_{j+1}$ and $x \notin mod(s)$.

Assume that x is not modified by subroutine s and x is defined in $regT_{j+1}$. Then x is also defined in $regV_j$, $regV_j(x)$ is a valid jump for s and different from $(\_,\_)_{new}$ and $InInit$, because otherwise condition T7 (e) or (f) of Def. 16.3.8 would be violated. Hence, the local variable x is defined in $regJ$ and $regJ(x) = regV_j(x)$, therefore $regJ(x) \sqsubseteq regT_{j+1}(x)$.   □

At the beginning of the verification of a method the new functions $enterJsr$ and $leaveJsr$ have to be initialized, so that we refine the $initVerify$ rule as follows:

> $initVerify(meth) = \ldots$
>   **forall** $s \in dom(enterJsr)$
> $enterJsr(s) := \emptyset$
>   **forall** $s \in dom(leaveJsr)$
> $leaveJsr(s) := \emptyset$

In the retrospective it is confirmed that verifying embedded subroutines is not trivial, whereas checking embedded subroutines posed no particular problems. This is the reason why we started with the checking machine before developing the verifier by imposing necessary and sufficient conditions which are checkable at link-time on the code.

Proof. (Main Theorem) Let any well-formed and well-typed Java program P be given, let $P_C = compile(P)$ for the compiler defined in Part II. By Theorem 16.5.2 P_C has a bytecode type assignment. Therefore by Theorem 17.1.2, P_C passes successfully the bytecode verifier in the diligent VM, so that it will be trustfully executed by the submachine *trustfulVM* of diligent VM without violating any run-time checks (by Theorem 16.4.1) and by Theorem 14.1.1 with the same semantical effect as P has on the machine *execJava* defined in Part I.   □

17.6 Verifying JVM$_{\mathcal{N}}$

Native methods cannot be verified because they are implemented in foreign languages. If a native method changes the state of the VM in an unsafe way, there could be type violations at run-time.

$verifyScheme_N(check) =$
  if $changed(0) \wedge isNative(meth_v)$ **then**
    if $check(meth_v)$ **then**
      $changed(0) := undef$
    else
      $halt :=$ `"Verification failed"`
  else
    $verifyScheme_C(propagate\,VM_E, succ_E, check_E)$

$diligent\,VM_N = diligentScheme(verify\,VM, trustful\,VM_N)$
  where $verify\,VM = verifyScheme_N(check_N)$

What our verifier ensures is that the only methods which can be declared as native methods are `equal` and `clone`. (The executable AsmGofer model in Appendix A contains further native methods).

18. The dynamic virtual machine

In this chapter we refine the virtual machines of the previous chapters to a dynamic machine that incorporates dynamic loading and linking of classes. This involves new rules for class loader methods and an extension of $switchVM_E$ to $switchVM_D$ to cope with referencing loaded classes (together with their superclasses) before they are linked.

The previous machines assume that a JVM program and all referenced classes are already loaded so that the class environment is static. However, the real JVM is dynamic: it loads and links classes as they are needed.

Dynamic loading [23, §5.3] is the process of finding a binary form, which during linking involving preparation and verification as described in Chapter 17, is integrated into the run-time state.

The environment as seen by a running JVM program, that is the set of loaded classes, is partitioned into separate name spaces. In JDK 1.2 there is one name space for classes that come from the local file system, and a separate name space for each network source. To each loaded class its loader is attached as part of the entire class name; in this way each class is placed into the "private" loader determined name space, which is taken into account when checking the type compatibility of class instances.

18.1 Initiating and defining loaders

A class loader, when invoked to load a class, might delegate the loading process to another class loader, i.e., there may be a chain of delegation. In such a case the first class loader is called an *initiating* loader. The loader which eventually loads the class and incorporates the class into the environment is called a *defining* loader. Two classes are equal iff they have the same name, where the loader part of the name refers to the defining loader. It is possible that two classes, loaded by different initiating loaders, are defined by the same loader. This is the reason why we have to attach the defining loader to the class name instead of the initiating loader.

If a class C references other classes, the defining loader of class C is used to load the references if they are not already loaded by that loader. For example, if C is defined by loader L and the super class of C is Object, then the loader L is used to load class Object. The loader L can load the class directly (becoming the defining loader) or it may delegate the loading to another loader. The JVM environment provides a system class loader which loads classes from the local file system.

Since the system loader does not delegate loading, all references of a class loaded by the system loader are also loaded by the system loader. Therefore, local classes, which are typically built-in classes, cannot reference non-local classes. This avoids the problem of type "spoofing" local classes.

18.2 Loading classes

When the JVM needs access to a particular class, it is up to a class loader to provide the class. Internally each class is represented as an instance of class Class. In JDK 1.2 the built-in system class loader is used to load classes from the local file system in a platform dependent manner. Additionally, Java programmers can define their own class loaders by subclassing the built-in class ClassLoader and implementing the loadClass method. The system class loader is an instance of this class. The programming interface is as follows:

```
public abstract class ClassLoader {
  protected final Class findLoadedClass(String name);
  protected final Class findSystemClass(String name)
    throws ClassNotFoundException;
  protected final Class defineClass(String name, byte[] data,
    int offset, int length) throws ClassFormatError;
  protected abstract Class loadClass(String name)
    throws ClassNotFoundException;
  protected final void resolveClass(Class c)
    throws NullPointerException;
}
```

The class loader takes care of loading and linking, although the name ClassLoader might suggest that it is only responsible for loading and not linking. User defined class loaders customize the load phase; class loaders do not differ in the way they link classes. Linking is done by the method resolveClass.

When a class has to be linked, then it must have been loaded before. When loading a class, all its non-loaded super classes (if any) must be loaded as well, from bottom to top in the inheritance hierarchy. During this step these classes are not linked. When a class is going to be linked, then during the link phase all its non linked super classes (if any) are linked from top to bottom in the inheritance tree.

In the JVM dynamic loading and linking is triggered by (constant pool) resolution. When the machine executes an instruction that references a class, field or method, it first checks whether the referenced class exists in the sense defined below. In case it does not, the JVM invokes the loadClass method of the class loader that defined the referencing class, to load the referenced class. If `loadClass` is called for a class that the loader has already loaded, then the method should simply return that class. The system class loader is implemented in that way. A class exists in the name space of a class loader, if the loader is an initiating or defining loader for that class.

As a consequence `loadClass` methods typically perform the following three steps, reflecting the programming interface defined above.

1. If the invoked class loader has already loaded the required class, it finds the previously defined class object using the method `findLoadedClass`. Upon successful search, `findLoadedClass` returns the previously defined class object (which is also returned by `loadClass`).
2. If `findLoadedClass` returns *null*, the system class loader is consulted using the method `findSystemClass`. This method tries to load the class from the local domain and to link it. If and when loading the class is successful, all (including the previously non-loaded) super classes are required to be loaded, as well. Furthermore, the `findSystemClass` method links the class and every non linked super class. If `findSystemClass` is successful, it returns the loaded and linked class object (which is also returned by `loadClass`), otherwise `findSystemClass` throws a `ClassNotFoundException`.
3. If no local class can be found (a `ClassNotFoundException` was thrown in the previous step), the class file is read from the origin of the referencing class and a class object is constructed from the read bytecodes using `defineClass`. Incorporating the new class into the run-time state triggers implicit loading of all super classes. Yet, at this time the loaded class and its super classes are *not* linked. If `defineClass` completes normally, it returns the constructed class object (which is also returned by `loadClass`), otherwise `defineClass` throws a `ClassFormatError`. In this case `loadClass` will also throw an exception.

Alternatively the class loader can delegate the loading to another class loader by invoking the `loadClass` method of that loader.

18.3 Dynamic semantics of the JVM$_\mathcal{D}$

The specification of dynamic loading and linking in the dynamic VM proceeds in three steps. First, we refine the run-time state. Second, we define loading of references. Third, we adapt the rules of the previous JVM models.

18.3.1 Refinement of the run-time state

Class loader instances are references. We use a universe Ld—a subset of the universe of references—for class loader instances. The system class loader $sysLd$ is a distinguished element of this subset.

$sysLd$: Ld
type $Ld = Ref$

Since each class loader has its own name space, a single JVM program can load multiple classes which have the same name. If classes with the same name have been loaded into different name spaces, the identity of the class loader that defined the class is needed to uniquely identify the class. As a consequence, we refine the notion of classes (and thereby of their fields and methods) by adding a loader component to their names. We refine the universe *Class* to include the loader information.

type $Class = (Ld, Name)$

The defining class loader (which incorporates the class into the JVM environment) is used as the loader component in all entries where the loader information is needed in a class file. For example, if class C is defined by loader L and C has syntactically a super class D, then the class file of C has an entry (L, D) for its super class. The loader L will be the initiating loader for D. Sometimes we write also D^L instead of (L, D). The same applies to all other entries in the class file. Later, we change the loader component of these entries if the defining loader differs from the initiating loader. From now on, we work only with classes which have a loader component and a class name.

State. Each class loader has its own name space. Elements of this name space are the classes the class loader has loaded. The dynamic function *ldEnv* keeps track of the loaded class object, which has been loaded under the given class name by the corresponding (initiating or defining) class loader instance. The name of the loaded class object (*classOf*) is always **Class**. A dynamic function *cOf* stores for a class instance the real name of the loaded class, i.e., the class name together with its defining loader.

$ldEnv : Class \rightarrow Ref$
$cOf \quad : Ref \rightarrow Class$

Initial values of dynamic functions needed for dynamic class loading are given at the end of this section. The following example illustrates loading of a class by different loaders.

Example 18.3.1. Let n be a class name, let L_1 and L_2 be initiating loaders for n, let L be the defining loader for n. Let r be the reference of the corresponding class object. Then, the dynamic functions *ldEnv*, *cOf*, and *classOf* have the following values:

$ldEnv(L_1, n) = r \quad cOf(r) \quad = (L, n)$
$ldEnv(L_2, n) = r \quad classOf(r) = (sysLd, \text{Class})$
$ldEnv(L, n) \ \ = r$

Since we have class names with the initiating loader and defining loader as the loader component, we have to transform a class name to a name with

Fig. 18.1 Ordering of class states

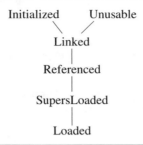

the defining loader as the loader component. As can be seen in the above example, for a class C we get the class which contains the defining loader, instead of the initiating loader, as its loader component by applying the following function *liftClass*:

$$liftClass(c) = cOf(ldEnv(c))$$

In the previous chapters the class state of a class could be *Referenced*, *Linked*, *Initialized*, and *Unusable*. In the dynamic machine we introduce two new states *Loaded* and *SupersLoaded*.

> **data** *ClassState* = ...
> | *Loaded* | *SupersLoaded*

The state *Loaded* means that the class is loaded. If a class has this state, then we know nothing about the class state of the super classes and of the referenced classes.

The state *SupersLoaded* is used if all super classes are loaded and the class state of all super classes is at least *SupersLoaded*. A class is in state *Referenced* if all super classes have at least state *Referenced* and all referenced classes have at least state *SupersLoaded*. Fig. 18.1 shows the ordering of the different class states.

Environment. When a class file is loaded, the class environment changes. The function *cEnv*: *Class* → *ClassFile* becomes dynamic. An external function *load* is used as a source for new class files on the local file system:

> *load*: (*ClassPath*, *Class*) → *Content*

Types. Changing the class environment changes all environment based derived functions, in particular all typing conditions. Since already loaded and verified classes should not become invalid, the class environment is only allowed to increase.

Type compatibility has to take different name spaces into account. Using the extension of a class to a class name with its defining loader, we define

Fig. 18.2 Refinement of the switch machine

$switchVM_D =$
$\quad switchVM_E$
$\quad$**case** $switch$ **of**
$\quad\quad InitClass(c) \rightarrow$ **if** $classState(c) < Referenced$ **then**
$\quad\quad\quad\quad\quad\quad\quad\quad\quad referenceClass(c)$
$\quad\quad Result(res) \rightarrow$
$\quad\quad\quad$ **if** $methNm(meth) =$ `"<cload>"` **then**
$\quad\quad\quad\quad ldEnv(reg(0), stringOf(reg(1))) := res(0)$

$referenceClass(c) =$
$\quad$ **if** $c =$ `Object` **then**
$\quad\quad classState(c) := Referenced$
$\quad$ **elseif** $classState(c) = SupersLoaded$ **then**
$\quad\quad$ **let** $supers = \{super(c)\} \cup implements(c)$
$\quad\quad$ **choose** $c' \in supers, classState(c') < Referenced$
$\quad\quad\quad referenceClass(c')$
$\quad\quad$ **ifnone**
$\quad\quad\quad loadReferences(c)$
$\quad$ **else** $loadSuperClasses(c)$

as mentioned above two classes to be equal iff they have the same name and the same defining loader. This guarantees that type spoofing problems as detected by Saraswat [30] do not occur in our model. The Saraswat example is given in Appendix A.

18.3.2 Loading references

In the dynamic machine a class can be in a class state less than *Referenced*. When such a class has to be initialized, then we first have to reference the class to reference all its super classes and to load all referenced classes. This is done by extending the switch machine $switchVM_E$ to $switchVM_D$ (see Fig. 18.2) where a class will be referenced if the state is less than *Referenced* (either *Loaded* or *SupersLoaded*).

If the class `Object` has to be referenced, then we set the class state immediately to *Referenced*, because `Object`[1] has no super class. If a class c different from `Object` has to be referenced, then we distinguish between the class states *SupersLoaded* and *Loaded*. If the state is *SupersLoaded*—meaning that at least all super classes have state *SupersLoaded*—we reference each super class which has not already been referenced. The invoked submachine *referenceClass* terminates its recursive calls because the inheritance hierarchy is finite. If there is no unreferenced super class, we load all references of

---

[1] `Object` means the class with name Object and loader component $sysLd$. The same applies to the other basic classes.

the class c, as defined by the submachine *loadReferences*. If the state of c is *Loaded*, then we first have to load the super classes of c, which is done by the machine *loadSuperClasses* described below (see Fig. 18.3).

This algorithm of referencing guarantees that the class state of a class becomes referenced only if all super classes are at least referenced and all referenced classes are at least in state *SupersLoaded*. Hence, this ensures that the class hierarchy is loaded completely with respect to all types which may occur during execution of the class. The following example illustrates why the class state *Loaded* is not sufficient for the referenced classes in our diligent machine.

Example 18.3.2. Let I be an interface. Let A be a class which implements I and let A be the super class of B. In the following code fragment the classes B and I are referenced, but A (the super class of B) is needed during verification to determine whether B is compatible to I.

> $\vdots$
> *InvokeStatic*$(B, B/getB())$
> *InvokeVirtual*(**void**, $I/m()$)

Fig. 18.3 specifies loading of super classes and references. The two machines *loadSuperClasses* and *loadReferences* in that figure are based on the scheme *loadClasses*. The scheme gets as its first argument a set of classes to load and the second argument is a machine which is executed if all these classes have at least state *SupersLoaded*. If there is any class which has not been loaded, then we load the class using the machine *callLoad*. This machine updates the *switch* function to call the method `<cload>` of the loader ld (the loader component of the class) and with the class name as argument.

> *callLoad*$(ld, cn) =$
> $\quad switch := Call(\texttt{<cload>}, [ld, cn])$

The method `<cload>(String)` is not a Java API method; it is a wrapper in our machine to call the `loadClass` method. The code of the method is as follows:

> *Load*(**addr**, 0)
> *Load*(**addr**, 1)
> *InvokeVirtual*(**Class**, `loadClass(String)`)
> *Return*(**addr**)

The method `<cload>` is similar to the method `<clinit>` which is also called only by the virtual machine. When the `<cload>` method returns, it has to continue at the same instruction it was invoked from. Therefore we extend the definition of *implicitCall* from Chapter 10 which is used in *switchVM$_C$*.

> *implicitCall*$(m) = methNm(m) \in \{$ `"<clinit>"`, `"<cload>"` $\}$

Fig. 18.3 Loading super classes and references

$loadClasses(cs, m) =$
 choose $c \in cs \setminus dom(ldEnv)$
  $callLoad(c)$
 ifnone
  choose $c \in cs, classState(liftClass(c)) = Loaded$
   $loadSuperClasses(liftClass(c))$
  ifnone m

$loadSuperClasses(c) =$
 $loadClasses(\{super(c)\} \cup implements(c), setSupersLoaded(c))$

$loadReferences(c) =$
 $loadClasses(directReferences(c), loadIndirectReferences(c))$

$setSupersLoaded(c) =$
 $classState(c) := SupersLoaded$
 $setDefiningLoadersForSupers(c)$

$loadIndirectReferences(c) =$
 $loadClasses(indirectReferences(c), setReferenced(c))$

$setReferenced(c) =$
 $classState(c) := Referenced$
 $setDefiningLoaders(c)$

Since we do not know and therefore cannot specify the possibly user defined
body for the `loadClass` method, our model can only reflect the result of its
execution, namely by specifying what happens when a `<cload>` method returns. If it returns normally, it has extended the loader environment. Therefore, the dynamic switch machine $switchVM_D$ in Fig. 18.2 sets—when the
method returns—the dynamic function $ldEnv$ for the current loader instance
(in register 0) and the name of the class to load (in register 1) with the reference of the created class object (returned in $res(0)$). Note that the function
$stringOf$ returns the string content of the corresponding reference.

The question arises whether we really need the wrapper function. Why
not simply call `loadClass` directly? We do not know anything about user
defined loaders. A loader may delegate the loading by invoking the `loadClass`
method of another loader. This loader may delegate again. However, the chain
of delegation is of no interest and we are only interested in the first (initiating)
loader and the last (defining) loader.

When a class is defined by a loader L, each class entry in the class file
contains L as the loader component. The loader L is the initiating loader
for all these references. At the time when the reference is loaded by L, we

can replace the loader component by L_d using the not furthermore specified submachine *setDefiningLoaders*, if L_d is the defining loader for the reference. This is what the machines in Fig. 18.3 are doing, as we are now going to explain in more detail.

The machine *loadSuperClasses* in Fig. 18.3 loads all super classes of the class c. If the class state of all super classes is at least *SupersLoaded*, then the machine *setSupersLoaded* sets the class state to *SupersLoaded* and the not furthermore specified machine *setDefiningLoadersForSupers* replaces the loader component for the super class entries (super class and implemented interfaces) in the class file with the defining loader. All other references are untouched, because at this time they are not necessarily loaded and the defining loader might be unknown.

Indirect references. An indirect reference is a class which appears only in the context of another reference. More precisely, classes in argument types of methods, and classes in return types of methods and fields are indirect references. The other references are called *direct*. Let us consider the following instruction in a class D:

$GetStatic(A, C/getA(B))$

The class C is a direct reference which has to be loaded by the same loader as D. The classes in the types A and B have to be handled in the same way as in the class C and are called indirect references. Thus we load the classes in A and B with the defining loader of C and not with the loader of D. This is the reason why we have to load the direct references before we load the indirect references. Otherwise we do not know the loader to load the indirect references. Note that the machine *setDefiningLoaders* takes also care of the difference between direct and indirect references when substituting the loader component.

Loading the references is done by *loadReferences* which first loads all direct references. If all direct references are loaded and the class state for all these is at least *SupersLoaded*, then the indirect references are loaded in the same way. Finally the class state is set to *Referenced* and the not furthermore specified machine *setDefiningLoaders* substitutes all loader components in the class file with the defining loader.

Example ($\rightsquigarrow$ CD) 18.3.3. The following example illustrates why we distinguish between direct and indirect references. Assume we have the following classes (for readability we extend class names by their loaders):

```
public class A^L extends B^{LA} {
   public A()       { m(); n(); }
   public void m() { }
   public void n() {
      try { super.getA().n(); }
      catch (LinkageError e) { ... }
```

```
    }
  }
  public classs B^{LA} extends A^{LA} {
    public A^{LA} getA() { return this; }
  }
  public class A^{LA} { }
```

There is an error in the Java program, because `super.getA()` in the method n returns the class A^{LA} and this class has no method n. The bytecode of the method n in class A^L is of special interest:

$$\vdots$$
$Load(\mathbf{addr}, 0)$
$InvokeSpecial(A, B/getA())$
$InvokeVirtual(\mathbf{void}, A/n())$
$$\vdots$$

There seems to be no error in the bytecode. The class B has a method $getA$ which returns A and A has a method n. The problem is that $B/getA$ returns A^{LA} and this class is not compatible to A^L.

If we load the references as above and take care of direct and indirect references, then our verifier has to verify the following annotated program:

$$\vdots$$
$Load(\mathbf{addr}, 0)$
$InvokeSpecial(A^{LA}, B^L/getA())$
$InvokeVirtual(\mathbf{void}, A^L/n())$
$$\vdots$$

Now, the verifier detects that A^{LA} is not compatible to A^L and rejects the program at the *InvokeVirtual* instruction.

Remark 18.3.1. The verifier in JDK 1.3 from Sun accepts the bytecode for the method n in class A^L and throws a `LinkageError` before calling the method $B/getA()$, although all classes have been already loaded and initialized.

18.3.3 The trustful JVM$_\mathcal{D}$

JVM$_\mathcal{D}$ extends JVM$_\mathcal{N}$ by the native methods for loading and resolving classes and by the native method `newInstance` which creates an instance for a given class object.

The *trustfulVM* for JVM$_\mathcal{D}$ is the one for JVM$_\mathcal{N}$, extended with the new *execVM$_D$* rule appearing in Fig. 18.4 and the new switch machine *switchVM$_D$* appearing in Fig. 18.2.

Fig. 18.4 Trustful execution of JVM$_\mathcal{D}$ instructions

$execVM_D =$
   $execVM_N$
   if $c = \texttt{ClassLoader}$ **then**
     $execClassLoader(m)$
   elseif $meth = \texttt{Class/newInstance()}$ **then**
     $meth := cOf(reg(0))/\texttt{<newInstance>()}$
   where $c/m = meth$

$trustfulVM_D = trustfulScheme_N(execVM_D, switchVM_D)$

Rules for the final methods of class `ClassLoader`. Fig. 18.5 shows the new rules of the dynamic VM for the final methods of class `ClassLoader`.

The method `findLoadedClass` is required to return the class object for a class previously loaded by the called class loader. If the class is not found, a *null* reference is returned.

The method `findSystemClass` attempts to find the named class by using the internal class loader $sysLd$.[2] If the system class is not found, a `ClassNotFoundException` is thrown (by *loadClass*). Otherwise the class is referenced and linked. Finally, the method returns the loaded class. Loading and linking is specified in Fig. 18.6.

The `defineClass` method tests whether the class name (argument 1) is already in the name space of the loader (argument 0). In such a case the exception `ClassFormatError` is thrown[3]. Otherwise the class—specified by the array (arguments 2, 3, and 4)—is defined and the machine *defineClass* returns the newly created class object.

The `resolveClass` method references and links the class specified by the reference of the class object. It throws a `NullPointerException` if the reference is *null*.

Note that there is no need to explicitly call `resolveClass`, because the virtual machine references and links the class—if not already done—before the class will be initialized.

The details on loading, defining, and linking are specified in Fig. 18.6. The *loadClass* machine tests whether the specified class exists on the local file system and either defines that class or throws a `ClassNotFoundException`.

The *defineClass* machine takes three arguments. The first argument is the binary representation of the class name (the second argument) to be defined. If the last argument is *True*, the new created class is returned by *defineClass*. If the class name coincides with the expected class name, a new class object

---

[2] The search is typically performed along the user's class path, described by the environment variable `CLASSPATH`.

[3] The JLS does not specify this case.

Fig. 18.5 Execution of `final` class loader methods

$execClassLoader(m) =$
  if $m = $ `findLoadedClass` **then**
    let $c = (reg(0), stringOf(reg(1)))$
    if $c \notin dom(ldEnv)$ **then**
      $switch := Result([null])$
    else
      $switch := Result([ldEnv(c)])$
  if $m = $ `findSystemClass` **then**
    let $c = (sysLd, stringOf(reg(1)))$
    if $c \notin dom(ldEnv)$ **then**
      $loadClass(classPath, c)$
    elseif $classState(c) < Referenced$ **then**
      $referenceClass(c)$
    elseif $classState(c) = Referenced$ **then**
      $linkClass(c)$
    else
      $switch := Result([ldEnv(c)])$
  if $m = $ `defineClass` **then**
    let $c = (reg(0), stringOf(reg(1)))$
    if $c \notin dom(ldEnv)$ **then**
      let $content = arrayContent(heap(reg(2)), reg(3), reg(4))$
      $defineClass(content, c, True)$
    else
      $raise(\,$`"ClassFormatError"`$\,)$
  if $m = $ `resolveClass` **then**
    let $r = reg(1)$
    if $r = null$ **then**
      $raise(\,$`"NullPointerException"`$\,)$
    else
      let $c = cOf(r)$
      if $classState(c) < Referenced$ **then**
        $referenceClass(c)$
      elseif $classState(c) = Referenced$ **then**
        $linkClass(c)$
      else
        $switch := Result([\,])$

is created and the corresponding dynamic functions are initialized properly. Otherwise a `ClassFormatError` is thrown.

The linking machine *linkClass* in Fig. 18.6 ensures that the class and its super classes are prepared. Note that the diligent VM has its own machine for linking, but in the trustful VM the class states *Referenced* and *Linked* differ only in preparation.

Rules for the final methods of class `Class`. If a program uses class loaders to load and define new classes, then the `loadClass` method returns the class object of the loaded class. New instances of the loaded classes can be created

Fig. 18.6 Loading and linking machines

$loadClass(classPath, c) =$
  if $c \notin dom(load(classPath))$ **then**
    $raise(\,$"`ClassNotFoundException`"$\,)$
  else
    $defineClass(load(classPath), c, False)$

$defineClass(content, c, returnClass) =$
    let $cf = analyze(content)$
    if $classNm(cf) \neq classNm(c)$ **then**
      $raise(\,$"`ClassFormatError`"$\,)$
    else create r
      $classState(c) := Loaded$
      $heap(r)\quad\ := Object(\texttt{Class}, \emptyset)$
      $cOf(r)\qquad := c$
      $cEnv(c)\quad\ := cf$
      $ldEnv(c)\quad := r$
      if $returnClass$ **then** $switch := Result([r])$

$linkClass(c) =$
  let $classes = \{super(c)\} \cup implements(c)$
  if $c = \texttt{Object} \vee \forall\, c' \in classes : classState(c') \geq Linked$ **then**
    $classState(c) := Linked$
    $prepareClass(c)$
  elseif $\neg cyclicInheritance(c)$ **then**
    choose $c' \in classes, classState(c') = Referenced$
      $linkClass(c')$
  else
    $halt := $ "`Cyclic Inheritance: `" $\cdot classNm(c)$

---

using the `newInstance` method of class `Class`. The stripped down signature of class `Class` is:

```
public final class Class{
  protected final Object newInstance();
}
```

The `newInstance` method has the same semantics as if in Java a new instance creation expression with an empty argument list is called. The method `newInstance` is called on the reference r where r is the class object. For such a given reference, the dynamic function cOf (see Fig. 18.6) returns the real class name.

We model `newInstance` as a native method where we update the dynamic function $meth$ to $cOf(r)/$`<newInstance>`$()$ with the effect, that this method will be executed in the next step. Without loss of generality we assume that each loaded class C contains the following code for that method:

> $New(C)$
> $Dupx(0, 1)$
> $InvokeSpecial(\texttt{void}, C/\texttt{<init>}())$
> $Return(\texttt{addr})$

We update the dynamic function *meth* instead of setting *switch* to call `<newInstance>`, because otherwise we would create a new frame for the method `<newInstance>`. After returning from the method `<newInstance>` the native method `newInstance` would call `<newInstance>` again and again, because the state after returning from `<newInstance>` would be the same as before invoking `<newInstance>`.

Initialization. Dynamic loading works correctly under the assumption that the classes `Object`, `ClassLoader`, `Class`, and `String` are pre-linked and that an instance of the class `ClassLoader`, namely *sysLd*, is created. Furthermore, there has to be a class object for each loaded class.

Assume that initially the dynamic function *heap* is defined only for *sysLd* and *heap*(*sysLd*) is an instance of `ClassLoader`. Additionally, the class state for the classes `Object`, `Class`, `ClassLoader`, and `String` is *Linked* and *cEnv* is defined for these classes. Then the initial class objects and the initial values for the corresponding dynamic functions can be obtained by applying the following rule:

> $initializeDynamicLoading(classes) =$
> **forall** $c \in classes$
>   **create** r
> $heap(r) \quad := Object(\texttt{Class}, \emptyset)$
> $cOf(r) \quad := c$
> $ldEnv(c) := r$

The dynamic VM starts execution by interpreting the instructions of the internal method `<entrypoint>` (see Chapter 10). The method `<entrypoint>`, which calls the `main` method of the class to execute, is defined in class `Object`. The initial attempt to call `main` of class *Main* discovers that the class state of *Main* is loaded. The virtual machine tries to initialize the class and transitively its super classes using *sysLd* (the system loader) as the current loader. Afterwards, the class and transitively its super classes are initialized, that is verified, prepared, linked, and initialized in the strict sense. Now, the method `main` can be called.

18.3.4 The defensive JVM$_\mathcal{D}$

The defensive JVM$_\mathcal{D}$ extends the defensive JVM$_\mathcal{N}$ by the native methods for dynamic loading.

> $check_D(c/m) =$
> $c = \texttt{ClassLoader} \wedge m \in \{\, \texttt{findLoadedClass}, \texttt{findSystemClass},$
> $\texttt{resolveClass}, \texttt{defineClass}\,\} \vee$
> $c/m = \texttt{Class}/\texttt{newInstance}() \vee$
> $check_N(c/m)$

$defensiveVM_D =$
  $defensiveScheme_N(check_D, trustfulVM_D)$

18.3.5 The diligent JVM$_\mathcal{D}$

The diligent JVM$_\mathcal{D}$ extends the diligent JVM$_\mathcal{N}$ by the new check function $check_D$ and the trustful machine $trustfulVM_D$.

$diligentVM_D = diligentScheme(verifyVM, trustfulVM_D)$
  where $verifyVM = verifyScheme_N(check_D)$

18.3.6 Exercises

Exercise 18.3.1. The *loadClass* machine is used by the native method findSystemClass. Why do we call *defineClass* with *False* as the last argument?

Exercise 18.3.2. The JLS uses loading constraints [23, §5.3.4] to detect type errors if there are classes with the same name defined by different loaders. Why do we not need loading constraints?

Exercise 18.3.3. The *loadClasses* scheme in Fig. 18.3 applies the *liftClass* function to class c. Why do we have to use *liftClass*(c) instead of c?

Exercise 18.3.4. Let A and B we classes. Consider the following instructions in class C defined by loader L:

- $New(B)$
- $GetField(B[\,], A/f)$
- $InvokeVirtual(B, A/m(\texttt{int}, C))$
- $InvokeStatic(\texttt{void}, B/m(\texttt{int}, A))$

Which loader will be used to load A, B, and C in the above instructions?

Exercise 18.3.5. The dynamic function *ldEnv* contains the relation between a class and its class object. Why do we update the dynamic function in *switchVM$_D$* (Fig. 18.2) and in *defineClass* (see Fig. 18.6)? What are the differences?

Exercise 18.3.6. Extend the formulation of the Main Theorem from the *diligentVM$_E$* to the dynamic *diligentVM$_D$* and prove the theorem from appropriate assumptions on the class loaders.

A. Executable Models

The ASM models introduced in this book are executable with AsmGofer [32] where all external functions (and predicates) can be computed which in the models are only abstractly specified. AsmGofer is an Abstract State Machine programming system; an extension of the functional programming environment Gofer [22] (more precisely TkGofer [36]—an extension of Gofer for graphical user interfaces). The AsmGofer tool was developed for executing the ASM models in this book, but it is a general interpreter for a large class of ASMs. AsmGofer allows to execute an ASM step by step. In each step the current state can be observed.

We defined graphical user interfaces (GUIs) for our models to simplify the interaction between the user and the AsmGofer interpreter. The source code of AsmGofer, installation instructions, and the sources of our ASM models are provided by the attached CD (see the README file in the root directory of the CD). All executable models have been developed by Joachim Schmid, Siemens Corporate Technology, Munich (see machines/files/license.term on the CD for further information).

There are precompiled binaries of AsmGofer for several popular operating systems like Linux, Solaris Sparc, and Microsoft Windows. For such operating systems, our executable models can be started directly from the CD without installing anything. Furthermore, there is an installation program for Microsoft Windows based platforms.

The following sections introduce the three graphical user interfaces for Java, the compiler from Java to bytecode, and the Java Virtual Machine. At the end of this chapter, the reader should be able to execute a Java program with our machine, compile it to bytecode, and execute that bytecode with our Java Virtual Machine.

A.1 Overview

The ASM models presented in this book are executable. Each model reads its input from files. The input format for the Java-ASM and the Compiler-ASM is the standard Java syntax. Given a Java program, the Compiler-ASM generates bytecode in a textual representation called *Jasmin* [24]. This textual representation of bytecode is the input for the JVM-ASM.

Fig. A.1 Relationship between different machines

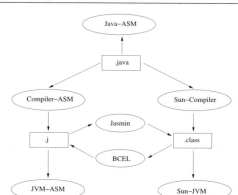

Usually, bytecode is stored in the binary representation called *class file*. However, we use the textual representation, because it is easier to read and to generate. There are several tools to convert between the binary and the textual representation. For example, *Jasmin* [24] and *BCEL* (Bytecode Engineering Library) [15], which are also provided by the attached CD.

Fig. A.1 gives an overview about the different file formats (denoted by rectangles) and shows the relationship between the ASM-machines in this book and the corresponding machines from Sun.

The source language is Java (suffix `.java`). The Java-ASM reads programs in the source language and executes them. There is no counterpart by Sun. The Compiler-ASM reads also programs in the source language Java and compiles them to bytecode in Jasmin syntax (suffix `.j`). On the other hand, the Sun-Compiler generates class files (suffix `.class`). The JVM-ASM and the Sun-JVM read input in Jasmin syntax and class files, respectively. Due to Jasmin and BCEL, there are several possibilities to use and mix the different machines and compilers.

A.2 Java

The ASM model for Java is available as an executable model with a graphical user interface. The GUI is like a debugger and can be used to observe the behavior of a Java program. Although we introduced different machines for Java, namely $execJava_I, \ldots, execJava_T$ (see Part I) it is not useful to execute only $Java_I$ statements, because each Java program contains at least one class and one method. Hence, there is only one GUI, which supports all features up to $Java_T$.

A.2.1 Completing the Java ASM

The Java specification [18] contains additional features which do not appear in our models, but they can all be handled in a routine manner using the method described in this book. Not supported are *packages*, *throws* clauses, switch statements, for loops, do while loops, the operators for bit manipulation >>=, >>>=, <<=, ^=, >>, >>>, <<, &=, |=, &, ~, ^, |, the increment operator ++, the decrement operator --, and the following special assignment operators *=, +=, -=, %=, and /=.

One could argue that a Java specification is complete only together with a specification of all API methods the language comes with. We specify and implement all Java API methods which are needed to execute the examples in the book. The file machines/predefined.java on the CD contains our environment for execution. This file is loaded at runtime. For example, our class Object provides the methods <init>, equals, notify, notifyAll, toString, and wait. Other supported classes and interfaces are:

- ArithmeticException
- ArrayIndexOutOfBoundsException
- ArrayStoreException
- ClassCastException
- Cloneable
- CloneNotSupportedException
- Comparable
- Error
- Exception
- ExceptionInInitializerError
- Float
- IllegalThreadStateException
- IndexOutOfBoundsException
- Integer
- InterruptedException
- LinkageError
- NoClassDefFoundError
- NullPointerException
- Number
- PrintStream
- Runnable
- RuntimeException
- String
- StringBuffer
- System
- Thread
- ThreadDeath
- Throwable

Note that these classes and interfaces are not defined completely, but they can be extended by the reader if he wishes to do so.

The primitive types `byte`, `short`, `int`, `long`, `float`, and `double` are supported by the type system, but not implemented according to the Java specification [19, §4.2]. The integral types are mapped to the AsmGofer type *Int* and the floating point types are mapped to the AsmGofer type *Float*.

A.2.2 Starting the machine

For the following steps, we assume that AsmGofer has been installed successfully (see instructions on the CD for further information) or there is a corresponding precompiled binary.[1] We further assume, that the executable ASM-models are located in the directory ~/jbook/machines which is the current working directory.

For a unix like environment, the command ./java calls AsmGofer and loads all necessary files for the Java machine. A user for Microsoft Windows should either type java in the *command prompt* or double click the file java.exe in the explorer. The output should look like the following:

```
joe:~/jbook/machines > ./java
=== AsmGofer v1.0.2 (TkGofer v2.0) ===
(with modules: guiMonad, widget, time, io, concurrent, asmvar)
Gofer Version 2.30a  Copyright (c) Mark P Jones 1991-1994

Reading script file "AsmGofer/Preludes/tk.prelude-all-asm":
Reading script file "files/jvm/lib/monad.gs":
:
Reading script file "files/gui/main.gs":

Gofer session for:
Reading script file "files/basic/types.gs":
:
files/java/gui/main.gs
? please wait (starting the GUI)
```

AsmGofer is an interpreter and is ready to use when the ? prompt appears. It is possible to use the interpreter in console mode, but we prefer using the GUI. The GUI (see Fig. A.2) will be automatically started by the script.

A.2.3 Introduction to the GUI

The GUI (see Fig. A.2) is divided into different parts. The main window contains the source code of the selected method. On startup this is the code

---

[1] Precompiled binaries are available for Microsoft Windows and for the unix-like operating systems Linux, cygwin under Microsoft Windows, and Solaris Sparc.

Fig. A.2 Java GUI

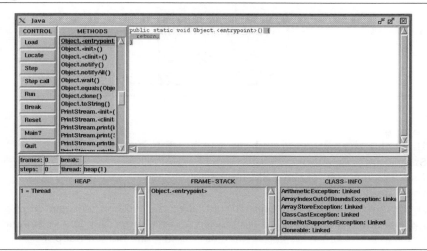

of the method `Object.<entrypoint>`. This method is used to call the main
method of the class to execute (if there is any program). Left to the source
window there is the `METHODS` frame. The frame contains all known methods
preceeded by their class name.

At the bottom there are three frames, namely `HEAP`, `FRAME-STACK`, and
`CLASS-INFO`. The `HEAP` frame displays the content of the dynamic function
heap in the notation *ref=value* where *ref* is the heap reference. Note that the
system thread is always present in the heap and has reference 1.

The frame `FRAME-STACK` displays the frame information of the dynamic
function *frames* and the current frame: the method name and the local variables of each frame. The first (top) element in the list is the current method
followed by the local variables, then the method which has called the current
method, and so on.

Information about loaded classes, their global (static) variables, and their
class state (dynamic function *classState*) is shown in the `CLASS-INFO` frame.

The fields `frames`, `steps`, `break`, and `thread` contain information about
the size of the current frame stack, the number of steps executed, the current
breakpoint (if there is any), and the current thread reference, respectively.
Breakpoints are described in Appendix A.2.5.

The frame `CONTROL` contains several buttons to load and execute a given
program step by step. In particular these are the following buttons:

– `Load`
    Opens the file manager to load a Java program. After loading the file the
    new classes and methods are shown in the corresponding frames.

Fig. A.3 Control execution

- `Locate`
  Highlights the method and phrase which will be executed next.
- `Step`
  Executes one step of the ASM model.
- `Step call`
  If the current phrase is a method call, then the method is executed completely. Afterwards, the GUI is updated and ready for the next command. Otherwise the behavior is the same as pressing the button `Step`.
- `Run`
  Executes the program until it terminates or a breakpoint is reached. During the run, the GUI is updated in each step and the user can stop and start the execution.
- `Break`
  Sets a breakpoint to the marked position. More information about breakpoints can be found in Appendix A.2.5.
- `Reset`
  Resets all dynamic functions to their initial values. This button can be used to restart the execution of a program.
- `Main?`
  Usually the first `main` method of the loaded classes is executed. If there are several classes, there might be several `main` methods. The button `Main?` lists all known signatures for `main` methods and the user can choose the method to execute. The method `Object.<entrypoint>` will be modified to call the corresponding `main` method.
- `Quit`
  Quits the GUI and leaves the AsmGofer interpreter.

A.2.4 Running an example

Start the Java interpreter as described in the last section and load the file `examples/java/Exercise6_2_2/Test.java`. The file contains an example for throwing and catching exceptions.

After loading the file, the `METHODS` frame contains the methods `<init>()`, `<clinit>()`, `test(int)` and the method `main` of class `Test`. The methods `<init>` and `<clinit>` are not present in the Java source code. They have been generated with default bodies, because each class needs these two methods. The code of `Object.<entrypoint>` has been modified to call the `main` method of class `Test` and to catch all exceptions. We do not support runtime arguments for the `main` method. Thus the method is called with argument `null`:

```
public static void Object.<entrypoint>() {
  try {
    Test.main(null);
  } catch (Throwable x){ }
  return;
}
```

After pressing the button `Run` the execution starts and the `Run` window (see Fig. A.3) appears. The window contains a slide to change the execution speed and four buttons to control the run:

- `cancel`
  Cancels the execution and closes the window. The execution can be continued by pressing the `Run` (or `step`) button again.
- `clear`
  Clears the current breakpoint (if there is any).
- `finish`
  Executes the program until it terminates or until the breakpoint is reached. During the execution the GUI is not updated and does not react to any user commands. This mode is for fast execution.
- `start` or `stop`
  Starts and stops the execution without closing the window.

During the run, the GUI is updated in each step. For example, Fig. A.4 shows the GUI while throwing an exception.

The `Run` window closes itself if no further execution is possible. The program can be executed again by resetting the state with the button `Reset` where each dynamic function is set to its initial value.

A.2.5 Breakpoints

Sometimes we are interested in local variables or heap values at special time points. For instance, in the above example, the state before executing the finally code. Breakpoints help to interrupt the execution (during `Run` or `Step call`) at certain positions in the source program.

Setting breakpoints. The GUI supports only one breakpoint. Therefore setting a new breakpoint removes the old breakpoint. To set a breakpoint, first select the corresponding method, mark the phrase, and press the button `Break`. The breakpoint is shown in the info field `break:`. The GUI stores the marked position and interrupts the execution during `Run` and `Step call` if the execution position is equal to the breakpoint.

Fig. A.4 Execution of Exercise 6.2.2

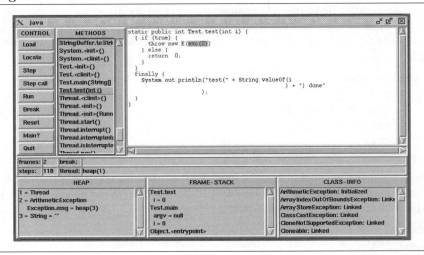

Removing breakpoints. The Run window in Fig. A.3 has a button `clear` which removes the breakpoint.

A.2.6 Examples on the CD

Java examples are located in the directory `machines/examples/java` on the CD. There is a directory for each example. In the directory there are the source files and either a file called `out` or a file `no_out`. The file `out` contains the output of the example when running it with our Java-ASM. If the file `no_out` is present, then the example does not produce an output.

A.3 Compiler

Fig. A.5 shows the GUI for the Compiler-ASM. The GUI can be used to load Java programs and to compile them into bytecode.

A.3.1 Completing the Compiler ASM

The compiler supports everything which is supported by the Java-ASM, except threads (excluding in particular the `synchronized` statement).

A.3.2 Starting the machine

Similar to the Java-ASM, the command `./compiler` (or for Microsoft Windows users the file `compiler.exe`) calls AsmGofer with all files necessary for the compiler. The output should look as follows:

Fig. A.5 Compiler GUI

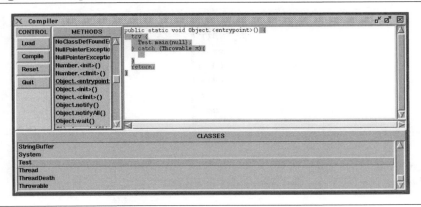

```
joe:~/jbook/machines > ./compiler
=== AsmGofer v1.0.2 (TkGofer v2.0) ===
(with modules: guiMonad, widget, time, io, concurrent, asmvar)
Gofer Version 2.30a  Copyright (c) Mark P Jones 1991-1994

Reading script file "AsmGofer/Preludes/tk.prelude-all-asm":
Reading script file "files/jvm/lib/monad.gs":
⋮
files/compiler/gui/main.gs
? please wait (starting the GUI)
```

The script automatically starts the GUI (Fig. A.5) after loading the files.

A.3.3 Introduction to the GUI

The GUI consists of four parts. Namely the CONTROL frame, the METHODS frame, the source window, and the CLASSES frame.

The METHODS frame shows all known methods preceeded by the corresponding class name. The source code of the selected method is shown in the source window in the middle. All known classes are displayed in the CLASSES frame. The CONTROL frame contains the following buttons:

- Load
  Opens the file manager to load a Java program. The first class of the program will be selected in the CLASSES frame.
- Compile
  Compiles the selected class (in the CLASSES frame) to bytecode in Jasmin syntax. The GUI opens the file manager and asks for a filename to store the bytecode. The default filename for a class with name n is $n.j$.

Fig. A.6 Execution language

– Quit
Leaves the GUI and the AsmGofer interpreter.

A.3.4 Examples on the CD

All examples in the java directory except the examples about threads can be used for the compiler. Other compiler examples are located on the CD in the directory `machines/examples/compiler`.

A.4 Java Virtual Machine

The ASM models for the Java Virtual Machine are available as executable models. We have three different machines. Namely the Trustful JVM, the Defensive JVM, and the Diligent JVM. The Trustful JVM (Part II) does not check anything, the Defensive JVM (Chapter 15) checks all instructions on the fly, and the Diligent JVM (Chapter 17) verifies a class before execution. The GUI is the same for all these machines.

In all JVM-ASMs the supported sublanguage can be selected (Fig. A.6). This means that the machine can execute instructions up to $JVM_{\mathcal{I}}$, or $JVM_{\mathcal{C}}$, $JVM_{\mathcal{O}}$, $JVM_{\mathcal{E}}$, $JVM_{\mathcal{N}}$, and $JVM_{\mathcal{D}}$. $JVM_{\mathcal{N}}$ is needed for output and $JVM_{\mathcal{D}}$ for dynamic loading (the Saraswat example described below, e.g.). Without the features of $JVM_{\mathcal{D}}$ the GUI loads all referenced classes, because otherwise we could not execute the given program. Initially the sublanguage is $JVM_{\mathcal{N}}$.

Switching from or to dynamic loading resets the machine to its initial state, because in dynamic mode each loaded class needs an instance of class `Class` which we create only in dynamic mode. Furthermore, loading references of a class can be delayed until the class needs to be linked. Hence, for examples about dynamic loading, first switch to dynamic mode and then load the example.

A.4.1 Completing the JVM ASM

The list of supported bytecode instructions is given in Appendix C.8. Similar to Java, to be complete, one should implement all Java API methods. We have implemented all the API methods which are needed for executing the examples in the book. The supported classes and interfaces are defined in the following two directories:

- machines/predefined.jvm/java/lang
- machines/predefined.jvm/java/io.

There are definitions for the following classes and interfaces:

- AbstractMethodError
- ArithmeticException
- Array
- ArrayIndexOutOfBoundsException
- ArrayStoreException
- Class
- ClassCastException
- ClassLoader
- ClassNotFoundException
- Cloneable
- CloneNotSupportedException
- Comparable
- Error
- Exception
- ExceptionInInitializerError
- Float
- IncompatibleClassChangeError
- Integer
- LinkageError
- NegativeArraySizeException
- NoClassDefFoundError
- NullPointerException
- Number
- PrintStream
- RuntimeException
- String
- StringBuffer
- System
- Throwable

Here too, the classes and interfaces are not defined completely, but can be extended easily. Furthermore, the primitive types are mapped to the AsmGofer types *Int* and *Float* as in Java and are not implemented according to the specification [23, §2.4].

A.4.2 Starting the machines

The JVM machines can be started similarly to the Java-ASM and the Compiler-ASM. The scripts are ./trustful, ./defensive, and ./diligent.[2] The output should look as follows:

```
joe:~/jbook/machines > ./diligent
=== AsmGofer v1.0.2 (TkGofer v2.0) ===
(with modules: guiMonad, widget, time, io, concurrent, asmvar)
Gofer Version 2.30a  Copyright (c) Mark P Jones 1991-1994

Reading script file "AsmGofer/Preludes/tk.prelude-all-asm":
Reading script file "files/jvm/lib/monad.gs":
⋮
files/jvm/gui/jvmgui.gs
? please wait (starting the GUI)
```

The scripts start the GUI (Fig. A.7) immediately after loading the files.

A.4.3 Introduction to the GUI

The JVM GUI consists of several frames and info fields. The frames HEAP, CLASS-INFO, STACK, and VARIABLES give information about the current run:

- HEAP
  Displays the content of the dynamic function *heap*. The notation is *ref* = *class* where *ref* is the heap reference. The system class loader has reference 1.
- CLASS-INFO
  Displays all loaded classes together with their class state and their global (static) variables. Note that a class name is shown together with the reference of its class loader when $JVM_{\mathcal{D}}$ is selected.
- STACK
  Displays all stack frames. A stack frame starts with the name of the method followed by the content of the corresponding stack. The stack values are denoted by $n = value$ where n equals 0 is the top stack element.
  During bytecode verification, the window displays the stack types ($opdT$) of the current verified instruction.
- VARIABLES
  Displays all local variables in the frame. The window is organized in the same way as the STACK window. The current method is always the first element. The variables are denoted by $n = value$ where n is the number of the variable.

---

[2] Users for Microsoft Windows should use the corresponding exe file (extension .exe).

Fig. A.7 Java Virtual Machine GUI

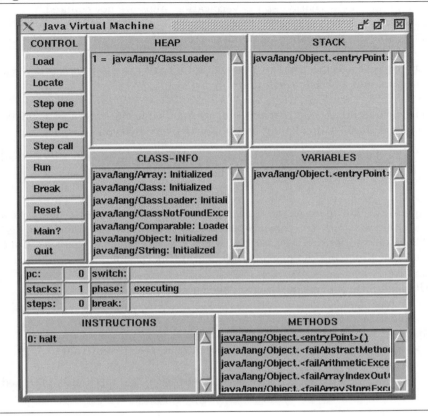

During bytecode verification, the window displays the local variable types
(*regT*) of the current verified instruction.

The INSTRUCTIONS frame at the bottom contains the bytecode instructions of the selected method in the METHODS frame. The METHODS frame shows
all known methods together with their class names.

Additionally, there are several info fields. These fields contain information
about dynamic functions like *pc* or *switch* and other information like the
current breakpoint. In particular, there are the following fields:

– pc
   The value of the dynamic function *pc*. During verification the field contains
   the *pc* of the currently verified instruction.
– stacks
   The number of stacks.

– steps

The number of execution steps. Verification steps are not counted.
– switch

The value of the dynamic function *switch*.
– phase

The current execution mode. Possible values are *executing, preparing verification*, and *bytecode verification*.
– break

The current breakpoint. Breakpoints are handled in the same way as breakpoints in Java. A breakpoint can be set to every bytecode instruction.

As for Java and Compiler GUI, there are buttons on the left side to load and execute a program. The buttons have the following behavior:

– Load

Opens the file manager to load a JVM program. The GUI manages a variable *classPath* to store the directories where the user loads classes. These directories are searched for when a class should be loaded during runtime. Resetting the machine resets also this variable.
– Locate

Highlights the current instruction and method.
– Step one

Executes one step.
– Step pc

Executes until the value of *pc* is different from the current value.
– Step call

If the current instruction is a method call, then the method is executed completely before the user gets back the control, otherwise the behavior is the same as Step one.
– Run

Starts the automatic run mode, as in Java.
– Break

Sets a breakpoint to the highlighted instruction.
– Reset

Resets all dynamic functions to their initial values. After resetting, the GUI is also in its initial state.
– Main?

The button displays a window with all main methods. The user can select the method to execute (as for Java).
– Quit

Quits the GUI and the AsmGofer interpreter.

A.4.4 Examples on the CD

The directory `machines/examples/jvm` contains examples for the Java Virtual Machine. These examples are mainly the examples of the Java part compiled with our compiler.

A.4.5 Dynamic Loading – Saraswat's Example

The class definitions below are similar to Saraswat's example [30]. For better readability we annotate class names with the defining loader.

The method invocation `rr.getR()` in the constructor of class RT^L is of special interest. The variable `rr` is of type RR^{sysLd}. Therefore, the result type of the method invocation is the result type of the method definition `getR()` in class RR^{sysLd}. The class RR^{sysLd} is loaded in such a way, that the result type of `getR()` will be R^{sysLd} (see definition below).

Let us reconsider the method invocation `rr.getR()` in the constructor of class RT^L. The result of the invocation is assigned to the variable `r`, which has declared type R^L. The assignment violates the type constraints of Java, if class R^{sysLd} (the result type of the invocation) is not compatible to R^L (the declared type of `r`). This is the case in our example, where L is supposed to be different from $sysLd$.

Earlier versions of the JDK did not detect a type error in the assignment `r = rr.getR()` even if L was different from $sysLd$. This error in the Sun verifier allowed type spoofing of local classes. In the example below, the Sun verifier verified the code of class RT^L with type R^L for variable `r`, although at run-time the type of `r` was R^{sysLd}. Our JVM with dynamic loading detects the type error when verifying the class RT^L.

```
public class RT^L {
  public  RT() {
    try {
      RR^{sysLd} rr = new  RR^{sysLd}();
      R^L       r  = rr.getR();
      r.r = 300960;
    } catch (Throwable e) {
      ...
    }
  }
}

public class RR^{sysLd} {
  public R^{sysLd} getR() {
    return new R^{sysLd}();
  }
}
```

```
public class R^{sysLd} {
 public String r = "abc";
}

public class R^L {
   public int r;
}
```

There are two questions to be addressed, namely whether (i) it is possible
to write bytecode, such that the above situation occurs, and (ii) how we can
show that with our machine the type error will be detected. In reproducing
Saraswat's example we are somehow handicapped by the fact that our machine supports only some Java API methods. For example, it is not possible
to load classes from a given URL.

In the following we describe how to write a class loader for the above example which can be used on our JVM. The presented class loader is a slightly
modified version of the class loader given by Saraswat in his example. For
simplicity we describe the classes in the source language and not in bytecode
directly. Therefore, the classes have to be compiled with the Sun compiler [3]
to bytecode. *BCEL* can then be used to translate the bytecode into Jasmin
syntax, which can be executed on our machine.

```
public abstract class LocalClassLoader extends ClassLoader {
   private String directory;
   public LocalClassLoader (String dir) {
    directory = dir;
   }
   protected Class loadClassFromFile(String name)
       throws ClassNotFoundException, IOException {
     FileInputStream f =
       new FileInputStream(directory + name + ".class");
     int bytecount = f.available();
     byte[] buffer = new byte[bytecount];
     try {
       f.read(buffer);
       return defineClass(name, buffer, 0, bytecount);
     }
     catch (Exception e) { ... }
   }
}
```

The class loader is initialized with a directory name, where the loader has
to look for classes. The method loadClassFromFile reads the content of
the given file name in that directory (if there is such a file). Afterwards, the

---

[3] Our compiler does not support the class ClassLoader.

method defines and returns the class. The following class extends the previous
class and defines the delegation to the system loader.

```
public class DelegatingLoader extends LocalClassLoader {
  public DelegatingLoader (String dir) { super(dir); }
  public synchronized Class loadClass(String name)
  throws ClassNotFoundException {
    try {
      if (name.equals("RR") || name.startsWith("java")) {
        return findSystemClass(name);
      }
      else
        return loadClassFromFile(name);
    } catch (Exception e) { ... }
  }
}
```

Assume that L is an instance of DelegatingLoader. If L has to load class
RT, it loads the class from the local file system, and L is the defining loader
for RT. The class R is referenced in RT, and therefore the class R will also
be loaded from the local file system and defined by L.

On the other hand, if L has to load class RR, then L delegates loading to
the system loader which will become the defining loader for that class. The
class contains also a reference R which is loaded and defined by the system
loader, too. Now, we have the situation described above.

The presented class LocalClassLoader compiled with JDK 1.2 and translated to Jasmin syntax with *BCEL* works also with our JVM. Note that our
implementation changes the suffix .class to .j. This allows to use the same
Java code for execution with JDK and for our JVM. Note also, that the
method available reports always size 0. Nevertheless, loading classes from
the local file system and defining them in this way, works fine in our implementation.

The directory machines/examples/jvm/Saraswat contains the above example. Example 18.3.3 deals also with dynamic loading.

B. Java

B.1 Rules

$$execJava = execJava_I$$
$$execJava_C$$
$$execJava_O$$
$$execJava_E$$
$$execJava_T$$

$$execJava_I =$$
$$execJavaExp_I$$
$$execJavaStm_I$$

$$execJava_C =$$
$$execJavaExp_C$$
$$execJavaStm_C$$

$$execJava_O =$$
$$execJavaExp_O$$

$$execJava_E =$$
$$execJavaExp_E$$
$$execJavaStm_E$$

$$execJava_T =$$
$$execJavaStm_T$$

$$context(pos) = \textbf{if } pos = firstPos \lor restbody/pos \in Bstm \cup Exp \textbf{ then}$$
$$restbody/pos$$
$$\textbf{else}$$
$$restbody/up(pos)$$

$$yieldUp(result) =$$
$$restbody := restbody[result/up(pos)]$$
$$pos \quad := up(pos)$$

$yield(result) =$
    $restbody := restbody[result/pos]$

$execJavaExp_I = \textbf{case } context(pos) \textbf{ of}$
    $lit \rightarrow yield(JLS(lit))$

    $loc \rightarrow yield(locals(loc))$

    $uop \, {}^{\alpha}exp \rightarrow pos := \alpha$
    $uop \blacktriangleright val \rightarrow yieldUp(JLS(uop, val))$

    ${}^{\alpha}exp_1 \; bop \; {}^{\beta}exp_2 \rightarrow pos := \alpha$
    $\blacktriangleright val \; bop \; {}^{\beta}exp \quad \rightarrow pos := \beta$
    ${}^{\alpha}val_1 \; bop \blacktriangleright val_2 \rightarrow \textbf{if } \neg(bop \in divMod \wedge isZero(val_2)) \textbf{ then}$
                        $yieldUp(JLS(bop, val_1, val_2))$

    $loc = {}^{\alpha}exp \rightarrow pos := \alpha$
    $loc = \blacktriangleright val \rightarrow locals := locals \oplus \{(loc, val)\}$
                    $yieldUp(val)$

    ${}^{\alpha}exp_0 \, ? \, {}^{\beta}exp_1 \, : \, {}^{\gamma}exp_2 \rightarrow pos := \alpha$
    $\blacktriangleright val \, ? \, {}^{\beta}exp_1 \, : \, {}^{\gamma}exp_2 \rightarrow \textbf{if } val \textbf{ then } pos := \beta \textbf{ else } pos := \gamma$
    ${}^{\alpha}True \, ? \blacktriangleright val \, : \, {}^{\gamma}exp \rightarrow yieldUp(val)$
    ${}^{\alpha}False \, ? \, {}^{\beta}exp \, : \blacktriangleright val \rightarrow yieldUp(val)$

$execJavaStm_I = \textbf{case } context(pos) \textbf{ of}$
   $;\qquad \rightarrow yield(Norm)$
   $^\alpha exp; \rightarrow pos := \alpha$
   $^\blacktriangleright val; \rightarrow yieldUp(Norm)$

   $\textbf{break } lab; \qquad\qquad\quad \rightarrow yield(Break(lab))$
   $\textbf{continue } lab; \qquad\qquad \rightarrow yield(Continue(lab))$
   $lab : {}^\alpha stm \qquad\qquad\quad \rightarrow pos := \alpha$
   $lab : {}^\blacktriangleright Norm \qquad\qquad \rightarrow yieldUp(Norm)$
   $lab : {}^\blacktriangleright Break(lab_b) \quad \rightarrow \textbf{if } lab = lab_b \textbf{ then } yieldUp(Norm)$
                         $\textbf{else } yieldUp(Break(lab_b))$
   $lab : {}^\blacktriangleright Continue(lab_c) \rightarrow \textbf{if } lab = lab_c \textbf{ then } yield(body/pos)$
                         $\textbf{else } yieldUp(Continue(lab_c))$
   $phrase(^\blacktriangleright abr) \rightarrow \textbf{if } pos \neq firstPos \wedge propagatesAbr(restbody/up(pos)) \textbf{ then}$
                        $yieldUp(abr)$

   $\{\,\} \qquad\qquad\qquad\qquad\qquad\qquad\qquad \rightarrow yield(Norm)$
   $\{^{\alpha_1} stm_1 \ldots {}^{\alpha_n} stm_n\} \qquad\qquad\quad \rightarrow pos := \alpha_1$
   $\{^{\alpha_1} Norm \ldots {}^\blacktriangleright Norm\} \qquad\qquad \rightarrow yieldUp(Norm)$
   $\{^{\alpha_1} Norm \ldots {}^\blacktriangleright Norm^{\alpha_{i+1}} stm_{i+1} \ldots {}^{\alpha_n} stm_n\} \rightarrow pos := \alpha_{i+1}$

   $\textbf{if } (^\alpha exp)\,^\beta stm_1 \textbf{ else }^\gamma stm_2 \rightarrow pos := \alpha$
   $\textbf{if } (^\blacktriangleright val)\,^\beta stm_1 \textbf{ else }^\gamma stm_2 \rightarrow \textbf{if } val \textbf{ then } pos := \beta \textbf{ else } pos := \gamma$
   $\textbf{if } (^\alpha True)^\blacktriangleright Norm \textbf{ else }^\gamma stm \rightarrow yieldUp(Norm)$
   $\textbf{if } (^\alpha False)^\beta stm \textbf{ else }^\blacktriangleright Norm \rightarrow yieldUp(Norm)$

   $\textbf{while } (^\alpha exp)\,^\beta stm \qquad \rightarrow pos := \alpha$
   $\textbf{while } (^\blacktriangleright val)\,^\beta stm \qquad \rightarrow \textbf{if } val \textbf{ then } pos := \beta \textbf{ else } yieldUp(Norm)$
   $\textbf{while } (^\alpha True)^\blacktriangleright Norm \rightarrow yieldUp(body/up(pos))$

   $Type\ x; \rightarrow yield(Norm)$

$execJavaExp_C = \textbf{case } context(pos) \textbf{ of}$
   $c.f \qquad\qquad \rightarrow \textbf{if } initialized(c) \textbf{ then } yield(globals(c/f)) \textbf{ else } initialize(c)$
   $c.f = {}^\alpha exp \rightarrow pos := \alpha$
   $c.f = {}^\blacktriangleright val \rightarrow \textbf{if } initialized(c) \textbf{ then}$
                  $globals(c/f) := val$
                  $yieldUp(val)$
              $\textbf{else } initialize(c)$

   $c.m^\alpha(exps) \rightarrow pos := \alpha$
   $c.m^\blacktriangleright(vals) \rightarrow \textbf{if } initialized(c) \textbf{ then } invokeMethod(up(pos), c/m, vals)$
                 $\textbf{else } initialize(c)$

   $(\,) \qquad\qquad\qquad\qquad\qquad\qquad \rightarrow yield([\,])$
   $(^{\alpha_1} exp_1, \ldots, {}^{\alpha_n} exp_n) \qquad\qquad \rightarrow pos := \alpha_1$
   $(^{\alpha_1} val_1, \ldots, {}^\blacktriangleright val_n) \qquad\qquad \rightarrow yieldUp([val_1, \ldots, val_n])$
   $(^{\alpha_1} val_1, \ldots, {}^\blacktriangleright val_i, {}^{\alpha_{i+1}} exp_{i+1} \ldots {}^{\alpha_n} exp_n) \rightarrow pos := \alpha_{i+1}$

$initialize(c) =$
  if $classState(c) = Linked$ **then**
    $classState(c) := InProgress$
    forall $f \in staticFields(c)$
      $globals(f) := defaultVal(type(f))$
    $invokeMethod(pos, c/\texttt{<clinit>}, [\,])$
  if $classState(c) = Linked$ **then**
    $initWait(c) \quad := \emptyset$
    $initThread(c) := thread$
  if $classState(c) = InProgress \wedge initThread(c) \neq thread$ **then**
    $exec(thread) := Waiting$
    $cont(thread) := (frames, (meth, restbody, pos, locals))$
    $initWait(c) \quad := initWait(c) \cup \{thread\}$
  if $classState(c) = Unusable$ **then**
    $fail(\texttt{NoClassDefFoundErr})$

$execJavaStm_C = $ **case** $context(pos)$ **of**
  $\texttt{static }{}^\alpha stm \rightarrow$ **let** $c = classNm(meth)$
    if $c = \texttt{Object} \vee initialized(super(c))$ **then** $pos := \alpha$
    else $initialize(super(c))$
  $\texttt{static }{}^\alpha Return \rightarrow yieldUp(Return)$

  $\texttt{return }{}^\alpha exp; \qquad \rightarrow pos := \alpha$
  $\texttt{return }{}^\blacktriangleright val; \qquad \rightarrow yieldUp(Return(val))$
  $\texttt{return}; \qquad\qquad \rightarrow yield(Return)$
  $lab : {}^\blacktriangleright Return \qquad \rightarrow yieldUp(Return)$
  $lab : {}^\blacktriangleright Return(val) \rightarrow yieldUp(Return(val))$
  $Return \qquad\qquad\quad \rightarrow$ **if** $pos = firstPos \wedge \neg null(frames)$ **then**
    $\qquad\qquad\qquad\qquad\qquad exitMethod(Norm)$
  $Return(val) \qquad\quad \rightarrow$ **if** $pos = firstPos \wedge \neg null(frames)$ **then**
    $\qquad\qquad\qquad\qquad\qquad exitMethod(val)$

  ${}^\blacktriangleright Norm; \rightarrow yieldUp(Norm)$

$invokeMethod(nextPos, c/m, values)$
  $\mid Native \in modifiers(c/m) =$
    $invokeNative(c/m, values)$
  $\mid$ **otherwise** $=$
    $frames \quad := push(frames, (meth, restbody, nextPos, locals))$
    $meth \quad\;\; := c/m$
    $restbody := body(c/m)$
    $pos \qquad := firstPos$
    $locals \quad\;\; := zip(argNames(c/m), values)$

$exitMethod(result) =$
  let $(oldMeth, oldPgm, oldPos, oldLocals) = top(frames)$
  $meth$ $:= oldMeth$
  pos $:= oldPos$
  $locals$ $:= oldLocals$
  $frames := pop(frames)$
  if $methNm(meth) =$ `"<clinit>"` $\land result = Norm$ **then**
    $restbody$ $:= oldPgm$
    $classState(classNm(meth)) := Initialized$
  elseif $methNm(meth) =$ `"<init>"` $\land result = Norm$ **then**
    $restbody := oldPgm[locals(\text{"this"})/oldPos]$
  else
    $restbody := oldPgm[result/oldPos]$

$execJavaExp_O =$ **case** $context(pos)$ **of**
  `this` $\rightarrow yield(locals(\text{"this"}))$

  `new` $c \rightarrow$ **if** $initialized(c)$ **then create** ref
              $heap(ref) := Object(c, \{(f, defaultVal(type(f)))$
                            $\mid f \in instanceFields(c)\})$
              $waitSet(ref) := \emptyset$
              $locks(ref)$ $:= 0$
              if $c \preceq_h$ **Thread then**
                $exec(ref) := NotStarted$
                $sync(ref) := [\,]$
                $interruptedFlag(ref) := False$
              $yield(ref)$
            else $initialize(c)$

  $^\alpha exp.c/f \rightarrow pos := \alpha$
  $^\blacktriangleright ref.c/f \rightarrow$ **if** $ref \neq null$ **then** $yieldUp(getField(ref, c/f))$

  $^\alpha exp_1.c/f = {}^\beta exp_2 \rightarrow pos := \alpha$
  $^\blacktriangleright ref.c/f = {}^\beta exp \rightarrow pos := \beta$
  $^\alpha ref.c/f = {}^\blacktriangleright val \rightarrow$ **if** $ref \neq null$ **then**
    $setField(ref, c/f, val)$
    $yieldUp(val)$

  $^\alpha exp$ `instanceof` $c \rightarrow pos := \alpha$
  $^\blacktriangleright ref$ `instanceof` $c \rightarrow yieldUp(ref \neq null \land classOf(ref) \preceq c)$

  $(c)^\alpha exp \rightarrow pos := \alpha$
  $(c)^\blacktriangleright ref \rightarrow$ **if** $ref = null \lor classOf(ref) \preceq c$ **then** $yieldUp(ref)$

  $^\alpha exp.c/m^\beta(exps) \rightarrow pos := \alpha$
  $^\blacktriangleright ref.c/m^\beta(exps) \rightarrow pos := \beta$
  $^\alpha ref.c/m^\blacktriangleright(vals) \rightarrow$ **if** $ref \neq null$ **then**
    let $c' =$ **case** $callKind(up(pos))$ **of**
            $Virtual \rightarrow lookup(classOf(ref), c/m)$
            $Super \rightarrow lookup(super(classNm(meth)), c/m)$
            $Special \rightarrow c$
    $invokeMethod(up(pos), c'/m, [ref] \cdot vals)$

$$failUp(exc) = yieldUp(\textbf{throw new } exc();)$$
$$fail(exc) \quad = yield(\textbf{throw new } exc();)$$

$execJavaStm_E = \textbf{case } context(pos) \textbf{ of}$
   $\textbf{throw } {}^\alpha exp; \rightarrow pos := \alpha$
   $\textbf{throw } {}^\blacktriangleright ref; \rightarrow \textbf{if } ref = null \textbf{ then } failUp(\texttt{NullPointerException})$
               $\textbf{else } yieldUp(Exc(ref))$

   $\textbf{try } {}^\alpha stm \textbf{ catch} \ldots \quad \rightarrow pos := \alpha$
   $\textbf{try } {}^\blacktriangleright Norm \textbf{ catch} \ldots \rightarrow yieldUp(Norm)$
   $\textbf{try } {}^\blacktriangleright Exc(ref) \textbf{ catch } (c_1\ x_1)\ {}^{\beta_1} stm_1 \ldots \textbf{catch } (c_n\ x_n)\ {}^{\beta_n} stm_n \rightarrow$
      $\textbf{if } \exists\, 1 \leq j \leq n : classOf(ref) \preceq_{\mathrm{h}} c_j \textbf{ then}$
         $\textbf{let } j = \min\{i \mid classOf(ref) \preceq_{\mathrm{h}} c_i\}$
         $pos \quad := \beta_j$
         $locals := locals \oplus \{(x_j, ref)\}$
      $\textbf{else } yieldUp(Exc(ref))$
   $\textbf{try } {}^\blacktriangleright abr \textbf{ catch } (c_1\ x_1)\ {}^{\beta_1} stm_1 \ldots \textbf{catch } (c_n\ x_n)\ {}^{\beta_n} stm_n \rightarrow yieldUp(abr)$
   $\textbf{try } {}^\alpha Exc(ref) \ldots \textbf{catch } (c_i\ x_i)\ {}^\blacktriangleright Norm \ldots \rightarrow yieldUp(Norm)$
   $\textbf{try } {}^\alpha Exc(ref) \ldots \textbf{catch } (c_i\ x_i)\ {}^\blacktriangleright abr \ldots \quad \rightarrow yieldUp(abr)$

   ${}^\alpha stm_1 \textbf{ finally } {}^\beta stm_2 \rightarrow pos := \alpha$
   ${}^\blacktriangleright Norm \textbf{ finally } {}^\beta stm \rightarrow pos := \beta$
   ${}^\blacktriangleright abr \textbf{ finally } {}^\beta stm \quad \rightarrow pos := \beta$
   ${}^\alpha s \textbf{ finally } {}^\blacktriangleright Norm \quad \rightarrow yieldUp(s)$
   ${}^\alpha s \textbf{ finally } {}^\blacktriangleright abr \quad \rightarrow yieldUp(abr)$

   $lab : {}^\blacktriangleright Exc(ref) \quad \rightarrow yieldUp(Exc(ref))$
   $\texttt{static } {}^\alpha Exc(ref) \rightarrow$
      $\textbf{if } classOf(ref) \preceq_{\mathrm{h}} \texttt{Error} \textbf{ then}$
         $yieldUp(Exc(ref))$
      $\textbf{else}$
         $failUp(\texttt{ExceptionInInitializerError})$
   $Exc(ref) \rightarrow \textbf{if } pos = firstPos \wedge \neg null(frames) \textbf{ then}$
            $exitMethod(Exc(ref))$
            $\textbf{if } methNm(meth) = \texttt{"<clinit>"} \textbf{ then}$
               $classState(classNm(meth)) := Unusable$

$execJavaExp_E = \textbf{case } context(pos) \textbf{ of}$
   ${}^\alpha val_1\ bop\ {}^\blacktriangleright val_2 \quad \rightarrow \textbf{if } bop \in divMod \wedge isZero(val_2) \textbf{ then}$
                   $failUp(\texttt{ArithmeticException})$
   ${}^\blacktriangleright ref.c/f \qquad\quad \rightarrow \textbf{if } ref = null \textbf{ then } failUp(\texttt{NullPointerException})$
   ${}^\alpha ref.c/f = {}^\blacktriangleright val \rightarrow \textbf{if } ref = null \textbf{ then } failUp(\texttt{NullPointerException})$
   ${}^\alpha ref.c/m\ {}^\blacktriangleright (vals) \rightarrow \textbf{if } ref = null \textbf{ then } failUp(\texttt{NullPointerException})$
   $(c)\ {}^\blacktriangleright ref \qquad\qquad \rightarrow \textbf{if } ref \neq null \wedge classOf(ref) \npreceq c \textbf{ then}$
                   $failUp(\texttt{ClassCastException})$

$releaseLock(phrase) =$
   $\textbf{let } [p] \cdot rest = sync(thread)$
   $sync(thread) := rest$
   $locks(p) \qquad := locks(p) - 1$
   $yieldUp(phrase)$

$killThread =$
  $waitSet(thread) := \emptyset$
  $exec(thread)\quad := Dead$
  forall $q \in waitSet(thread)$
    $exec(q) := Notified$

$execJavaStm_T = \textbf{case } context(pos) \textbf{ of}$
  synchronized $(^{\alpha}exp)^{\beta}stm \rightarrow pos := \alpha$
  synchronized $(^{\blacktriangleright}ref)^{\beta}stm \rightarrow$
    if $ref = null$ **then** $failUp(\texttt{NullPointerException})$
    else
      if $ref \in sync(thread)$ **then**
        $sync(thread) := [ref] \cdot sync(thread)$
        $locks(ref)\quad := locks(ref) + 1$
        $pos\qquad\quad := \beta$
      else
        $exec(thread)\qquad := Synchronizing$
        $syncObj(thread) := ref$
        $cont(thread)\qquad := (frames, (meth, restbody, \beta, locals))$
  synchronized $(^{\alpha}ref)^{\blacktriangleright}Norm \rightarrow releaseLock(Norm)$
  synchronized $(^{\alpha}ref)^{\blacktriangleright}abr\quad \rightarrow releaseLock(abr)$

  static $^{\blacktriangleright}abr \rightarrow notifyThreadsWaitingForInitialization$
  $abr \rightarrow \textbf{if } pos = firstPos \wedge null(frames) \textbf{ then } killThread$

$notifyThreadsWaitingForInitialization =$
  let $c = classNm(meth)$
  $initWait(c)\quad := \emptyset$
  $initThread(c) := undef$
  forall $q \in initWait(c)$
    $exec(q) := Active$

$execJavaThread =$
  choose $q \in dom(exec), runnable(q)$
    if $q = thread \wedge exec(q) = Active$ **then**
      $execJava$
    else
      if $exec(thread) = Active$ **then**
        $cont(thread) := (frames, (meth, restbody, pos, locals))$
      $thread := q$
      $run(q)$

$run(q) =$
  $switchCont(q)$
  if $exec(q) = Synchronizing$ **then**
    $synchronize(q)$
  if $exec(q) = Notified$ **then**
    $wakeup(q)$

$switchCont(q) =$
  let $(frames', (meth', restbody', pos', locals')) = cont(q)$
  $exec(q) := Active$
  $meth   := meth'$
  $restbody := restbody'$
  $pos   := pos'$
  $locals   := locals'$
  $frames   := frames'$

$synchronize(q) =$
  $sync(q)   := [syncObj(q)] \cdot sync(q)$
  $locks(syncObj(q)) := 1$

$wakeup(q) =$
  $locks(waitObj(q)) := occurrences(waitObj(q), sync(q))$

$invokeNative(meth, values)$
  $\mid\ meth = \text{Thread/start()}$ $= start(values(0))$
  $\mid\ meth = \text{Thread/interrupt()}$ $= interrupt(values(0))$
  $\mid\ meth = \text{Thread/interrupted()}$ $= interrupted$
  $\mid\ meth = \text{Thread/isInterrupted()}$ $= isInterrupted(values(0))$
  $\mid\ meth = \text{Object/wait()}$ $= wait(values(0))$
  $\mid\ meth = \text{Object/notify()}$ $= notify(values(0))$
  $\mid\ meth = \text{Object/notifyAll()}$ $= notifyAll(values(0))$

$start(ref) =$
  if $exec(ref) \neq NotStarted$ **then**
    $fail(\text{IllegalThreadStateException})$
  else
    let $q   = getField(ref, \text{Thread/ "target"})$
        $meth = lookup(classOf(q), \text{Thread/run()})/\text{run()}$
    $exec(ref) := Active$
    $cont(ref) := ([], (meth, body(meth), firstPos, \{(\text{"this"}, q)\}))$
    $yieldUp(Norm)$

$interrupt(q) =$
  $yieldUp(Norm)$
  if $exec(q) = Waiting \land \neg classInitialization(q)$ **then**
    let $(frames', (meth', restbody', pos', locals')) = cont(q)$
    let $fail = restbody'[\textbf{throw new } \text{InterruptedException}(); /pos']$
    let $ref = waitObj(q)$
    $waitSet(ref) := waitSet(ref) \setminus \{q\}$
    $exec(q)   := Notified$
    $cont(q)   := (frames', (meth', fail, pos', locals'))$
    $interruptedFlag(q) := False$
  else
    $interruptedFlag(q) := True$

$interrupted =$
  if $interruptedFlag(thread)$ **then**
    $interruptedFlag(thread) := False$
    $yield(True)$
  else
    $yield(False)$

$isInterrupted(q) =$
  if $interruptedFlag(q)$ **then**
    $yieldUp(True)$
  else
    $yieldUp(False)$

$wait(ref) =$
  if $ref \notin sync(thread)$ **then**
    $fail(\texttt{IllegalMonitorStateException})$
  else
    let $ret = restbody[Norm/up(pos)]$
    $waitSet(ref)$ $:= waitSet(ref) \cup \{thread\}$
    $locks(ref)$ $:= 0$
    $exec(thread)$ $:= Waiting$
    $waitObj(thread) := ref$
    $cont(thread)$ $:= (frames, (meth, ret, up(pos), locals))$
    $yieldUp(Norm)$

$notify(ref) =$
  if $ref \notin sync(thread)$ **then**
    $fail(\texttt{IllegalMonitorStateException})$
  else
    $yieldUp(Norm)$
    choose $q \in waitSet(ref)$
      $waitSet(ref) := waitSet(ref) \setminus \{q\}$
      $exec(q)$ $:= Notified$

$notifyAll(ref) =$
  if $ref \notin sync(thread)$ **then**
    $fail(\texttt{IllegalMonitorStateException})$
  else
    $waitSet(ref) := \emptyset$
    $yieldUp(Norm)$
    forall $q \in waitSet(ref)$
      $exec(q) := Notified$

B.2 Arrays

Grammar:

$$
\begin{aligned}
Exp &:= \dots \mid Exp[Exp] \\
Asgn &:= \dots \mid Exp[Exp] = Exp \\
Invk &:= \dots \mid \textbf{new } Exp[Exp_1] \dots [Exp_n]
\end{aligned}
$$

Heap structure:

$$\textbf{data } Heap= Object(Class, Map(Class/Field, Val))$$
$$\mid Array(Type, [Val])$$

$$classOf(ref) = \textbf{case } heap(ref) \textbf{ of}$$
$$Array(t, elems) \rightarrow Array(t)$$
$$Object(c, fields) \rightarrow c$$

Execution rules for arrays:

$$execJava_{Array} = \textbf{case } context(pos) \textbf{ of}$$
$$^{\alpha}exp_1[^{\beta}exp_2] \rightarrow pos := \alpha$$
$$^{\blacktriangleright}ref[^{\beta}exp] \quad \rightarrow pos := \beta$$
$$^{\alpha}ref[^{\blacktriangleright}i] \qquad \rightarrow \textbf{if } ref = null \textbf{ then } fail(\texttt{NullPointerException})$$
$$\textbf{elseif } i < 0 \vee i \geq arraySize(ref) \textbf{ then}$$
$$fail(\texttt{IndexOutOfBoundsException})$$
$$\textbf{else}$$
$$yieldUp(getElement(ref, i))$$

$$^{\alpha}exp_1[^{\beta}exp_2] = {}^{\gamma}exp_3 \rightarrow pos := \alpha$$
$$^{\blacktriangleright}ref[^{\beta}exp_2] = {}^{\gamma}exp_3 \rightarrow pos := \beta$$
$$^{\alpha}ref[^{\blacktriangleright}i] = {}^{\gamma}exp_3 \quad \rightarrow pos := \gamma$$
$$^{\alpha}ref[^{\beta}i] = {}^{\blacktriangleright}val \quad \rightarrow$$
$$\quad \textbf{if } ref = null \textbf{ then}$$
$$\quad\quad fail(\texttt{NullPointerException})$$
$$\quad \textbf{elseif } i < 0 \vee i \geq arraySize(ref) \textbf{ then}$$
$$\quad\quad fail(\texttt{IndexOutOfBoundsException})$$
$$\quad \textbf{elseif } val \in Ref \wedge classOf(val) \not\preceq c \textbf{ then}$$
$$\quad\quad fail(\texttt{ArrayStoreException})$$
$$\quad \textbf{else}$$
$$\quad\quad setElement(ref, i, val)$$
$$\quad\quad yieldUp(val)$$
$$\quad \textbf{where } Array(c, \_) = heap(ref)$$

$$\textbf{new } t[^{\alpha_1}exp_1] \ldots [^{\alpha_n}exp_n] \rightarrow pos := \alpha_1$$
$$\textbf{new } t[^{\alpha_1}dim_1] \ldots [^{\blacktriangleright}dim_n] \rightarrow$$
$$\quad \textbf{if } \exists 1 \leq j \leq n : dim_j < 0 \textbf{ then}$$
$$\quad\quad fail(\texttt{NegativeArraySizeException})$$
$$\quad \textbf{else}$$
$$\quad\quad \textbf{let } ref := createArray(t, n, [dim_1, \ldots, dim_n])$$
$$\quad\quad yieldUp(ref)$$
$$\textbf{new } t[^{\alpha_1}dim_1] \ldots [^{\blacktriangleright}dim_i][^{\alpha_{i+1}}exp_{i+1}] \ldots [^{\alpha_n}exp_n] \rightarrow pos := \alpha_{i+1}$$

Array functions:

$createArray(Array(t), d, [i] \cdot is) = \textbf{create } ref$
    $waitSet(ref) := \emptyset$
    $locks(ref) := 0$
    $\textbf{if } d = 1 \textbf{ then}$
        $heap(ref) := Array(t, take(i, repeat(defaultVal(t))))$
        $result(ref)$
    $\textbf{else}$
        $\textbf{let } elems := \textbf{forall } x \in [1..i]$
           $\textbf{let } r := createArray(t, d - 1, is)$
           $result(r)$
        $heap(ref) := Array(t, elems)$
        $result(ref)$

$getElement(ref, i) = elems(i)$
   $\textbf{where } Array(t, elems) = heap(ref)$

$setElement(ref, i, e) =$
   $heap(ref) := Array(t, take(i, elems) \cdot [e] \cdot drop(i + 1, elems))$
$\textbf{where } Array(t, elems) = heap(ref)$

$arraySize(ref) = length(elems)$
   $\textbf{where } Array(t, elems) = heap(ref)$

C. JVM

C.1 Trustful execution

$execVM_I(instr) =$
 case $instr$ **of**

$Prim(p)$	$\rightarrow$	**let** $(opd', ws) = split(opd, argSize(p))$
		if $p \in divMod \Rightarrow sndArgIsNotZero(ws)$ **then**
		$opd := opd' \cdot JVMS(p, ws)$
		$pc\ \ := pc + 1$
$Dupx(s_1, s_2)$	$\rightarrow$	**let** $(opd', [ws_1, ws_2]) = splits(opd, [s_1, s_2])$
		$opd := opd' \cdot ws_2 \cdot ws_1 \cdot ws_2$
		$pc\ \ := pc + 1$
$Pop(s)$	$\rightarrow$	**let** $(opd', ws) = split(opd, s)$
		$opd := opd'$
		$pc\ \ := pc + 1$
$Load(t, x)$	$\rightarrow$	**if** $size(t) = 1$ **then** $opd := opd \cdot [reg(x)]$
		else $opd := opd \cdot [reg(x), reg(x + 1)]$
		$pc := pc + 1$
$Store(t, x)$	$\rightarrow$	**let** $(opd', ws) = split(opd, size(t))$
		if $size(t) = 1$ **then** $reg := reg \oplus \{(x, ws(0))\}$
		else $reg := reg \oplus \{(x, ws(0)), (x + 1, ws(1))\}$
		$opd := opd'$
		$pc\ \ := pc + 1$
$Goto(o)$	$\rightarrow$	$pc := o$
$Cond(p, o)$	$\rightarrow$	**let** $(opd', ws) = split(opd, argSize(p))$
		$opd := opd'$
		if $JVMS(p, ws)$ **then** $pc := o$ **else** $pc := pc + 1$
$Halt$	$\rightarrow$	$halt :=$ `"Halt"`

$$execVM_C(instr) =$$
$$execVM_I(instr)$$

case $instr$ **of**

$\quad GetStatic(\_, c/f) \rightarrow$ **if** $initialized(c)$ **then**
$$\qquad\qquad opd := opd \cdot globals(c/f)$$
$$\qquad\qquad pc \;\;:= pc + 1$$
$\qquad\qquad$ **else** $switch := InitClass(c)$

$\quad PutStatic(\_, c/f) \rightarrow$ **if** $initialized(c)$ **then**
$\qquad\qquad$ **let** $(opd', ws) = split(opd, size(c/f))$
$$\qquad\qquad globals(c/f) := ws$$
$$\qquad\qquad opd := opd'$$
$$\qquad\qquad pc \;\;:= pc + 1$$
$\qquad\qquad$ **else** $switch := InitClass(c)$

$\quad InvokeStatic(\_, c/m) \rightarrow$ **if** $initialized(c)$ **then**
$\qquad\qquad$ **let** $(opd', ws) = split(opd, argSize(c/m))$
$$\qquad\qquad opd \;\;\;\; := opd'$$
$$\qquad\qquad switch := Call(c/m, ws)$$
$\qquad\qquad$ **else** $switch := InitClass(c)$

$\quad Return(t) \rightarrow$ **let** $(opd', ws) = split(opd, size(t))$
$$\qquad\qquad switch := Result(ws)$$

$$switchVM_C =$$

case $switch$ **of**

$\quad Call(meth, args) \rightarrow$ **if** $\neg isAbstract(meth)$ **then**
$$\qquad\qquad pushFrame(meth, args)$$
$$\qquad\qquad switch := Noswitch$$

$\quad Result(res) \;\; \rightarrow$ **if** $implicitCall(meth)$ **then** $popFrame(0, [])$
$\qquad\qquad$ **else** $popFrame(1, res)$
$$\qquad\qquad switch := Noswitch$$

$\quad InitClass(c) \rightarrow$ **if** $classState(c) = Linked$ **then**
$$\qquad\qquad classState(c) := Initialized$$
$\qquad\qquad$ **forall** $f \in staticFields(c)$
$$\qquad\qquad\quad globals(c/f) := default(type(c/f))$$
$$\qquad\qquad pushFrame(c/\texttt{<clinit>}())$$
$\qquad\qquad$ **if** $c = \texttt{Object} \vee initialized(super(c))$ **then**
$$\qquad\qquad\quad switch := Noswitch$$
$\qquad\qquad$ **else**
$$\qquad\qquad\quad switch := InitClass(super(c))$$

$$pushFrame(newMeth, args) =$$
$$\quad stack := stack \cdot [(pc, reg, opd, meth)]$$
$$\quad meth := newMeth$$
$$\quad pc \;\;\;\; := 0$$
$$\quad opd \;\;\; := []$$
$$\quad reg \;\;\; := makeRegs(args)$$

$$popFrame(offset, result) =$$
$\quad$ **let** $(stack', [(pc', reg', opd', meth')]) = split(stack, 1)$
$$\quad pc \;\;\;\; := pc' + offset$$
$$\quad reg \;\;\; := reg'$$
$$\quad opd \;\;\; := opd' \cdot result$$
$$\quad meth := meth'$$
$$\quad stack := stack'$$

$execVM_O(instr) =$
$\quad execVM_C(instr)$
$\quad \textbf{case } instr \textbf{ of}$
$\quad\quad New(c) \rightarrow$
$\quad\quad\quad \textbf{if } initialized(c) \textbf{ then create } r$
$\quad\quad\quad\quad heap(r) := Object(c, \{(f, defaultVal(f)) \mid f \in instanceFields(c)\})$
$\quad\quad\quad\quad opd := opd \cdot [r]$
$\quad\quad\quad\quad pc \;\; := pc + 1$
$\quad\quad\quad \textbf{else } switch := InitClass(c)$
$\quad\quad GetField(\_, c/f) \rightarrow \textbf{let } (opd', [r]) = split(opd, 1)$
$\quad\quad\quad\quad\quad\quad\quad\quad\quad \textbf{if } r \neq null \textbf{ then}$
$\quad\quad\quad\quad\quad\quad\quad\quad\quad\quad opd := opd' \cdot getField(r, c/f)$
$\quad\quad\quad\quad\quad\quad\quad\quad\quad\quad pc \;\; := pc + 1$
$\quad\quad PutField(\_, c/f) \rightarrow \textbf{let } (opd', [r] \cdot ws) = split(opd, 1 + size(c/f))$
$\quad\quad\quad\quad\quad\quad\quad\quad\quad \textbf{if } r \neq null \textbf{ then}$
$\quad\quad\quad\quad\quad\quad\quad\quad\quad\quad setField(r, c/f, ws)$
$\quad\quad\quad\quad\quad\quad\quad\quad\quad\quad pc \;\; := pc + 1$
$\quad\quad\quad\quad\quad\quad\quad\quad\quad\quad opd := opd'$
$\quad\quad InvokeSpecial(\_, c/m) \rightarrow$
$\quad\quad\quad \textbf{let } (opd', [r] \cdot ws) = split(opd, 1 + argSize(c/m))$
$\quad\quad\quad \textbf{if } r \neq null \textbf{ then}$
$\quad\quad\quad\quad opd \quad := opd'$
$\quad\quad\quad\quad switch := Call(c/m, [r] \cdot ws)$
$\quad\quad InvokeVirtual(\_, c/m) \rightarrow$
$\quad\quad\quad \textbf{let } (opd', [r] \cdot ws) = split(opd, 1 + argSize(c/m))$
$\quad\quad\quad \textbf{if } r \neq null \textbf{ then}$
$\quad\quad\quad\quad opd \quad := opd'$
$\quad\quad\quad\quad switch := Call(lookup(classOf(r), c/m), [r] \cdot ws)$

$\quad\quad InstanceOf(c) \rightarrow \textbf{let } (opd', [r]) = split(opd, 1)$
$\quad\quad\quad\quad\quad\quad\quad\quad\quad opd := opd' \cdot (r \neq null \wedge classOf(r) \sqsubseteq c)$
$\quad\quad\quad\quad\quad\quad\quad\quad\quad pc \;\; := pc + 1$
$\quad\quad Checkcast(c) \;\; \rightarrow \textbf{let } r = top(opd)$
$\quad\quad\quad\quad\quad\quad\quad\quad\quad \textbf{if } r = null \vee classOf(r) \sqsubseteq c \textbf{ then}$
$\quad\quad\quad\quad\quad\quad\quad\quad\quad\quad pc := pc + 1$

$switchVM_E =$
  $switchVM_C$
  case $switch$ **of**
    $Call(meth, args) \rightarrow$ **if** $isAbstract(meth)$ **then**
                  $raise(\,\texttt{"AbstractMethodError"}\,)$
    $InitClass(c) \rightarrow$ **if** $unusable(c)$ **then**
                  $raise(\,\texttt{"NoClassDefFoundError"}\,)$
    $Throw(r) \rightarrow$ **if** $\neg escapes(meth, pc, classOf(r))$ **then**
                  let $exc = handler(meth, pc, classOf(r))$
                  $pc \quad := handle(exc)$
                  $opd \quad := [r]$
                  $switch := Noswitch$
                else
                  if $methNm(meth) = \texttt{"<clinit>"}$ **then**
                    if $\neg(classOf(r) \preceq_{\mathrm{h}} \textbf{Error})$ **then**
                      $raise(\,\texttt{"ExceptionInInitializerError"}\,)$
                      $pc := undef$
                    else $switch := ThrowInit(r)$
                  else $popFrame(0, [\,])$
    $ThrowInit(r) \rightarrow$ **let** $c = classNm(meth)$
                  $classState(c) := Unusable$
                  $popFrame(0, [\,])$
                  if $\neg superInit(top(stack), c)$ **then**
                    $switch := Throw(r)$

$superInit((\_,\_,\_, m), c) =$
  $methNm(m) = \texttt{"<clinit>"} \wedge super(classNm(m)) = c$

$execVM_E(instr) =$
  $execVM_O(instr)$
  case $instr$ **of**
    $Athrow \rightarrow$ **let** $[r] = take(opd, 1)$
              if $r \neq null$ **then** $switch := Throw(r)$
              else $raise(\,\texttt{"NullPointerException"}\,)$
    $Jsr(s) \rightarrow opd := opd \cdot [pc + 1]$
          $pc \quad := s$
    $Ret(x) \rightarrow pc := reg(x)$
    $Prim(p) \rightarrow$ **let** $ws = take(opd, argSize(p))$
              if $p \in divMod \wedge sndArgIsZero(ws)$ **then**
                $raise(\,\texttt{"ArithmeticException"}\,)$
    $GetField(\_, c/f) \rightarrow$ **let** $[r] = take(opd, 1)$
                  if $r = null$ **then** $raise(\,\texttt{"NullPointerException"}\,)$
    $PutField(\_, c/f) \rightarrow$ **let** $[r] \cdot ws = take(opd, 1 + size(c/f))$
                  if $r = null$ **then** $raise(\,\texttt{"NullPointerException"}\,)$
    $InvokeSpecial(\_, c/m) \rightarrow$
      let $[r] \cdot ws = take(opd, 1 + argSize(c/m))$
      if $r = null$ **then** $raise(\,\texttt{"NullPointerException"}\,)$
    $InvokeVirtual(\_, c/m) \rightarrow$
      let $[r] \cdot ws = take(opd, 1 + argSize(c/m))$
      if $r = null$ **then** $raise(\,\texttt{"NullPointerException"}\,)$
    $Checkcast(c) \rightarrow$ **let** $r = top(opd)$
                  if $r \neq 0 \wedge \neg(classOf(r) \sqsubseteq c)$ **then**
                    $raise(\,\texttt{"ClassCastException"}\,)$

$exec\,VM_N =$
  if $meth =$ Object/ equals then
    $switch := Result(reg(0) = reg(1))$
  elseif $meth =$ Object/ clone then
    let $r = reg(0)$
    if $classOf(r) \preceq_h$ Cloneable then
      create r'
        $heap(r') := heap(r)$
        $switch \quad := Result(r')$
    else
      $raise($ "CloneNotSupportedException" $)$

$switch\,VM_D =$
  $switch\,VM_E$
  case $switch$ of
    $InitClass(c) \rightarrow$ if $classState(c) < Referenced$ then
                      $referenceClass(c)$
    $Result(res) \rightarrow$
      if $methNm(meth) =$ "<cload>" then
      $ldEnv(reg(0), stringOf(reg(1))) := res(0)$

$referenceClass(c) =$
  if $c =$ Object then
    $classState(c) := Referenced$
  elseif $classState(c) = SupersLoaded$ then
    let $supers = \{super(c)\} \cup implements(c)$
    choose $c' \in supers, classState(c') < Referenced$
      $referenceClass(c')$
    ifnone
      $loadReferences(c)$
  else $loadSuperClasses(c)$

$loadClasses(cs, m) =$
$\quad$ **choose** $c \in cs \setminus dom(ldEnv)$
$\quad\quad callLoad(c)$
$\quad$ **ifnone**
$\quad\quad$ **choose** $c \in cs, classState(liftClass(c)) = Loaded$
$\quad\quad\quad loadSuperClasses(liftClass(c))$
$\quad\quad$ **ifnone** m

$loadSuperClasses(c) =$
$\quad loadClasses(\{super(c)\} \cup implements(c), setSupersLoaded(c))$

$loadReferences(c) =$
$\quad loadClasses(directReferences(c), loadIndirectReferences(c))$

$setSupersLoaded(c) =$
$\quad classState(c) := SupersLoaded$
$\quad setDefiningLoadersForSupers(c)$

$loadIndirectReferences(c) =$
$\quad loadClasses(indirectReferences(c), setReferenced(c))$

$setReferenced(c) =$
$\quad classState(c) := Referenced$
$\quad setDefiningLoaders(c)$

$callLoad(ld, cn) =$
$\quad switch := Call(\text{<cload>}, [ld, cn])$

$execVM_D =$
$\quad execVM_N$
$\quad$ **if** $c = \text{ClassLoader}$ **then**
$\quad\quad execClassLoader(m)$
$\quad$ **elseif** $meth = \text{Class}/\text{newInstance}()$ **then**
$\quad\quad meth := cOf(reg(0))/\text{<newInstance>}()$
where $c/m = meth$

$execClassLoader(m) =$
   if $m =$ `findLoadedClass` **then**
      let $c = (reg(0), stringOf(reg(1)))$
      if $c \notin dom(ldEnv)$ **then**
         $switch := Result([null])$
      else
         $switch := Result([ldEnv(c)])$
   if $m =$ `findSystemClass` **then**
      let $c = (sysLd, stringOf(reg(1)))$
      if $c \notin dom(ldEnv)$ **then**
         $loadClass(classPath, c)$
      elseif $classState(c) < Referenced$ **then**
         $referenceClass(c)$
      elseif $classState(c) = Referenced$ **then**
         $linkClass(c)$
      else
         $switch := Result([ldEnv(c)])$
   if $m =$ `defineClass` **then**
      let $c = (reg(0), stringOf(reg(1)))$
      if $c \notin dom(ldEnv)$ **then**
         let $content = arrayContent(heap(reg(2)), reg(3), reg(4))$
         $defineClass(content, c, True)$
      else
         $raise($ `"ClassFormatError"` $)$
   if $m =$ `resolveClass` **then**
      let $r = reg(1)$
      if $r = null$ **then**
         $raise($ `"NullPointerException"` $)$
      else
         let $c = cOf(r)$
         if $classState(c) < Referenced$ **then**
            $referenceClass(c)$
         elseif $classState(c) = Referenced$ **then**
            $linkClass(c)$
         else
            $switch := Result([])$

$loadClass(classPath, c) =$
   if $c \notin dom(load(classPath))$ **then**
      $raise($ `"ClassNotFoundException"` $)$
   else
      $defineClass(load(classPath), c, False)$

$defineClass(content, c, returnClass) =$
    let $cf = analyze(content)$
    if $classNm(cf) \neq classNm(c)$ **then**
      $raise(\,\texttt{"ClassFormatError"}\,)$
    else create r
      $classState(c) := Loaded$
      $heap(r) \qquad := Object(\texttt{Class}, \emptyset)$
      $cOf(r) \qquad\;\; := c$
      $cEnv(c) \qquad := cf$
      $ldEnv(c) \qquad := r$
      if $returnClass$ **then** $switch := Result([r])$

$linkClass(c) =$
  let $classes = \{super(c)\} \cup implements(c)$
  if $c = \texttt{Object} \vee \forall c' \in classes : classState(c') \geq Linked$ **then**
    $classState(c) := Linked$
    $prepareClass(c)$
  elseif $\neg cyclicInheritance(c)$ **then**
    choose $c' \in classes, classState(c') = Referenced$
      $linkClass(c')$
  else
    $halt := \texttt{"Cyclic Inheritance: "} \cdot classNm(c)$

$prepareClass(c) =$
  forall $f \in staticFields(c)$
    $globals(c/f) := defaultVal(type(c/f))$

$trustfulVM_I = execVM_I(code(pc))$

$trustfulScheme_C(execVM, switchVM) =$
  if $switch = Noswitch$ **then**
    $execVM(code(pc))$
  else
    $switchVM$

$trustfulVM_C = trustfulScheme_C(execVM_C, switchVM_C)$

$trustfulVM_O = trustfulScheme_C(execVM_O, switchVM_C)$

$trustfulVM_E = trustfulScheme_C(execVM_E, switchVM_E)$

$trustfulScheme_N(nativeVM, switchVM) =$
  if $switch = Noswitch \wedge isNative(meth)$ **then**
    $nativeVM$
  else
    $trustfulScheme_C(execVM_E, switchVM)$

$trustfulVM_N = trustfulScheme_N(execVM_N, switchVM_E)$

$trustfulVM_D = trustfulScheme_N(execVM_D, switchVM_D)$

C.2 Defensive execution

$pushFrame(c/m, args) =$
    $stack := stack \cdot [(pc, reg, opd, meth)]$
    $meth := c/m$
    $pc \quad := 0$
    $opd \quad := []$
    $reg \quad := makeRegs(args)$
    if $methNm(m) =$ `"<init>"` **then**
      let $[r] \cdot \_ = args$
      if $c =$ `Object` **then**
        $initState(r) := Complete$
      else
        $initState(r) := InInit$

$execVM_E(instr) =$
    $execVM_O(instr)$
    case $instr$ **of**
      $\ldots$
      $Jsr(s) \rightarrow opd := opd \cdot [(pc + 1, \mathrm{retAddr}(s))]$
                $pc \quad := s$
      $\ldots$

$defensiveScheme_I(check, trustfulVM) =$
    if $\neg validCodeIndex(code, pc) \vee$
      $\neg check(instr, maxOpd, pc, type(reg), type(opd))$ **then**
        $halt :=$ `"Runtime check failed"`
    else
      $trustfulVM$

$defensiveVM_I = defensiveScheme_I(check_I, trustfulVM_I)$

$defensiveVM_C = defensiveScheme_C(check_C, trustfulVM_C)$

$defensiveScheme_C(check, trustfulVM) =$
    if $switch = Noswitch$ **then**
      $defensiveScheme_I(check(meth), trustfulVM)$
    else
      $trustfulVM$

$defensiveVM_O = defensiveScheme_C(check_O, trustfulVM_O)$

$defensiveVM_E = defensiveScheme_C(check_E, trustfulVM_E)$

$defensiveScheme_N(check, trustfulVM) =$
    if $isNative(meth)$ **then**
      if $check(meth)$ **then** $trustfulVM$
      else $halt :=$ `"unknown native method"`
    else
      $defensiveScheme_C(check_E, trustfulVM)$

$$defensiveVM_N = defensiveScheme_N(check_N, trustfulVM_N)$$

$$defensiveVM_D =$$
$$\quad defensiveScheme_N(check_D, trustfulVM_D)$$

C.3 Diligent execution

$propagateVM_I(code, succ, pc) =$
    forall $(s, regS, opdS) \in succ(code(pc), pc, regV_{pc}, opdV_{pc})$
      $propagateSucc(code, s, regS, opdS)$

$propagateSucc(code, s, regS, opdS) =$
    if $s \notin dom(visited)$ **then**
      if $validCodeIndex(code, s)$ **then**
        $regV_s \qquad := \{(x, t) \mid (x, t) \in regS, validReg(t, s)\}$
        $opdV_s \qquad := [\textbf{if } validOpd(t, s) \textbf{ then } t \textbf{ else } \text{unusable} \mid t \in opdS]$
        $visited(s) \quad := True$
        $changed(s) := True$
      else
        $halt :=$ "Verification failed (invalid code index)"
    elseif $regS \sqsubseteq_{reg} regV_s \wedge opdS \sqsubseteq_{seq} opdV_s$ **then**
      skip
    elseif $length(opdS) = length(opdV_s)$ **then**
      $regV_s \qquad := regV_s \sqcup_{reg} regS$
      $opdV_s \qquad := opdV_s \sqcup_{opd} opdS$
      $changed(s) := True$
    else
      $halt :=$ "Propagate failed"

$initVerify(meth) =$
    $visited(0) \quad := True$
    $changed(0) := True$
    $regV_0 \qquad := formals(meth)$
    $opdV_0 \qquad := []$
    forall $i \in dom(visited), i \neq 0$
      $visited(i) \quad := undef$
      $changed(i) := undef$
      $regV_i \qquad := undef$
      $opdV_i \qquad := undef$
    forall $s \in dom(enterJsr)$
      $enterJsr(s) := \emptyset$
    forall $s \in dom(leaveJsr)$
      $leaveJsr(s) := \emptyset$

$switchVM_C =$
    $\ldots$
    case *switch* **of**
      $InitClass(c) \rightarrow$ **if** $classState(c) = Referenced$ **then**
                    $linkClass(c)$

$linkClass(c) =$
  let $classes = \{super(c)\} \cup implements(c)$
  if $c = \texttt{Object} \vee \forall\, c' \in classes : classState(c') \geq Linked$ **then**
    $prepareVerify(c)$
  elseif $\neg cyclicInheritance(c)$ **then**
    choose $c' \in classes, classState(c') = Referenced$
      $linkClass(c')$
  else
    $halt := \texttt{"Cyclic Inheritance: "} \cdot classNm(c)$

$prepareVerify(c) =$
  if $constraintViolation(c)$ **then**
    $halt := violationMsg(classNm(c))$
  else
    let $verifyMeths' = [(c/m) \mid m \in dom(methods(cEnv(c))),$
                             $\neg null(code(c/m))]$
    $verifyMeths := verifyMeths'$
    $verifyClass := c$
    $initVerify(top(verifyMeths'))$
    $prepareClass(c)$

$propagateVM_E(code, succ, pc) =$
  $propagateVM_I(code, succ, pc)$
  case $code(pc)$ **of**
    $Jsr(s) \rightarrow enterJsr(s) := \{pc\} \cup enterJsr(s)$
            forall $(i, x) \in leaveJsr(s), i \notin dom(changed)$
              if $regV_i(x) = \texttt{retAddr}(s)$ **then**
                  $propagateJsr(code, pc, s, i)$
    $Ret(x) \rightarrow$ **let** $\texttt{retAddr}(s) = regV_{pc}(x)$
            $leaveJsr(s) := \{(pc, x)\} \cup leaveJsr(s)$
            forall $j \in enterJsr(s), j \notin dom(changed)$
              $propagateJsr(code, j, s, pc)$

$propagateJsr(code, j, s, i) =$
  $propagateSucc(code, j + 1, regJ \oplus mod(s) \lhd regV_i, opdV_i)$ **where**
    $regJ = \{(x, t) \mid (x, t) \in mod(s) \lhd regV_j,$
                 $validJump(t, s) \wedge t \neq (\_, \_)_{new} \wedge t \neq InInit\}$

$diligentVM_I =$
  if $dom(changed) \neq \emptyset$ **then**
    $verifyScheme_I(code, maxOpd, propagateVM_I, succ_I, check_I)$
  else
    $trustfulVM_I$

$verifyScheme_I(code, maxOpd, propagateVM, succ, check) =$
  choose $pc \in dom(changed)$
    if $check(code(pc), maxOpd, pc, regV_{pc}, opdV_{pc})$ **then**
      $changed(pc) := undef$
      $propagateVM(code, succ, pc)$
    else
      $halt := \texttt{"Verification failed"}$

$$diligentScheme(verifyVM, execVM) =$$
$$\quad \textbf{if } \neg isChecked \textbf{ then}$$
$$\quad\quad verifyVM$$
$$\quad \textbf{else}$$
$$\quad\quad execVM$$

$$diligentVM_C = diligentScheme(verifyVM, trustfulVM_C)$$
$$\quad \textbf{where } verifyVM = verifyScheme_C(propagateVM_I, succ_C, check_C)$$

$$verifyScheme_C(propagateVM, succ, check) =$$
$$\quad \textbf{if } dom(changed) \neq \emptyset \textbf{ then}$$
$$\quad\quad verifyScheme_I(code(meth_v), maxOpd(meth_v), propagateVM,$$
$$\quad\quad\quad\quad\quad\quad\quad succ(meth_v), check(meth_v))$$
$$\quad \textbf{else}$$
$$\quad\quad \textbf{let } verifyMeths' = drop(verifyMeths, 1)$$
$$\quad\quad verifyMeths := verifyMeths'$$
$$\quad\quad \textbf{if } length(verifyMeths') > 0 \textbf{ then}$$
$$\quad\quad\quad initVerify(top(verifyMeths'))$$
$$\quad\quad \textbf{else}$$
$$\quad\quad\quad classState(verifyClass) := Linked$$

$$diligentVM_O = diligentScheme(verifyVM, trustfulVM_O)$$
$$\quad \textbf{where } verifyVM = verifyScheme_C(propagateVM_I, succ_O, check_O)$$

$$diligentVM_E = diligentScheme(verifyVM, trustfulVM_E)$$
$$\quad \textbf{where } verifyVM = verifyScheme_C(propagateVM_E, succ_E, check_E)$$

$$verifyScheme_N(check) =$$
$$\quad \textbf{if } changed(0) \wedge isNative(meth_v) \textbf{ then}$$
$$\quad\quad \textbf{if } check(meth_v) \textbf{ then}$$
$$\quad\quad\quad changed(0) := undef$$
$$\quad\quad \textbf{else}$$
$$\quad\quad\quad halt := \texttt{"Verification failed"}$$
$$\quad \textbf{else}$$
$$\quad\quad verifyScheme_C(propagateVM_E, succ_E, check_E)$$

$$diligentVM_N = diligentScheme(verifyVM, trustfulVM_N)$$
$$\quad \textbf{where } verifyVM = verifyScheme_N(check_N)$$

$$diligentVM_D = diligentScheme(verifyVM, trustfulVM_D)$$
$$\quad \textbf{where } verifyVM = verifyScheme_N(check_D)$$

C.4 Check functions

$check_I(instr, maxOpd, pc, regT, opdT) =$
   case $instr$ **of**
      $Prim(p) \rightarrow opdT \sqsubseteq_{\text{suf}} argTypes(p) \land$
                    $\neg overflow(maxOpd, opdT, retSize(p) - argSize(p))$
      $Dupx(s_1, s_2) \rightarrow$ **let** $[ts_1, ts_2] = tops(opdT, [s_1, s_2])$
                $length(opdT) \geq s_1 + s_2 \land$
                $\neg overflow(maxOpd, opdT, s_2) \land$
                $validTypeSeq(ts_1) \land validTypeSeq(ts_2)$
      $Pop(s) \rightarrow length(opdT) \geq s$
      $Load(t, x) \rightarrow$
         if $size(t) = 1$ **then** $[regT(x)] \sqsubseteq_{\text{mv}} t \land \neg overflow(maxOpd, opdT, 1)$
         else $[regT(x), regT(x + 1)] \sqsubseteq_{\text{mv}} t \land \neg overflow(maxOpd, opdT, 2)$
      $Store(t, \_) \rightarrow opdT \sqsubseteq_{\text{suf}} t$
      $Goto(o) \quad\ \rightarrow True$
      $Cond(p, o) \rightarrow opdT \sqsubseteq_{\text{suf}} argTypes(p)$
      $Halt \quad\quad\ \rightarrow True$

$check_C(meth)(instr, maxOpd, pc, regT, opdT) =$
   $check_I(instr, maxOpd, pc, regT, opdT) \lor$
   case $instr$ **of**
      $GetStatic(t, c/f) \quad\ \rightarrow \neg overflow(maxOpd, opdT, size(t))$
      $PutStatic(t, c/f) \quad\ \rightarrow opdT \sqsubseteq_{\text{suf}} t$
      $InvokeStatic(t, c/m) \rightarrow opdT \sqsubseteq_{\text{suf}} argTypes(c/m) \land$
                            $\neg overflow(maxOpd, opdT, size(t) -$
                                           $argSize(c/m))$
      $Return(t) \quad\quad\quad\quad\ \rightarrow opdT \sqsubseteq_{\text{suf}} returnType(meth) \land$
                                     $returnType(meth) \sqsubseteq_{\text{mv}} t$

$check_O(meth)(instr, maxOpd, pc, regT, opdT) =$
   $check_C(meth)(instr, maxOpd, pc, regT, opdT) \land endinit(meth, instr, regT) \lor$
   case $instr$ **of**
      $New(c) \rightarrow \neg overflow(maxOpd, opdT, 1)$
      $GetField(t, c/f) \rightarrow opdT \sqsubseteq_{\text{suf}} c \land \neg overflow(maxOpd, opdT, size(t) - 1)$
      $PutField(t, c/f) \rightarrow opdT \sqsubseteq_{\text{suf}} c \cdot t$
      $InvokeSpecial(\_, c/m) \rightarrow$
         let $[c'] \cdot \_ = take(opdT, 1 + argSize(c/m))$
         $length(opdT) > argSize(c/m) \land$
         $opdT \sqsubseteq_{\text{suf}} argTypes(c/m) \land$
         $\neg overflow(maxOpd, opdT, retSize(c/m) - argSize(c/m) - 1) \land$
         if $methNm(m) = $ `"<init>"` **then**
            $initCompatible(meth, c', c)$
         else $c' \sqsubseteq c$
      $InvokeVirtual(\_, c/m) \rightarrow$
         $opdT \sqsubseteq_{\text{suf}} c \cdot argTypes(c/m) \land$
         $\neg overflow(maxOpd, opdT, retSize(c/m) - argSize(c/m) - 1)$
      $InstanceOf(c) \rightarrow opdT \sqsubseteq_{\text{suf}}$ `Object`
      $Checkcast(c) \quad \rightarrow opdT \sqsubseteq_{\text{suf}}$ `Object`

$check_E(meth)(instr, maxOpd, pc, regT, opdT) =$
    $check_O(meth)(instr, maxOpd, pc, regT, opdT) \lor$
    case $instr$ **of**
        $Store(\mathbf{addr}, x) \rightarrow length(opdT) > 0 \land isRetAddr(top(opdT))$
        $Athrow \qquad\quad \rightarrow opdT \sqsubseteq_{\mathrm{suf}} \mathbf{Throwable}$
        $Jsr(o) \qquad\quad\ \rightarrow \neg overflow(maxOpd, opdT, 1)$
        $Ret(x) \qquad\quad\ \rightarrow isRetAddr(regT(x))$

$check_N(c/m) =$
    $c/m = \mathbf{Object}/\,\mathbf{equals}\ \lor$
    $c/m = \mathbf{Object}/\,\mathbf{clone}$

$check_D(c/m) =$
    $c = \mathbf{ClassLoader} \land m \in \{\,\mathbf{findLoadedClass}, \mathbf{findSystemClass},$
                            $\mathbf{resolveClass}, \mathbf{defineClass}\,\} \lor$
    $c/m = \mathbf{Class}/\,\mathbf{newInstance}()\ \lor$
    $check_N(c/m)$

C.5 Successor functions

$succ_I(instr, pc, regT, opdT) =$
    case $instr$ **of**
        $Prim(p) \rightarrow \{(pc + 1, regT, drop(opdT, argSize(p)) \cdot returnType(p))\}$
        $Dupx(s_1, s_2) \rightarrow$
            $\{(pc + 1, regT, drop(opdT, s_1 + s_2)\cdot$
                            $take(opdT, s_2) \cdot take(opdT, s_1 + s_2))\}$
        $Pop(s) \rightarrow \{(pc + 1, regT, drop(opdT, s))\}$
        $Load(t, x) \rightarrow$
            if $size(t) = 1$ **then**
                $\{(pc + 1, regT, opdT \cdot [regT(x)])\}$
            else
                $\{(pc + 1, regT, opdT \cdot [regT(x), regT(x + 1)])\}$
        $Store(t, x) \rightarrow$
            if $size(t) = 1$ **then**
                $\{(pc + 1, regT \oplus \{(x, top(opdT))\}, drop(opdT, 1))\}$
            else
                $\{(pc + 1, regT \oplus \{(x, t_0), (x + 1, t_1)\}, drop(opdT, 2))\}$
            where $[t_0, t_1] = take(opdT, 2)$
        $Goto(o) \quad \rightarrow \{(o, regT, opdT)\}$
        $Cond(p, o) \rightarrow \{(pc + 1, regT, drop(opdT, argSize(p))),$
                        $(o, regT, drop(opdT, argSize(p)))\}$

$succ_C(meth)(instr, pc, regT, opdT) =$
    $succ_I(instr, pc, regT, opdT) \cup$
    case $instr$ **of**
        $GetStatic(t, c/f) \quad \rightarrow \{(pc + 1, regT, opdT \cdot t)\}$
        $PutStatic(t, c/f) \quad \rightarrow \{(pc + 1, regT, drop(opdT, size(t)))\}$
        $InvokeStatic(t, c/m) \rightarrow \{(pc + 1, regT, drop(opdT, argSize(c/m)) \cdot t)\}$
        $Return(mt) \qquad\quad \rightarrow \emptyset$

$succ_O(meth)(instr, pc, regT, opdT) =$
$\quad succ_C(meth)(instr, pc, regT, opdT) \cup$
$\quad$ **case** $instr$ **of**
$\qquad New(c) \rightarrow \{(pc+1, regS, opdS \cdot [(c, pc)_{new}])\}$
$\qquad\quad$ **where** $regS = \{(x, t) \mid (x, t) \in regT, t \neq (c, pc)_{new}\}$
$\qquad\qquad\qquad opdS = [\textbf{if } t = (c, pc)_{new} \textbf{ then unusable else } t \mid t \in opdT]$
$\qquad GetField(t, c/f) \rightarrow \{(pc+1, regT, drop(opdT, 1) \cdot t)\}$
$\qquad PutField(t, c/f) \rightarrow \{(pc+1, regT, drop(opdT, 1 + size(t)))\}$
$\qquad InvokeSpecial(t, c/m) \rightarrow$
$\qquad\quad$ **let** $opdT' = drop(opdT, 1 + argSize(c/m)) \cdot t$
$\qquad\quad$ **if** $methNm(m) = \text{"<init>"}$ **then**
$\qquad\qquad$ **case** $top(drop(opdT, argSize(c/m)))$ **of**
$\qquad\qquad\quad (c, o)_{new} \rightarrow \{(pc+1, regT[c/(c, o)_{new}], opdT'[c/(c, o)_{new}])\}$
$\qquad\qquad\quad InInit \quad \rightarrow$ **let** $c/\_ = meth$
$\qquad\qquad\qquad\qquad\qquad \{(pc+1, regT[c/InInit], opdT'[c/InInit])\}$
$\qquad\quad$ **else**
$\qquad\qquad\qquad \{(pc+1, regT, opdT')\}$
$\qquad InvokeVirtual(t, c/m) \rightarrow$
$\qquad\quad$ **let** $opdT' = drop(opdT, 1 + argSize(c/m)) \cdot t$
$\qquad\quad \{(pc+1, regT, opdT')\}$
$\qquad InstanceOf(c) \rightarrow \{(pc+1, regT, drop(opdT, 1) \cdot [\textbf{int}])\}$
$\qquad Checkcast(t) \rightarrow \{(pc+1, regT, drop(opdT, 1) \cdot t)\}$

$succ_E(meth)(instr, pc, regT, opdT) =$
$\quad succ_O(meth)(instr, pc, regT, opdT) \cup allhandlers(instr, meth, pc, regT) \cup$
$\quad$ **case** $instr$ **of**
$\qquad Athrow \rightarrow \emptyset$
$\qquad Jsr(s) \quad \rightarrow \{(s, regT, opdT \cdot [\textbf{retAddr}(s)])\}$
$\qquad Ret(x) \rightarrow \emptyset$

C.6 Constraints

$constraintViolation(c) =$
$\quad$ **if** $isInterface(c)$ **then** $\neg validInterface(c)$
$\quad$ **else** $\neg validClass(c)$

$validInterface(c) =$
$\quad isAbstract(c) \wedge super(c) = \texttt{Object} \wedge$
$\quad \forall c' \in implements(c): accessible(c, c') \wedge isInterface(c') \wedge$
$\quad \forall m \in dom(methods(cEnv(c))): validIMeth(c/m, code(c/m)) \wedge$
$\quad checkEqualVisibleSigs(c)$

$validClass(c) =$
$\quad (c = \texttt{Object} \vee super(c) \neq undef \wedge accessible(c, super(c))) \wedge$
$\quad \forall c' \in implements(c): accessible(c, c') \wedge isInterface(c') \wedge$
$\quad \forall m \in dom(methods(cEnv(c))): validCMeth(c/m, code(c/m)) \wedge$
$\quad checkEqualVisibleSigs(c)$

$validIMeth(c/m, code) =$
  let $mods = modifiers(c/m)$
  let $len\ \ \ = length(code)$
  if $methNm(m) = $ `"<clinit>"` **then**
    $Abstract \notin mods\ \wedge$
    $\forall\, instr \in code : validInstr(c/m, maxReg(c/m), instr, len)$
  else
    $Abstract \in mods\ \wedge\ null(code)\ \wedge\ Private \notin mods\ \wedge$
    $\forall\, m' \in overrideMethods(c/m) : checkOverride(c/m, m')$

$validCMeth(c/m, code) =$
  let $mods = modifiers(c/m)$
  let $len\ \ \ = length(code)$
  $null(code) = (Native \in mods\ \vee\ Abstract \in mods)\ \wedge$
  $\neg(Abstract \in mods\ \wedge\ Private \in mods)\ \wedge$
  $\forall\, instr \in code : validInstr(c/m, maxReg(c/m), instr, len)\ \wedge$
  $\forall\, m' \in overrideMethods(c/m) : checkOverride(c/m, m')$

$checkOverride(m, m') = \dots$ *(see Constraint 4.1.10)*

$checkEqualVisibleSigs = \dots$ *(see Constraint 4.1.11)*

$validInstr(ctx/m, maxReg, instr, len) =$
  $validAccess(ctx, instr)\ \wedge$
  case $instr$ **of**

$Goto(pc)$	$\rightarrow pc \geq 0 \wedge pc < len$
$Cond(p, pc)$	$\rightarrow pc \geq 0 \wedge pc < len$
$Load(t, x)$	$\rightarrow x \geq 0 \wedge x \leq maxReg - size(t)\ \wedge$
$Store(t, x)$	$\rightarrow x \geq 0 \wedge x \leq maxReg - size(t)\ \wedge$
	$(x \neq 0 \vee methNm(m) \neq$ `"<init>"` $)$

$GetStatic(t, c/f) \rightarrow isStatic(c/f) \wedge type(c/f) = t$
$PutStatic(t, c/f) \rightarrow isStatic(c/f) \wedge type(c/f) = t$
$InvokeStatic(t, c/m) \rightarrow$
  $head(methNm(m)) \neq\, '<' \wedge\ isStatic(c/m) \wedge \neg isInterface(c)\ \wedge$
  $returnType(c/m) = t$
$GetField(t, c/f) \rightarrow \neg isStatic(c/f) \wedge type(c/f) = t$
$PutField(t, c/f) \rightarrow \neg isStatic(c/f) \wedge type(c/f) = t$
$InvokeSpecial(t, c/m) \rightarrow$
  $methNm(m) = $ `"<init>"` $\vee\ c \in supers(ctx)\ \wedge$
  $returnType(c/m) = t \wedge \neg isStatic(c/m) \wedge \neg isInterface(c)$
$InvokeVirtual(t, c/m) \rightarrow$
  $methNm(m) \neq$ `"<init>"` $\wedge \neg isStatic(c/m) \wedge returnType(c/m) = t$
$NewArray(t, d) \rightarrow d \leq arrayDim(t) \wedge d \leq 255$
$New(c)\ \ \ \ \ \ \ \ \ \ \ \rightarrow \neg isAbstract(c)$
$Jsr(o)\ \ \ \ \ \ \ \ \ \ \ \ \rightarrow o \geq 0 \wedge o < len$
$Ret(x)\ \ \ \ \ \ \ \ \ \ \ \ \rightarrow x \geq 0 \wedge x < maxReg$

$validAccess(ctx, instr) =$
    case $instr$ **of**

$GetStatic(t, c/f)$	$\rightarrow accessible(ctx, c/f) \wedge accessible(ctx, t)$
$PutStatic(t, c/f)$	$\rightarrow accessible(ctx, c/f) \wedge accessible(ctx, t)$
$InvokeStatic(t, c/m)$	$\rightarrow accessible(ctx, c/m) \wedge accessible(ctx, t)$
$GetField(t, c/f)$	$\rightarrow accessible(ctx, c/f) \wedge accessible(ctx, t)$
$PutField(t, c/f)$	$\rightarrow accessible(ctx, c/f) \wedge accessible(ctx, t)$
$InvokeSpecial(t, c/m)$	$\rightarrow accessible(ctx, c/m) \wedge accessible(ctx, t)$
$InvokeVirtual(t, c/m)$	$\rightarrow accessible(ctx, c/m) \wedge accessible(ctx, t)$
$New(c)$	$\rightarrow accessible(ctx, c)$

$arrayDim(Array(t)) = 1 + arrayDim(t)$
$arrayDim(\_)\qquad\quad = 1$

$violationMsg(cn) =$
    `"Constraint Violation: class "` $\cdot\ cn$

C.7 Arrays

New instructions (extension to type $Instr$):

data $Instr = \ldots$
    | $NewArray(Type, Dimension)$
    | $ArrayLength$
    | $AStore(ArrayMoveType)$
    | $ALoad(ArrayMoveType)$

Array move types:

data $ArrayMoveType =$ byte | short | char | int |
                                        long | float | double | Object

Conversion from array move types to verify types

$type_{vt}($byte$)\quad = [$int$]$
$type_{vt}($char$)\quad = [$int$]$
$type_{vt}($short$)\quad = [$int$]$
$type_{vt}($int$)\quad = [$int$]$
$type_{vt}($float$)\quad = [$float$]$
$type_{vt}($long$)\quad = [$lowLong, highLong$]$
$type_{vt}($double$) = [$lowDouble, highDouble$]$
$type_{vt}($Object$) = [$Object$]$

Heap structure:

data Heap $= Object(Class, Map(Class/Field, Val)) \mid Array(Type, Val^*)$

$typeOf(r) =$
    if $(r = null)$ **then** Null
    else case $heap(r)$ **of**
              $Array(t, vs) \rightarrow Array(t)$
              $Object(c, fields) \rightarrow$ **case** $initState(r)$ **of**
                                      $New(pc)\quad \rightarrow (c, pc)_{new}$
                                      $InInit\quad\ \rightarrow InInit$
                                      $Complete \rightarrow c$

Extension to $exec\,VM_O$:

$exec\,VM_O(instr) = \ldots$
  case $instr$ **of**
    $NewArray(t, d) \rightarrow$
      let $(opd', ds) = split(opd, d)$
      if $\forall\, i \in ds : i \geq 0$ **then**
        let $r := createArray(t, d, ds)$
        $opd := opd' \cdot [r]$
        $pc\ \ := pc + 1$
    $ArrayLength \rightarrow$
      let $(opd', [r]) = split(opd, 1)$
      if $\neg(r = null)$ **then**
        $opd := opd' \cdot [arraySize(r)]$
        $pc\ \ := pc + 1$
    $ALoad(t) \rightarrow$
      let $(opd', [r, i]) = split(opd, 2)$
      if $\neg(r = null) \wedge i \geq 0 \wedge i < arraySize(r)$ **then**
        $opd := opd' \cdot getElement(r, i)$
        $pc\ \ := pc + 1$
    $AStore(t) \rightarrow$
      let $(opd', [[r, i], v]) = splits(opd, [2, size(t)])$
      if $\neg(r = null) \wedge i \geq 0 \wedge i < arraySize(r)\ \wedge$
        $(t \neq \texttt{Object} \vee v = null \vee [classOf(v)] \sqsubseteq_{\text{seq}} arrayType(r))$ **then**
          $heap(r) := setElement(r, i, v)$
          $opd\ \ \ \ \ \ := opd'$
          $pc\ \ \ \ \ \ \ \ := pc + 1$

Extension to $exec\,VM_E$:

$exec\,VM_E(instr) = \ldots$
  case $instr$ **of**
    $NewArray(t, d) \rightarrow$
      let $ds = take(opd, d)$
      if $\exists\, i \in ds : i < 0$ **then**
        $raise(\texttt{"NegativeArraySizeException"})$
    $ArrayLength \rightarrow$
      if $top(opd) = null$ **then**
        $raise(\texttt{"NullPointerException"})$
    $ALoad(t) \rightarrow$
      let $[r, i] = take(opd, 2)$
      if $r = null$ **then**
        $raise(\texttt{"NullPointerException"})$
      elseif $i < 0 \vee i \geq arraySize(r)$ **then**
        $raise(\texttt{"ArrayIndexOutOfBoundsException"})$
    $AStore(t) \rightarrow$
      let $[[r, i], v] = tops(opd, [2, size(t)])$
      if $r = null$ **then**
        $raise(\texttt{"NullPointerException"})$
      elseif $i < 0 \vee i \geq arraySize(r)$ **then**
        $raise(\texttt{"ArrayIndexOutOfBoundsException"})$
      elseif $t = \texttt{Object} \wedge v \neq null\ \wedge$
          $\neg([classOf(v)] \sqsubseteq_{\text{seq}} arrayType(r))$ **then**
        $raise(\texttt{"ArrayStoreException"})$

Extension to $check_O$:

$$check_O(meth)(instr, maxOpd, pc, regT, opdT) = \ldots \vee$$
$\quad$ **case** $instr$ **of**
$\quad\quad NewArray(t, d) \rightarrow opdT \sqsubseteq_{\text{suf}} copy(d)(\texttt{int})$
$\quad\quad ArrayLength \quad\rightarrow length(opdT) > 0 \wedge isArray(top(opdT))$
$\quad\quad ALoad(t) \quad\quad\rightarrow opdT \sqsubseteq_{\text{suf}} [Array(type_{\text{vt}}(t)), \texttt{int}]$
$\quad\quad AStore(t) \quad\quad\rightarrow opdT \sqsubseteq_{\text{suf}} [Array(type_{\text{vt}}(t)), \texttt{int}] \cdot type_{\text{vt}}(t)$

Extension to $succ_O$:

$$succ_O(meth)(instr, pc, regT, opdT) = \ldots \cup$$
$\quad$ **case** $instr$ **of**
$\quad\quad NewArray(t, d) \rightarrow$
$\quad\quad\quad \{(pc + 1, regT, drop(opdT, d) \cdot [Array(t)])\}$
$\quad\quad ArrayLength \rightarrow$
$\quad\quad\quad \{(pc + 1, regT, drop(opdT, 1) \cdot [\texttt{int}])\}$
$\quad\quad ALoad(\texttt{Object}) \rightarrow$
$\quad\quad\quad$ **let** $[arr, i] = take(opdT, 2)$
$\quad\quad\quad \{(pc + 1, regT, drop(opdT, 2) \cdot [arrayElemType(arr)])\}$
$\quad\quad ALoad(t) \rightarrow$
$\quad\quad\quad \{(pc + 1, regT, drop(opdT, 2) \cdot type_{\text{vt}}(t))\}$
$\quad\quad AStore(t) \rightarrow$
$\quad\quad\quad \{(pc + 1, regT, drop(opdT, 2 + size(t)))\}$

Array functions:

$$createArray(t, d, [i] \cdot is) =$$
$\quad$ **create** r
$\quad\quad$ **if** $d = 1$ **then**
$\quad\quad\quad heap(r) := Array(t, copy(i)(defaultVal(t)))$
$\quad\quad\quad result(r)$
$\quad\quad$ **else**
$\quad\quad\quad$ **let** $Array(elemType) = t$
$\quad\quad\quad$ **let** $vs := $ **forall** $x \in [1..i]$
$\quad\quad\quad\quad$ **let** $r := createArray(elemType, d - 1, is)$
$\quad\quad\quad\quad result([r])$
$\quad\quad\quad heap(r) := Array(t, vs)$
$\quad\quad\quad result(r)$

$arrayType(r) = t$
$\quad$ **where** $Array(t, arr) = heap(r)$

$isArray(Array([\texttt{int}])) \qquad\qquad\qquad\qquad = True$
$isArray(Array([\texttt{lowLong}, \texttt{highLong}])) \qquad = True$
$isArray(Array([\texttt{float}])) \qquad\qquad\qquad\quad = True$
$isArray(Array([\texttt{lowDouble}, \texttt{highDouble}])) = True$
$isArray(t) \qquad\qquad\qquad\qquad\qquad\quad = t \sqsubseteq Array([\texttt{Object}])$

$arrayElemType(Array([t])) = t$
$arrayElemType(\texttt{Null}) \qquad = \texttt{Null}$
$arrayElemType(rs) \qquad\quad = \sqcup\{arrayElemType(r) \mid r \in rs\}$

Example C.7.1. The following legal Java program is rejected be some byte-code verifiers:

```
public class Test {
  public static void main(String[] argv) {
    int[][] a = null;
    a[0] = new int[0];
  }
}
```

The program should be accepted. At run-time, a `NullPointerException` will be thrown, because the variable `a` is a null pointer when the array element `a[0]` is assigned.

C.8 Abstract versus real instructions

Bytecode instruction	Abstract instruction
aaload	$ALoad(\texttt{Object})$
aastore	$AStore(\texttt{Object})$
aconst_null	$Prim(\texttt{null})$
aload_0	$Load(\texttt{addr}, 0)$
aload_1	$Load(\texttt{addr}, 1)$
aload_2	$Load(\texttt{addr}, 2)$
aload_3	$Load(\texttt{addr}, 3)$
aload n	$Load(\texttt{addr}, n)$
anewarray t	$NewArray(t, 1)$
areturn	$Return(\texttt{addr})$
arraylength	$ArrayLength$
astore_0	$Store(\texttt{addr}, 0)$
astore_1	$Store(\texttt{addr}, 1)$
astore_2	$Store(\texttt{addr}, 2)$
astore_3	$Store(\texttt{addr}, 3)$
astore n	$Store(\texttt{addr}, n)$
athrow	$Athrow$
baload	$ALoad(\texttt{byte})$
bastore	$AStore(\texttt{byte})$
bipush n	$Prim(n)$
caload	$ALoad(\texttt{char})$
castore	$AStore(\texttt{char})$
checkcast c	$Checkcast(c)$
d2f	$Prim(\texttt{d2f})$
d2i	$Prim(\texttt{d2i})$
d2l	$Prim(\texttt{d2l})$
dadd	$Prim(\texttt{dadd})$
daload	$ALoad(\texttt{double})$
dastore	$AStore(\texttt{double})$
dcmpg	$Prim(\texttt{dcmpg})$
dcmpl	$Prim(\texttt{dcmpl})$
dconst_0	$Prim(0.0)$
dconst_1	$Prim(1.0)$
ddiv	$Prim(\texttt{ddiv})$
dload_0	$Load(\texttt{double}, 0)$
dload_1	$Load(\texttt{double}, 1)$
dload_2	$Load(\texttt{double}, 2)$
dload_3	$Load(\texttt{double}, 3)$

Bytecode instruction	Abstract instruction
dload n	$Load(\text{double}, n)$
dmul	$Prim(\text{dmul})$
dneg	$Prim(\text{dneg})$
drem	$Prim(\text{drem})$ (not implemented)
dreturn	$Return(\text{double})$
dstore_0	$Store(\text{double}, 0)$
dstore_1	$Store(\text{double}, 1)$
dstore_2	$Store(\text{double}, 2)$
dstore_3	$Store(\text{double}, 3)$
dstore n	$Store(\text{double}, n)$
dsub	$Prim(\text{dsub})$
dup2_x1	$Dupx(1, 2)$
dup2_x2	$Dupx(2, 2)$
dup2	$Dupx(0, 2)$
dup_x1	$Dupx(1, 1)$
dup_x2	$Dupx(2, 1)$
dup	$Dupx(0, 1)$
f2d	$Prim(\text{f2d})$
f2i	$Prim(\text{f2i})$
f2l	$Prim(\text{f2l})$
fadd	$Prim(\text{fadd})$
faload	$ALoad(\text{float})$
fastore	$AStore(\text{float})$
fcmpg	$Prim(\text{fcmpg})$
fcmpl	$Prim(\text{fcmpl})$
fconst_0	$Prim(0.0F)$
fconst_1	$Prim(1.0F)$
fconst_2	$Prim(2.0F)$
fdiv	$Prim(\text{fdiv})$
fload_0	$Load(\text{float}, 0)$
fload_1	$Load(\text{float}, 1)$
fload_2	$Load(\text{float}, 2)$
fload_3	$Load(\text{float}, 3)$
fload n	$Load(\text{float}, n)$
fmul	$Prim(\text{fmul})$
fneg	$Prim(\text{fneg})$
frem	$Prim(\text{frem})$ (not implemented)
freturn	$Return(\text{float})$
fstore_0	$Store(\text{float}, 0)$
fstore_1	$Store(\text{float}, 1)$

Bytecode instruction	Abstract instruction
fstore_2	$Store(\texttt{float}, 2)$
fstore_3	$Store(\texttt{float}, 3)$
fstore n	$Store(\texttt{float}, n)$
fsub	$Prim(\texttt{fsub})$
getfield fref t	$GetField(t, \mathit{fref})$
getstatic fref t	$GetStatic(t, \mathit{fref})$
goto_w o	$Goto(o)$
goto o	$Goto(o)$
i2b	$Prim(\texttt{i2b})$
i2c	$Prim(\texttt{i2c})$
i2d	$Prim(\texttt{i2d})$
i2f	$Prim(\texttt{i2f})$
i2l	$Prim(\texttt{i2l})$
i2s	$Prim(\texttt{i2s})$
iadd	$Prim(\texttt{iadd})$
iaload	$ALoad(\texttt{int})$
iand	$Prim(\texttt{iand})$ (not implemented)
iastore	$AStore(\texttt{int})$
iconst_0	$Prim(0)$
iconst_1	$Prim(1)$
iconst_2	$Prim(2)$
iconst_3	$Prim(3)$
iconst_4	$Prim(4)$
iconst_5	$Prim(5)$
iconst_m1	$Prim(-1)$
idiv	$Prim(\texttt{idiv})$
if_acmpeq l	$Cond(\texttt{if\_acmpeq}, l)$
if_acmpne l	$Cond(\texttt{if\_acmpne}, l)$
if_icmpeq l	$Cond(\texttt{if\_icmpeq}, l)$
if_icmpge l	$Cond(\texttt{if\_icmpge}, l)$
if_icmpgt l	$Cond(\texttt{if\_icmpgt}, l)$
if_icmple l	$Cond(\texttt{if\_icmple}, l)$
if_icmplt l	$Cond(\texttt{if\_icmplt}, l)$
if_icmpne l	$Cond(\texttt{if\_icmpne}, l)$
ifeq l	$Cond(\texttt{if\_eq}, l)$
ifge l	$Cond(\texttt{if\_ge}, l)$
ifgt l	$Cond(\texttt{if\_gt}, l)$
ifle l	$Cond(\texttt{if\_le}, l)$
iflt l	$Cond(\texttt{if\_lt}, l)$
ifne l	$Cond(\texttt{if\_ne}, l)$

Bytecode instruction	Abstract instruction
ifnonnull l	$Cond(\texttt{ifnonnull}, l)$
ifnull l	$Cond(\texttt{ifnull}, l)$
iinc n i	$IInc(n, i)$ (not described)
iload_0	$Load(\texttt{int}, 0)$
iload_1	$Load(\texttt{int}, 1)$
iload_2	$Load(\texttt{int}, 2)$
iload_3	$Load(\texttt{int}, 3)$
iload n	$Load(\texttt{int}, n)$
imul	$Prim(\texttt{imul})$
ineg	$Prim(\texttt{ineg})$
instanceof c	$Instanceof(c)$
invokeinterface $mref/rt$	$InvokeVirtual(rt, mref)$
invokespecial $mref/rt$	$InvokeSpecial(rt, mref)$
invokestatic $mref/rt$	$InvokeStatic(rt, mref)$
invokevirtual $mref/rt$	$InvokeVirtual(rt, mref)$
ior	$Prim(\texttt{ior})$ (not implemented)
irem	$Prim(\texttt{irem})$
ireturn	$Return(\texttt{int})$
ishl	$Prim(\texttt{ishl})$ (not implemented)
ishr	$Prim(\texttt{ishr})$ (not implemented)
istore_0	$Store(\texttt{int}, 0)$
istore_1	$Store(\texttt{int}, 1)$
istore_2	$Store(\texttt{int}, 2)$
istore_3	$Store(\texttt{int}, 3)$
istore n	$Store(\texttt{int}, n)$
isub	$Prim(\texttt{isub})$
iushr	$Prim(\texttt{iushr})$ (not implemented)
ixor	$Prim(\texttt{ixor})$ (not implemented)
jsr_w s	$Jsr(s)$
jsr s	$Jsr(s)$
l2d	$Prim(\texttt{l2d})$
l2f	$Prim(\texttt{l2f})$
l2i	$Prim(\texttt{l2i})$
ladd	$Prim(\texttt{ladd})$
laload	$ALoad(\texttt{long})$
land	$Prim(\texttt{land})$
lastore	$AStore(\texttt{long})$
lcmp	$Prim(\texttt{lcmp})$
lconst_0	$Prim(0L)$
lconst_1	$Prim(1L)$

Bytecode instruction	Abstract instruction
ldc2_w n	$Prim(n)$
ldc_w n	$Prim(n)$
ldc n	$Prim(n)$
ldiv	$Prim(\texttt{ldiv})$
lload_0	$Load(\texttt{long}, 0)$
lload_1	$Load(\texttt{long}, 1)$
lload_2	$Load(\texttt{long}, 2)$
lload_3	$Load(\texttt{long}, 3)$
lload n	$Load(\texttt{long}, n)$
lmul	$Prim(\texttt{lmul})$
lneg	$Prim(\texttt{lneg})$
lookupswitch	not supported
lor	$Prim(\texttt{lor})$ (not implemented)
lrem	$Prim(\texttt{lrem})$ (not implemented)
lreturn	$Return(\texttt{long})$
lshl	$Prim(\texttt{lshl})$ (not implemented)
lshr	$Prim(\texttt{lshr})$ (not implemented)
lstore_0	$Store(\texttt{long}, 0)$
lstore_1	$Store(\texttt{long}, 1)$
lstore_2	$Store(\texttt{long}, 2)$
lstore_3	$Store(\texttt{long}, 3)$
lstore n	$Store(\texttt{long}, n)$
lsub	$Prim(\texttt{lsub})$
lushr	$Prim(\texttt{lushr})$ (not implemented)
lxor	$Prim(\texttt{lxor})$ (not implemented)
monitorenter	not supported
monitorexit	not supported
multianewarray t d	$NewArray(t, d)$
newarray t	$NewArray(t, 1)$
new c	$New(c)$
nop	Nop (not described)
pop2	$Pop(2)$
pop	$Pop(1)$
putfield fref t	$PutField(t, \mathit{fref})$
putstatic fref t	$PutStatic(t, \mathit{fref})$
return	$Return(\texttt{void})$
ret n	$Ret(n)$
saload	$ALoad(\texttt{short})$
sastore	$AStore(\texttt{short})$
sipush	$Prim(n)$

Bytecode instruction	Abstract instruction
swap	*Swap* (not described)
tableswitch	not supported
wide	not supported

D. Compiler

D.1 Compilation functions

$$\begin{aligned}
\mathcal{E}(lit) &= Prim(lit) \\
\mathcal{E}(loc) &= Load(\mathcal{T}(loc), \overline{loc}) \\
\mathcal{E}(loc = exp) &= \mathcal{E}(exp) \cdot Dupx(0, size(\mathcal{T}(exp))) \cdot Store(\mathcal{T}(exp), \overline{loc}) \\
\mathcal{E}(!\ exp) &= \mathcal{B}_1(exp, \text{una}_1) \cdot Prim(1) \cdot Goto(\text{una}_2) \cdot \\
&\quad \text{una}_1 \cdot Prim(0) \cdot \text{una}_2 \\
\mathcal{E}(uop\ exp) &= \mathcal{E}(exp) \cdot Prim(uop) \\
\mathcal{E}(exp_1\ bop\ exp_2) &= \mathcal{E}(exp_1) \cdot \mathcal{E}(exp_2) \cdot Prim(bop) \\
\mathcal{E}(exp_0\ ?\ exp_1\ :\ exp_2) &= \mathcal{B}_1(exp_0, \text{if}_1) \cdot \mathcal{E}(exp_2) \cdot Goto(\text{if}_2) \cdot \text{if}_1 \cdot \mathcal{E}(exp_1) \cdot \text{if}_2
\end{aligned}$$

$$\begin{aligned}
\mathcal{S}(;) &= \epsilon \\
\mathcal{S}(exp;) &= \mathcal{E}(exp) \cdot Pop(size(\mathcal{T}(exp))) \\
\mathcal{S}(\{stm_1 \ldots stm_n\}) &= \mathcal{S}(stm_1) \cdot \ldots \cdot \mathcal{S}(stm_n) \\
\mathcal{S}(\text{if } (exp)\ stm_1\ \text{else}\ stm_2) &= \mathcal{B}_1(exp, \text{if}_1) \cdot \mathcal{S}(stm_2) \cdot Goto(\text{if}_2) \cdot \\
&\quad \text{if}_1 \cdot \mathcal{S}(stm_1) \cdot \text{if}_2 \\
\mathcal{S}(\text{while } (exp)\ stm) &= Goto(\text{while}_1) \cdot \text{while}_2 \cdot \mathcal{S}(stm) \cdot \\
&\quad \text{while}_1 \cdot \mathcal{B}_1(exp, \text{while}_2) \\
\mathcal{S}(lab : stm) &= lab_c \cdot \mathcal{S}(stm) \cdot lab_b \\
\mathcal{S}(\text{continue } lab;) &= \textbf{let } [\text{fin}_1, \ldots, \text{fin}_n] = \textit{finallyLabsUntil}(lab) \\
&\quad Jsr(\text{fin}_1) \cdot \ldots \cdot Jsr(\text{fin}_n) \cdot Goto(lab_c) \\
\mathcal{S}(\text{break } lab;) &= \textbf{let } [\text{fin}_1, \ldots, \text{fin}_n] = \textit{finallyLabsUntil}(lab) \\
&\quad Jsr(\text{fin}_1) \cdot \ldots \cdot Jsr(\text{fin}_n) \cdot Goto(lab_b)
\end{aligned}$$

$$\begin{aligned}
\mathcal{B}_1(\textbf{true}, lab) &= Goto(lab) \\
\mathcal{B}_1(\textbf{false}, lab) &= \epsilon \\
\mathcal{B}_1(!\ exp, lab) &= \mathcal{B}_0(exp, lab) \\
\mathcal{B}_1(exp_0\ ?\ exp_1\ :\ exp_2, lab) &= \mathcal{B}_1(exp_0, \text{if}_1) \cdot \mathcal{B}_1(exp_2, lab) \cdot Goto(\text{if}_2) \cdot \\
&\quad \text{if}_1 \cdot \mathcal{B}_1(exp_1, lab) \cdot \text{if}_2 \\
\mathcal{B}_1(exp, lab) &= \mathcal{E}(exp) \cdot Cond(\textbf{ifne}, lab)
\end{aligned}$$

$$\begin{aligned}
\mathcal{B}_0(\textbf{true}, lab) &= \epsilon \\
\mathcal{B}_0(\textbf{false}, lab) &= Goto(lab) \\
\mathcal{B}_0(!\ exp, lab) &= \mathcal{B}_1(exp, lab) \\
\mathcal{B}_0(exp_0\ ?\ exp_1\ :\ exp_2, lab) &= \mathcal{B}_1(exp_0, \text{if}_1) \cdot \mathcal{B}_0(exp_2, lab) \cdot Goto(\text{if}_2) \cdot \\
&\quad \text{if}_1 \cdot \mathcal{B}_0(exp_1, lab) \cdot \text{if}_2 \\
\mathcal{B}_0(exp, lab) &= \mathcal{E}(exp) \cdot Cond(\textbf{ifeq}, lab)
\end{aligned}$$

$$\mathcal{E}(c.f) \qquad = GetStatic(\mathcal{T}(c/f), c/f)$$
$$\mathcal{E}(c.f = exp) = \mathcal{E}(exp) \cdot Dupx(0, size(\mathcal{T}(exp))) \cdot PutStatic(\mathcal{T}(c/f), c/f)$$
$$\mathcal{E}(c.m(exps)) = \mathcal{E}(exps) \cdot InvokeStatic(\mathcal{T}(c/m), c/m)$$

$$\mathcal{E}((exp_1, \ldots, exp_n)) = \mathcal{E}(exp_1) \cdot \ldots \cdot \mathcal{E}(exp_n)$$

$$\mathcal{S}(\text{static } stm) = \mathcal{S}(stm)$$
$$\mathcal{S}(\text{return; }) \qquad = \textbf{let } [fin_1, \ldots, fin_n] = finallyLabs$$
$$\qquad\qquad\qquad\qquad Jsr(fin_1) \cdot \ldots \cdot Jsr(fin_n) \cdot Return(\textbf{void})$$
$$\mathcal{S}(\text{return } exp;) =$$
$$\quad \textbf{if } finallyCodeToExec \textbf{ then}$$
$$\qquad \mathcal{E}(exp) \cdot Store(\mathcal{T}(exp), \overline{var}) \cdot$$
$$\qquad \textbf{let } [fin_1, \ldots, fin_n] = finallyLabs$$
$$\qquad Jsr(fin_1) \cdot \ldots \cdot Jsr(fin_n) \cdot Load(\mathcal{T}(exp), \overline{var}) \cdot Return(\mathcal{T}(exp))$$
$$\quad \textbf{else}$$
$$\qquad \mathcal{E}(exp) \cdot Return(\mathcal{T}(exp))$$

$$\mathcal{E}(\textbf{this}) \qquad\qquad = Load(\textbf{addr}, 0)$$
$$\mathcal{E}(\textbf{new } c) \qquad\quad = New(c) \cdot Dupx(0, 1)$$
$$\mathcal{E}(exp.c/f) \qquad\quad = \mathcal{E}(exp) \cdot GetField(\mathcal{T}(c/f), c/f)$$
$$\mathcal{E}(exp_1.c/f = exp_2) = \mathcal{E}(exp_1) \cdot \mathcal{E}(exp_2) \cdot Dupx(1, size(\mathcal{T}(c/f))) \cdot$$
$$\qquad\qquad\qquad\qquad PutField(\mathcal{T}(c/f), c/f)$$
$$\mathcal{E}(exp.c/m(exps)) \quad = \mathcal{E}(exp) \cdot \mathcal{E}(exps) \cdot$$
$$\qquad\qquad\qquad\qquad \textbf{case } callKind(exp.c/m) \textbf{ of}$$
$$\qquad\qquad\qquad\qquad\quad Virtual \rightarrow InvokeVirtual(\mathcal{T}(c/m), c/m)$$
$$\qquad\qquad\qquad\qquad\quad Super \;\; \rightarrow InvokeSpecial(\mathcal{T}(c/m), c/m)$$
$$\qquad\qquad\qquad\qquad\quad Special \rightarrow InvokeSpecial(\mathcal{T}(c/m), c/m)$$

$$\mathcal{E}(exp \textbf{ instanceof } c) = \mathcal{E}(exp) \cdot InstanceOf(c)$$
$$\mathcal{E}((c)exp) \qquad\qquad = \mathcal{E}(exp) \cdot Checkcast(c)$$

$$\mathcal{S}(\textbf{throw } exp;) = \mathcal{E}(exp) \cdot Athrow$$
$$\mathcal{S}(\textbf{try } stm \textbf{ catch } (c_1 \, x_1) \, stm_1 \ldots \textbf{ catch } (c_n \, x_n) \, stm_n) =$$
$$\quad \text{try} \cdot \mathcal{S}(stm) \cdot \text{tryEnd} \cdot Goto(\text{end}) \cdot$$
$$\quad \text{handle}_1 \cdot Store(\textbf{addr}, \overline{x_1}) \cdot \mathcal{S}(stm_1) \cdot Goto(\text{end}) \cdot$$
$$\qquad \vdots$$
$$\quad \text{handle}_n \cdot Store(\textbf{addr}, \overline{x_n}) \cdot \mathcal{S}(stm_n) \cdot Goto(\text{end}) \cdot$$
$$\quad \text{end}$$
$$\mathcal{S}(stm_1 \textbf{ finally } stm_2) =$$
$$\quad \text{try}_f \cdot \mathcal{S}(stm_1) \cdot Jsr(\text{fin}) \cdot Goto(\text{end}) \cdot$$
$$\quad \text{default} \cdot Store(\textbf{addr}, \overline{exc}) \cdot Jsr(\text{fin}) \cdot Load(\textbf{addr}, \overline{exc}) \cdot Athrow \cdot$$
$$\quad \text{fin} \cdot Store(\textbf{addr}, \overline{ret}) \cdot \mathcal{S}(stm_2) \cdot Ret(\overline{ret}) \cdot$$
$$\quad \text{end}$$

$\mathcal{X}(\textbf{try } stm \textbf{ catch } (c_1\ x_1)\ stm_1 \ldots \textbf{ catch } (c_n\ x_n)\ stm_n\ ) =$
    $\mathcal{X}(stm)\cdot$
    $\mathcal{X}(stm_1)\cdot Exc(\text{try}, \text{tryEnd}, \text{handle}_1, c_1)\cdot$
    $\vdots$
    $\mathcal{X}(stm_n)\cdot Exc(\text{try}, \text{tryEnd}, \text{handle}_n, c_n)$
$\mathcal{X}(stm_1 \textbf{ finally } stm_2) =$
    $\mathcal{X}(stm_1)\cdot Exc(\text{try}_f, \text{default}, \text{default}, \textbf{Throwable})\cdot \mathcal{X}(stm_2)$
$\mathcal{X}(\{stm_1 \ldots stm_n\})\qquad = \mathcal{X}(stm_1)\cdot \ldots \cdot \mathcal{X}(stm_n)$
$\mathcal{X}(\textbf{if } (exp)\ stm_1 \textbf{ else } stm_2) = \mathcal{X}(stm_1)\cdot \mathcal{X}(stm_2)$
$\mathcal{X}(\textbf{while } (exp)\ stm)\qquad = \mathcal{X}(stm)$
$\mathcal{X}(lab :\ stm)\qquad\qquad = \mathcal{X}(stm)$
$\mathcal{X}(\textbf{static } stm)\qquad\quad = \mathcal{X}(stm)$
$\mathcal{X}(\_)\qquad\qquad\qquad = \epsilon$

D.2 maxOpd

$opdSize(phrase) = \textbf{case } phrase \textbf{ of}$

lit	$\rightarrow s$
loc	$\rightarrow s$
$loc = exp$	$\rightarrow max(opdSize(exp), 2 * s)$
$uop\ exp$	$\rightarrow max(opdSize(exp), s)$
$exp_1\ bop\ exp_2$	$\rightarrow max(opdExps([exp_1, exp_2]), s)$
$exp_1 ?\ exp_2 :\ exp_3$	$\rightarrow max(opdSize(exp_1),$
	$\qquad max(opdSize(exp_2), opdSize(exp_3)))$
$exp;$	$\rightarrow opdSize(exp)$
$\{stm_1 \ldots stm_n\}$	$\rightarrow opdStms([stm_1, \ldots, stm_n])$
$\textbf{if } (exp)\ stm_1 \textbf{ else } stm_2$	$\rightarrow max(opdSize(exp), opdStms([stm_1, stm_2]))$
$\textbf{while } (exp)\ stm$	$\rightarrow max(opdSize(exp), opdSize(stm))$
$lab :\ stm$	$\rightarrow opdSize(stm)$
$c.f$	$\rightarrow s$
$c.f = exp$	$\rightarrow max(opdSize(exp), 2 * s)$
$c.m(exps)$	$\rightarrow max(opdSize(exps), s)$
$(exp_1, \ldots, exp_n)$	$\rightarrow opdExps([exp_1, \ldots, exp_n])$
$\textbf{static } stm$	$\rightarrow opdSize(stm)$
$\textbf{return } exp;$	$\rightarrow opdSize(exp)$
$\textbf{this}$	$\rightarrow 1$
$\textbf{new } c(exps)$	$\rightarrow 2 + opdSize(exps)$
$exp.c/f$	$\rightarrow max(opdSize(exp), s)$
$exp_1.c/f = exp_2$	$\rightarrow max(opdExps([exp_1, exp_2]), 1 + 2 * s)$
$exp.c/m(exps)$	$\rightarrow max(opdExps([exp, exps]), s)$
$exp \textbf{ instanceof } c$	$\rightarrow opdSize(exp)$
$(c)exp$	$\rightarrow opdSize(exp)$
$\textbf{throw } exp;$	$\rightarrow opdSize(exp)$

$\textbf{try } stm \textbf{ catch } (c_1\ loc_1)\ stm_1 \ldots \textbf{ catch } (c_n\ loc_n)\ stm_n\ \rightarrow$
    $max(opdSize(stm), max(1, opdStms([stm_1, \ldots, stm_n])))$
$stm_1 \textbf{ finally } stm_2 \rightarrow max(opdSize(stm_1), max(1, opdSize(stm_2)))$

$exp_1[exp_2]$	$\rightarrow max(opdExps([exp_1, exp_2]), s)$
$exp_1[exp_2] = exp_3$	$\rightarrow max(opdExps([exp_1, exp_2, exp_3]), 2 + 2 * s)$
$\textbf{new } t[d_1] \ldots [d_n]$	$\rightarrow max(1, opdExps([d_1, \ldots, d_n]))$
$\textbf{otherwise}$	$\rightarrow 0$

$\textbf{where } s = size(\mathcal{T}(phrase))$

$$opdExps([\,]) \qquad\qquad = 0$$
$$opdExps([exp] \cdot exps) = max(opdSize(exp), size(\mathcal{T}(exp)) + opdExps(exps))$$

$$opdStms([\,]) \qquad\qquad = 0$$
$$opdStms([stm] \cdot stms) = max(opdSize(stm), opdStms(stms))$$

D.3 Arrays

$$\mathcal{E}(exp_1[exp_2]) \qquad\quad = \mathcal{E}(exp_1) \cdot \mathcal{E}(exp_2) \cdot ALoad(\mathcal{T}(exp_1[exp_2]))$$
$$\mathcal{E}(exp_1[exp_2] = exp_3) = \mathcal{E}(exp_1) \cdot \mathcal{E}(exp_2) \cdot \mathcal{E}(exp_3) \cdot$$
$$\qquad\qquad\qquad\qquad\quad Dupx(2, size(\mathcal{T}(exp_1[exp_2]))) \cdot AStore(\mathcal{T}(exp_3))$$
$$\mathcal{E}(\textbf{new } t[d_1]\dots[d_n]) \;= \mathcal{E}(d_1) \cdot \dots \cdot \mathcal{E}(d_n) \cdot NewArray(t, n)$$

References

1. K. Achatz and W. Schulte. A formal OO method inspired by Fusion and Object-Z. In J. P. Bowen, M. G. Hinchey, and D. Till, editors, *ZUM'97: The Z Formal Specification*, number 1212 in Lecture Notes in Computer Science, pages 92–111. Springer-Verlag, 1997.
2. J. Alves-Foss, editor. *Formal Syntax and Semantics of Java(tm)*. Number 1523 in Lecture Notes in Computer Science. Springer-Verlag, 1999.
3. E. Börger. High level system design and analysis using Abstract State Machines. In D. Hutter, W. Stephan, P. Traverso, and M. Ullmann, editors, *Current Trends in Applied Formal Methods (FM-Trends 98)*, number 1641 in Lecture Notes in Computer Science, pages 1–43. Springer-Verlag, 1999.
4. E. Börger. Abstract state machines at the cusp of the millenium. In *Abstract State Machines ASM'2000*, number 1912 in Lecture Notes in Computer Science. Springer-Verlag, 2000.
5. E. Börger and I. Durdanovic. Correctness of compiling Occam to transputer code. *The Computer Journal*, 39:52–92, 1996.
6. E. Börger and D. Rosenzweig. The WAM—definition and compiler correctness. In L. Plümer C. Beierle, editor, *Logic Programming: Formal Methods and Practical Applications*, pages 20–90. Elsevier Science B.V./North-Holland, 1995.
7. E. Börger and J. Schmid. Composition and submachine concepts. In P. G. Clote and H. Schwichtenberg, editors, *Computer Science Logic (CSL 2000)*, number 1862 in Lecture Notes in Computer Science, pages 41–60. Springer-Verlag, 2000.
8. E. Börger and W. Schulte. Defining the Java Virtual Machine as platform for provably correct Java compilation. In L. Brim, J. Gruska, and J. Zlatuska, editors, *MFCS'98*, number 1450 in Lecture Notes in Computer Science, pages 17–35. Springer-Verlag, 1998.
9. E. Börger and W. Schulte. A programmer friendly modular definition of the semantics of Java. In Alves-Foss [2], pages 353–404. Extended Abstract in: R. Berghammer and F. Simon, editors, Programming Languages and Fundamentals of Programming, University of Kiel (Germany) TR 9717, 1997, pages 175–181.
10. E. Börger and W. Schulte. Initialization problems for Java. *Software – Principles and Tools*, 19(4):175–178, 2000.
11. E. Börger and W. Schulte. Modular design for the Java Virtual Machine architecture. In E. Börger, editor, *Architecture Design and Validation Methods*, pages 297–357. Springer-Verlag, 2000.
12. E. Börger and W. Schulte. A practical method for specification and analysis of exception handling — a Java JVM case study. *IEEE Transactions of Software Engineering*, 26(10), 2000.
13. R. M. Cohen. Defensive Java Virtual Machine version 0.5 alpha release. http://www.cli.com/software/djvm/, 1997.

14. Java Developer Connection. Bug parade, 1999. http://developer.java.sun.com/developer/bugParade/.

15. M. Dahm. JavaClass. Technical report, FU Berlin, 2000. http://www.inf.fu-berlin.de/~dahm/JavaClass/.

16. S. N. Freund and J. C. Mitchell. Specification and verification of Java bytecode subroutines and exceptions. Technical Report CS-TN-99-91, Stanford University, 1999.

17. S. N. Freund and J. C. Mitchell. The type system for object initialization in the Java bytecode language. *ACM Transactions on Programming Languages and Systems*, 21(6):1196–1250, 1999.

18. J. Gosling, B. Joy, and G. Steele. *The Java(tm) Language Specification*. Addison Wesley, 1996.

19. J. Gosling, B. Joy, G. Steele, and G. Bracha. *The Java(tm) Language Specification*. Addison Wesley, second edition, 2000.

20. Y. Gurevich. Evolving algebras 1993: Lipari guide. In E. Börger, editor, *Specification and Validation Methods*, pages 9–36. Oxford University Press, 1995.

21. P. H. Hartel and L. Moreau. Formalising the safety of Java, the Java Virtual Machine and Java Card. 2001. Submitted to ACM Computing Surveys.

22. M. P. Jones. Gofer distribution 2.30, 1993. http://www.cse.ogi.edu/~mpj/goferarc/.

23. T. Lindholm and F. Yellin. *The Java(tm) Virtual Machine Specification*. Addison Wesley, second edition, 1999.

24. J. Meyer and T. Downing. *Java Virtual Machine*. O'Reilly & Associates, Inc., 1997.

25. Sun Microsystems. Connected, limited device configuration, specification 1.0, Java 2 platform micro edition, 2000.

26. R. O'Callahan. A simple, comprehensive type system for Java bytecode subroutines. In *POPL '99. Proc. 26th ACM Symposium on Principles of Programming Languages*, pages 70–78, 1999.

27. Z. Qian. A formal specification of Java(tm) Virtual Machine for objects, methods and subroutines. In Alves-Foss [2], pages 271–311.

28. Z. Qian. Standard fixpoint iteration for Java bytecode verification. *ACM Transactions on Programming Languages and Systems*, 200? To appear.

29. Z. Qian, A. Goldberg, and A. Coglio. A formal specification of Java class loading. In *Proceedings of the Conference on Object-Oriented Programming, Systems, Languages and Application (OOPSLA-00)*, volume 35 of *ACM Sigplan Notices*, pages 325–336. ACM Press, 2000.

30. V. Saraswat. Java is not type-safe. Technical report, AT&T, Research, 1997. http://www.research.att.com/~vj/bug.html.

31. G. Schellhorn. *Verifikation abstrakter Zustandsmaschinen*. PhD thesis, University of Ulm, 1999. For an English version see http://www.informatik.uni-ulm.de/pm/kiv/papers/verif-asms-english.ps.gz.

32. J. Schmid. Executing ASM specifications with AsmGofer, 1999. Web pages at http://www.tydo.de/AsmGofer.

33. R. Stärk. Formal foundations of Java. Course notes, University of Fribourg, 1999.

34. R. Stata and M. Abadi. A type system for Java bytecode subroutines. *ACM Transactions on Programming Languages and Systems*, 21(1):90–137, 1999.

35. A. Tozawa and M. Hagya. Formalization and analysis of class loading in Java. *Higher Order and Symbolic Computation*, 200? To appear.

36. T. Vullinghs, W. Schulte, and T. Schwinn. An introduction to TkGofer, 1996. Web pages at http://pllab.kaist.ac.kr/seminar/haha/tkgofer2.0-html/user.html.

List of Figures

1.1	Dependency Graph	5
1.2	Language oriented decomposition of Java/JVM	6
1.3	Multiple thread Java machine execJavaThread	7
1.4	Security oriented decomposition of the JVM	8
1.5	Decomposing trustfulVMs into execVMs and switchVMs	9
1.6	Decomposing diligent JVMs into trustfulVMs and verifyVMs	10
1.7	Decomposing verifyVMs into propagateVMs, checks, succs	11
1.8	Decomposing defensiveVMs into trustfulVMs and checks	12
2.1	Control state ASM diagrams	16
2.2	The semantics of ASM rules	24
3.1	Syntax of $\text{Java}_\mathcal{I}$	35
3.2	Execution of $\text{Java}_\mathcal{I}$ expressions	41
3.3	Execution of $\text{Java}_\mathcal{I}$ statements	42
4.1	Syntax of a Java class	48
4.2	Syntax of a Java interface	49
4.3	Syntax of $\text{Java}_\mathcal{C}$	50
4.4	Execution of $\text{Java}_\mathcal{C}$ expressions	64
4.5	Execution of $\text{Java}_\mathcal{C}$ statements	66
5.1	Syntax of $\text{Java}_\mathcal{O}$	73
5.2	Execution of $\text{Java}_\mathcal{O}$ expressions	81
6.1	Syntax of $\text{Java}_\mathcal{E}$	88
6.2	Execution of $\text{Java}_\mathcal{E}$ statements	91
6.3	Execution of $\text{Java}_\mathcal{E}$ expressions	92
7.1	Syntax of $\text{Java}_\mathcal{T}$	96
7.2	Execution of $\text{Java}_\mathcal{T}$ statements	99
9.1	Trustful execution of $\text{JVM}_\mathcal{I}$ instructions	141
9.2	Compilation of $\text{Java}_\mathcal{I}$ expressions	144
9.3	Compilation of $\text{Java}_\mathcal{I}$ expressions for control flow	144
9.4	Compilation of $\text{Java}_\mathcal{I}$ statements	144

10.1   Trustful execution of JVM$_\mathcal{C}$ instructions 151
10.2   Trustful switch machine 152
10.3   Compilation of Java$_\mathcal{C}$ expressions/statements 153

11.1   Trustful execution of JVM$_\mathcal{O}$ instructions..................... 156
11.2   Compilation of Java$_\mathcal{O}$ expressions 158

12.1   Switch machine for JVM$_\mathcal{E}$ 161
12.2   Trustful execution of JVM$_\mathcal{E}$ instructions 162
12.3   Compilation of Java$_\mathcal{E}$ abruption statements 164
12.4   Definition of Java$_\mathcal{E}$ exception tables 164

15.1   Defensive JVM interpreter 210
15.2   Checking JVM$_\mathcal{I}$ instructions 212
15.3   Checking JVM$_\mathcal{C}$ instructions 214
15.4   Checking JVM$_\mathcal{O}$ instructions 218
15.5   Pushing a new JVM$_\mathcal{O}$ frame 219
15.6   Checking JVM$_\mathcal{E}$ instructions 220

16.1   A polymorphic subroutine 225
16.2   Breaking out of a subroutine to the top level 225
16.3   Breaking out of a subroutine to an enclosing subroutine 225
16.4   Jumping out of a subroutine with an exception handler 226
16.5   Which variables are modified by the subroutine? 226
16.6   Inconsistencies in Sun's JDK 1.2 verifier 226
16.7   A valid Java program rejected by Sun's JDK 1.2 verifier 227
16.8   A valid Java program rejected by all known verifiers............ 227
16.9   Another Java program rejected by all known verifiers........... 227
16.10 Why sets of reference types 229
16.11 A piece of the Java type hierarchy 230
16.12 Successors for JVM$_\mathcal{I}$ instructions 232
16.13 Successors for JVM$_\mathcal{C}$ instructions 233
16.14 Successors for JVM$_\mathcal{O}$ instructions 234
16.15 Successors for JVM$_\mathcal{E}$ instructions 235
16.16 Some instructions do not throw exceptions 235
16.17 Successors are monotonic 235
16.18 Violation of T7 (e) 241
16.19 Violation of T7 (f) 241
16.20 Violation of T7 (f) 243
16.21 Violation of T8 243
16.22 Certifying compilation of Java$_\mathcal{I}$ expressions 257
16.23 Certifying compilation of Java$_\mathcal{I}$ statements.................... 257
16.24 Certifying compilation of Java$_\mathcal{I}$ expressions for control flow 258
16.25 Certifying compilation of Java$_\mathcal{C}$ expressions/statements 258
16.26 Certifying compilation of Java$_\mathcal{O}$ expressions 259

16.27 Certifying compilation of Java$_\mathcal{E}$ statements 259
16.28 Certifying compilation of Java$_\mathcal{E}$ abruptions statements 260
16.29 The general pattern for abruptions statements 260

18.1 Ordering of class states 293
18.2 Refinement of the switch machine 294
18.3 Loading super classes and references 296
18.4 Trustful execution of JVM$_\mathcal{D}$ instructions 299
18.5 Execution of **final** class loader methods 300
18.6 Loading and linking machines 301

A.1 Relationship between different machines 306
A.2 Screenshot Java GUI 309
A.3 Screenshot control execution speed 310
A.4 Screenshot Java example 312
A.5 Screenshot compiler GUI 313
A.6 Screenshot select JVM subset 314
A.7 Screenshot JVM GUI 317

List of Tables

3.1   The primitive types of Java 34
3.2   Unary operators for operands of primitive type 36
3.3   Binary operators for operands of primitive type............... 36
3.4   Type constraints for expressions of $\text{Java}_\mathcal{I}$ 37
3.5   Type constraints after introduction of primitive type casts 38
3.6   Derived language constructs............................... 44

4.1   Type constraints for $\text{Java}_\mathcal{C}$ 59
4.2   Type constraints after introduction of primitive type casts 61

5.1   Binary operators for references 72
5.2   Type constraints for $\text{Java}_\mathcal{O}$............................... 78
5.3   Type constraints after introduction of primitive type casts 78

6.1   Type constraints for $\text{Java}_\mathcal{E}$ 89

8.1   The direct subexpressions of an expression 114
8.2   The predecessors of expressions and statements 115
8.3   Reachability constraints 118
8.4   Definite assignment for boolean expressions 122
8.5   Definite assignment for arbitrary expressions 123
8.6   Definite assignment for statements 124

Index

; 42, 144, 325, 361
<clinit> 61
<cload> 295
<init> 77
<newInstance> 302
? : 41, 144, 324, 361
$\mathcal{T}$ 37
· 27
⊲ 28
◁ 28
$\mathcal{A}$ 255
$\mathcal{A}_0$ 255
$\mathcal{A}_1$ 255
$\mathcal{B}_0$ 144, 258, 361
$\mathcal{B}_1$ 144, 258, 361
$\mathcal{E}$ 144, 257, 361
$\mathcal{P}$ 255
$\mathcal{S}$ 144, 257, 361
$\mathcal{V}$ 256
⊕ 28
$\prec_\mu$ 113, 115
$\prec_d$ 47, 48
$\prec_h$ 48
$\preceq$ 33, 71, 84
$\preceq_h$ 48
⊔ 277, 283
$\sqcup_{opd}$ 277
$\sqcup_{reg}$ 277
⊑ 127, 216, 230
$\sqsubseteq_{mv}$ 213, 214, 217
$\sqsubseteq_{pre}$ 112
$\sqsubseteq_{reg}$ 222
$\sqsubseteq_{seq}$ 222
$\sqsubseteq_{suf}$ 211

Abr 62, 89
access violation 351
accessible
– element 53, 54
– type 50
Active 97

addr 155
after 121
allhandlers 236
ALoad 351, 352, 353, 355
Args 150
arity 18
Array 216, 230, 332, 351
array 71, 231, 332, 364
arrayDim 351
arrayElemType 353
ArrayLength 351, 352, 353, 355
ArrayMoveType 351
arraySize 333
arrayType 353
Asgn 35, 50, 73
ASM 23
– run 25
AStore 351, 352, 353, 355
Athrow 159, 355
– defensive machine 220, 348
– diligent machine 235, 349
– trustful machine 162, 338

before 121
beg 169
binary operator 41, 92, 144, 324, 328, 361
Block 35
block 42, 144, 325, 361
– exception table 164, 363
body 62
boolean 39
boolean 144, 361
Break 42, 62, 89, 325
break 42, 144, 164, 325, 361
break(α, lab) 123
Bstm 35
byte 39, 351

Call 150
– trustful machine 152, 161, 336, 338

callLoad   295, 340
cEnv   148
CFile   148
changed   275
char   39, 351
check$_I$ 212, 347
check$_O$ 353
check$_C$ 214, 347
check$_D$ 302, 348
check$_E$ 220, 348
check$_N$ 221, 348
check$_O$ 218, 347
Checkcast   155, 355
– defensive machine   218, 347
– diligent machine   234, 349
– trustful machine   156, 162, 337, 338
checkEqualVisibleSigs   350
checkOverride   350
Class   50, 216, 230, 292
class   71
– field   51, 64, 153, 325, 362
classcast   81, 92, 158, 327, 328, 362
ClassFile   148
classInitialization   104
classNm   148
classOf   80, 332
ClassState   62, 293
– diligent machine   281
– trustful machine   150, 160
classState   62, 151
Code   140
code   140, 149
cOf   292
compile
– $\mathcal{B}_0$ 144, 361
– $\mathcal{B}_1$ 144, 361
– $\mathcal{E}$ 144, 361
– $\mathcal{S}$ 144, 361
– ;   144, 361
– ? :   144, 361
– **break**   144, 164, 361
– **continue**   144, 164, 361
– **false**   144, 361
– **if then else**   144, 361
– **instanceof**   158, 362
– **new**   158, 362
– **return**   153, 164, 362
– **static**   153
– **this**   158, 362
– **throw**   164, 362
– **true**   144, 361
– **try catch**   164, 362
– **try finally**   164, 362

– **while**   144, 361
– array   364
– binary operator   144, 361
– block   144, 361
– boolean   144, 361
– classcast   158, 362
– expression   144, 361
– field   153, 158, 362
– invocation   153, 158, 362
– label   144, 361
– literal   144, 361
– new array   364
– statement   144, 361
– unary operator   144, 361
– variable   144, 361
Complete   217
Cond   139, 357
– constraints   350
– defensive machine   212, 347
– diligent machine   232, 348
– trustful machine   141, 335
constant   18, 19
constraints   349, 350
constraintViolation   349
cont   96
context   40, 323
Continue   42, 62, 89, 325
continue   42, 144, 164, 325, 361
copy   27
createArray   333, 353

Dead   97
defaultVal   79, 150
defensive machine   209
– *Athrow*   220, 348
– *Checkcast*   218, 347
– *Cond*   212, 347
– *Dupx*   212, 347
– *GetField*   218, 347
– *GetStatic*   214, 347
– *Goto*   212, 347
– *Halt*   212, 347
– *InstanceOf*   218, 347
– *InvokeSpecial*   218, 347
– *InvokeStatic*   214, 347
– *InvokeVirtual*   218, 347
– *JVM$_C$*   213
– *JVM$_E$*   219
– *JVM$_I$*   210
– *JVM$_N$*   221
– *JVM$_O$*   214
– *Jsr*   220, 343, 348
– *Load*   212, 347

- *New*   218, 347
- *Pop*   212, 347
- *Prim*   212, 347
- *PutField*   218, 347
- *PutStatic*   214, 347
- *Ret*   220, 348
- *Return*   214, 347
- *Store*   212, 220, 347, 348
defensiveScheme$_C$ 214, 343
defensiveScheme$_I$ 210, 343
defensiveScheme$_N$ 221, 343
defensiveVM$_C$ 213, 343
defensiveVM$_E$ 220, 343
defensiveVM$_I$ 210, 343
defensiveVM$_O$ 214, 343
defensiveVM$_D$ 303, 344
defensiveVM$_N$ 221, 344
defineClass   301, 342
defining loader   289
definite assignment   121
diligent machine   273
- *Athrow*   235, 349
- *Checkcast*   234, 349
- *ClassState*   281
- *Cond*   232, 348
- *Dupx*   232, 348
- *GetField*   234, 349
- *GetStatic*   233, 348
- *Goto*   232, 348
- *InstanceOf*   234, 349
- *InvokeSpecial*   234, 349
- *InvokeStatic*   233, 348
- *InvokeVirtual*   234, 349
- *JVM$_C$*   279
- *JVM$_E$*   283
- *JVM$_I$*   275
- *JVM$_N$*   286
- *JVM$_O$*   283
- *Jsr*   235, 284, 345, 349
- *Load*   232, 348
- *New*   234, 349
- *Pop*   232, 348
- *Prim*   232, 348
- *PutField*   234, 349
- *PutStatic*   233, 348
- *Ret*   235, 284, 345, 349
- *Return*   233, 348
- *Store*   232, 348
diligentScheme   280, 346
diligentVM$_C$ 280, 346
diligentVM$_E$ 284, 346
diligentVM$_I$ 276, 345
diligentVM$_N$ 287, 346

diligentVM$_O$ 283, 346
diligentVM$_D$ 303, 346
direct reference   297
direct subexpression   114
double   39, 139, 351
drop   27
Dupx   139, 356
- defensive machine   212, 347
- diligent machine   232, 348
- trustful machine   141, 335
dynamic loading   289
- *InitClass*   294, 339
- *Result*   294, 339

element
- accessible   53, 54
end   169
endinit   219
equation   21
escapes   160
Exc   89, 91, 159, 328
exception   88
exception table
- **if then else**   164, 363
- **static**   164, 363
- **try finally**   164, 363
- **try**   164, 363
- **while**   164, 363
- block   164, 363
- label   164, 363
excs   149
exec   97
execClassLoader   300, 341
execJava   31, 323
execJava$_C$ 63, 323
execJava$_E$ 90, 323
execJava$_I$ 39, 323
execJava$_O$ 80, 323
execJava$_T$ 98, 323
execJava$_{Array}$ 332
execJavaExp$_C$ 64, 325
execJavaExp$_E$ 92, 328
execJavaExp$_I$ 41, 324
execJavaExp$_O$ 81, 327
execJavaStm$_C$ 66, 326
execJavaStm$_E$ 91, 328
execJavaStm$_I$ 42, 325
execJavaStm$_T$ 99, 329
execJavaThread   101, 329
execVM$_C$ 151, 336
execVM$_E$ 162, 220, 338, 343, 352
execVM$_I$ 141, 335
execVM$_N$ 166, 339

exec VM$_O$ 156, 337, 352
exec VM$_D$ 299, 340
exitMethod   66, 82, 327
Exp   35, 50, 73
expression
– ? :   41, 144, 324, 361
– **false**   144, 361
– **instanceof**   81, 158, 327, 362
– **new**   81, 158, 327, 362
– **this**   81, 158, 327, 362
– **true**   144, 361
– array   332, 364
– binary operator   41, 92, 144, 324,
  328, 361
– boolean   144, 361
– classcast   81, 92, 158, 327, 328, 362
– compile   144, 361
– direct subexpression   114
– field   64, 81, 92, 153, 158, 325, 327,
  328, 362
– invocation   64, 81, 92, 153, 158, 325,
  327, 328, 362
– literal   41, 144, 324, 361
– new array   332, 364
– statement   42, 66, 325, 326
– unary operator   41, 144, 324, 361
– variable   41, 144, 324, 361
Exps   50

fail   90, 161, 328
failUp   90, 328
False   18, 39
false   144, 361
false   121
FDec   149
Field   50
field   64, 81, 92, 153, 158, 325, 327, 328,
  362
– class   51, 64, 325
– instance   51, 81, 92, 327, 328
fields   148
FieldTab   149
finally   91, 328
firstPos   39, 64
float   39, 139, 211, 216, 351
floating point   33
formals   281, 283
formula   20
Frame   62, 149
frame
– in a state   127
– parent   127
frames   62

frames$_n^q$ 111
from   159
function
– controlled   17
– derived   17
– domain of   19
– dynamic   16, 18
– interaction   17
– monitored   17
– static   16, 18

getElement   333
GetField   155
– access violation   351
– constraints   350
– defensive machine   218, 347
– diligent machine   234, 349
– trustful machine   156, 162, 337, 338
getField   82
GetStatic   147
– access violation   351
– constraints   350
– defensive machine   214, 347
– diligent machine   233, 348
– trustful machine   151, 336
globals   62, 150
Goto   139, 357
– constraints   350
– defensive machine   212, 347
– diligent machine   232, 348
– trustful machine   141, 335

Halt   139
– defensive machine   212, 347
– trustful machine   141, 335
handle   159
handler   160
Heap   80, 156, 332, 351
heap   80, 156
highDouble   211, 216
highLong   211, 216

if then else   42, 144, 325, 361
– exception table   164, 363
IInc   358
implements   148
implicitCall   152, 295
indirect reference   297
inheritance   48
InInit   216, 217
init sequence   246
InitClass   150
– dynamic loading   294, 339
– trustful machine   152, 161, 336, 338

initCompatible   219
initialize   64, 92, 101, 326
Initialized   62, 150
initialized   62, 100, 151
initializeDynamicLoading   302
initiating loader   289
InitState   217
initState   217
initThread   100
initVerify   281, 286, 344
initWait   100
InProgress   62
instance
 − field   51, 81, 92, 158, 327, 328, 362
 − invocation   81, 92, 158, 327, 328, 362
 − method   52
instanceFields   79
InstanceOf   155
 − defensive machine   218, 347
 − diligent machine   234, 349
 − trustful machine   156, 337
Instanceof   358
instanceof   81, 158, 327, 362
Instr   139, 147, 155, 159, 351
Instr$_C$ 147
Instr$_E$ 159
Instr$_I$ 139
Instr$_O$ 155
int   39, 139, 211, 216, 351
integral   33
Interface   216, 230
interface   71
interrupt   104, 330
interrupted   104, 331
interruptedFlag   97
Invk   50, 73
invocation   64, 81, 92, 153, 158, 325,
    327, 328, 362
 − instance   81, 92, 327, 328
 − static   64, 325
invokeMethod   65, 326
invokeNative   103, 330
InvokeSpecial   155, 358
 − access violation   351
 − constraints   350
 − defensive machine   218, 347
 − diligent machine   234, 349
 − trustful machine   156, 162, 337, 338
InvokeStatic   147, 358
 − access violation   351
 − constraints   350
 − defensive machine   214, 347
 − diligent machine   233, 348

 − trustful machine   151, 336
InvokeVirtual   155, 358
 − access violation   351
 − constraints   350
 − defensive machine   218, 347
 − diligent machine   234, 349
 − trustful machine   156, 162, 337, 338
isArray   353
isChecked   280
isHigh   212, 217
isInterface   148
isInterrupted   104, 331
isRetAddr   220

javaOpd   170
Jsr   159, 358
 − constraints   350
 − defensive machine   220, 343, 348
 − diligent machine   235, 284, 345, 349
 − trustful machine   162, 338
JVM$_C$
 − defensive machine   213
 − diligent machine   279
 − trustful machine   147
JVM$_E$
 − defensive machine   219
 − diligent machine   283
 − trustful machine   159
JVM$_I$
 − defensive machine   210
 − diligent machine   275
 − trustful machine   139
JVM$_N$
 − defensive machine   221
 − diligent machine   286
 − trustful machine   165
JVM$_O$
 − defensive machine   214
 − diligent machine   283
 − trustful machine   155
jvmVal   169

killThread   99, 329
Kind   75

label   42, 66, 144, 325, 326, 361
 − exception table   164, 363
Ld   292
ldEnv   292
length   27
liftClass   293
linkClass   282, 345
 − trustful machine   301, 342
Linked   62, 150

literal   33, 41, 144, 324, 361
Load   139, 355
– constraints   350
– defensive machine   212, 347
– diligent machine   232, 348
– trustful machine   141, 335
load   293
loadClass   301, 341
loadClasses   296, 340
Loaded   293
loadIndirectReferences   296, 340
loadReferences   296, 340
loadSuperClasses   296, 340
Locals   39
locals   39
$locals_n^q$ 111
location   23
locked   106, 107
locks   96
`long`   39, 139, 351
lookup   79
`lowDouble`   211, 216
`lowLong`   211, 216

makeRegs   153
Map   28
match   160
maxOpd   149, 213, 363
maxReg   149
MDec   149
Meth   50
meth   62, 149
$meth_n^q$ 111
$meth_v$ 280
method
– instance   52
– signature   51
– static   52
methods   148
MethTab   149
mod   238, 264
modifiers   148, 149
MoveType   139, 147, 155
MSig   51, 148

New   155, 217, 359
– access violation   351
– constraints   350
– defensive machine   218, 347
– diligent machine   234, 349
– trustful machine   156, 337
`new`   81, 158, 327, 362
new array   332, 364

NewArray   351, 352, 353, 355, 359
– constraints   350
Nop   359
normal   117
Noswitch   150
Notified   97
notified   106
notify   105, 331
notifyAll   105, 331
notifyThreadsWaitingForInitialization
    101, 329
NotStarted   97
`Null`   216, 230
null   27, 80
numeric   33

Object   80, 156, 332, 351
`Object`   351
Offset   139
opd   140
opdExps   364
opdSize   363
opdStms   364
opdV   275
overflow   212

Pc   140
pc   140
Phrase   35, 38, 50
phrase
– thread enters   112
– thread evaluates   113
– thread is inside   112
Pop   139, 359
– defensive machine   212, 347
– diligent machine   232, 348
– trustful machine   141, 335
pop   27
popFrame   153, 336
pos   38
pos_n^q 111
position
– constructor invocation   115
– initialization invocation   115
– method invocation   114
– predecessor   113
Powerset   28
predecessor   113
prepareClass   282, 342
prepareVerify   282, 345
Prim   139, 355
– defensive machine   212, 347
– diligent machine   232, 348

– trustful machine   141, 162, 335, 338
primitive   33
propagateJsr   284, 345
propagatesAbr   43, 65, 92, 99
propagateSucc   277, 344
propagateVM$_E$ 284, 345
propagateVM$_I$ 276, 344
push   27
pushFrame   152, 219, 336, 343
PutField   155, 359
– access violation   351
– constraints   350
– defensive machine   218, 347
– diligent machine   234, 349
– trustful machine   156, 162, 337, 338
PutStatic   147, 359
– access violation   351
– constraints   350
– defensive machine   214, 347
– diligent machine   233, 348
– trustful machine   151, 336

raise   161
reachable   117
reachable   237
Ref   80
reference   217
reference   71
– is used   128
referenceClass   294, 339
Referenced   281
reg   140
RegNo   139
regV   275
relation
– *subtype*   33
– inheritance   48
releaseLock   98, 328
restbody   38
restbody$_n^q$ 111
Result   150
– dynamic loading   294, 339
– trustful machine   152, 336
Ret   159, 359
– constraints   350
– defensive machine   220, 348
– diligent machine   235, 284, 345, 349
– trustful machine   162, 338
retAddr   220
Return   62, 89, 147, 355
– defensive machine   214, 347
– diligent machine   233, 348
– trustful machine   151, 336

return   66, 153, 164, 326, 362
return   51, 56, 71
returnType   149
rule   22
– block   22
– call   23
– conditional   22
– definite assignment   121
– definition   23
– forall   23
– let   23
– parametrized   17
– schema   17
– skip   22
– update   22
run   102, 329
run   25
run method   115
runnable   102

setElement   333
setField   82
setReferenced   296, 340
setSupersLoaded   296, 340
short   39, 351
signature
– method   51
Size   139
Special   75
split   27
splits   28
stack   149
stack map   252
start   103, 330
state   18
statement
– ;   42, 144, 325, 361
– **break**   42, 144, 164, 325, 361
– **continue**   42, 144, 164, 325, 361
– **finally**   91, 328
– **if then else**   42, 144, 325, 361
– **return**   66, 153, 164, 326, 362
– **static**   66, 153, 326
– **synchronized**   99, 329
– **throw**   91, 164, 328, 362
– **try catch**   164, 362
– **try finally**   164, 362
– **try**   91, 328
– **while**   42, 144, 325, 361
– block   42, 144, 325, 361
– compile   144, 361
– expression   42, 66, 325, 326
– label   42, 66, 144, 325, 326, 361

static 66, 153, 326
− exception table   164, 363
static
− invocation   64, 153, 325, 362
− method   52
staticFields   64, 150
Stm   35, 88, 96
Store   139, 355
− constraints   350
− defensive machine   212, 220, 347, 348
− diligent machine   232, 348
− trustful machine   141, 335
stringOf   296
subtype   33
$succ_C$ 233, 348
$succ_E$ 235, 349
$succ_I$ 232, 348
$succ_O$ 234, 349, 353
Super   75
super   62, 148
SupersLoaded   293
superuniverse   18
Swap   360
Switch   150, 160
switch   150
switchCont   102, 330
$switchVM_C$ 152, 281, 336, 344
$switchVM_E$ 161, 338
$switchVM_D$ 294, 339
sync   96
syncFromCont   106
synchronize   102, 330
synchronized   99, 329
Synchronizing   97
synchronizing   106
syncObj   97
sysLd   292

take   27
term   19
− closed   19
− interpretation of   20
this   81, 158, 327, 362
thread   98
thread
− previous step   113
ThreadState   97
Throw   160
− trustful machine   161, 338
throw   91, 164, 328, 362
ThrowInit   160
− trustful machine   161, 338

top   27
tops   28
True   18, 39
true   144, 361
true   121
trustful machine
− *Athrow*   162, 338
− *Call*   152, 161, 336, 338
− *Checkcast*   156, 162, 337, 338
− *ClassState*   150, 160
− *Cond*   141, 335
− *Dupx*   141, 335
− *GetField*   156, 162, 337, 338
− *GetStatic*   151, 336
− *Goto*   141, 335
− *Halt*   141, 335
− *InitClass*   152, 161, 336, 338
− *InstanceOf*   156, 337
− *InvokeSpecial*   156, 162, 337, 338
− *InvokeStatic*   151, 336
− *InvokeVirtual*   156, 162, 337, 338
− JVM_C 147
− JVM_E 159
− JVM_I 139
− JVM_N 165
− JVM_O 155
− *Jsr*   162, 338
− *Load*   141, 335
− *New*   156, 337
− *Pop*   141, 335
− *Prim*   141, 162, 335, 338
− *PutField*   156, 162, 337, 338
− *PutStatic*   151, 336
− *Result*   152, 336
− *Ret*   162, 338
− *Return*   151, 336
− *Store*   141, 335
− *Throw*   161, 338
− *ThrowInit*   161, 338
− *linkClass*   301, 342
$trustfulScheme_C$ 151, 342
$trustfulScheme_N$ 165, 342
$trustfulVM_C$ 151, 342
$trustfulVM_E$ 159, 342
$trustfulVM_I$ 141, 342
$trustfulVM_N$ 165, 342
$trustfulVM_O$ 157, 342
$trustfulVM_D$ 299, 342
try   91, 328
− exception table   164, 363
try catch   164, 362
try finally   164, 362
− exception table   164, 363

typ   159
type   79, 149, 217
type
– accessible   50
– array   71, 231
– class   71
– floating point   33
– frame   211
– integral   33
– interface   71
– numeric   33
– primitive   33
– reference   71
– return   51, 56, 71
typeOf   217, 351

unary operator   41, 144, 324, 361
undef   18
universe   19
Unusable   62, 160
unusable   216
unusable   160
up   40
update   23
– consistent set   24
– firing   25
update set   23
upper bound   230
upto   159

Val   39, 80, 150
validAccess   351
validClass   349
validCMeth   350
validCodeIndex   210
validIMeth   350
validInstr   350
validInterface   349
validJump   284
validOpd   276
validReg   276
validTypeSeq   212
variable   19, 41, 144, 324, 361
– assignment   20
vars   121
verifyClass   280
verifyMeths   280
verifyScheme$_C$ 281, 346
verifyScheme$_I$ 276, 345
verifyScheme$_N$ 287, 346
VerifyType   216, 220, 230
violationMsg   351
Virtual   75

visited   275
vocabulary   18
void   147

wait   105, 331
Waiting   97
waiting   106
waitObj   97
waitSet   97
wakeup   102, 330
while   42, 144, 325, 361
– exception table   164, 363
Word   211
WordType   211, 217, 220

yield   40, 323, 324
yieldUp   40, 323

zip   28

Printing: Mercedes-Druck, Berlin
Binding: Buchbinderei Lüderitz & Bauer, Berlin